Field Research on Translation and Interpreting

Benjamins Translation Library (BTL)

ISSN 0929-7316

The Benjamins Translation Library (BTL) aims to stimulate research and training in Translation & Interpreting Studies – taken very broadly to encompass the many different forms and manifestations of translational phenomena, among them cultural translation, localization, adaptation, literary translation, specialized translation, audiovisual translation, audio-description, transcreation, transediting, conference interpreting, and interpreting in community settings in the spoken and signed modalities.

For an overview of all books published in this series, please see
benjamins.com/catalog/btl

General Editor

Roberto A. Valdeón
University of Oviedo

Associate Editor

Franz Pöchhacker
University of Vienna

Honorary Editors

Yves Gambier
University of Turku
& Immanuel Kant Baltic Federal University

Gideon Toury
Tel Aviv University

Advisory Board

Cecilia Alvstad
Høgskolen i Østfold

Georges L. Bastin
University of Montreal

Dirk Delabastita
University of Namur

Daniel Gile
Université Paris 3 - Sorbonne Nouvelle

Arnt Lykke Jakobsen
Copenhagen Business School

Krisztina Károly
Eötvös Lorand University

Kobus Marais
University of the Free State

Christopher D. Mellinger
University of North Carolina at Charlotte

Jan Pedersen
Stockholm University

Nike K. Pokorn
University of Ljubljana

Luc van Doorslaer
University of Tartu & KU Leuven

Meifang Zhang
University of Macau

Volume 165

Field Research on Translation and Interpreting
Edited by Regina Rogl, Daniela Schlager and Hanna Risku

Field Research on Translation and Interpreting

Edited by

Regina Rogl
Daniela Schlager
Hanna Risku
University of Vienna

John Benjamins Publishing Company
Amsterdam / Philadelphia

∞™ The paper used in this publication meets the minimum requirements of
the American National Standard for Information Sciences – Permanence
of Paper for Printed Library Materials, ANSI z39.48-1984.

Research results from: Austrian Science Fund (FWF):
10.55776/P33132. Published with the support of the Austrian Science
Fund (FWF): 10.55776/PUB1200.

DOI 10.1075/btl.165

Cataloging-in-Publication Data available from Library of Congress:
LCCN 2025004533 (PRINT) / 2025004534 (E-BOOK)

ISBN 978 90 272 2030 1 (HB)
ISBN 978 90 272 4485 7 (E-BOOK)

© 2025 – John Benjamins B.V.

This publication is licensed, unless otherwise indicated, under the terms of the Creative
Commons Attribution-Non-Commercial 4.0 International (CC BY-NC 4.0) license
(https://creativecommons.org/licenses/by-nc/4.0/), which permits use, sharing, adaptation,
distribution, and reproduction in any medium or format, provided you give appropriate credit
to the original author(s) and source, provide a link to the Creative Commons license, and
indicate any attribution changes. Use for commercial purposes is not permitted.

John Benjamins Publishing Company · https://benjamins.com

Table of contents

INTRODUCTION Searching and researching the field of translation
and interpreting   1
Regina Rogl, Daniela Schlager & Hanna Risku

PART I. **Delving into specific ethnographic approaches**
CHAPTER 1. Translating at work: Identifying and contextualizing
paraprofessional translatoriality in organizations   36
Kaisa Koskinen

CHAPTER 2. Linguistic ethnography in interpreting studies   55
Jemina Napier

CHAPTER 3. Retrospective ethnography and remembrance: A narrative
of UNOG field missions   74
Lucía Ruiz Rosendo & Alma Barghout

PART II. **Centering on positionality, reflexivity and ethics**
CHAPTER 4. Affective labor in the simultaneous interpreting of prayer:
An autoethnographic re-analysis   98
Sari Hokkanen

CHAPTER 5. 'Going native' during field research on multilingual legislation:
Methodological and ethical strategies   117
Cornelia Staudinger

CHAPTER 6. Practisearcher meets 'non-professionals': A journey of conducting
reflexive translation and interpreting research in an NGO   137
Vanessa Steinkogler

CHAPTER 7. The field diary as a resource for (auto)ethnographies of translation
and interpreting   157
Lucile Davier

CHAPTER 8. Beyond ethical clearance in field research: In search of situated
and reflexive ethics   179
Aurélien Riondel

PART III. Zooming in on processes and materiality

CHAPTER 9. Co-constructing cognitive artifacts in the translation workplace 200
Raphael Sannholm

CHAPTER 10. Revision files as cognitive ethnographic data: Artefact analysis of file and software features combined with systemic functional discourse analysis 226
Annamari Korhonen

CHAPTER 11. Thinking with actor-network theory to unearth the (in)visibility of translation in a journalistic setting 251
Marlie van Rooyen

PART IV. Integrating marginalised groups and phenomena

CHAPTER 12. Field research on reading translated fiction: Methodological considerations and challenges 278
Duygu Tekgül-Akın

CHAPTER 13. What translation and interpreting practices do: Field research on human differentiation in a German reception centre for refugees 297
Dilek Dizdar & Tomasz Rozmysłowicz

CHAPTER 14. Lives in translation: Listening to the voices of asylum seekers 320
Marija Todorova

CHAPTER 15. Exploring interspecies translation and interpreting through multispecies ethnography 338
Xany Jansen van Vuuren

Index 363

Introduction

Searching and researching the field of translation and interpreting

Regina Rogl, Daniela Schlager & Hanna Risku
University of Vienna

1. Introduction

Our journey into the methodological approach of field research began with our theoretical work on the concept of the situatedness of translation (from Risku 2000 and 2002 to Risku and Rogl 2021). The situated view on translation draws, for example, on embodied, embedded, enacted, extended and affective (4EA) approaches to cognition as well as on converging sociological frameworks that look at how actors and their practices and products are embedded in societies and social situations. These socio-cognitive views assume that human activities cannot be explained without taking into account the parallel bodily, material and social processes in which they occur. To take this theoretical stance seriously, we turned to field research and the call to "follow the actors" (Latour 2005: 12) "in the wild" (Hutchins 1995) in our empirical, ethnographic translation research projects (Risku 2004; Risku and Pircher 2006; Rogl 2022; research projects *Extended Translation* 2014–2017 and *Rethinking Translation Expertise* 2021–2025).

We have recently again been in close contact with the daily hustle and bustle in the offices of many young and seasoned translation practitioners, where we got to know their working procedures, their social networks and their sources of joy and sorrow. Needless to say, we are immensely grateful to all those colleagues in the field who opened their doors for us. The deeper we delve into the field research approach, the more clearly we recognise its challenges and specificities. Given this, we decided to initiate a dedicated conference (*Field Research on Translation and Interpreting*; FIRE-TI 2022 in Vienna) and, ultimately, to compile this volume dedicated to field research within our discipline. Both at the conference and in the preparations for this book, the discussions on the different definitions and experiences of what constitutes field research or, indeed, the field itself were most inspiring. As translation and interpreting (T&I) scholars increasingly leave their offices and labs and gather data in the field, data collection methods con-

https://doi.org/10.1075/btl.165.int
Available under the CC BY-NC 4.0 license. © 2025 John Benjamins Publishing Company

tinue to evolve, incorporating a broader range of creative techniques and technological tools. With the emergence of global T&I networks and the COVID-19 pandemic, the concept of 'the field' has taken on new digital and analogue dimensions and can encompass a wide spectrum, spanning from very specific to increasingly broad interpretations.

In this introductory chapter, we discuss the field research approach and the concept of the field in T&I (research). We reflect on some common themes in the chapters in this book, including both methodological and conceptual issues. It seems to us that the contributing authors have succeeded in unearthing many critical dimensions of T&I that question and disrupt the boundaries of T&I (research) as we now know it. Consequently, we conclude with a discussion of the potential in T&I field research that thus became visible.

2. Of field research and fieldwork

Kapiszewski, MacLean and Read (2015:1) describe 'field research' as the act of "leaving one's home institution in order to acquire data, information, or insights that significantly inform one's research". The aim of field research is to collect data that is intricately intertwined with the situations and settings in which the phenomena under study unfold. To be able to do so, field researchers familiarise and engage themselves with the settings they study to varying extents, ranging from frequent visits to complete immersion in the field. They occupy roles that lie on a continuum from insider to outsider and may even change roles during their research (see, e.g., Hokkanen, Chapter 4; Staudinger, Chapter 5; Davier, Chapter 7, this volume). The methods they use can vary from participant observation or participatory research to less immersive data gathering methods like video recordings, the collection of email communication or field interviews. Their presence in the field allows them not only to gather highly context-, setting- and situation-specific data during their visits to the field, but also to interpret this data through the prism of their own interactions, experiences and perceptions. Field research is therefore a reflexive and interpretive process that evolves based on events and interactions unfolding within the field at a given time. Data collection using questionnaires, source and target texts, newspaper articles, recorded interpreted speech or even experiments is thus only considered part of a field research methodology if it is undertaken in the actual setting and situation where the relevant practices occur or if it serves as a supplement to the main data.

As 'field research' hinges on the realisation of 'fieldwork', these two terms are frequently used interchangeably. In this volume, we adhere to the distinction made by Bailey (2018), wherein 'field research' characterises the overall research design, while 'fieldwork' specifically denotes "the portion of research that is conducted in the location, referred to as a setting, of interest" (Bailey 2018:243). Accordingly, our understanding of field research as an overall research design that involves engagement with the studied setting outside the confines of the research institution is intentionally broad to avoid automatically equating 'field research' and 'ethnographic fieldwork'. In the past, empirical social research often conflated field research with observational research. The understanding of 'observation' was primarily influenced by the ethnographic research tradition, which involves a researcher's physical presence and extended immersion in the field, including a comprehensive documentation of events, circumstances and artefacts as well as the attempt to acquire an 'emic' perspective (Pike 1967:37–72) of the activities and constructions of meaning in the chosen setting. Over time, this initial and rather rigid understanding of field research has evolved to encompass all practical research steps that enable both direct and indirect access to relevant data from the field (Nowotny and Knorr 2015:83). Thus, while the contribution of ethnography to field research has been highly influential, 'ethnographic fieldwork' can be viewed as a specific approach within the broader spectrum of field research methodologies.

The same conflation of field research and ethnographic research can sometimes be observed in translation and interpreting studies (TIS). In TIS methodological literature, standard course books frequently lack dedicated sections on field research. Scholarly knowledge on 'fieldwork', 'field relations' or 'field research ethics' is either scattered over publications on case study designs or limited to chapters on ethnographic research and is thus often overlooked by researchers who carry out research in the field but do not subscribe to an ethnographic approach. In this sense, TIS may encounter challenges similar to those outlined by Kapiszewski, MacRegan and Read (2015:x) for the field of political science: we often only pass on our experiences of doing field research in an "informal and piecemeal" manner, resulting in an "inefficient and inevitably incomplete" transmission of methodological knowledge (Kapiszwski, MacRegan, and Read 2015:x). We see this volume as an attempt to fill this gap and provide a space for field researchers to share their experiential knowledge.

In TIS, field research has been called for or introduced as an indispensable enrichment to various methodological needs and from various epistemological starting points. In interpreting research, the need to venture into the field during data collection is almost unavoidable if the aim is to acquire data that strongly depends on the interpreting setting (e.g., a hospital, school, court or conference) and the participants (e.g., patients, doctors, teachers, parents, judges or defendants) — situations that are by nature difficult to simulate. Even if the aim is to analyse recorded speech, the researcher will need to collaborate with people or institutions in 'real-life' settings, be it to instruct someone on what and how to record or to negotiate access.

Both in interpreting and translation research, different theoretical frameworks have led to greater consideration of field methodologies. This is particularly evident in sociological approaches, which underscore the societal, cultural and organisational embeddedness of T&I practices while also focussing on questions of agency. With its emphasis on following actors throughout the spaces in which they build and maintain relationships with human and non-human entities, actor-network theory (ANT) has, for instance, been one of the frameworks that has drawn more researchers to step into the field. Field research has likewise been accorded an increasingly important role in areas with a strong focus on interactional and organisational dynamics that are easier to grasp in people's 'lifeworlds', such as T&I workplace and ergonomics research (see, e.g., Risku, Rogl, and Milošević 2017 for an overview), or the sociolinguistic paradigm in interpreting studies. From a cognitive T&I research perspective, the notion of the situated nature of action and cognition (cf. Hutchins 1995; Suchman 2007) has equally culminated in a new methodological focus on field research (Hubscher-Davidson 2011; Risku 2017).

While various research endeavours with different methodological and conceptual approaches might require the researcher to step out of their own office or lab, it should be stressed that a substantial amount of the conceptual and methodological groundwork for field research in TIS has been laid in ethnographic approaches. Over the last two decades, ethnographic fieldwork has garnered increased attention in our discipline. Recently published overviews (e.g., Angelelli 2015; Asare 2016; Buzelin 2022; Risku et al. 2022) and a dedicated special issue edited by Marin-Lacarta and Yu (2023a) illustrate the diversity of methodological approaches even within the framework of ethnography. These articles specify the unique conceptual focus of ethnographic research and provide valuable insights into the practical and ethical challenges that ethnographers encounter. Marin-Lacarta and Yu (2023b: 151) also highlight the diversity of settings where ethnographic fieldwork has been an integral and transformative component of the research design, including:

> interpreting in healthcare settings (Baraldi and Gavioli 2007), institutional translation (LeBlanc 2014; Koskinen 2008), non-government organisations (Tesseur 2022), translation agencies (Olohan and Davitti 2017; LeBlanc 2013), institutional conference interpreting (Duflou 2016), online translation communities (Lu and Lu 2022; Yu 2022, 2019), and literary translation grants and publishers (Marin-Lacarta 2019; Marin-Lacarta and Vargas-Urpí 2019, 2018; Buzelin 2015).

Ethnographic approaches essentially only began to gain traction in TIS in the early 2000s, after anthropology went through a period of significant introspection marked by the 'representational crisis' (see, e.g., Spencer 2007) and 'reflexive turn' and culminating in what has been referred to as a certain "self-abjection" in the field (Lather 2007). Gupta and Ferguson (1997: 2) delineated a series of key developments in ethnographic field research in anthropology and sociology (for a detailed discussion, see also LeCompte 2002), which, it can be argued, can also be seen in recent field research in TIS (as evidenced in various chapters in this volume). These developments include a critique of essentialist concepts of culture (e.g., Wolf 2002 on hybrid in-between spaces; Cronin and Simon 2014 on the city as translation zone; Fheodoroff 2022 on agent-centred translation zones), the exploration of the interactions that shape fieldwork experiences (e.g., Milošević and Risku 2020), the establishment of ethnography as a genre of writing (a debate that Buzelin [2022: 41] describes as sorely lacking in TIS), reflections on the textual genre of field notes (e.g., Davier, Chapter 7, this volume) and an inquiry into the nature of the concept of 'the field' itself (see Section 3). At the same time, recent TIS field research has explored how field methods can be tailored to the particularities of T&I practices (e.g., Koskinen, Chapter 1; Napier, Chapter 2, this volume), while also asking how TIS could enrich field research in other disciplines (Koskinen, Chapter 1, this volume).

In this volume, our perspective extends beyond ethnographic field research, embracing a deliberately broader scope. When compiling the chapters, our goal was to cover a variety of issues that are integral to field research on T&I. These include the dynamics of the researcher's presence in the field, engaging with actors in the chosen setting, reflecting on what it means to adopt an interpretative approach, issues of positionality, and navigating ethical considerations in research designs that involve closely following actors or practices. These elements are echoed in diverse approaches to field research and are not only relevant for observational research but also, for instance, for 'field interviews', which often involve initial site visits to build rapport, on-site interviews and informal interactions in office spaces or during interim result presentations. Conducting field interviews in the interviewees' work environments thus often yields richer insights due to the contextual depth they provide. Our choice to maintain this broad perspective is therefore quite intentional, as we aim to address concerns that may be relevant to any researchers engaged in establishing field relationships, exploring the idiosyncrasies of the research sites and reflecting on their own role in the co-construction of knowledge.

3. In search of 'the field'

In TIS, the term 'field' can carry different meanings. We use it to classify specific disciplinary areas such as 'the interpreting studies field' or practice areas like 'the audiovisual translation field'. It can likewise be subject to an even narrower understanding such as 'field interpreting' (see Ruiz Rosendo and Barghout, Chapter 3, this volume) or serve as a theoretical concept like Bourdieu's (e.g., 1993) field theory. Last but not least, it can also be used to denote a methodological concept, which is what we focus on in this volume.

The conceptualisation of the 'field' within the specific context being studied constitutes a fundamental question in every field research project. Researchers face the challenge of determining where their 'field' begins and ends, and how this delineation can be substantiated. The 'field' is the place we go to gather data, which is why it has long been viewed as little more than a "data reservoir" (Nowotny and Knorr 2015: 82, our translation). However, researchers should critically reflect on their constitutive role in deciding which data they consider to be part of the field and relevant in the data collection process.

Notions of 'the field' are heavily influenced by traditional ethnographic research principles such as the need for researchers to physically 'be there' and immerse themselves in a particular location. In the 1980s and 1990s, however, this notion of 'the field' as a singular, localisable entity began to be challenged in anthropology and related fields for a range of conceptual and practical reasons. Gupta and Ferguson (1997: 3), for instance, highlight the existential crises that anthropology went through from the 1970s to the 1990s. This period was marked by a growing awareness that traditional ethnography was no longer keeping up with the changing methodological, theoretical and political needs of a field that had undergone a postcolonial turn and seen the advent of (post-)critical ethnography (Lather 2007). These emerging perspectives highlighted the researcher's part in shaping and bodily co-constructing knowledge, introducing a move towards reflexivity. They simultaneously challenged the often still prevailing assumptions of researcher neutrality and objectivity and placed an emphasis on examining power structures in the field, between researchers and participants, and also within institutional research. At the same time, this period saw a critical reassessment of prevailing, largely essentialist, ideas of culture that were also the base for traditional conceptualisations of 'the field', namely that a social or cultural group would somehow be confined to a single locality with clearly defined boundaries that a researcher would then supposedly be capable of pinpointing (Gupta and Ferguson 1997: 4). Yet, as Amit (2000: 6) explains,

> in a world of infinite interconnections and overlapping contexts, the ethnographic field cannot simply exist, awaiting discovery. It has to be laboriously constructed, prised apart from all the other possibilities for contextualization to which its constituent relationships and connections could also be referred.

This shift in how societies and 'cultures' were conceptualised within the social sciences was accompanied by significant transformations within the societies themselves. While ethnographic field research was initially designed for the study of "supposedly small-scale societies" (Gupta and Ferguson 1997: 3), the emergence of "an interconnected world in which people, objects, and ideas are rapidly shifting and refuse to stay in place" (Gupta and Ferguson 1997: 4) prompted many social scientists to move away from a notion of the 'field' as an easily identifiable, geographically confined and stable entity. Instead, they tried to accommodate how people inhabit and move between multiple physical, virtual, cultural and linguistic spaces (LeCompte 2002: 288) and take into account their multiple, and possibly contradictory, subjectivities and identities (Warf and Arias 2009: 6). As several chapters in this volume illustrate, ongoing societal transformations, crises and global events persistently influence how field researchers can approach and engage with field sites that are in a constant state of flux. While extending the scope of fieldwork to embrace global connections, field researchers also still face the challenge of not losing sight of the distinctive significance of the local.

Another relic from traditional ethnographic imperatives of fieldwork is an understanding of 'the field' as a location distant from the researchers' homes where they would immerse themselves for an extended period of time. As Caputo (2000) points out, the further the location of this site, the more legitimate the 'field' was often considered. In anthropology, this principle has been strong enough to serve as a basis for academic boundary work in that it has been used to delineate those scholars whose research is considered "'real' fieldwork" (Caputo 2000: 20–21) or in that it impacts academic staff decisions based on researchers' geographic specialisation areas (Caputo 2000: 20). Yet, as Amit (2000: 2) notes, this notion of travelling away from 'home' and fully immersing oneself in a remote field did not even necessarily align with the research realities in more traditional ethnography. Researchers would return home on a regular basis or at the end of a full observation day because it was more convenient, because they might also have caregiving responsibilities or because (as in organisational research) it simply would not make much sense for them to stay after office hours. They might also spread their time across teaching duties, committee work and visits to the field site. It thus seems critical to deliberate on a field concept that actually mirrors lived field research practice (see also Günel and Watanabe's [2024] concept of "patchwork ethnography").

For the aforementioned reasons, it makes sense to understand field sites not as physically bounded in one single place, but rather as a patchwork of potentially evolving spaces that could include physical, virtual or maybe even conceptually delineated spaces and mirror the nature of people's mobilities and interconnected practices. To ascertain which spaces matter in a specific research project, one more enlightening approach is to trace the trajectories of actors, objects and relations across the diverse spaces they navigate (see, e.g., the influential 'multi-sited ethnography' proposed by Marcus [1995], which has significantly expanded the understanding of the 'field' in the social sciences).

What the researcher can focus on in field research always involves choices. When multiple events occur at the same time, observers may struggle to decide where to focus their attention (Koskinen 2008: 45). Furthermore, even if field researchers could record everything that is happening, the sheer volume and complexity of such rich, multi-layered data would render it unfeasible for full processing and interpretation. Ultimately, interpretative research is inherently selective. In this sense, a 'field' is never predetermined or pre-existent but always 'constructed' or, as Coleman and Hellermann (2011: 3) put it, it is never really "natural" but always "made". While Marcus' (1995) approach has often been understood as an attempt at *following* relations that emerge somewhat naturally, some research endeavours require considerable construction effort (Coleman and Hellermann 2011). In his more recent work, Marcus (2011) suggests that researchers should not merely *follow* informants, objects and practices, since this would mean "simply submitting themselves to a track laid out for them rather than actively choosing and constituting their ethnographic path" (Coleman and Hellermann 2011: 3). Instead, he proposes viewing 'fields' that are naturally disjunctive as "distributed knowledge systems" (Marcus 2011: 23).

Ferguson (2011), in contrast, notes that globalisation, mobility and the interconnectedness of contemporary societies do not constitute entirely unprecedented phenomena. He questions the necessity of developing entirely new methodologies in response to societal shifts, proposing instead a reorientation towards alternative analytical units (Ferguson 2011: 197–198) by either shifting the focus from the search for *a* field to 'relations' or conceptualising the 'field' or 'object of study' as a 'set of practices'. Both of these options have been taken up in T&I field research. In her ethnographic work on European Union institutions, Koskinen (2008: 44) characterises her understanding of culture as inherently relational. ANT-inspired translation research has shown how tracing emerging assemblages may uncover hidden instances of translation (e.g., Van Rooyen, Chapter 11, this volume), while Olohan (2021) has illustrated how translation can be conceptualised from a praxeological perspective, thereby providing a more tangible starting point for field research journeys aimed at uncovering T&I practices.

Another attempt at adapting the conceptualisation of 'the field' to today's methodological needs that has been taken up in translation research (see, e.g., Hsiao 2014; Li 2015; Wongseree 2017; Rogl 2022) can be found in Hine's (2016) work on an ethnography that is capable of accommodating the online–offline continuities of everyday practices. Over the last decade, researchers have developed various, somewhat overlapping, strategies for tracing such activities and conceived their 'fields' as "online", "multi-modal", "multi-sited", "blended", "networked" or "connective", with the latter constituting Hine's own suggestion in which

> the frames of meaning-making for online activities are acknowledged to be multiple, and the connections which the ethnographer chooses to pursue therefore have to be viewed as strategic choices rather than as dictated by the prior boundaries of the field as an autonomous agent. (Hine 2016:562)

'Closeness' to a field also does not always have to be a purely geographical notion. It can also mean closeness in terms of a researcher's own personal and professional knowledge and experiences. Koskinen (2008:52) notes that, similar to other organisational or work-related field research, T&I field research is frequently undertaken by researchers who are (or were) part of the settings being studied. This semi-insider position helps so-called 'practisearchers' to gain access to the field, establish rapport with its members and better understand or relate to the events and dynamics within the setting (for an early mention of "practisearchers", see Gile 1994; for a more detailed discussion on what this means for a field researcher's positionality, see Koskinen 2008 and Chapter 1, this volume). However, many researchers experience this dual role as troubling, e.g., when it comes to reflecting on their own positioning and subjectivities (see Section 4).

Field research has often been compared to a journey. As noted above, this journey does not necessarily involve physical displacements: it can also refer to an experiential or emotional journey in which field researchers bodily experience and construct their own understandings of what they perceive in the field (Amit 2000:7).

4. Current methodological and conceptual issues

Every field research journey is different. Each project varies in its location and duration, involves unique participants and relations, and differs in its approaches, conceptual backgrounds, methods and data types. In this volume, we see a broad variety of settings — from national and international institutions (e.g., Napier, Chapter 2; Ruiz Rosendo and Barghout, Chapter 3; Staudinger, Chapter 5) via language service providers (e.g., Sannholm, Chapter 9; Korhonen, Chapter 10) to human or animal welfare institutions (e.g., Steinkogler, Chapter 6; Davier, Chapter 7; Jansen van Vuuren, Chapter 15), refugee contexts (e.g., Dizdar and Rozmysłowicz, Chapter 13; Todorova, Chapter 14), radio station newsrooms (Van Rooyen, Chapter 11), churches (Hokkanen, Chapter 4) and book clubs (Tekgül-Akın, Chapter 12). The researchers navigated online and offline sites, observed and talked to diverse actors and opted for different degrees of researcher involvement in approaching their fields.

Many of the chapters in this volume explicitly adopt ethnographic approaches (e.g., Koskinen, Chapter 1; Napier, Chapter 2; Ruiz Rosendo and Barghout, Chapter 3; Hokkanen, Chapter 4; Staudinger, Chapter 5; Steinkogler, Chapter 6; Davier, Chapter 7; Sannholm, Chapter 9; Korhonen, Chapter 10; Tekgül-Akın, Chapter 12; Dizdar and Rozmysłowicz, Chapter 13; Todorova, Chapter 14; Jansen van Vuuren, Chapter 15). Nonetheless, they also exhibit substantial diversity in their specific methodological approaches to ethnography: some chapters draw from the rich traditions of anthropology and cultural studies, while others venture into cognitive ethnography and more fine-grained, micro-level methodologies. Various data sources and methods (e.g., participant observation; interviews; field notes and diaries; artefact and document analysis) are employed and discussed, both in analogue and digital data collection contexts. Some authors go on a journey into their own past and use retrospective ethnography (Ruiz Rosendo and Barghout, Chapter 3) or revisit previous projects (Napier, Chapter 2; Hokkanen, Chapter 4), while others delve into topics of general relevance to fieldwork and field studies (Riondel, Chapter 8) such as issues related to research ethics and self-reflexivity.

Despite this variety of approaches and settings, sooner or later most field researchers have to deal with similar methodological and conceptual issues. The common ground here seems to lie in the complex and messy dynamics inherent in field research, which is a journey into the unknown, without a straightforward path and a definite end.

This 'messiness' might, in part, be traceable to the nature of the subject under investigation: human experience is complex and thus difficult to study or even grasp, especially when researchers aim at a comprehensive, nuanced understanding (as is often the case in field research). Moreover, experiences do not stand still, waiting to be 'discovered' and analysed. People, relationships and practices evolve and change during the investigation, and so do the researchers, and they are all likely to be influenced by their interaction with each other. Field research with an interest in human beings (and also non-human animals; see Jansen van Vuuren, Chapter 15, this volume), their experiences, emotions and processes of meaning-making thus means navigating through the uncertainties and constantly changing conditions that characterise life.

Moreover, researchers are not just external observers of this social world, they are an integral part of it. Scientific practices are embedded in societal, cultural and economic contexts that substantially influence them. As has been shown by the *laboratory studies* approach in science and technology studies (for an overview, see Knorr-Cetina 1995), the fact that knowledge is actively and interactively constructed — and not merely discovered — applies not only to qualitative or field research. It has been shown to also significantly impact the production of scientific knowledge even in the context of rigid quantitative or experimental research. This social construction implies multiple perspectives and thus multiple 'realities'. Whereas this subjectivity and contingency are seen in many areas of research as confounding factors and efforts are made to suppress them, the field research tradition considers them to be central components and, indeed, as epistemological tools. Consequently, reflexivity takes on an important role and becomes a resource in the research process. This aspect also makes field research methodologically challenging: multiple perspectives have to be considered, hardly anything can be generalised, and everything is highly context-specific — there is no 'one-size-fits-all', and researchers are instead required to make context- and situation-specific decisions in every phase of the research process from the development of research questions and preparation for field access to the interpretation of data and documentation of results.

Many of these decisions are discussed in the contributions to this volume. Overarching, recurring and closely interrelated themes include the role and position of the researcher, relationships with the field and participants as well as ethical considerations. These are often not clear-cut or stable but multifaceted and dynamic. Indeed, many authors reflect not on *one* but on *several* — fluid — roles and positions that they have to manage and that have a significant impact on what they can actually observe in a particular setting, how their relationships with people in the field will develop and what ethical choices they will have to make.

A common dual role in T&I research is that of the 'practisearcher' (see Section 3), which means that the researchers are not only researchers but also trained and/or practising translators or interpreters, which influences their general perspective and potentially introduces biases and ethical challenges. Steinkogler (Chapter 6, this volume), whose study participants are non-professional and para-professional translators and interpreters, discusses, for example, the challenge and importance of not imposing her own professional standards on the participants and remaining sensitive to their experiences and perceptions. Other researchers actively function as translators or interpreters in their chosen settings within the framework of autoethnographic approaches or participant observations (Ruiz Rosendo and Barghout, Chapter 3; Hokkanen, Chapter 4; Staudinger, Chapter 5; Davier, Chapter 7). Being both researcher and research subject at the same time introduces an even greater risk of role conflicts and often makes the management of field relationships more challenging and sensitive. Some authors also explicitly take a committed, socially engaged stance towards their research projects, which are inspired by their own strong support and deep personal engagement for issues such as refugee aid (Todorova, Chapter 14), veganism (Davier, Chapter 7) or animal welfare (Jansen van Vuuren, Chapter 15). Their dual role as researchers and activists (or triple role if they are also practising translators or interpreters) again provides them with a specific perspective and presents benefits as well as challenges.

Not only can researchers have multiple roles, the roles themselves can also evolve and change. Some authors specifically discuss such transformative experiences during or after their fieldwork, demonstrating that 'insider' or 'outsider' positions and 'emic' or 'etic' perspectives are not stable or mutually exclusive categories but rather nuances in a continuum. Staudinger (Chapter 5), for example, reflects on 'going native' in the field. Her role evolved from that of an external researcher to a partial insider and, ultimately, a full member of the group she was studying, making reflexivity as an ongoing practice essential. Hokkanen (Chapter 4), on the other hand, moved from being an insider to a (partial) outsider after her fieldwork and subsequently reflects on her previous position in the field. She puts her deep personal commitment to her role as an autoethnographer and church interpreter at the heart of her analysis and re-examines it several years later from her now-changed emotional and theoretical perspective. Instead of silencing her private selves, she thus makes her subjective positionality an essential resource in the construction of knowledge and also demonstrates that it can be fruitful to approach past studies from a new perspective (similar to Napier, Chapter 2, in this volume). Staudinger's (Chapter 5) and Hokkanen's (Chapter 4) research objects — the revision of legislative drafts by in-house translators in a government institution vs. simultaneous church interpreting of prayer by volunteer members of a religious community — could be seen as quasi opposites. However, they do have a common denominator: they question the insider-outsider dichotomy and see researcher positionality as a dynamic spectrum, allowing for multiple, equally insightful interpretations of the data, deeply connected to their respective positions, with the etic—emic axis constituting just one of the relevant coordinates. Davier (Chapter 7), in turn, adds an important point to this discussion by addressing the notion that the entanglement of different researcher roles not only affects how a researcher lives these roles but also how they evolve during fieldwork. She reports, for instance, that being deeply involved as a volunteer translator and researcher in an organisation promoting vegetarianism and veganism strengthened her own vegan identity.

Discussions on researcher reflexivity often centre on social categories such as gender, age, occupation, education, language or class and only rarely include reflections on emotion (Punch 2012). However, as showcased in the chapters by Hokkanen (Chapter 4) and Davier (Chapter 7), researchers' emotions are not absent from (field) research and can be fruitfully analysed under the umbrella of reflexivity. Affect as "embodied meaning-making" (Hokkanen and Koskinen 2016: 83) plays a vital role in understanding the phenomena being studied and is thus a relevant, albeit largely neglected, factor in the production of knowledge in our field. It would certainly be enriching to see the impact of affect and emotions included in researchers' self-reflections more often.

Some of the chapters (Hokkanen, Chapter 4; Staudinger, Chapter 5; Davier, Chapter 7) highlight the benefits of using field diaries as a tool for self-reflection. Field diaries not only support ongoing reflection and transparency, they also chronicle the researcher's evolving position and relationships within the field. They are instrumental in documenting and guiding methodological and ethical decisions as the research project evolves. As emphasised by Davier (Chapter 7), they can also have a 'cathartic' function, offering a means to process emotions. Overall, field diaries are undoubtedly an effective tool for recognising and documenting not only the situatedness, embeddedness, embodiment and affectivity of the individuals in the field but also of one's self as a researcher.

Reflexivity in field research is closely tied to ethical considerations, which are of the utmost importance both in seemingly non-sensitive settings as well as in contexts that involve marginalised and potentially vulnerable groups (e.g., Dizdar and Rozmysłowicz, Chapter 13; Todorova, Chapter 14) or in closed-off, highly confidential settings such as the UN field missions explored by Ruiz Rosendo and Barghout (Chapter 3). It becomes clear that ethical considerations touch upon all phases of the research process, which raises questions about the adequacy of standardised ethical procedures such as ethics board approval or informed consent. These often fail to capture the dynamics of fieldwork or the context-specific understandings of ethical conduct. In some cases, they might even have a counterproductive effect by creating a superficial "facade of ethics" (Marzano 2012: 445) which suggests that all ethical questions have been resolved at the beginning of the study and do not need further consideration as the research progresses (see Riondel, Chapter 8, this volume). It would seem that for "mediating messiness" (Billo and Hiemstra 2013; see also Goodnough 2008; Krane 2016; Salovaara 2018; Clift et al. 2019) also in ethical terms, field researchers need to go beyond ethical committees or signed consent sheets. In this regard, Marzano (2012) and Riondel (Chapter 8) propose alternative approaches which are more flexible and responsive to the unique challenges of field research. Marzano advocates "relational ethics" (Ellis 2007) or "ethics of care" (Noddings 2003), prioritising emotional connections, empathy and mutual respect over rules as the foundation for ethical conduct. In a similar vein, Riondel (Chapter 8) argues for a more situated and reflexive approach to ethics, where ethical decisions are made on a case-by-case basis and continually reassessed throughout the research process. Such an approach enables researchers to tailor their strategies specifically to each unique and changing context. Moreover, both Marzano (2012) and Riondel (Chapter 8) emphasise the importance of not just avoiding harm but actively seeking to do good and consider potential benefits for participants.

In addition to these inherent challenges of field research, external challenges also arise. Just as the rules of ethics committees often have quantitative or experimental foundations, so too do the funding logics behind the allocation of research grants. As Cheek (2018) notes, the ongoing "marketization" of research entails a metric-based approach to evaluate whether "research products" (Cheek 2018: 577) are 'valuable'. Qualitative research often defies measurement, which can lead to its marginalisation — and often not being funded at all — or to a pressure to conform to these rather narrow criteria. This pressure can result in a standardisation of qualitative methods and potentially sideline innovative or unconventional approaches. Adapting to this business-oriented environment while maintaining the integrity and purpose of qualitative inquiry can be a difficult balancing act. Thus, alongside the complexities of navigating through the social world being studied, field researchers face another orientation challenge, namely that of manoeuvring through the intricate and competitive "research marketplace" (Cheek 2018; see also Carey and Swanson 2003).

The global COVID-19 pandemic exacerbated these challenges and introduced new ones. Fieldwork during this time became even more unpredictable and challenging. Researchers had to be more flexible and adaptive than ever before, dealing with their own and (potential) participants' altered and sometimes precarious work and life circumstances, adjusting to rapidly changing travel and contact restrictions, and coping with uncertain resources both in terms of funding and staff. This situation created logistical, ethical and emotional difficulties.

From a logistics perspective, it was initially unclear how long the crisis would dominate our living and working conditions. Many researchers found themselves having to cope with the "uncertain future of pandemic postponing" (Nyoni and Agbaje 2022: 70), continuously setting new dates and plans — often only to have to postpone them again. This was the case for our own *Rethinking Translation Expertise (Retrex)* project, too: our entire research design was based on the premise that we could be present on site in the workplaces. As a result, we had to postpone the start of our project, ultimately delaying it by 18 months and pushing the limits of the Austrian Science Fund which funds our research. Planning within the team was also not without difficulties as we had to face several changes and challenges in our private and working lives and were rarely able to see each other face-to-face during this time.

As it became clear that the pandemic was not going to end soon, many researchers had to resign themselves to either abandoning their projects or redesigning their research. If the field was still accessible in some way, they had to adapt key steps — such as field access, building relationships with participants, data collection, or even the research question — to the pandemic conditions. These steps already require flexibility and adaptability in a non-pandemic setting, but this was intensified during the pandemic: "[T]he pandemic has made contingency planning a central part of our research designs" (Krause et al. 2021:265). This contingency planning was also crucial because (field) researchers still faced pressure to continue producing. For many, this situation presented quite an emotional burden (MacLean et al. 2020:1–2; Davier, Chapter 7, this volume).

A more fundamental issue that arose for some researchers (including our team) was one of an ethical nature. Is my research really so important that I must somehow push through with it in light of the global crisis, the immense suffering it has caused and the many inequalities it has exacerbated (cf. MacLean et al. 2020:2)? While this big question can also be posed in the context of other global issues and crises, it had concrete methodological implications during the COVID pandemic. For example, we had pangs of conscience about approaching potential observation sites, questioning whether it was appropriate to ask translation agencies if we could shadow them onsite as soon as it was possible again given the assumption that they probably had more pressing concerns at that time. The problem of field access during the pandemic is addressed in this volume in the chapter by Davier (Chapter 7), for whom it presented a major challenge. Contrary to her original plan, she had to conduct most of her data collection remotely in a field that was changing so drastically and with relationships becoming so loose that she questions whether it is even justified to speak of a 'field' at all.

Even when field access remained possible, new ethical and methodological concerns arose. When on-site research was feasible, consideration had to be given to minimising health risks for both the researcher and the people in the field. Protecting study participants from potential dangers is generally a mandate in (field) research, but for researchers in TIS this had previously rarely entailed dealing with highly contagious and potentially fatal diseases. When fieldwork had to be conducted remotely, researchers faced the challenge of devising new, digitised approaches, familiarising themselves with hardware and software tools that allow remote data collection and dealing with technical issues. Many also questioned whether the quality of their field relationships — and their research in general — would suffer due to the use of remote digital methods (Krause et al. 2021; Watson and Lupton 2022). Furthermore, fieldwork in virtual spaces generally presents its own specific challenges, which also need to be considered, even when not undertaken out of pandemic necessity (see, e.g., Rogl 2022: 161–226; Huang, Cadwell, and Sasamoto 2023).

On a more positive note, the pandemic did also bring with it certain opportunities for research. In some cases, the use of digital methods produces insights that would be difficult to obtain through analogue means. The increased reliance on digital tools, which has continued to some extent in the aftermath of the pandemic, might also make research projects more feasible in the long term (e.g., by bridging larger geographical distances; cf. Watson and Lupton 2022). Last but not least, the significant changes in people's personal and professional lives raised intriguing new questions for research: How do people — in our case, those involved in T&I — cope with the altered conditions? Will some of these changes have a lasting impact on their fields (see, e.g., Cheung 2022; Liu and Cheung 2022)? And who, if not field researchers, is best equipped to investigate these questions?

Although we hope that such circumstances will not return in the foreseeable future, there remains much to be learned from them regarding our handling of crises and the unforeseen. Research, and particularly field research, is always embedded within a societal and lifeworld context and is thus affected by the crises we experience collectively and individually. For Dizdar and Rozmysłowicz (Chapter 13, this volume), it was a more recent crisis that confounded their field access. The Russian invasion of Ukraine significantly restricted their ability to conduct onsite research at an asylum reception centre, with the exceedingly high acute occupancy at the centre making it unfeasible to carry out all the planned field visits.

As the considerations above clearly show, navigating complexity and messiness is key in field research. In communicating our research, we have to translate this complexity and messiness into language and often face the challenge that the experiences and constructions of meaning encountered in the field do not fit into neat, clear-cut boxes. This is not limited to methodological questions: it can also include the terms, categories and approaches we draw on to make sense of the phenomena we observe. Even (or particularly?) fundamental concepts like 'translation' and 'interpreting' sometimes create difficulties and require reflection and refinement. Accordingly, many of the authors in this volume question, expand, redefine and create various terms and concepts or adopt new approaches to capture the lived realities outside of academia as precisely as possible.

It can also be argued that T&I are practices of mediating messiness — often, but not necessarily, related to language. Some chapters in this volume specifically focus on ways to study language use in the field, enabling fine-grained analyses of collaborative meaning-making processes (Koskinen, Chapter 1; Napier,

Chapter 2; Korhonen, Chapter 10; Dizdar and Rozmysłowicz, Chapter 13). Both Koskinen (Chapter 1) and Napier (Chapter 2) discuss the potentials of 'linguistic ethnography' (LE, or, in Koskinen's case, specifically 'translatorial linguistic ethnography'), which combines ethnographic principles with linguistic analysis, granting central importance to language practices while still maintaining the holistic, context-sensitive ethnographic perspective. Using an LE framework helps to zoom in on the nuances of translator- or interpreter-mediated communication and other linguistically realised interactions in the field, thus achieving a deeper understanding of language and translation as "artefacts in the socio-cultural context" (Koskinen, Chapter 1). In a similar vein, although not within an LE framework, Korhonen (Chapter 10) employs artefact analysis and systemic functional linguistics to explore cognitive collaboration in translation revision, aiming to enhance cognitive ethnographic methodology. Dizdar and Rozmysłow-icz (Chapter 13) also take a closer look at language, specifically its impact on shaping social dynamics and identities within institutional settings like refugee reception centres. Here, individuals are categorised, among other factors, based on their languages, and this process of 'human differentiation' is conducted predominantly by linguistic means.

The concepts of 'translation' or 'interpreting' themselves are linguistically manifested in the field, and translating them into academic writing poses its own challenges. Our 'etic' scholarly conceptualisations of T&I do not always correspond with both the 'emic' understandings and the multifaceted and intricate practices in the field. One example is the blurring of lines between translating and interpreting (and translators and interpreters): many individuals handle both tasks, the activities often overlap, and they are often not distinguished in naming terms. Consequently, some authors (Koskinen, Chapter 1; Dizdar and Rozmysłowicz, Chapter 13; Todorova, Chapter 14; Jansen van Vuuren, Chapter 15) have chosen to use 'translation' as an umbrella term for both translation and interpreting, even though this is uncommon in current TIS discourse in English.[1] While this might introduce a certain degree of ambiguity in some instances, it ultimately reflects an inductive use of the term and aligns more closely with the realities encountered in the field. The lines between translation and interpreting and other, non-translatorial, activities are also often blurred in the field, for instance, in the realm of paraprofessional translation. To capture such phenomena that deviate from our prototypical conceptions of 'translating' and 'interpreting' without oversimplifying their nuances, may require alternative terms such as 'translatoriality' (Koskinen, Chapter 1). Broad definitions of trans-

---

1. Unlike, e.g., in German, where 'Translation' encompasses both 'Übersetzen' (translating) and 'Dolmetschen' (interpreting).

lation are also evident in the work of Van Rooyen (Chapter 11), Todorova (Chapter 14) and Jansen van Vuuren (Chapter 15). Jansen van Vuuren's ecosemiotic perspective (Chapter 15) includes the interpretation of non-verbal communication between humans and non-humans, for Todorova (Chapter 14), translation involves the transformation of meaning through various means such as cultural exchange and integration in culinary community events, while Van Rooyen (Chapter 11) includes the more abstract concept of translation specific to ANT.

In a related development, not only are the conceptions of 'translating' and 'interpreting' being challenged and expanded but also those of the relevant actors. The long-standing focus on professional translators in translation studies (Grbić and Kujamäki 2019) is gradually shifting, with increasing attention being given in recent years to non- and paraprofessional translators and interpreters and other involved actors. Many of the translators/interpreters studied in the chapters in this volume are not prototypical 'professionals' (e.g., Steinkogler, Chapter 6; Van Rooyen, Chapter 11; Dizdar and Rozmysłowicz, Chapter 13; Todorova, Chapter 14; Jansen van Vuuren, Chapter 15). Tekgül-Akın (Chapter 12) goes one step further by focusing her study not on the actors involved in the production process but on the recipients, i.e., the readers. Research into paraprofessional translation and interpreting appears in particular to be gaining momentum. As Koskinen (Chapter 1) argues, the field research approach seems particularly suited in this area, since translatorial practices that are not (or only barely) visibly institutionalised (even less than professional translation and interpreting) might not even be identified using other methods, and a context-sensitive perspective is needed to examine their diverse manifestations in detail. Van Rooyen's chapter (Chapter 11) illustrates how tracing such invisible paraprofessional translation practices can be made to work in an observational study.

Similarly, the intricacies of translatorial collaboration often remain invisible outside of field research. The complex interplay of translators with their social and material environments in the translation process is particularly highlighted by approaches like distributed cognition (Sannholm, Chapter 9; Korhonen, Chapter 10) or actor-network theory (Van Rooyen, Chapter 11), which share several commonalities that lie at the intersection of sociological and cognitive research interests (cf. Risku and Rogl 2022). By emphasising non-human elements or artefacts — such as objects and tools — and locating agency or cognition not in a single person but in a web of interactions between humans and non-human elements, these approaches challenge traditional notions of what constitutes an 'actor' (see Risku 2024). Here, agency extends beyond individual capacities and, in the case of ANT, is explicitly attributed to 'non-human actors' as well. From an ecosemiotic perspective, Jansen van Vuuren (Chapter 15) also stresses the importance of recognising both human and non-human agency in T&I processes, particularly the agency of non-human animals. She suggests focusing more on the commonalities and continuities between humans and non-humans rather than their differences. Overall, field research seems to contribute to expanding the inclusivity of T&I studies by showcasing the diversity of practice which does not necessarily conform to academic definitions or adhere to disciplinary boundaries.

5. Tapping the potentials of field research

We would like to conclude this introduction by summarising the relevance of T&I field research for the further development of TIS as a discipline. In doing so, we highlight nine specific motivations for utilising field research approaches: from contextualisation to cooperation between industry and academia.

Contextualisation

Field research makes it possible to understand the sociocultural contexts in which T&I relevant activities take place. It allows us to see how specific situations influence actors, activities and processes of meaning-making, and how the actors in turn influence the situations. Field research facilitates insights into specific contexts of action with their origins, developments, possibilities and limits. It can thus prevent oversimplifications and generalisations.

Authenticity

Field research helps to acquire data that are closely connected to their source location. It ranges from the direct observation of activities that would mostly have taken place even without the researchers being present to the collection of written correspondence between participants as the communication unfolds and interviews with participants in their usual locations. It offers us insights into activities and their social and material circumstances. Regarding research on translation revision, Mossop (2007:17) notes, for example, that most empirical studies still take place *in vitro*, usually within a university campus. He stresses the need to study revision in the workplace during the actual production process noting that otherwise the subjects' decisions might be influenced by the fact that they know their output will never be delivered to a client. Screen actions can be recorded, and emails to and from colleagues, clients and subject experts can be examined, thus complementing the aforementioned set of methodological tools more traditionally associated with field research, even if traditional process research methods such as thinking aloud and recording of conversations may not always be practical in an office setting.

Field research thus allows us to empirically reappraise previous research results that might be based on more distant verbal rationalisations and to compare real-time and real-life/work situations with ideal representations, previous plans and retrospective memories and explanations. It can reveal telling differences between what is expressed as a norm and what is actually done, thus permitting analyses of the reasons for the differences between normative views or idealisations and the usual course of events. At the same time, in the direct context of action, we learn how actors see, describe, justify and legitimise their decisions, thus enabling us to analyse which values and ideologies are connected to these justifications.

Developmental perspective

Since field research can include long-term immersion in or several data collection visits to the field over a long period of time, it can make changes in behaviour, attitudes, working methods or conditions visible.

Innovation

Given its generally inductive approach, field research can reveal new aspects and phenomena whose relevance had not been recognised in previous theoretical and empirical enquiries. It can broaden our horizons through rich encounters with the participants. New processes, practices, roles and materials or even completely new questions and topics can arise that might not have been considered when planning data sources and acquisition methods. Such discoveries are not only worthwhile on their own, they also open up new research questions and hypotheses, which can then be included in further studies like large-scale surveys and experiments.

Explanation

Field research is also well suited as a follow-up project to surveys and experiments that reveal certain general correlations but may not be able to provide any information about their context and backgrounds. While quantitative studies can describe the relationships between specific predefined variables, qualitative field research can seek to understand why actors behave in a specific way in certain contexts, how and why specific decisions are made, and thus also how and why T&I products, actors and situations have become the way they are today. Field, lab, survey and other research can act as complements and/or correctives for each other, challenging and testing each other's insights and jointly contributing to the development of the discipline.

Participant perspective

The longer, more frequent or more intense a researcher's presence in the field, the greater their proximity to and insights into how the participants think and how they perceive and experience their situations. Such insider perspectives potentially differ significantly from previous scientific assumptions, which can lead to scholarly reconceptualisations and updates.

Transformational power

Field research can change the field. At the individual level, a participant might find it rewarding and insightful to voice their experiences and reflect on their practices, which in turn might inspire them to tackle a problem differently or adopt a new perspective. At the organisational level, becoming aware of research questions and findings can prompt organisations to initiate strategic development processes. At the societal level, while we need to be aware that uncritical approaches to field research can produce highly problematic results (e.g., reinforcing ableism; exoticising, essentialist, exploitative or extractivist stances), we still believe that field research can unearth injustice or silenced voices and identify factors that can be used to improve the situation.

Didactic relevance

Regularly investigating practice on the ground helps to update teaching contents and curricula (see, e.g., Ruiz Rosendo and Barghout, Chapter 3, this volume). Bringing the insights acquired through field research into our study programmes can empower students by making them aware of current developments in practice and providing them with the opportunity to reflect on how they want to deal with them.

Research-practice cooperation

Field research can stimulate the exchange of experiences between research and practice, potentially expanding the horizons on both sides. The collaboration and insights gained can inspire practitioners, researchers, teachers, students or repre-

6. The contributions in this volume

The chapters in this volume are grouped into four parts. The first part presents specific methodological approaches in T&I field research and is followed by a part that deals with the critical issues of positionality, reflexivity and ethics in the respective authors' research projects. The chapters in the third part showcase the utilisation of particular data types, with a specific focus on artefacts, non-human actors and distributed agency. The final part potentially challenges established TIS boundaries and focal points by integrating marginalised groups and phenomena.

Part I. Delving into specific ethnographic approaches

Field research is often ethnographic. However, ethnography is not a uniform approach. Variables such as research interests, data granularity or available data types can influence the choice of a particular ethnographic approach. The chapters brought together in Part I of this volume explore the advantages and hurdles of selected ethnographic approaches that prove promising for our field.

In her chapter, Kaisa **Koskinen** encourages us to study the everyday management of multilinguality, irrespective of whether the participants would see their activities as T&I or not. Such translatoriality is omnipresent in many aspects of life, and Koskinen focuses here on paraprofessional translation as the translatorial actions of non-translators/-interpreters in work contexts where organisational agendas depend on being able to deal with multilingualism. For this purpose, she collaborates with scholars in international business and management and organisation studies. In the framework of what she refers to as translatorial linguistic ethnography, Koskinen suggests utilising creative practices of data acquisition and combining methods from different research traditions — from questionnaires to the analysis of physical spaces and material environments — and including participants as co-researchers in the projects.

Jemina **Napier** connects with Kaisa Koskinen's chapter by delving deeper into linguistic ethnography (LE). She demonstrates how LE uniquely combines linguistic and ethnographic methods to explore social and communicative dynamics across different interpreting settings. Napier argues for the transformative potential of LE within the field of interpreting studies, particularly in its ability to shed light on language use in context as well as the consequences and perceptions of language choices. The chapter provides an overview of LE and its application in the analysis of interpreter-mediated interactions. It then revisits examples from previous research from an LE perspective, drawing on Napier's extensive prior studies in the domain of sign language interpreting research. In discussing which of her previous work could be framed as following an LE approach, Napier not only clarifies what qualifies as LE and what does not. She also illustrates the potential of LE for gaining a deeper understanding of interpreting as a "complex languaging practice".

Lucía **Ruiz Rosendo** and Alma **Barghout** employ retrospective reflexive ethnography and the concept of 'past presencing' to investigate interpreting practices in UN field missions. Their methodological approach leverages 'remembered data' from UN interpreters who have served in field missions, with a particular focus on the extensive first-hand experiences of one of the authors. The chapter underscores the value of (auto-)ethnographic accounts in enriching our understanding of the role and challenges faced by interpreters in field missions, thereby contributing to the development and implementation of targeted training programs for UN interpreters. In particular, Ruiz Rosendo and Barghout show how the retrospective analysis of field data can help explore interpreting practices in settings that are highly sensitive in nature and thus typically closed off to field researchers.

Part II. Centring on positionality, reflexivity and ethics

The chapters in Part II focus on reflexive journeys of field researchers in which they experience changing perspectives and encounter difficult ethical choices.

Sari **Hokkanen** reanalyses her field notes from an earlier autoethnographic research project on church interpreting from a drastically different personal perspective after several years. She initially considered taking the easy route to reporting results by ignoring the radical changes in her positionality and carrying out a "quasi-objective", "matter-of-fact analysis" of her data. In the end, however, she decided to do the opposite and systematically analyse her changed researcher position from member to non-member of the religious community that she studied, as she realised that this shift enabled her to arrive at the current insights in the first place. This re-interpretation brought to the fore a reconceptualisation of her research object, the affective aspects of volunteer, faith-related interpreting. Having previously taken her emotional involvement in interpreting as "authentic and divinely inspired", she now applies the theoretical approach of affective labour to discuss how interpreters manage affects to align with the expectations of the social context, and how deep and surface acting help interpreters in emotional self-regulation. Her chapter highlights the importance of reflexivity regarding multiple researcher postures, past vs. current selves, private selves vs. service roles.

Whereas Hokkanen started her autoethnography as a full member of the context she studied and now re-analyses her data from the position of a non-member, Cornelia **Staudinger**'s analysis describes the opposite situation. In her field research on linguistic revision and legal review of legislative drafts in the Swiss federal administration, she evolves from outsider to partial and ultimately full insider and member in the context studied. In Staudinger's case, the changes already happen during the research project itself, so that the data gathered and analysed in the first phases of the research project rely on her views as an outsider, whereas later in the project, she juggles the researcher and participant roles in parallel, now gathering and analysing data from her own changed work context. Her chapter thus deals with very concrete challenges of reflecting on one's own role, communicating transparently and applying conscious strategies to manage benefits and risks associated with becoming an insider.

Vanessa **Steinkogler** discusses issues of reflexivity and positionality by employing the concept of 'boundary work'. Drawing on her experiences from an ethnographic study at an Austrian NGO, she reflects on the relationships between herself and the participants, how they perceive and categorise each other, and how these boundaries develop during her research process. Even before entering the field, she expected methodological and ethical challenges due to her role as a 'practisearcher' in a setting with mainly non- and paraprofessional interpreters and translators. In the course of her fieldwork, however, her initial dual role evolved into multiple roles, which further complicated the navigation of boundaries and power asymmetries, and required her to constantly adjust her approach to build rapport and trust while maintaining her research objectives. Steinkogler emphasises the importance of reflexive practices, especially in the context of research into non-professional interpreting and translation, where relational dynamics between researchers and participants are particularly complex.

Lucile **Davier** puts a specific tool centre stage. Her chapter provides an in-depth exploration of the use of field diaries in (auto-)ethnographic research, emphasising their role as a tool for reflexivity. She discusses several benefits of field diaries using examples from her own autoethnographic study as a volunteer translator in a Swiss veganism organisation. For her, being deeply committed to the cause herself and having to face severe challenges in fieldwork due to the COVID-19 pandemic, the diary proved crucial. However, it can be helpful for other field research contexts as well by providing a medium for continuous self-reflection which can improve the quality of data collection and ethical conduct while still in the field, aid in developing analytical ideas, document authentic embodied experiences which often deviate from original plans, and have a cathartic role by channelling the researchers' thoughts and emotions, especially when things (seem to) go wrong.

Aurélien **Riondel**'s chapter critically examines current practices of ethical clearance in field research, advocating for a more nuanced, situated and reflexive approach to ethics in our field. He challenges the standardised processes overseen by research ethics committees (RECs), arguing that these often fail to accommodate the unique, evolving and cyclical nature of qualitative field research. He proposes a dynamic approach where ethical considerations are continually reevaluated and adapted to the specific context of each study, illustrating his argument with examples and experiences from his interview study on translation revision. Emphasising the importance of reflexivity, Riondel discusses how researchers can engage in ongoing ethical deliberation, documenting and contemplating ethical decisions throughout the research process, rather than merely complying with predefined rules. His work underscores the need for a balance between formal ethical regulations and a deeper, more thoughtful engagement with ethical issues, encouraging researchers to contribute positively to their field of study while maintaining a respectful and beneficial relationship with participants.

Part III.   Zooming in on processes and materiality

Following the examination of specific ethnographic tools and the field researcher's role in terms of positionality and reflexivity, this part delves into the methodological application of specific analytical units, in particular artefacts and processes, and explores how these can be conceptualised and operationalised within a field research framework.

Raphael **Sannholm** reports on his ethnographic fieldwork conducted in the Swedish translation office of an international language services provider. Focussing on a single instance of workplace interaction, the study meticulously explores the exchanges between two professional translators as they engage in the task of assessing a client-specific workplace document. Sannholm examines this example utilising conversation analysis to delve into the collective construction and maintenance of material resources as cognitive artefacts. With distributed cognition as central theoretical framework, his chapter provides a comprehensive examination of how cognitive artefacts like client-specific guidelines are interactively constructed, embedded in larger socio-cultural systems and used to organise practices in translation workplaces, offering insights into the interplay between collaborative processes and material resources.

The distributed aspect of translation work also lies at the centre of Annamari **Korhonen**'s chapter. She explores the use of two data sources and two analysis methods to study how cognitive work is distributed between translators and revisers. First, she utilises artefact analysis to examine how the formatting and software features of the revision files impact cognitive work. Here, she shows how those features guide the revisers' focus, potentially limiting their ability to edit certain textual features. She then complements the analysis by using revision files from the translation software as data, examining them through systemic functional discourse analysis. Here, she focusses on comments on the translated text, analysing shifts in thematic, ideational and interpersonal aspects. Through her explorative combination of artefact and discourse analysis, she is able to integrate both material and social aspects in her investigation of the distribution of work.

Marlie **van Rooyen** explores the role of translation in South African community radio stations. Utilising actor-network theory (ANT) as a conceptual and analytical lens, she embarks on a methodological journey to unveil hidden instances of translation as a fresh news item is being crafted and takes shape. Her research demonstrates how translation in journalistic settings is often invisible, embedded within the daily activities of news production and overshadowed by other journalistic practices, while involving a complex interplay of human and non-human actors. Van Rooyen illustrates how ANT can be used to meticulously trace the distribution and redistribution of agency among various actors, including journalists, diverse types of texts and other artefacts in the translation process, while simultaneously making the temporal dimension of the observed practices methodologically tangible.

Part IV.   Integrating marginalised groups and phenomena

In the fourth and final part of this volume, the chapters highlight fieldwork that focusses on groups and actors situated at the periphery, whether in the broader context of our societies or within the field of translation studies.

Duygu **Tekgül-Akın** reports on her experiences of using ethnography to study reading groups' encounters with translated fiction. This chapter brings to light the notable gap in studies that address the perspectives of translation end-users, particularly in literary translation research. Tekgül-Akın examines the advantages and hurdles she encountered in conducting field research to gain insights into how readers perceive and interpret translated works. Her chapter discusses a range of methodological issues, including ethical dilemmas and the logistical complexities of inquiring into reader attitudes in reading groups. In particular, Tekgül-Akın discusses her challenges of negotiating the potential tensions between her own positionality and multiple subjectivities on the one hand, and the readers' perceptions and attributions to her as "the cultural Other" or as someone with the authority of a researcher, on the other. Furthermore, adapting to the challenges posed by the COVID-19 pandemic, Tekgül-Akın delves into the emerging area of online research with readers, highlighting its potential drawbacks and charting possible directions for future investigations.

While Tekgül-Akın shifts our focus to a group previously peripheral in our field of research, the subsequent two chapters delve into field research with groups that tend to suffer marginalisation in our societies. For their field study at a German reception centre for refugees, Dilek **Dizdar** and Tomasz **Rozmysłowicz** introduce a theoretical framework based on "human differentiation". They aim at an understanding of T&I practices beyond facilitating communication by showing that these can contribute to the construction of differences between people. In the reception process, asylum seekers are sorted into language categories for translation purposes, affecting their further experiences and institutional treatment. The authors demonstrate how ethnographic methods like participant observation, interviews and document collection help to zoom in on this (often complex and problematic) differentiation process and the role that T&I play in it. They also discuss the challenges of recruiting interpreters in reception centres, which often involves internal recruitment from among asylum seekers or staff, leading to role conflicts and additional differentiation.

Marija **Todorova** highlights the role of interpreting and (self-)translation practices for the integration process. Her research focusses on asylum seekers and refugees in Hong Kong, involving in-depth interviews with asylum-seeking women and participant observation of community events aiming at interaction and cultural exchange between asylum seekers, refugees and the local population. Such events involve activities like food sharing and storytelling which can be understood as (self-)translation practices. Todorova dives into the methodological intricacies of conducting research with marginalised groups, addressing issues such as reflecting on power asymmetries, establishing relationships with the participants and representing their perspectives. She emphasises ethical sensitivity, methodological flexibility and the critical role of the researcher's positionality in studying and interpreting the complex realities of the participants' lives.

Finally, Xany **Jansen van Vuuren**'s study involves participants who have barely been researched in translation studies so far: non-human animals. She approaches interactions between humans and non-humans from an ecosemiotic perspective, viewing all forms of interpretation of signs as translational processes, including non-verbal communication between humans and, as in her case, horses. In the field under study, which consists of animal welfare outreach events in South Africa, a large number of such multispecies interactions take place, in addition to multilingual and multicultural communication resulting from the country's diverse background. Jansen van Vuuren aims at a comprehensive understanding of these manifold T&I processes by employing a multispecies ethnographic research design. Overall, she advocates for more inclusive, post-anthropocentric approaches in translation studies including non-verbal and interspecies communication and treating humans and non-human animals as equal agents in the field.

Acknowledgements

We would like to express our gratitude to Antonia Baumann, Celia Martín de León and the anonymous reviewers for their invaluable feedback on this introduction.

References

Amit, Vered. 2000. "Constructing the Field." In *Constructing the Field: Ethnographic Fieldwork in the Contemporary World*, ed. by Vered Amit, 1–18. London & New York: Routledge.

Angelelli, Claudia V. 2015. "Ethnographic Methods." In *Routledge Encyclopedia of Interpreting Studies*, ed. by Franz Pöchhacker, 148–150. London & New York: Routledge.

Asare, Edmund. 2016. "Ethnography of Communication." In *Researching Translation and Interpreting*, ed. by Claudia V. Angelelli, and Brian J. Baer, 212–219. London & New York: Routledge.

Bailey, Carol A. 2018. *A Guide to Qualitative Field Research*. 3rd edition. Thousand Oaks: Sage.

Baraldi, Claudio, and Laura Gavioli. 2007. "Dialogue Interpreting as Intercultural Mediation: An Analysis in Healthcare Multicultural Settings." In *Dialogue and Culture*, ed. by Marion Grein, and Edda Weigand, 155–175. Amsterdam & Philadelphia: John Benjamins.

Billo, Emily, and Nancy Hiemstra. 2013. "Mediating Messiness: Expanding Ideas of Flexibility, Reflexivity, and Embodiment in Fieldwork." *Gender, Place & Culture* 20 (3): 313–328.

Bourdieu, Pierre. 1993. *The Field of Cultural Production: Essays on Art and Literature*. Edited and introduced by Randal Johnson. New York: Columbia University Press.

Buzelin, Hélène. 2015. "Traduire pour le Centre national du livre." *Contextes: Revue de sociologie de la littérature*.

Buzelin, Hélène. 2022. "Ethnography in Translation Studies: An Object and a Research Methodology." *Slovo.ru: Baltic accent* 13 (1): 32–47.

Caputo, Virginia. 2000. "At 'Home' and 'Away': Reconfiguring the Field for Late Twentieth-Century Anthropology." In *Constructing the Field: Ethnographic Fieldwork in the Contemporary World*, ed. by Vered Amit, 19–31. London & New York: Routledge.

Carey, Martha A., and Janice Swanson. 2003. "Funding for Qualitative Research." *Qualitative Health Research* 13 (6): 852–856.

Cheek, Julianne. 2018. "The Marketization of Research: Implications for Qualitative Inquiry." In *The SAGE Handbook of Qualitative Research*, ed. by Norman K. Denzin, and Yvonna S. Lincoln, 569–599. Los Angeles, London & New Delhi: Sage.

Cheung, Andrew K. F. (ed). 2022. "Teaching and Practice of Distant Interpreting in the Pandemic Era." Special issue, *INContext* 2(2). https://www.incontextjournal.org/index .php/incontext/issue/view/3

Clift, Bryan C., Julie Gore, Sheree Bekker, Ioannis Costas Batlle, Katharina Chudzikowski, and Jenny Hatchard (eds). 2019. *Myths, Methods, and Messiness: Insights for Qualitative Research Analysis*. Bath: University of Bath.

Coleman, Simon, and Pauline von Hellerman. 2011. "Introduction: Queries, Collaborations, Calibrations." In *Multi-Sited Ethnography: Problems and Possibilities in the Translocation of Research Methods*, ed. by Simon Coleman, and Pauline von Hellerman, 1–15. London & New York: Routledge.

Cronin, Michael, and Sherry Simon. 2014. "Introduction: The City as Translation Zone." *Translation Studies* 7 (2): 119–132.

Duflou, Veerle. 2016. *Be(com)ing a Conference Interpreter: An Ethnography of EU Interpreters as a Professional Community*. Amsterdam & Philadelphia: John Benjamins.

Ellis, Carolyn. 2007. "Telling Secrets, Revealing Lives: Relational Ethics in Research with Intimate Others." *Qualitative Inquiry* 13 (1): 3–29.

Ferguson, James. 2011. "Novelty and Method: Reflections on Global Fieldwork." In *Multi-Sited Ethnography: Problems and Possibilities in the Translocation of Research Methods*, ed. by Simon Coleman, and Pauline von Hellerman, 194–207. London & New York: Routledge.

Fheodoroff, Marlene. 2022. "The Agent-Centred Translation Zone: Researching the People Within Translational Spaces." *Translation in Society* 1 (2): 177–199.

Gile, Daniel. 1994. "Opening Up in Interpretation Studies." In *Translation Studies as an Interdiscipline: Selected Papers from the Translation Studies Congress, Vienna, 9–12 September 1992*, ed. by Mary Snell-Hornby, Franz Pöchhacker, and Klaus Kaindl, 149–158. Amsterdam & Philadelphia: John Benjamins.

Goodnough, Karen. 2008. "Dealing with Messiness and Uncertainty in Practitioner Research: The Nature of Participatory Action Research." *Canadian Journal of Education* 31 (2): 431–458.

Grbić, Nadja, and Pekka Kujamäki. 2019. "Professional vs Non-Professional? How Boundary Work Shapes Research Agendas in Translation and Interpreting Studies." In *Moving Boundaries in Translation Studies*, ed. by Helle V. Dam, Matilde N. Brøgger, and Karen K. Zethsen, 113–131. London & New York: Routledge.

Günel, Gökçe, and Chika Watanabe. 2024. "Patchwork Ethnography." *American Ethnologist* 51 (1): 131–139.

Gupta, Akhil, and James Ferguson. 1997. "Discipline and Practice: 'The Field' as Site, Method, and Location in Anthropology." In *Anthropological Locations: Boundaries and Grounds of a Field Science*, ed. by Akhil Gupta, and James Ferguson, 1–46. Berkeley, Los Angeles & London: University of California Press.

Hine, Christine. 2016. "Ethnographies of Online Communities and Social Media: Modes, Varieties, Affordances." In *The SAGE Handbook of Online Research Methods*, ed. by Nigel Fielding, Raymond M. Lee, and Grant Blank, 556–576. Los Angeles & London: Sage.

Hokkanen, Sari, and Kaisa Koskinen. 2016. "Affect as a Hinge: The Translator's Experiencing Self as a Sociocognitive Interface." In *Cognitive Space: Exploring the Situational Interface*, ed. by Maureen Ehrensberger-Dow, and Birgitta Englund Dimitrova, 78–96. Amsterdam & Philadelphia: John Benjamins.

Hsiao, Chi-hua. 2014. "The Cultural Translation of U.S. Television Programs and Movies: Subtitle Groups as Cultural Brokers in China." Dissertation, University of California.

Huang, Boyi, Patrick Cadwell, and Ryoko Sasamoto. 2023. "Challenging Ethical Issues of Online Ethnography: Reflections from Researching in an Online Translator Community." *The Translator* 29 (2): 157–174.

Hubscher-Davidson, Severine. 2011. "A Discussion of Ethnographic Research Methods and Their Relevance for Translation Process Research." *Across Languages and Cultures* 12 (1): 1–18.

Hutchins, Edwin. 1995. *Cognition in the Wild*. Cambridge: MIT Press.

Kapiszewski, Diana, Lauren M. MacLean, and Benjamin Lelan Read. 2015. *Field Research in Political Science: Practices and Principles*. Cambridge: Cambridge University Press.

Knorr-Cetina, Karin. 1995. "Laboratory Studies: The Cultural Approach to the Study of Science." In *Handbook of Science and Technology Studies*, ed. by Sheila Jasanoff, Gerald E. Markle, James C. Petersen, and Trevor Pinch, 140–166. Thousand Oaks, London & New Delhi: Sage.

Koskinen, Kaisa. 2008. *An Ethnographic Study of EU Translation*. Manchester: St. Jerome.

Krane, Vikki. 2016. "Embracing the Messiness of Qualitative Research: Challenges and Opportunities for Qualitative Researchers in Sport and Exercise." In *Routledge Handbook of Qualitative Research in Sport and Exercise*, ed. by Brett Smith, and Andrew C. Sparkes, 472–475. London & New York: Routledge.

Krause, Peter, Ora Szekely, Mia Bloom, Fotini Christia, Sarah Zukerman Daly, Chappell Lawson, Zoe Marks, Aidan Milliff, Kacie Miura, Richard Nielsen, William Reno, Emil Aslan Souleimanov, and Aliyu Zakayo. 2021. "COVID-19 and Fieldwork: Challenges and Solutions." *PS: Political Science & Politics* 54 (2): 264–269.

Lather, Patti. 2007. "Postmodernism, Post-Structuralism and Post(Critical) Ethnography: Of Ruins, Aporias and Angels." In *Handbook of Ethnography*, 2nd edition, ed. by Paul Atkinson, Amanda Coffey, Sara Delamont, John Lofland, and Lyn Lofland, 477–492. London: Sage.

Latour, Bruno. 2005. *Reassembling the Social: An Introduction to Actor-Network Theory*. Oxford: Oxford University Press.

LeBlanc, Matthieu. 2013. "Translators on Translation Memory (TM). Results of an Ethnographic Study in Three Translation Services and Agencies." *The International Journal for Translation and Interpreting Research* 5 (2): 1–13.

LeBlanc, Matthieu. 2014. "Traduction, bilinguisme et langue de travail: une étude de cas au sein de la fonction publique fédérale canadienne." *Meta* 59 (3): 537–556.

LeCompte, Margaret. D. 2002. "The Transformation of Ethnographic Practices: Past and Current Challenges." *Qualitative Research* 2 (3): 283–299.

Li, Dang. 2015. "Amateur Translation and the Development of a Participatory Culture in China: A Netnographic Study of the Last Fantasy Fansubbing Group." Dissertation, School of Arts, Languages and Cultures, University of Manchester.

Liu, Kanglong, and Andrew K. F. Cheung. (eds). 2022. *Translation and Interpreting in the Age of COVID-19*. Singapore: Springer.

Lu, Sijing, and Siwen Lu. 2022. "Methodological Concerns in Online Translation Community Research: A Reflexive Netnography on Translator's Communal Habitus." *Perspectives* 30 (4): 695–710.

MacLean, Lauren M., Nabila Rahman, Robin L. Turner, and Jack Corbett. 2020. "Disrupted Fieldwork: Navigating Innovation, Redesign, and Ethics during an Ongoing Pandemic." *Qualitative and Multi-Method Research* 18 (2): 1–8.

Marcus, George E. 1995. "Ethnography in/of the World System: The Emergence of Multi-Sited Ethnography." *Annual Review of Anthropology* 24: 95–117.

Marcus, George E. 2011. "Multi-Sited Ethnography: Five or Six Things I Know About It Now." In *Multi-Sited Ethnography: Problems and Possibilities in the Translocation of Research Methods*, ed. by Simon Coleman, and Pauline von Hellerman, 16–32. London & New York: Routledge.

Marin-Lacarta, Maialen. 2019. "Characteristics of a Digital Literary Translation Publisher: Revisiting Bourdieu's Mapping of the Publishing Field." *The Translator* 25 (1): 27–41.

Marin-Lacarta, Maialen, and Mireia Vargas-Urpí. 2018. "When the Translator Does More Than Translate: A Case Study of Translator Roles in a Digital Publishing Initiative." *Hermes: Journal of Language and Communication Studies* 58: 117–137.

Marin-Lacarta, Maialen, and Mireia Vargas-Urpí. 2019. "Translators Revising Translators: A Fruitful Alliance." *Perspectives* 27 (3): 404–418.

Marin-Lacarta, Maialen, and Chuan Yu. (eds). 2023a. "Ethnographic Research in Translation and Interpreting Studies." Special issue, *The Translator* 29 (2).

Marin-Lacarta, Maialen, and Chuan Yu. 2023b. "Ethnographic Research in Translation and Interpreting Studies." *The Translator* 29 (2): 147–156.

Marzano, Marco. 2012. "Informed Consent." In *The SAGE Handbook of Interview Research: The Complexity of the Craft*, 2nd edition, ed. by Jaber F. Gubrium, James A. Holstein, Amir B. Marvasti, and Karyn D. McKinney, 443–456. Thousand Oaks: Sage.

Milošević, Jelena, and Hanna Risku. 2020. "Situated Cognition and the Ethnographic Study of Translation Processes: Translation Scholars as Outsiders, Consultants and Passionate Participants." *Linguistica Antverpiensia* 19: 111–131.

Mossop, Brian. 2007. "Empirical Studies of Revision: What We Know and Need to Know." *The Journal of Specialised Translation* 8: 5–20.

Noddings, Nel. 2003. *Caring: A Relational Approach to Ethics & Moral Education*. Berkeley: University of California Press.

Nowotny, Helga, and Karin D. Knorr. (1975) 2015. "Die Feldforschung." In *Techniken der empirischen Sozialforschung. Band 2: Untersuchungsformen*, ed. by Jürgen van Koolwijk, and Maria Wieken-Mayser, 82–112. München: Oldenbourg Wissenschaftsverlag.

Nyoni, Phefumula, and Olaide Agbaje. 2022. "Fieldwork Dynamics in a Higher Education Setting amid the COVID-19 Pandemic." *Critical Studies in Teaching and Learning* 10 (1): 63–77.

Olohan, Maeve. 2021. *Translation and Practice Theory*. London & New York: Routledge.

Olohan, Maeve, and Elena Davitti. 2017. "Dynamics of Trusting in Translation Project Management: Leaps of Faith and Balancing Acts." *Journal of Contemporary Ethnography* 46 (4): 391–416.

Pike, Kenneth L. 1967. *Language in Relation to a Unified Theory of Structure of Human Behavior.* 2nd rev. edition. The Hague: Mouton.

Punch, Samantha. 2012. "Hidden Struggles of Fieldwork: Exploring the Role and Use of Field Diaries." *Emotion, Space and Society* 5 (2): 86–93.

Risku, Hanna. 2000. "Situated Translation und Situated Cognition: ungleiche Schwestern." In *Translationswissenschaft. Festschrift für Mary Snell-Hornby zum 60. Geburtstag,* ed. by Mira Kadrić, Klaus Kaindl, and Franz Pöchhacker, 81–91. Tübingen: Stauffenburg.

Risku, Hanna. 2002. "Situatedness in Translation Studies." *Cognitive Systems Research* 3 (3): 523–533.

Risku, Hanna. 2004. *Translationsmanagement. Interkulturelle Fachkommunikation im Informationszeitalter.* Tübingen: Narr.

Risku, Hanna. 2017. "Ethnographies of Translation and Situated Cognition." In *The Handbook of Translation and Cognition,* ed. by John W. Schwieter, and Aline Ferreira, 290–310. Oxford: Wiley-Blackwell.

Risku, Hanna. 2024. "Reflections on Individualized and Extended Translator Studies." In *Translation als Gestaltung: Beiträge für Klaus Kaindl zur translatorischen Theorie und Praxis,* ed. by Mira Kadrić, Waltraud Kolb, and Sonja Pöllabauer, 65–74. Tübingen: Narr.

Risku, Hanna, Maija Hirvonen, Regina Rogl, and Jelena Milošević. 2022. Ethnographic Research. In *The Routledge Handbook of Translation and Methodology,* ed. by Federico Zanettin, and Christopher Rundle, 324–339. London & New York: Routledge.

Risku, Hanna, and Richard Pircher. 2006. "Translatory Cooperation: Roles, Skills and Coordination in Intercultural Text Design." In *Übersetzen –Translating – Traduire: Towards a "Social Turn"?,* ed. by Michaela Wolf, 253–264. Münster: LIT.

Risku, Hanna, and Regina Rogl. 2021. "Translation and Situated, Embodied, Distributed, Embedded and Extended Cognition." In *The Routledge Handbook of Translation and Cognition,* ed. by Fábio Alves, and Arnt L. Jakobsen, 478–499. London & New York: Routledge.

Risku, Hanna, and Regina Rogl. 2022. "Praxis and Process Meet Halfway: The Convergence of Sociological and Cognitive Approaches in Translation Studies." *The International Journal of Translation and Interpreting Research* 14 (2): 32–49.

Risku, Hanna, Regina Rogl, and Jelena Milošević. 2017. "Introduction. Translation Practice in the Field: Current Research on Socio-Cognitive Processes." *Translation Spaces* 6 (1): 3–26.

Rogl, Regina. 2022. "Die Verwobenheit von technischen Strukturen und sozialen Praxen im Kontext gemeinschaftsbasierter Übersetzung im Web 2.0." Dissertation, University of Vienna.

Salovaara, Perttu. 2018. "Accounting for the Messiness of the Research Process: The Fieldpath Approach." *Qualitative Research in Organizations and Management* 13 (4): 315–332.

Spencer, Jonathan. 2007. "Ethnography After Postmodernism." In *Handbook of Ethnography,* 2nd edition, ed. by Paul Atkinson, Amanda Coffey, Sara Delamont, John Lofland, and Lyn Lofland, 443–452. London: Sage.

Suchman, Lucy. 2007. *Human-Machine Reconfigurations: Plans and Situated Actions.* 2nd edition. Cambridge: Cambridge University Press.

Tesseur, Wine. 2022. *Translation as Social Justice: Translation Policies and Practices in Non-Governmental Organisations.* London & New York: Routledge.

Warf, Barney, and Santa Arias. 2009. "Introduction: The Reinsertion of Space in the Humanities and Social Sciences." In *The Spatial Turn: Interdisciplinary Perspectives*, ed. by Barney Warf, and Santa Arias, 1–10. London & New York: Routledge.

Watson, Ash, and Deborah Lupton. 2022. "Remote Fieldwork in Homes During the COVID-19 Pandemic: Video-Call Ethnography and Map Drawing Methods." *International Journal of Qualitative Methods* 21: 1–12.

Wolf, Michaela. 2002. "Culture as Translation: Ethnographic Models of Representation in Translation Studies." In *Crosscultural Transgressions: Research Models in Translation Studies II. Historical and Ideological Issues*, ed. by Theo Hermans, 180–192. Manchester: St. Jerome.

Wongseree, Thandao. 2017. "Understanding Thai Fansubbing: Collaboration in Fan Communities Translating a Korean TV Show." Dissertation, School of Applied Language and Intercultural Studies, Dublin City University.

Yu, Chuan. 2019. "Negotiating Identity Roles During the Process of Online Collaborative Translation: An Ethnographic Approach." *Translation Studies* 12 (2): 231–252.

Yu, Chuan. 2022. *Online Collaborative Translation in China and Beyond: Community, Practice, and Identity*. London & New York: Routledge.

PART I

Delving into specific ethnographic approaches

CHAPTER 1

Translating at work
Identifying and contextualizing paraprofessional translatoriality in organizations

Kaisa Koskinen
Tampere University

This chapter is a proposal for a research agenda that focuses on a particular context of translation work: everyday management of multilinguality in organizations by people who have been employed in another capacity but end up engaging in translatorial actions to move organizational agendas forward and get their work done. The agenda builds on work already done in translation studies and is developed in collaboration with scholars in international business and management and organization studies. As this widespread and contextually embedded practice is only becoming identified and studied, the chapter argues for embedded approaches that focus on extended fieldwork, and offers ideas for creative and exploratory methods to enrich data collection and to invite participants to collaborate and co-research this phenomenon.

Keywords: paraprofessional translation, translatoriality, translatorial linguistic ethnography, fieldwork methods, contextualization, workplace studies

1. Introduction

Non-professional, volunteer and activist translation has gained increasing atten-tion in translation studies in the past decade or so. As translation studies has intensified its interest in contexts of translation beyond the remit of professional translation industry, it has become evident that also professionals of other fields often engage in translating at work, some of them extensively. This translation work is distinct from professional translation, for example due to the non-necessity to follow professional translation norms and to the varied competence levels and translation concepts of those involved in it. At the same time, the con-text of work, with its functional orientation and participants' labor relations and

https://doi.org/10.1075/btl.165.01kos
Available under the CC BY-NC 4.0 license. © 2025 John Benjamins Publishing Company

organizational roles, is in many ways also different from non-professional translating in volunteer contexts, making this sector of translating at work distinct from both professional and non-professional translation. Several scholars (Pym 2011: 87; Tyulenev 2014: 75; Koskela, Koskinen, and Pilke 2017; Piekkari, Tietze, and Koskinen 2020) have started to categorize a distinct object of study, *paraprofessional translation*, to account for

- written and oral rerendering of content across languages,
- at work,
- by people in their professional/paid capacity that is other than translating/interpreting.

Although research into paraprofessional translation is still scarce, anecdotal evidence suggests that it is likely to be a widespread activity and to span across the spectrum of organizations. Today's work context is often multilingual, and paraprofessional translation practices emerge to manage this multilinguality, to create community and to move forward with the tasks at hand. It needs to be underlined that 'translation' is here to be understood in both its written and oral modes, and also extending to other modes such as gestures, visualizations and other communicative solutions. One can find clear distinctions between interpreting and translating in organizations, but in multilingual organizational life this binary division is not always clear-cut in ways the professional world draws the distinction.

In this chapter, I argue for the continued development of this research branch in general and for the need for ethnographic fieldwork in different workplaces in particular. Fieldwork is particularly important for a number of reasons. First, our understanding of the many faces of paraprofessional translation is at an exploratory phase and the area is largely under-researched with some notable exceptions: some early work has looked into paraprofessional public service interpreting (e.g., Pöchhacker and Kadrić 1999), and a lot of recent research has focused on journalistic translation (e.g., Davier and Conway 2019). With limited data on many other contexts, it is therefore necessary to gather extensive descriptive data and collect the understandings of the practitioners themselves before we rush into conclusions about its nature. Second, due to often non-existent organizational management of paraprofessional translation and limited normative pressure (in comparison to more codified professional practices), paraprofessional translation is likely to vary in different contexts, and paraprofessional translators may have developed idiosyncratic ways of dealing with the tasks. Hence the need for the kinds of context-sensitive approaches that extensive fieldwork can provide. Third, paraprofessional translation activities are not always identified as such by practitioners, limiting the usability of interview and survey data and creating a need for immersive observational studies. Fourth, the practices encountered in the field may well also challenge the perceived notions of what constitutes good or successful translatoriality that the researcher — often with a background in professional translation and interpreting as a trainer or practitioner, or both — may embrace, and the ethnographic principle of entering the field with an open mind to learn what is going on from the perspective of the members of the work community is a useful and necessary antidote to rushed interpretations (see also Steinkogler's account of her experiences "as an interested learner" regarding the paraprofessional interpreting practices she studied; Chapter 6, this volume).

Recognizing and identifying paraprofessional translation is not straightforward. These language practices can often contain fragmentary and fleeting moments of translation and may depict innovative ways of onboarding everyone across languages (Koskela, Koskinen, and Pilke 2017). This is in stark contrast to professional translation assignments that typically begin with a finalized text or utterance to be paraphrased in another language in its entirety and the task being given to a separate in-house department or sent to an outsourced translation partner. Hence the necessity to begin by having an open mind about how translation manifests itself in the various everyday activities in the workplace. Because also researchers will have their preconceived notions of what is and what is not translation, and because these may not always fit the realities in the field, I have found it useful to shift terminology. I propose that the concept of *translatoriality* will help the researcher to keep an open mind and ear to micro-moments of translation that neither the participants nor the researcher may necessarily immediately perceive as translating.

This chapter is conceptual-methodological in nature. In the following, I will first further clarify how I understand the two core concepts, paraprofessional translation and translatoriality, and then develop a research agenda that will allow us to build an understanding of how they evolve in real-life contexts in organizations. Building on my earlier work (Koskinen 2020a; see also Koskinen 2008), I advocate for a particularly focused form of ethnographic enquiry, namely *translatorial linguistic ethnography*, and I argue that a combination of creative and exploratory fieldwork methods beyond observation and interviewing might be beneficial in teasing out not only the existing realities of paraprofessional translation but also its largely still untapped potential in organizational processes.

This potential has already been identified in organization and management studies and international business (e.g., Ciuk, James, and Śliwa 2019; Piekkari, Tietze, and Koskinen 2020; Røvik 2023). The potential for contributions from translation studies to these fields lies particularly in the combined understanding of actors and their contextual realities that has for long been developed in sociological approaches to translation and increasingly also in cognitive translation studies (Risku and Rogl 2022). Another particular strength of translation studies within this interdisciplinary area of study is its fine-tuned understanding and vocabulary for a comparative analysis of textual data in several languages (Tietze, Koskinen, and Piekkari 2022: 135). It is indeed a corner stone of translatorial linguistic ethnography to also include translations among its data sets and to treat them as ethnographic artifacts in a manner similar to other datasets (Koskinen 2020a; see also Koskinen 2008: 119–145). In this chapter, however, a particular emphasis is put on various creative and exploratory methods than can enhance data collection in the field. In this discussion, I will build on my own previous work, mainly within the realm of professional translation, as well as that of some other scholars, to begin to develop a methodological tool box for researching paraprofessional translation.

2. Paraprofessional translation

Paraprofessional translators can be defined as follows: they are people who translate as part of their regular work in another professional capacity. Or, to quote Sergei Tyulenev's definition of paratranslators, "people whose jobs are not directly translation- or interpreting-related who do translate or interpret" (Tyulenev 2014: 75). This activity can be voluntary, creating affinities to non-professional translation practices where participants undertake translation according to their own choosing. Or it can be something that a person is asked to do on a regular basis because of their linguistic skills and proven competences, bringing their task description close to in-house translators who often also engage in other activities (see e.g., Kuznik 2016). Some of them *are* professional translators by training but have been hired in another capacity. Some paraprofessional translators actively seek these roles because they enjoy it. They are often called boundary spanners in international business literature (see, e.g., Barner-Rasmussen et al. 2014), that is, valuable connectors between different organizational silos or in-between organizations. High-profile boundary spanners have been studied extensively, but the value of the shop-floor boundary spanners who guarantee information flows across languages may well go entirely unnoticed in the organization and by scholars alike (see, however, e.g., Humonen and Angouri 2023). Sometimes organizational translation tasks are seen as menial work and passed on to the lowest-raking junior colleagues (Ciuk, Koskinen, and Śliwa, forthcoming), but just as well it may be the local manager who engages in strategic paraprofessional translation (Logemann and Piekkari 2015). Depending on their professional status and occupational role, paraprofessional translators such as the CEO studied by Logemann and Piekkari may exert significant agency in and through their translation work and use it strategically to forward particular organizational or personal goals. Professional translators, particularly in today's complex networks of out-sourced translation, several steps removed from the organization, will rarely have the will or the means to produce similarly agentic translations. Indeed, a recent survey demonstrated the participating translators' self-concept to lean heavily towards fidelity: "despite a fundamentally assistive and adaptive role awareness, mediation, co-creation and advising do not feature large in the way the translators regard their role" (Massey and Wieder 2019: 74).

The above overview already indicates that paraprofessional translation may take forms different from professional translation, it can take many shapes, and its status in different organizations can vary. What distinguishes it from *non*-professional translation is the organizational context and the labor relation (on work vs. labor see Zwischenberger and Alfer 2022). Employment brings with it a particular contractual and economic bind, a social identity and a functional and hierarchical role (Meyer, Becker, and Van Dijk 2006). This bind creates a commitment, that is, "a force that binds an individual to a target (social or non-social) and to a course of action of relevance to that target" (Meyer, Becker, and Van Dijk 2006: 666). This commitment can take many forms. Meyer and Allen (1997) differentiate between affective commitment where employees maintain an attachment to a given target because they want to, normative commitment where they do so because they feel they should, and continuance commitment which is based on a necessity or willingness to not sever the connection. These commitments lead to more or less positive workplace behaviors and emotional reactions, but they all share the fundamental element of delineating one's course of actions with the organizational targets (Meyer, Becker, and Van Dijk 2006: 667).

This target-orientedness of organizational behavior links paraprofessional translation to functional orientations in translation studies. The theory of translatorial action developed by Justa Holz-Mänttäri in the 1980s (Holz-Mänttäri 1984) to account for professional translation as an expert profession can therefore also be applied to the analysis of paraprofessional translation practices (Koskinen 2017; Ciuk, James, and Śliwa 2019). With its focus on various actors involved as well as the fundamental role of the goal of the communication, the theory of translatorial action allows the researcher to break free of delimiting notions of equivalence and expectations of straight-forward similarity between the source-language and the target-language textual renderings. This framework valorizes the outcomes of the communication and posits the translator as the expert who has the competences to make informed decisions about which translatorial actions to use. It therefore gears the analysis towards viewing paraprofessional translators not as 'less competent' for not being professional translators but as resourceful experts of their own organizational goals and actions and to recognizing and valuing the many translatorial strategies they use in organizational life. These may include, for example, onboarding by summarizing (Koskela, Koskinen, and Pilke 2017) or resorting to multimodal solutions such as drawing, gestures or movements (Ciuk, Koskinen, and Śliwa, forthcoming). More often than not, paraprofessional translation may also be collaborative in nature (Ciuk, James, and Śliwa 2019). The paraprofessional forms of collaboration/translaboration deserve further research and theorization in a manner similar to online collaborative translation in non-professional and professional contexts (Zwischenberger and Alfer 2022).

It is not too surprising that existing, as yet unpublished, interview data depicts a lot of variation in terms of both paraprofessional translation practices and translation beliefs (Ciuk, Koskinen, and Śliwa, forthcoming). In contrast to professional translators, those engaged in paraprofessional translation do not seem to consider "translatorship" (Svahn 2020) a central part of their "social identity" at work, that is, one's "sense of self and one's similarity to a collective or its members" (see Meyer, Becker, and Van Dijk 2006: 667). It follows that paraprofessional translation practices cannot be expected to be constrained by professional codes of practice in a manner similar to professional translation. Instead, those engaged in paraprofessional translation may well extend the ethical codes and norms of their own profession into their translatorial actions as well. This we do not yet know, and more research on paraprofessional translators' commitments, social identifications, translation ideology and translation beliefs is needed.

As mentioned above, journalistic translation practices are the area of paraprofessional translation that has been most extensively covered by research. 'Journalation' (the convergence of translator and journalist roles) and the international circulation of news and media content has generated valuable insights into this particular context (see, e.g., Davier and Conway 2019). Once we accumulate more insights into organizational paraprofessional translation practices, we can begin to discern similarities and differences between paraprofessional translation in the media and that in other organizational contexts.

3. Translatoriality

In recent years, translation studies has seen numerous proposals for an "extended concept of translation" (Zwischenberger and Alfer 2022) with varying degrees of extension, from a by now widespread explicit inclusion of intersemiotic modes of translation to posthuman (e.g., Cronin 2021) and bio-semiotic theories (Marais 2019) and more. This proliferation of explicitations of the translation concept is a welcome development not only for increasing the transparency of what we scholars are talking about when we talk about translation but also as a reminder that our research participants will have their internalized translation concepts. While these may not always be verbalized nor even conscious, they will have a bearing on their views and comments as well as their practices.

When rethinking translation in the context of organizations, I have found it useful to return to Sandra Halverson's classic work on prototype theory and the idea of translation as a fuzzy concept (Halverson 2000). Her work allows us to appreciate that different conceptualizations can co-exist even among a seemingly homogenous group of people. The further we move away from the prototypical kernel features shared by all, the more we also enter a gray area of 'more or less translatorial' cases. In studying translation in organizations, a further complication arises from the fact that in organization and management studies the term translation is commonly used to denote change processes such as adopting a new management practice. In interdisciplinary work it has therefore sometimes been necessary to differentiate conceptually between "interlingual" and "metaphorical" translation (Piekkari, Tietze, and Koskinen 2020) to remind the readers in these fields of the existence and independent relevance of the movement across languages. In practice, as most translation scholars will readily accept, the interlingual, intercultural and interorganizational processes tend to be intertwined.

While it is surely relevant to study both interlingual and other kinds of translation work in organizations, my take on translation studies is less expansionist than that of some other commentators in that I see the contribution of translation studies best placed in exploring language practices, focusing on written and oral renderings, and accompanying these with various technological, intermodal and embodied extensions of verbal communication as and when they arise in empirical fieldwork.

This means that my translation concept, were I to enter a field site, would center on verbalizations within or between languages (i.e., intralingual and interlingual types) and I would be eager to also observe and understand what kinds of non-verbal resources the organization members employ in their translation work. There is no reason to assume that this would match the translation concept of all participants. This kind of potential misalignment between the researcher and the members is a challenge, particularly for interview studies: how to communicate the object of study and how to interpret the responses? This is why observational fieldwork is so crucial at this early stage when the features of paraprofessional translation are not yet well known, and also the researcher will need to enter the field with an open mind, prepared to work on their own translation concept as they acquire more knowledge of what is actually going on in the everyday life of the organization.

Another workaround to avoid conceptual misalignment is to propose new terminology. If the term 'translation' with its long history and varied usage is a hindrance in analysis, a neologism may offer new avenues for thought. For example, my co-authored article on oral translation practices in a bilingual meeting — i.e., paraprofessional translation — (Koskela, Koskinen, and Pilke 2017) was an outcome of a joint process of trying to define what constitutes translation in a flexilingual meeting where participants engaged in free-flowing translanguaging practices.[1] Rather than trying to define fixed borders of translating and non-translating, we talked about translatorial and non-translatorial turns and defined their translatoriality through collective deliberation. This allowed us to recognize the agile ways in which participants, particularly the chair, used translatorial tactics in ensuring that everyone stayed onboard without needing to extend the meeting by the tedious repetition of all content in various languages.

Translatoriality is a mouthful, but it has become a key concept in my research during the past decade. The more I have moved away from professional translation to observe translational phenomena in other contexts (Koskinen 2012), in historical periods prior to the rise of a translation and interpreting profession (Koskinen 2018) and, notably, paraprofessional translation in organizations, the more I have needed a conceptualization that can account for the muddy everyday life of dealing with multilingualism amidst organizational practices. Translatoriality covers not only the more obvious practices of providing full texts in more than one language, but also the continuums of translatoriality, the fragments of repetition and traces of other languages and self-translation by speakers (Kolehmainen, Koskinen, and Riionheimo 2015).

In addition to productively side-stepping questions of the translation concept, translatoriality carries no value judgement about who does the translating and how, not getting stuck in the perennial questions of the translation profession about who should be considered a professional translator, how we should define translation quality and what the acceptable conditions for this work are. Any of these can and potentially should be asked also in the context of paraprofessional translation, but any pre-set criteria of expected behavior or creating a sense of being critically assessed among participants would seriously compromise our ability to fully account for paraprofessional translation. Translatoriality is what it is, and it is not to be measured against our preconceived expectations originating from professional translation. It is a different creature, it is translation in the wild.

---

1. 'Translanguaging' is another neologism that aims to chart a wide territory of multilingual repertoires. It has gained ground in sociolinguistics, often overriding earlier usage of code-switching. Definitions of translanguaging tend to be rather fluid, reducing its applicability for research purposes where differentiating between switching between codes *with* versus *without* translation elements is central. On 'translanguaging' versus 'translatoriality', see Koskinen and Kinnunen (2022). On translanguaging in boundary spanning, see Barner-Rasmussen and Langinier (2020).

Translatoriality also has no in-built emancipatory agenda. One of its obvious benefits is that it creates a conceptual linkage to the theory of translatorial action discussed in the above section. Theoretically, this kind of robustness is welcome, as it avoids the risk of bringing in potentially clashing presuppositions and implicit ideologies from many directions. It needs to be stated, however, that my take on translatorial action is different from its original formulation precisely in the question of emancipation (see Koskinen 2018). Holz-Mänttäri's theorizations were explicitly aimed at improving the status of professional translators by rebranding them as experts in translatorial action, and taking this theory to explain translation practices performed by others than these experts — translation in the wild — can be seen as hijacking the theory (on the emancipatory undercurrent in translation studies see also Zwischenberger and Alfer 2022).

4. Introducing translatorial linguistic ethnography

During the past 15 years, ethnography has become one standard methodological choice in translation studies, favored by many PhD researchers in particular (e.g., Tesseur 2015; Hokkanen 2016; Pedersen 2019), signaling a generational change in the disciplinary approaches. Ethnography is not, however, one method but can be practiced in many ways. The current popularity of ethnography as a keyword — a search in *Translation Studies Bibliography* gives 210 hits (20.2.2023) — hides a multitude of approaches to ethnographic fieldwork (see Buzelin 2022). At a metalevel, ethnography has always had a two-track appearance in TS, a socio-cognitive one as pioneered by Hanna Risku (2004) and a socio-cultural one (Koskinen 2008).

Indeed, ethnographic fieldwork has been identified as a bridging element between cognitive translation studies and sociology of translation, both of which have a keen interest to understand translation work and to study workplace activities (Risku and Rogl 2022). But while all ethnography relies on an immersive approach to fieldwork (see, e.g., Risku et al. 2022:325), the socio-cognitive and socio-cultural approaches to doing ethnography are not identical in their research orientation, ethos or practical tool kit. Within the cognitive branch, microethnography as described by Risku et al. (2022), with its observation protocols and video recordings as well as the aim to study minute details of interaction, is rather far removed from socio-cultural ethnography that aims to understand the cultural practices, social identities and beliefs of the members through an open-ended inquiry to their lived experiences. In the latter case, ethnography is more an epistemology than a method (Buzelin 2022; Humonen and Angouri 2023), with all the implications for iterativity of fieldwork, knowledge creation, researcher position and the nature of academic research in general that this entails. A full engagement with this epistemological view is quite rare in translation studies publications (see, however, e.g., Hokkanen 2016, 2017).

Cognitive ethnography as practiced by Risku and her research team builds on the now classic work of Edwin Hutchins (1995) who argued for doing basic research on human cognition not only through laboratory experiments but also in real life settings and who maintained that human cognition is always culturally embedded. With its anthropologically designed fieldwork practices cognitive ethnography shares many of the tenets of socio-cultural ethnography. This makes it a bridge approach between sociology of translation and cognitive translation studies (see Risku and Rogl 2022). Risku and Rogl (2022) posit this quite optimistically as a convergence of the two, but in reality cognitive ethnography also needs to balance between two opposing epistemological requirements, one quite far in the qualitative end of the spectrum and the other deeply embedded in the empirical research paradigm of controlled laboratory designs and statistical analysis. Because of its affinity to cognitive (translation) studies, cognitive ethnography naturally also tends to employ the ethnographic toolkit to shed new light to themes and research problems generated within the cognitive paradigm (Hutchins 1995; Hubscher-Davidson 2011), whereas socio-cultural ethnography tends to build on theories and research agendas developed in the social sciences (e.g., power, role, agency, habitus).

The varied theoretical paradigms, epistemological expectations and different interpretations of what ethnography is and should be can create tensions in the discipline. It is therefore a welcome development that more fine-tuned labels are being created to better signal what kind of a theoretical and methodological basis a particular project has and what it aims to achieve. In this chapter, I wish to participate in this development by proposing a particular kind of ethnography, that is, translatorial linguistic ethnography, a term I will attempt to unpack below.

Back in 2004 when I was working on my own first ethnographic project (Koskinen 2008), my main worry was whether I dare label it ethnography or not. At that time the classic anthropological model was quite overpowering. While many other fields had started developing their own ways of doing ethnography, in translation studies there were few examples available of any kind of ethnographic methodology. The most daring moment in my project was to move away from diminutive solutions such as 'ethnographically-oriented' to boldly use the label 'ethnography', and thinking about variants of ethnography did not appear relevant at the time. Peter Flynn, who was working on a similar project on literary translation, aligned his PhD project with the then new approach of linguistic ethnography (Flynn 2005) as did Moira Inghilleri (2006) in her study of interpreting in asylum procedures. Had I been aware of their choices at the time, I would probably have followed suit in a manner similar to Wine Tesseur (2015) in her PhD on translation practices at Amnesty International, using the label of linguistic ethnography to add to terminological cohesion (see also Tesseur 2017). These projects are not paradigmatically connected or aligned theoretically or methodologically, but they all share the desire to also study translations as artifacts in the socio-cultural context (see also Napier, Chapter 2, on linguistic ethnography in interpreting studies). In that sense the label of *linguistic* ethnography is quite apt.

The more recent proposal for a particular *translatorial* linguistic ethnography (Koskinen 2020a) aims to underline the potential of translated data as ethnographic data. The proposal was originally targeted at researchers outside translation studies, to cater for the growing interest in studying paraprofessional translation in management studies and international business. These fields traditionally rely heavily on interview data, and a methodology that focuses on immersive fieldwork on the one hand and on a detailed analysis of translation data on the other hand has been seen as a new opening among scholars in language-sensitive management research (Humonen and Angouri 2023: 84).

Counterintuitively, the idea of actually studying oral or written translations as ethnographic data is not that common in translation studies either, at least not in the socio-cultural track where actors, processes and contexts are studied more than products (i.e., the translations themselves). And since written translating, in particular, is rather unobservable as a social practice unless conducted in teams where actions and meanings are constructed in negotiations (see the microethnographic approach in Korhonen and Hirvonen 2021), many socio-cultural ethnographies end up relying heavily on interview and focus group data. Interviews of informants are, of course, one standard method in ethnography, but excessive reliance on them tilts the project away from what is going on and towards what is being verbalized and put on display in talk.

While not aiming to ban interviewing from the fieldworker's tool kit, translatorial linguistic ethnography is a call to surround these constructed and researcher-led interactions, on the one hand, with the kind of contextual knowledge that can be acquired from immersive site visits and, on the other hand, with the traces of processes, policies and positionalities left in the translation paper trail. While these two may seemingly appear antagonistic, they are in fact closely intertwined. It has long been known that context is a defining feature of translation; translation solutions can be viewed as evidence of context. This intertwined or 'fractal' nature of physical and institutional surroundings, verbalizations and the minutiae of translation shifts was a key finding of my study of translation work in the European Union (Koskinen 2008: 149–150). Similar context-sensitive research is currently needed for paraprofessional translation work.

5. Doing translatorial linguistic ethnography

5.1 Identifying paraprofessional translation

In studying paraprofessional translation and other instances of translation in the wild, the first challenge is to identify where, when and by whom this activity happens. In present day workplaces, full monolinguality is rare if not non-existent. Multilingualism can take many forms. While languages can exist side by side, more often than not multilingual usage leads to reverbalizations of a particular content in another language. In fieldwork, the co-existence of more than one language can therefore be used as a strong methodological indicator of potential translatoriality and a signal of likely paraprofessional translation. To capture these moments and to identify which situations and events to observe and whom to follow to capture them, the researcher needs to spend time in the field doing traditional observation and writing field notes. This kind of non-obtrusive observation is at the heart of ethnography. In researching paraprofessional translation it is of the utmost importance for the researcher to capture and collect all kinds of translatoriality, also the borderline cases in terms of the researcher's own translation concept.

In fieldwork, these moments of translatoriality can be observed as they evolve, especially in oral interaction. But as discussed above much of written translation is actually quite non-observable. In fieldwork there is therefore a need to complement the traditional observation + field notes method of ethnography with some other approaches. Methodologically, translatorial linguistic ethnography is open to many directions. Interviewing and the analysis of translations as ethnographic artifacts, as discussed above, are obvious extensions to observation, but also other, more creative solutions can be employed.

5.2 Creative and exploratory practices

Already in 2008, one tool I used was a questionnaire (Koskinen 2008, Appendix 2) that aimed to probe details of everyday life (such as where the Finnish EU translators considered their home to be, who they had lunch with during the previous week, or which media they followed regularly). The questionnaire was first developed as a scaffolding tool to alleviate my anxiety about failing as a fieldworker and coming home empty-handed. It was thanks to the anonymous reviewer of the book manuscript who underlined the insights provided by the responses to the questionnaire that allowed me to fully appreciate the usability of this unorthodox, quantitatively tilted tool in a qualitative enquiry. In the analysis, the questionnaire responses and field observations and discussions entered into a fruitful dialogue. For example, the question of who the participants had recently had lunch with depicted a rather closed bubble: Finnish translators were mainly mingling with their Finnish colleagues. The physical surroundings and the observations of everyday practices provided an explanation: in the unit's current location at the time, a freight lift conveniently connected them directly with the downstairs canteen, and in line with normal office behavior they popped into some offices close by (all occupied by other Finns) for company and then went downstairs. This way they did not accidentally meet the colleagues from other units on their way for lunch. The end result fed into a creation of a tightly-knit monocultural unit that was not only because of any introverted preferences of these translators but also because of the architectural characteristics of their office space (see Koskinen 2008: 95–96). In paraprofessional contexts, a questionnaire on the use of different languages and the roles and contexts where the respondents find themselves operating across languages could reveal interesting insights into the daily practices as well as their language biographies. The questionnaire format might also work well to probe the mental translation concept and also to introduce respondents to the ideas of translatoriality. An example of a questionnaire on translation students' translation concepts can be found in Kumpulainen 2016 (Appendices 3 and 4).

Another element in that early fieldwork was to combine an analysis of the physical place with the relational and cultural space the EU translators occupied (Koskinen 2008: 61–80). An interpretive analysis of the material environment is a standard feature of ethnographic fieldwork, but it is not often foregrounded in translation studies' ethnographies. Integrating the increasingly extensive body of work on cities as sites of translation by Sherry Simon and others will enhance the analysis of the sense of place and deepen the context-sensitivity of ethnography (for methodological advice see Simon 2019; on spaces and places see also Koskinen 2020b: 117–141). Practical applications of contextualizing methods also include the linguistic landscapes approach that focusses on analyzing languages which are visible in a particular place (Koskinen 2012). Traditionally this has centered around signage in the cityscape, but there is no reason why it could not be applied to workplaces as well (e.g., Hanauer 2009). The EU translation units signaled their background through national flag stickers and touristic posters of their home countries (Koskinen 2008: 74). In paraprofessional contexts the display of particular languages or cultures in office walls or desktops offers insights into their status and participants' identity work. These artifacts could also be discussed in interviews.

Indeed, another approach that can be used to capture the material context of work is artifact analysis (Risku 2004: 147–172). This analysis focuses on the tools used by participants, and their affordances and the affects they create. Contemporary professional translation practices are technology-driven and embedded in multiple techno-social systems. Paraprofessional translation is likely to be more varied in the extent to which technological applications are available and wanted. While professional computer-assisted translation tools may be rarely used, machine translation solutions are known to have permeated many workplaces for both very sophisticated and advanced usage (Nurminen 2019), and as a handy ad hoc tool in everyday communication.

Recent advances in practice research (Olohan 2021) and exploratory practice (Hanks 2017) as well as a growing ethos of co-researching and citizen science bring new opportunities to fieldwork (see, e.g., Vaattovaara, forthcoming). Workplace studies focusing on fieldwork benefit from a close affinity with participants, creating possibilities for engaging them in co-researching activities, from data collection to analysis, and also in action research initiatives that aim at improving paraprofessional translation practices in the organization. This kind of organic and dialogic fieldwork is a retake on an earlier plea for public translation studies (Koskinen 2010). Public translation studies, a concept adapted from Michael Burawoy's (2004) classic notion of public sociology, fits nicely with the ethos of ethnographic fieldwork as it entails a full-body experience in the context and activity under study and supports the development of embedded, embodied and affective research designs where both the researchers and the members co-create joint activities.

In some cases, this kind of joint experimentation between researchers and participants can develop into artistic research, that is, research and innovation that builds on artistic practice. For example, in audio description for the theatre, some experiments have resulted in the integration of the audio describers into the team devising the performance (Fryer 2018). In paraprofessional translation contexts in organizations, selling extremely creative methods to either the organizational gatekeepers or the participants may prove difficult. It always makes sense to try to create a good match between context and methods. Still, playful data collection methods and invitations to share have been known to work well. The project of collecting love letters and hate mail from professional translators was met with unexpected enthusiasm (Koskinen and Ruokonen 2017; Ruokonen and Koskinen 2017), and Mary Nurminen's innovative idea of collecting stories of machine translation usage in non-professional and paraprofessional contexts has been a success (Nurminen n.d.). In today's workplaces time is at a premium, and creating an affective bond and joyful motivation may significantly improve the possibilities of gaining insightful data. One needs to keep in mind, though, that this kind of prompting steers the ethnographic project away from observing events as they occur naturally. The roles of the researcher and the co-researching participants in these kinds of activities where new knowledge and understanding are created need to be constantly reflected upon in all stages of the process.

6. Conclusions

In this chapter I have aimed to highlight the affordances of two conceptual avenues for further research: paraprofessional translation practices and translatoriality, and the linked methodological avenues, in particularly the framework of translatorial linguistic ethnography. The insights stem from my previous (field)work on professional translators, but my aim has been to be forward-looking and to offer new ideas for future research and hopefully supporting those currently engaged in field research, in professional, non-professional or paraprofessional translation. Approaches such as co-researching and explorative practice research bring avenues for collaboration with those we study and enable bringing knowledge back to those we learned it with in ways that support the further development of public translation studies. Exploring the material, spatial and visual aspects of the research site can give new understandings and interpretations of practices. And finally, a socio-cultural analysis of translations as artifacts allows us to benefit from the rich tradition of comparative textual analysis in translation studies and to enrich field data analysis by allowing for a triangulation or cross-pollination of observations, verbalizations and translation products into a holistic understanding of the translatorial realities we aim to uncover.

The call for immersive ethnographic fieldwork and co-researching practices responds to current research needs in the area of paraprofessional translation whose practices and beliefs are still largely uncharted. At the same time, it is a reminder of the continued relevance of context-sensitive research in the age of big data. To understand embedded, embodied and affective translatorial practices in their many contexts and varied shapes we need to engage in embedded, embodied and affective research that takes many shapes.

References

Barner-Rasmussen, Wilhelm, Mats Ehrnrooth, Alexei Koveshnikov, and Kristiina Mäkelä. 2014. "Cultural and Language Skills as Resources for Boundary Spanning within the MNC." *Journal of International Business Studies* 45 (7): 886–905.

Barner-Rasmussen, Wilhelm, and Hélène Langinier. 2020. "Exploring Translanguaging in International Business. Towards a Comparison of Highly Context-Embedded Practices." In *Managing Multilingual Workplaces: Methodological, Empirical and Pedagogic Perspectives*, ed. by Sierk Horn, Philippe Lecomte, and Susanne Tietze, 105–121. New York: Routledge.

Burawoy, Michail. 2004. "Public Sociologies: Contradictions, Dilemmas, and Possibilities." *Social Forces* 82 (4): 1603–1618.

Buzelin, Hélène. 2022. "Ethnography in Translation Studies: An Object and a Research Methodology." *Slovo.ru: baltic accent* 13 (1): 32–47.

Ciuk, Sylwia, Philip James, and Martina Śliwa. 2019. "Micropolitical Dynamics of Interlingual Translation Processes in an MNC Subsidiary." *British Journal of Management* 30 (4): 926–942.

Ciuk, Sylwia, Kaisa Koskinen, and Martyna Śliwa. Forthcoming. "Translation Practices and Beliefs Among Organizational Paraprofessional Translators: A Conceptual Framework." Unpublished article manuscript.

Cronin, Michael. 2021. "Translation and Posthumanism." In *The Routledge Handbook of Translation and Ethics*, ed. by Kaisa Koskinen, and Nike K. Pokorn, 279–293. London: Routledge.

Davier, Lucile, and Kyle Conway (eds). 2019. *Journalism and Translation in the Era of Convergence*. Amsterdam & Philadelphia: John Benjamins.

Flynn, Peter. 2005. "A Linguistic Ethnography of Literary Translation: Irish Poems and Dutch-speaking Translators." Doctoral dissertation, Ghent University.

Fryer, Louise. 2018. "The Independent Audio Describer Is Dead: Long Live Audio Description!" *Journal of Audiovisual Translation* 1 (1): 170–186.

Halverson, Sandra. 2000. "Prototype Effects in the 'Translation' Category." In *Translation in Context. Selected Papers from the EST Congress, Granada 1998*, ed. by Andrew Chesterman, Natividad Gallardo San Salvador, and Yves Gambier, 3–16. Amsterdam & Philadelphia: John Benjamins.

Hanauer, David I. 2009. "Science and the Linguistic Landscape: A Genre Analysis of Representational Wall Space in a Microbiology Laboratory." In *Linguistic Landscape. Expanding the Scenery*, ed. by Elana Shohamy, and Durk Gorter, 287–301. New York: Routledge.

Hanks, Judith. 2017. *Exploratory Practice in Language Teaching. Puzzling about Principles and Practices*. London: Palgrave Macmillan.

Hokkanen, Sari. 2016. "To Serve and to Experience: An Autoethnographic Study of Simultaneous Church Interpreting." Doctoral dissertation, University of Tampere.

Hokkanen, Sari. 2017. "Analyzing Personal Embodied Experiences: Autoethnography, Feelings, and Fieldwork." *Translation & Interpreting* 9 (1): 24–35.

Holz-Mänttäri, Justa. 1984. *Translatorisches Handeln. Theorie und Methode*. Helsinki: Suomalainen tiedeakatemia.

Hubscher-Davidson, Séverine. 2011. "A Discussion of Ethnographic Research Methods and their Relevance for Translation Process Research." *Across Languages and Cultures* 12 (1): 1–18.

Humonen, Kristina, and Jo Angouri. 2023. "Revisiting Ethnography and Reflexivity for Language-sensitive Workplace Research." In *Understanding the Dynamics of Language and Multilingualism in Professional Contexts: Advances in Language-Sensitive Management Research*, ed. by Philippe Lecomte, Mary Vigier, Claudine Gaibrois, and Betty Beeler, 84–101. Cheltenham & Northhampton, MA: Edward Elgar.

Hutchins, Edwin. 1995. *Cognition in the Wild*. Cambridge, MA & London: The MIT Press.

Inghilleri, Moira. 2006. "Macro Social Theory, Linguistic Ethnography and Interpreting Research." *Linguistica Antverpiensia* 5: 57–68.

Kolehmainen, Leena, Kaisa Koskinen, and Helka Riionheimo. 2015. "Arjen näkymätön kääntäminen: translatorisen toiminnan jatkumot [Invisible Everyday Translation: Continua of Translatorial Action]." *Virittäjä* 3: 372–400.

Korhonen, Annamari, and Maija Hirvonen. 2021. "Joint Creative Process in Translation: Socially Distributed Cognition in Two Production Contexts." *Cognitive Linguistic Studies* 8 (2): 251–276.

Koskela, Merja, Kaisa Koskinen, and Nina Pilke. 2017. "Bilingual Formal Meeting as a Context of Translatoriality." *Target* 29 (3): 464–485.

Koskinen, Kaisa. 2008. *Translating Institutions: An Ethnographic Study of EU Translation*. Manchester: St. Jerome/Routledge.

Koskinen, Kaisa. 2010. "What Matters to Translation Studies? On the Role of Public Translation Studies." In *Why Translation Studies Matters*, ed. by Daniel Gile, Gyde Hansen, and Nike K. Pokorn, 15–26. Amsterdam & Philadelphia: John Benjamins.

Koskinen, Kaisa. 2012. "Linguistic Landscape as a Translational Space. The Case of Hervanta." In *Language, Space and Power: Urban Entanglements*, ed. by Jani Vuolteenaho, Andrew Newby, Lieven Ameel, and Maggie Scott, 73–92. https://helda.helsinki.fi/handle/10138/38600

Koskinen, Kaisa. 2017. "Translatorial Action in Non-Professional Translation Communities: The Tampere City Council in 1875." In *Communities of Translation and Interpreting*, ed. by Kristiina Taivalkoski-Shilov, Liisa Tiittula, and Maarit Koponen, 37–61. Montreal: Éditions québécoises de l'œuvre.

Koskinen, Kaisa. 2020a. "Translatorial Linguistic Ethnography in Organizations." In *Managing Multilingual Workplaces: Methodological, Empirical and Pedagogic Perspectives*, ed. by Sierk Horn, Philippe Lecomte, and Susanne Tietze, 60–77. New York: Routledge.

Koskinen, Kaisa. 2020b. *Translation and Affect*. Amsterdam & Philadelphia: John Benjamins.

Koskinen, Kaisa, and Tuija Kinnunen. 2022. "Mediation in FL Learning: From Translation to Translatoriality." *Stridon: Studies in Translation and Interpreting* 2 (1): 5–29.

Koskinen, Kaisa, and Minna Ruokonen. 2017. "Love Letters or Hate Mail? Translators' Technology Acceptance in the Light of Their Emotional Narratives." In *Human Issues in Translation Technology*, ed. by Dorothy Kenny, 8–24. London: Routledge.

Kumpulainen, Minna. 2016. "Learning Translation. An Empirical Study into the Acquisition of Interlingual Text Production Skills." Doctoral dissertation, Joensuu: University of Eastern Finland.

Kuznik, Anna. 2016. "Work Content of In-House Translators in Small and Medium-sized Industrial Enterprises. Observing Real Work Situations." *Journal of Specialized Translation* 25. https://www.jostrans.org/issue25/art_kuznik.php

Logemann, Minna, and Rebecca Piekkari. 2015. "Localize or Local Lies? The Power of Language and Translation in the Multinational Corporation." *Critical Perspectives on International Business* 11 (1): 30–53.

Marais, Kobus. 2019. *A (Bio)Semiotic Theory of Translation: The Emergence of Social-Cultural Reality*. London: Routledge.

Massey, Gary, and Regine Wieder. 2019. "Quality Assurance in Translation and Corporate Communications: Exploring an Interdisciplinary Interface." In *Quality Assurance and Assessment Practices in Translation and Interpreting. Advances in Linguistics and Communication Studies*, ed. by Elsa Huertas Barros, Sonia Vandepitte, and Emilia Iglesias Fernández, 57–87. Hershey, PA: IGI Global.

Meyer, John P., and Natalie J. Allen. 1997. *Commitment in the Workplace: Theory, Research, and Application*. Newbury Park, CA: Sage.

Meyer, John P., Thomas E. Becker, and Rolf Van Dijk. 2006. "Social Identities and Commitments at Work: Toward an Integrative Model." *Journal of Organizational Behavior* 27: 665–683.

Nurminen, Mary. n.d. *Machine Translation stories*. Blog. https://mt-stories.com/

Nurminen, Mary. 2019. "Decision-making, Risk, and Gist Machine Translation in the Work of Patent Professionals." In *Proceedings of the 8th Workshop on Patent and Scientific Literature Translation*, ed. by Takehito Utsuro, Katsuhito Sudoh and Takashi Tsunakawa, 32–42. Dublin: European Association for Machine Translation.

Olohan, Maeve. 2021. *Translation and Practice Theory*. London and New York: Routledge.

Pedersen, Daniel. 2019. "Managing Transcreation Projects. An Ethnographic Study." In *Translation Practice in the Field: Current Research on Socio-cognitive Processes*, ed. by Hanna Risku, Regina Rogl, and Jelena Milosevic, 43–59. Amsterdam & Philadelphia: John Benjamins.

Piekkari, Rebecca, Susanne Tietze, and Kaisa Koskinen. 2020. "Metaphorical and Interlingual Translation in Moving Organizational Practices Across Languages." *Organization Studies* 41 (9): 1311–1332.

Pöchhacker, Franz, and Mira Kadrić. 1999. The Hospital Cleaner as Healthcare Interpreter. A Case Study. *The Translator* 5 (2): 161–178.

Pym, Anthony. 2011. "Translation Research Terms: A Tentative Glossary for Moments of Perplexity and Dispute." In *Translation Research Projects 3*, ed. by Anthony Pym, 75–110. Tarragona: Intercultural Studies Group.

Risku, Hanna. 2004. *Translationsmanagement. Interkulturelle Fachkommunikation im Informationszeitalter* [*Translation Management. Intercultural Specialized Translation in the Age of Information*]. Tübingen: Narr.

Risku, Hanna, Maija Hirvonen, Regina Rogl, and Jelena Milosevic. 2022. "Ethnographic Research." In *The Routledge Handbook of Translation and Methodology*, ed. by Federico Zanettin, and Christopher Rundle, 324–339. London: Routledge.

Risku, Hanna, and Regina Rogl. 2022. "Praxis and Process Meet Halfway: The Convergence of Sociological and Cognitive Approaches in Translation Studies." *Translation & Interpreting* 14 (2): 32–49.

Røvik, Kjell-Arne. 2023. *A Translation Theory of Knowledge Transfer: Learning Across Organizational Borders*. Oxford: Oxford University Press.

Ruokonen, Minna, and Kaisa Koskinen. 2017. "Dancing with Technology. Translators' Narratives on the Dance of Human and Machinic Agency in Translation Work." *The Translator* 23 (3): 310–323.

Simon, Sherry. 2019. *Translation Sites: A Field Guide*. London & New York: Routledge.

Svahn, Elin. 2020. "The Dynamics of Extratextual Translatorship in Contemporary Sweden." Doctoral dissertation, University of Stockholm.

Tesseur, Wine. 2015. "Transformation Through Translation: Translation Policies at Amnesty International." Doctoral dissertation, Aston University, Birmingham.

Tesseur, Wine. 2017. "Incorporating Translation into Sociolinguistic Research: Translation Policy in an International Non-Governmental Organization." *Journal of Sociolinguistics* 21 (5): 629–649.

Tietze, Susanne, Kaisa Koskinen, and Rebecca Piekkari. 2022. "Translation Approaches within Organisation Studies." In *Translation beyond Translation Studies*, ed. by Kobus Marais, 119–139. London: Bloomsbury.

Tyulenev, Sergey. 2014. *Translation and Society. An Introduction*. Abingdon & New York: Routledge.

Vaattovaara, Johanna. Forthcoming. "Exploring Connections between Exploratory Practice and Citizen Science as Forms of Inclusive Research." In "Advances in Inclusive Practitioner Research: Challenging Principles and Practices", ed. by Assia Slimani-Rolls, Cori Crane, Judith Hanks, and Inés Miller, special issue, *Language Teaching Research*.

Zwischenberger, Cornelia, and Alexa Alfer. 2022. "Translaboration: Translation and Labour." *Translation in Society* 1 (2): 200–223.

CHAPTER 2

Linguistic ethnography in interpreting studies

Jemina Napier
Heriot-Watt University

Linguistic ethnography (LE) combines linguistic and ethnographic
approaches to understand how social and communicative processes operate
in a range of settings. The core goal of LE is to examine language use in
context, thus various qualitative interpreting studies could be considered as
LE studies. I give an overview of LE and how it can be used to examine
interpreter-mediated interactions, highlighting examples from previous
interpreting research that could be considered as LE and drawing on
examples from my own studies of sign language interpreter-mediated
communication. I propose the affordances of examining interpreter-
mediated communication through the framework of LE encompassing
multi-methods approaches, which could re-frame what we mean by
mediated communication and contribute to a changing paradigm in
interpreting studies.

Keywords: qualitative research, multi-methods, linguistic ethnography,
interpreting studies, sign language interpreting

1. Introduction

The term linguistic ethnography (LE) is an umbrella term for "a growing body
of research by scholars who combine linguistic and ethnographic approaches in
order to understand how social and communicative processes operate in a range
of settings and contexts" (Shaw, Copland, and Snell 2015: 1). The core goal of LE is
to examine language use in context, so by that very definition, various qualitative
research conducted within interpreting studies (IS) could be considered as falling
under this umbrella.[1]

---

1. This is an idea that I first suggested in my inaugural lecture as Visiting Chair Professor for
the Centre for Translation Studies (CETRA) Research Summer School at the University of Leuven, Antwerp, Belgium in 2018, and then expanded on during my keynote presentation at the
FIRE-TI online conference in 2022.

https://doi.org/10.1075/btl.165.02nap
Available under the CC BY-NC 4.0 license. © 2025 John Benjamins Publishing Company

This chapter provides an overview of LE and how it can be used to examine interpreter-mediated interactions and will highlight previous interpreting research that could be considered within this framework. I give examples from my own studies of professional sign language interpreter-mediated communication in different settings that could be considered as research conducted within a LE framework; and I also propose the affordances of examining interpreter-mediated communication through the framework of LE, encompassing multi-methods approaches. Finally, I explore how re-framing our approach to IS through LE may also lead to a re-framing of what we mean by mediated communication and contribute to a changing paradigm in IS.

2. Using linguistic ethnography as a framework

Anyone familiar with ethnography will know that a traditional view of ethnography typically focuses on questions of agency in specific situations. Although perceptions of what constitutes ethnography and fieldwork are changing (see Introduction, this volume), ethnography is typically considered to involve the researcher spending considerable time in the field, observing behaviours, cultural norms and cultural practices and documenting fieldwork through taking field-notes about observations, interviewing people and filming or audio-recording in a whole range of different ways (Starfield 2010). This type of longitudinal ethnography is not always possible in IS, due to the sensitive nature of observing interpreting assignments in some institutional contexts and the challenge of getting permissions from all involved (Bendazzoli 2016), but there are some exceptions (see Hale and Napier 2013 and Dong 2016, 2023 for examples). Nevertheless, ethnographic principles can easily be applied (Hale and Napier 2013), for example through the use of "yo-yo fieldwork" (Wulff 2002) where the researcher regularly moves in and out of the field and may conduct participant observation in many local sites.

Marin-Lacarta and Yu (2023:148–149) argue that ethnography goes beyond data collection and analysis. They suggest that rather than using an ethnographic *approach*, use of the term ethnographic *framework* better captures the "multifaceted and transdisciplinary nature [of ethnography] ... and encompasses the conceptual, theoretical and methodological elements ... [that] guides the design of an ethnographic research project". They go on to suggest that "understanding ethnography as a research framework is, in our view, the most inclusive perspective, as the principles that characterise ethnography as a research framework influence the way we do ethnography, the way we interpret data and write about it, and the way in which new theoretical development is grounded" (Marin-Lacarta and Yu 2023:148).

There is also a strong expectation in ethnography of reflexivity, whereby the researcher is aware of, and analyses, the dynamics between themselves as a researcher and the participants (Copland and Creese 2015). Blackledge (2011) highlights the fact that ethnographers can benefit from the analytical frameworks provided by linguists (such as discourse analysis, conversation analysis, narrative analysis), while linguists can benefit from the processes of reflexive sensitivity required when doing ethnography. LE includes interpretive approaches from anthropology, applied linguistics, cultural studies and sociology (Blackledge 2011) and draws heavily on strands of linguistic anthropology, including ethnography of communication, interactional sociolinguistics and micro-ethnography (Rampton et al. 2004; Rampton 2007; Creese 2008). Analysis using a LE framework provides the opportunity to examine interaction in the context of the wider social world by using observational techniques as would be expected in ethnography, while drawing on concepts from applied linguistics and sociolinguistics (Rampton et al. 2004).

Integrating linguistic analyses into the use of ethnography provides the opportunity to observe interactions with a focus on language use and ideologies and the impact of language choices. Thus, in combining these two approaches, LE examines language use in context and provides a way to bring contextualised insight into communication practices. LE provides a holistic, in-situ perspective on language practices, and one theme of LE seeks to examine complex relationships between language practices and perceptions about language practices, and whether practices mirror perceptions. One nice example is the actual use of translanguaging strategies and humour in workplace relations in butcher's businesses, and perceptions of the positive benefits of using translanguaging and humour strategically to benefit everyday practices of buying and selling (Creese, Blackledge, and Hu 2018).

Rampton (2007) suggests that the foundation of LE requires understanding of the fact that meaning is created through language used within social relations, interactions and institutional norms, and that people who are taking part in a dialogue or conversation (interlocutors) construe meaning through their own thought worlds and linguistic repertoires, so ethnographic observations are required for a fine-grain examination of the creation of meaning in sites of encounter.

One of the beauties of LE is that researchers can draw on methodological approaches that meet their needs and interests (Rampton 2007) and combine analytical approaches rather than relying on only one approach or framework (Rampton et al. 2002). A central tenet of LE is the use of participant observation, whereby the researcher is placed at the 'heart of the research' and tries to enter the 'life-worlds' of those individuals whose everyday languaging practices are under observation (Rampton 2007; Tusting and Maybin 2007). As such, the researcher immerses themselves into what is happening and is actively involved in the social action under study, which requires sensitivity to their level of involvement with participants. One good example is Blackledge and Creese's (2019) observations of communication in food marketplaces where they would literally just wander around these food markets listening to people, recording people (with their permission) and documenting the way that people interacted and bartered for goods over a long period of time. They observed the relationships between people, the way they spoke to each other and how they spoke differently to different people at different times.

As such, LE offers a practical and theoretical response to the consideration of language, communication and interaction in the wider social world (Wetherell 2007), and various authors advocate that LE is the ideal framework for interdisciplinary research concerning language and communication (Tusting and Maybin 2007; Blackledge 2011; Shaw, Copland, and Snell 2015).

3. How can LE be used to examine interpreter-mediated interactions?

If LE offers us the opportunity to get much closer to the level of detail of interaction and the power dynamics involved than purely doing discourse or conversational analysis, or solely observing or talking to people about experiences of languaging, surely this combined method is an appropriate framework to apply to examine interpreter-mediated interactions (see also Koskinen, Chapter 1, on 'translatorial linguistic ethnography')? In IS, we have drawn heavily on linguistics and especially applied and sociolinguistics to understand the fine detail of interaction management when mediated through interpreters and the role of interpreters in mediated encounters (see for example, Wadensjö 1998; Roy 2000; Baraldi and Gavioli 2012; Sarangi 2023). In the same way that LE is a suitable framework for interdisciplinary research, IS is also becoming increasingly interdisciplinary (Pöchhacker 2004; Ehrensberger-Dow, Göpferich, and O'Brien 2015; de Pedro Ricoy and Napier 2017).

We can see a strong alignment between LE and IS as we consider interpreters as actors in a social, cultural and institutional context in which other players contribute to shaping the nature of the communication. Like LE, IS commonly draws on tools from other disciplines, such as: sociology (frames reference and footing which describe speaker/hearer/signer/watcher roles, Goffman 1981); and sociolinguistics (dialogic communication where meaning is negotiated in interaction, Bakhtin 1981; ethnography of communication examining communication in its social and cultural context, Hymes 1974).

Combining ethnography with detailed linguistic analysis is not a new approach in IS. There have been many sociolinguistic explorations of the role of interpreters or interpreting in action that draw on ethnographic principles (e.g., Biagini 2016; Duflou 2016). So, by the very definition of LE, various qualitative research conducted within IS could be considered as falling under this umbrella. We can tease this out a little more by reviewing examples of published studies of interpreter-mediated communication that refer to interpreters as actors in the social/cultural/institutional context, being participants in interaction and one of the interlocutors within a communicative context, with recognition of the power dynamics at play — which are the core principles of LE.

As noted by Marin-Lacarta and Yu (2023), many interpreting scholars were pioneers in applying ethnography within translation studies. Here I highlight a few studies that I suggest could be clearly situated within not just an ethnographic, but a LE framework. All of these studies combine fieldwork observations, filming/audio-recording, sociolinguistic analyses, and interviews with interpreters and/or interlocutors.

The most obvious is Angelelli's (2004) study of healthcare interpreting where she observed and followed interpreters between assignments in a hospital for an extended period of time. She audio-recorded all the interpreter-mediated consultations between doctors and patients, took fieldnotes, interviewed the interpreters when walking between assignments and also spoke to doctors and other healthcare professionals. Angelelli's study gave an insightful and up-close examination of interpreting practices in a healthcare setting, perceptions about interpreting practices, and whether actual practices reflect interpreters and healthcare professionals' perceptions.

There are several other examples where researchers have conducted fieldwork in context, observing interpreters working in that institutional setting, audio- or video-recording and analysing their language/interpreting practices as well as discussing those practices with interpreters (and sometimes other interlocutors) through interviews. These include: Berk-Seligson's (1990) and Hale's (2004) studies of courtroom interpreting; Davitti's (2015) analysis of parent-teacher meetings; Cox's (2015) observations of hospital emergency department interpreting; Bartłomiejczyk's (2017) consideration of interpreters' role and visibility in the EU parliament; Slettebakk Berge's (2018, 2023) research on educational interpreting in the classroom with deaf students; Compton's (2020) exploration of parent involvement in individualised education plan meetings for multilingual deaf children facilitated by interpreters; Hansen's (2020) examination of video-mediated interpreting in hospital encounters; and Torkpoor et al.'s (2022) study of interpreter role in dementia assessments, to name a few. These are all studies that could easily be classified as LE studies because they are observing and analysing language (interpreting) in practice and perceptions of that practice. Interestingly though, none of these studies referred to using a LE framework.

As also observed by Koskinen (2020), LE is not a framework that is typically used to examine interpreting practices. Three notable exceptions where LE is explicitly mentioned are the work of Inghilleri (2006) who examined the interpreter's role in the political asylum system in the UK, Dickinson (2017) who analysed sign language interpreting in the workplace in the UK, and Van Hest and Jacobs (2022) who conducted a multilingual study of communication mediated by professional or non-professional interpreters in an abortion clinic and two immigration law firms in Belgium. Retrospectively, however, all the studies I have described above could be considered as LE studies.

4. My research on sign language interpreter-mediated communication

LE is increasingly being applied to the study of signed language usage, including national, urban, rural, village, emerging and home signed languages; sign-sign and sign-spoken language contact; multilingual sign language practices; language socialisation processes in signing deaf children; and sign language ideologies. Using LE has expanded and enriched our understandings of how new sign languages emerge, how people acquire sign languages, how people negotiate communication with varying degrees of access to the environment, and how their experiences of these situations are represented in metalinguistic discourse (including in explicitly articulated language ideologies) (see Hou and Kusters 2019; Kusters and Hou 2020).

Aside from Dickinson's (2017) work as mentioned above, there have been no other specifically named LE studies of sign language interpreting practices. Being inspired by the work of deaf studies and sign language linguistics researchers in applying LE to their own work (e.g., Hou 2020; Kusters, Sahasrabudhe, and Gopalakrishnan 2016; Goico 2020; Moriarty 2020; Puupponen et al. 2024), and with reference to the fact that Kusters and Hou (2020) suggest that many studies of signed languages could be re-classified as LE studies, I began to reflect on my own studies of sign language interpreter-mediated communication. My research has often combined observations, linguistic analyses, interviews and focus groups, so I wondered whether these could also be re-defined as LE studies. I have selected a few of my own qualitative studies of sign language interpreting in different social (institutional) settings, none of which were originally framed as LE studies, to review whether in fact they could have been articulated in that way.

4.1 Social setting: Healthcare

Two combined projects explored deaf Australians' access to healthcare information. The first was commissioned by the National Auslan Interpreter Booking and Payment Service (NABS) to explore what access needs deaf people had outside of sign language interpreting provision in doctor or hospital appointments that NABS were already providing. For example, if a deaf person was diagnosed with diabetes could they access information through leaflets, websites, nutritional workshops or diabetes support groups post-diagnosis? A total of 72 in-depth semi-structured interviews were conducted with deaf Auslan users, in 9 metropolitan and regional locations across Australia (Napier and Kidd 2013; Napier et al. 2014a). A related study, co-funded by NABS and the Australian Research Council[2] explored access to healthcare information through discussion in focus groups with deaf community members and sign language interpreters of gaps in the Auslan lexicon for healthcare terminology. The study also involved analyses of authentic and simulated sign language interpreter-mediated healthcare appointments with post-appointment interviews with the interpreters on their perceptions of the interpreting practice to compare with findings of actual interpreting practice (Napier, Major, and Ferrara 2011; Major et al. 2012; Major and Napier 2012, 2019; Major 2013, 2014, 2024; Napier et al. 2014b). The findings from both studies revealed the lexical gaps, as well as lexical and discourse strategies used by interpreters in the healthcare context.

4.2 Social setting: Workplace

Research in the workplace context involved analysis of an authentic interpreter-mediated presentation by a deaf professional presenting at a conference, starting with interviews with, and reflections of, the presenter and two interpreters prior to the assignment, filming of the actual assignment, then post-assignment interviews and reflections to examine the nature of cooperation between the deaf presenter and interpreters (Napier 2007; Napier, Carmichael, and Wiltshire 2008). This project confirmed the strategies used throughout an interpreting assignment by each of the three participants with the goal of producing a cooperative, seamless interpretation of a presentation in Auslan. Another project focused on deaf people's access and inclusion at work through interpreters, using surveys, focus groups and interviews with deaf employees, business owners and self-employed people, hearing employers and interpreters, as well as analyses of simulated

---

2. Funded by the Australian Research Council, Linkage Projects Scheme, grant #LP0882270, 2008–10.

interpreter-mediated job interviews (Napier et al. 2020; Sheikh et al. 2021; Sommer Lindsay, Cameron, and Napier 2023).[3] This research delved into the perceptions of what deaf people need from interpreters when they are seeking work, but also in how they maintain relationships at work.

4.3 Are these LE studies?

I am not convinced that these studies in healthcare and workplace contexts would be classified as LE studies because although they do collect different forms of data, involve analysis of interpreter-mediated interaction in practice through different lenses, and were gleaning perceptions of interpreting practices, there is still something missing in LE terms. In all of these studies, although they do get close to thinking about what happens in interpreted interaction, they did not get to that level of detail of the local interpreter-mediated action in context through extensive participant observations. The studies collected separate data sets, the results of which were triangulated, but the interviews were somewhat divorced from the everyday reality of interpreting provision. Reflections on information access or interpreting practice were either retrospective based on prior experiences, or on one-off case studies of one recent experience of interpreter-mediated interaction rather than repeated observations, and were not designed within an ethnographic framework conceptually, theoretically or methodologically (cf. Marin-Lacarta and Yu 2023). Also, the critical analysis of the role that interpreters have to play in the interaction as social actors was also missing. It is more appropriate that these studies are considered as mixed or multi- methods studies.

There is no real consensus on the definition of mixed methods (Morse and Niehaus 2009), but it is generally agreed that mixed methods research combines different methods (Johnson, Onwuegbuzie, and Turner 2007), that some would refer to as 'multi-methods' (Brewer and Hunter 2006). Cresswell and Plano Clark (2023) suggest that mixed methods studies combine use of both qualitative and quantitative methods, while multi-methods use at least two methods within the same qualitative or quantitative methodological paradigm. Mixed and multi-methods support triangulation of research findings by examining research questions through different theoretical and methodological lenses, and thus provide validation of findings (Johnson, Onwuegbuzie, and Turner 2007).

The benefits of using mixed and multi-methods in examining interpreting has been highlighted elsewhere (Pöchhacker 2011; Napier and Hale 2023), and it has

---

3. DESIGNS project, funded through ERASMUS+ Agreement No. 2016-1-IE-01-KA202–016895.

been stressed that the complexity of interpreter-mediated communication warrants multi-faceted approaches to conducting research in this field.

So, how do we distinguish between qualitative multi-method studies and LE studies? LE encompasses multi-methods but there is another significant layer to the analysis: conceptually, methodologically, theoretically and analytically. Thus, utilising multi-methods is not enough to justify defining a project as a LE study.

When applying LE to the analysis of interpreting, Koskinen (2020:64) suggests we can "follow" the translation/interpretation from beginning to end and consider the role of the interpreter as actor and their agency in making interpreting decisions. Inghilleri (2006) notes that interpreters are embedded in social and political processes and this impacts on the actual and potential discursive moves within interpreter-mediated interactions. Therefore, interpreters as critical actors in the contexts may contribute to the production or reproduction of the existing social order. Decisions made by interpreters will be influenced by the social and political contexts in which they work as well as the training they have undertaken. Interpreters cannot remove themselves from the social order; they are the linchpin to communication happening between people that do not share the same language; they are co-constructors of meaning.

The increasing body of research on interpreting has contributed to our understanding of the pivotal role of interpreters in interactions. So, if we are giving consideration to this fundamental role and the level of involvement of interpreters in contributing to the success of communication, this is where LE comes in: we need to examine the whole social context; not just the interpreted interaction in the local context but also within the wider social context.

As such, I now review two other previous studies of sign language interpreter-mediated communication of mine that were not originally classified as LE studies, but now in hindsight could be considered this way due to the nature of the research design and the approach to analysis.

5. Re-framing my studies of sign language interpreter-mediated communication as LE

Two of my projects that could be re-framed as LE studies focus on different social/institutional contexts: (1) the political institution and (2) the legal institution.

5.1 Political institution

The first project was conducted in the European Parliament (EP) with the goal of evaluating the feasibility of deaf European citizens accessing their Member of the

European Parliament (MEP) via interpreter-mediated calls through audio-video link.[4]

The project took place over four key stages including a survey of deaf people and interpreters, as well as observations to explore whether deaf people could actually make contact with their MEP and European institutions through video-based interpreting services (Napier, Skinner, and Turner 2017, 2018). A case study was held on one day with multi-site repeated observations: (a) in the European Parliament observing hearing people taking calls from deaf people in MEP offices; (b) observations of deaf people making calls to the EP; (c) observations of the interpreters who were mediating the calls in a video interpreting call centre; (d) observations of re-speakers providing simultaneous production of captions through a video relay platform. The calls were as authentic as they could be; although the calls had been arranged from deaf people to MEPs through video relay interpreting services, for the hearing people who received the calls and for the interpreters who were mediating the calls, they were genuine, spontaneous calls.

Field notes were taken during the observations as well as recordings of the video-mediated calls through the video interpreter platform. The observations were followed up with interviews and focus groups with all participants, plus discourse analyses of the interpreter-mediated video calls and reflections on the methodology (Napier et al. 2018).

One of the critical things in conducting a study like this is that we were not only examining the interpreted interactions followed by interviews (i.e., multi-methods), but we were in the 'the field' doing observations, following people around and talking to people as communication transpired. In this study one integral focus was on the role of interpreters in contributing to the success of the communication in the wider social context of politics where there are clear power dynamics at play; especially between hearing people who are receiving cold calls from deaf people calling to request that MEPs represented them on a particular issue in their constituency. Our focus was on interpreters and telecommunications relay services as a tool for deaf political participation and citizenship (Turner et al. 2016), and the active sociolinguistic decisions made by interpreters in mediating video calls in order to enable political participation of deaf citizens (Napier, Skinner, and Turner 2018). Thus, given the combined theoretical, methodological and analytical framework used this could be viewed as a LE study.

---

4. INSIGN project, funded by the European Commission Directorate-General Justice (JUST/2013/RTSL/PR/0015/A4).

5.2 Legal institution

The second project is a longitudinal study that took place in Australia over 10 years across five stages, with a focus on whether it is feasible for deaf signers to serve as jurors in adversarial courtrooms and participate in jury deliberations through sign language interpreters. Before this series of connected studies, deaf people were only permitted to serve as jurors in the United States. Stage 1 compared deaf and hearing jurors' comprehension of jury directions using a quasi-experimental study (Napier and Spencer 2007, 2008, 2017; Napier, Spencer, and Sabolcec 2009),[5] and Stage 2 involved a survey and interviews with interpreters and legal personnel about their perceptions as to whether deaf people can serve as jurors (Napier and McEwin 2015).[6] Stages 3, 4 and 5 were designed as part of an ethnographic study. In Stage 3, members of the team spent a week at a courthouse in the United States where they conducted participant observations of a jury empanelment process involving a deaf juror, followed by interviews with the interpreter involved, the prospective deaf juror, various legal personnel in the court building and deaf people who had previously served as jurors in the vicinity (Napier et al. 2022; Napier and Russell forthcoming).

The findings of this study confirmed the need to conduct a more fine-grained analysis of interpreter-mediated interaction in jury deliberations, but it was not possible to gain access to a jury deliberation room in an authentic trial with a deaf juror serving. So, Stage 4 involved creating a simulation of a courtroom trial and jury deliberations involving a deaf juror and sign language interpreters, which took place over 3 days.[7] The trial and the deliberations were filmed, observational fieldnotes were taken, and follow-up interviews were conducted with the hearing jurors, the deaf juror, the interpreters, the legal personnel in the trial, and the actors who had played the defendant and witness. Subsequently, a discourse analysis was carried out on the deliberations to examine the turn-taking that took place mediated by interpreters, drawing on complementary data from the interviews to compare the actual practice with the perceptions of the experience (Hale et al. 2017). Stage 5 of the project involved focus groups with stakeholder groups (Spencer et al. 2017a, 2017b; Napier et al. 2019) to reflect on the findings from the

---

5. Commissioned and part-funded by the New South Wales Law Reform Commission with matched funding from a Macquarie University External Collaborative Research Grants Scheme, 2006.

6. Funded through a Macquarie University New Staff (Returning from Maternity Leave) Grant, 2009.

7. The 3-year project was funded through a grant from the Australian Research Council Linkage Program 2012, Round 2 (LP120200261).

previous stages of research; discuss the implications of the findings; and explore what recommendations could be made for policy, practice and law reform.[8]

A review of the methodology used has positioned this study as using mixed methods (Napier and Hale 2023), but in retrospect I believe that it could be re-framed as a LE study due to the extensive use of observations and comparisons of whether the actual interpreting practice mirrored perceptions of the practice. The conceptual and theoretical framework and combination of methods, data sets and analyses, allowed for examination of the role of the interpreter in impacting the outcomes of an adversarial trial using jurors, whether positively or negatively. The linguistic analyses confirmed the minimal involvement of interpreters in the jury deliberation, the fact that spontaneous turn-taking in the deliberations was not negatively impacted by the presence of interpreters, and in fact contributed to the smooth flow of discussion. Observations provided insights into the physical and metaphorical positioning of the interpreters in relation to the jurors and other people in the courtroom and jury deliberation room, and the interviews served to confirm the interlocutors' perceptions of how the jury experience can actually be enhanced by having a deaf juror and interpreters present. A LE framework provided the opportunity in Stages 3–4 of this longitudinal study to examine interaction in the context of courtroom trials: Using observational techniques and reflections on perceptions of experience as would be expected in ethnography, examination of the role of interpreters as social actors in the wider context of the legal system, sociolinguistic analysis of interpreter-mediated interactions, and comparisons of the actual with the perceived interpreting practices. This amalgamation of ethnography with linguistic concepts and analytical techniques suggests that this study was in fact conducted within a LE framework.

6. Re-thinking our approach to IS through LE

In reviewing the synergies between LE and IS, a key question for us to consider is whether we can make more use of LE as a novel framework to examine engagement with alternative forms of mediated communication across different social/institutional settings. It would seem that LE can provide an appropriate framework to add layers to the sociolinguistic work that has been conducted in IS to scrutinise the 'communicative pas de trois' between interpreters and interlocutors who use different languages (Wadensjö 1998; Yuan 2022).

---

8. The evidence from this project has actually led to law reform in three different countries: the Australian Capital Territory, Ireland and the UK to allow deaf people to serve as jurors. To date, several deaf people have now actively participated in jury service with interpreters in Ireland and the UK.

Although there is much work that has been done to examine 'interpreting as interaction' (Wadensjö 1998) and the close detail of interpreter-mediated interactive exchanges in context, utilising ethnographic observations through the LE framework is of value. In Sections 2 and 3, I discussed traditional approaches to ethnography, and how IS can draw on ethnography to examine interpreting in the local context. Thus, although it may be more challenging to apply traditional prolonged ethnography in interpreting settings, it is possible to move in and out of the field as suggested by Wulff (2002) and re-enter a particular institutional setting (such as a hospital or workplace, cf. Angelelli 2004; Dickinson 2017) on a regular basis to conduct observations. The same principle could be applied perhaps to conducting observations with one interpreter and following them across different sites over a fixed period of time.

A review of studies of other interpreting scholars, as well as my own, has demonstrated that it is possible to re-frame these projects as LE studies, as they embed the principles of LE by incorporating both an ethnographic framework and linguistic analyses, and most critically contrast actual interpreting practice with perceptions of interpreting practice.

This examination of LE with respect to IS confirms that if we design studies to examine interpreter-mediated interactions in the sites of encounter through a *linguistic ethnographic lens*, then we could achieve a more robust understanding of interpreting practice through a closer look at local action and interaction embedded in a wider social world; and a more in-depth understanding of interpreting as a complex languaging practice. As such, I would suggest that it is time for another paradigm shift in interpreting studies.

References

Angelelli, Claudia. 2004. *Medical Interpreting and Cross-Cultural Communication*. Cambridge: Cambridge University Press.

Bakhtin, Mikhail M. 1981. *The Dialogic Imagination: Four Essays*. Austin: University of Texas Press.

Baraldi, Claudio, and Laura Gavioli (eds). 2012. *Coordinating Participation in Dialogue Interpreting*. Amsterdam & Philadelphia: John Benjamins.

Bartłomiejczyk, Magdalena. 2017. "The Interpreter's Visibility in the European Parliament." *Interpreting* 19 (2): 159–185.

Bendazzoli, Claudio. 2016. "The Ethnography of Interpreter-Mediated Communication: Methodological Challenges in Fieldwork." In *Addressing Methodological Challenges in Interpreting Studies Research*, ed. by Claudio Bendazzoli, and Claudia Monacelli, 3–30. Cambridge: Cambridge Scholars.

Berk-Seligson, Susan. 1990. *The Bilingual Courtroom: Court Interpreters in the Judicial Process*. Chicago: University of Chicago Press.

Biagini, Marta. 2016. "Revisiting Ethnography for Dialogue Interpreting Research." In *Addressing Methodological Challenges in Interpreting Studies Research*, ed. by Claudio Bendazzoli, and Claudia Monacelli, 61–86. Cambridge: Cambridge Scholars.

Blackledge, Adrian. 2011. "Linguistic Ethnography." In *Bourdieu, Language & Linguistics*, ed. by Michael James Grenfell, 121–146. London: Continuum.

Blackledge, Adrian, and Angela Creese. 2019. *Voices of a City Market: An Ethnography*. Bristol: Multilingual Matters.

Brewer, John, and Albert Hunter. 2006. *Foundations of Multimethod Research: Synthesizing Styles*. Thousand Oaks: Sage.

Compton, Sarah. 2020. "Interpreter-Mediated Interactions: Parent Participation in Individualized Education Plan Meetings for Deaf Students from Multilingual Homes." *Journal of Language, Identity & Education* 19 (4): 227–245.

Copland, Fiona, and Angela Creese. 2015. *Linguistic Ethnography: Collecting, Analysing and Presenting Data*. London: Sage.

Cox, Antoon. 2015. "Ethnographic Research on Ad Hoc Interpreting in a Linguistically Diverse Emergency Department: The Challenges of Data Collection." *New Voices in Translation Studies* 12: 30–49.

Creese, Angela. 2008. "Linguistic Ethnography." In *Encyclopaedia of Language and Education: Research Methods in Language and Education*, 2nd edition, ed. by Nancy H. Hornberger, 229–241. Berlin: Springer Press.

Creese, Angela, Adrian Blackledge, and Rachel Hu. 2018. "Translanguaging and Translation: The Construction of Social Difference Across City Spaces." *International Journal of Bilingual Education and Bilingualism* 21 (7): 841–852.

Cresswell, John W., and Vicki L. Plano Clark. 2023. "Revisiting Mixed Methods Research Designs Twenty Years Later." In *The Sage Handbook of Mixed Methods Research Design*, ed. by Cheryl N. Poth, 21–36. London: Sage.

Davitti, Elena. 2015. "Interpreter-Mediated Parent-Teacher Talk." In *Linking Discourse Studies to Professional Practice*, ed. by Lubie Grujicic-Alatriste, 176–200. Clevedon: Multilingual Matters.

de Pedro Ricoy, Raquel, and Jemina Napier. 2017. "Introduction: Innovations in Interpreting Research Methods." *International Journal of Translation & Interpreting Research* 9 (1): 1–3.

Dickinson, Jules. 2017. *Sign Language Interpreting in the Workplace*. Washington, DC: Gallaudet University Press.

Dong, Jiqing. 2016. "(Re)constructing the Model of Interpreting Professionalism through Institutional Work: The Perceived Impact of Agencies on Interpreters' Work Practices." Unpublished doctoral dissertation, Heriot-Watt University.

Dong, Jiqing. 2023. "'Can you work for us as an interpreter?' An Ethnography of Navigating Tensions and Emotions Within an Interpreting Agency." *The Translator* 29 (2): 175–192.

Duflou, Veerle. 2016. *Be(com)ing a Conference Interpreter: An Ethnography of EU Interpreters as a Professional Community*. Amsterdam & Philadelphia: John Benjamins.

Chapter 2. Linguistic ethnography in interpreting studies

Ehrensberger-Dow, Maureen, Susanne Göpferich, and Sharon O'Brien (eds). 2015. *Interdisciplinarity in Translation and Interpreting Process Research*. Amsterdam & Philadelphia: John Benjamins.

Goffman, Erving. 1981. *Forms of Talk*. Philadelphia: University of Pennsylvania Press.

Goico, Sara. 2020. "A Linguistic Ethnography Approach to the Study of Deaf Youth and Local Signs in Iquitos, Peru." *Sign Language Studies* 20 (4): 619–643.

Hale, Sandra. 2004. *The Discourse of Court Interpreting. Discourse Practices of the Law, the Witness and the Interpreter*. Amsterdam & Philadelphia: John Benjamins.

Hale, Sandra, and Jemina Napier. 2013. *Research Methods in Interpreting: A Practical Resource*. London: Bloomsbury.

Hale, Sandra, Mehera San Roque, David Spencer, and Jemina Napier. 2017. "Deaf Citizens as Jurors in Australian Courts: Participating Via Professional Interpreters." *International Journal of Speech, Language & the Law* 24 (2): 151–176.

Hansen, Jessica P. B. (2020). "Video-Mediated Interpreting: The Interactional Accomplishment of Interpreting in Video-Mediated Environments." Unpublished doctoral dissertation, University of Oslo.

Hou, Lynne. 2020. "Who Signs? Language Ideologies about Deaf and Hearing Child Signers in One Family in Mexico." *Sign Language Studies* 20 (4): 664–690.

Hou, Lynne, and Annelies Kusters. 2019. "Sign Languages." In *The Routledge Handbook of Linguistic Ethnography*, ed. by Karin Tusting, 340–355. New York: Routledge.

Hymes, Dell. 1974. *Foundations in Sociolinguistics: An Ethnographic Approach*. Philadelphia: University of Pennsylvania Press.

Inghilleri, Moira. 2006. "Macro Social Theory, Linguistic Ethnography and Interpreting Research." *Linguistica Antverpiensia* 5: 57–68.

Johnson, R. Burke, Anthony J. Onwuegbuzie, and Lisa A. Turner. 2007. "Toward a Definition of Mixed Methods Research." *Journal of Mixed Methods Research* 1 (2): 112–133.

Koskinen, Kaisa. 2020. "Translatorial Linguistic Ethnography in Organisations." In *Managing Multilingual Workplaces: Methodological, Empirical and Pedagogic Perspectives*, ed. by Sierke Horn, Philippe Lecomte, and Susanne Tietze, 60–77. London: Routledge.

Kusters, Annelies, and Lynn Hou. 2020. "Linguistic Ethnography and Sign Language Studies." *Sign Language Studies* 20 (4): 561–571.

Kusters, Annelies, Sujit Sahasrabudhe, and Amaresh Gopalakrishnan. 2016. "*A Reflexive Report on Filmmaking within a Linguistic Ethnography with Deaf and Hearing People in Mumbai*." MMG Working Paper (16–04). https://pure.mpg.de/rest/items/item_2357815_2 /component/file_2357813/content

Major, George. 2013. "Healthcare Interpreting as Relational Practice." Unpublished doctoral dissertation, Macquarie University.

Major, George. 2014. "'Sorry, Could You Explain That?' Clarification Requests in Interpreted Healthcare Interaction." In *Investigations in Healthcare Interpreting*, ed. by Brenda Nicodemus, and Melanie Metzger, 32–69. Washington, DC: Gallaudet University Press.

Major, George. 2024. "Healthcare Interpreting as Relational Practice: Understanding the Interpreter's Role in Facilitating Rapport in Health Interactions." *Interpreting and Society* 4 (2): 115–136.

Major, George, and Jemina Napier. 2012. "Interpreting and Knowledge Mediation in the Healthcare Setting: What Do We Really Mean By 'Accuracy'?" *Linguistica Antverpiensia* 11, 207–226.

Major, George, and Jemina Napier. 2019. "'I'm There Sometimes as a Just in Case': Examining Role Fluidity in Healthcare Interpreting." In *Multicultural Health Translation, Interpreting and Communication*, ed. by Meng Ji, Mustapha Taibi, and Ineke Creeze, 183–204. London: Routledge.

Major, George, Jemina Napier, Lindsay Ferrara, and Trevor Johnston. 2012. "Exploring Lexical Gaps in Australian Sign Language for the Purposes of Health Communication." *Communication & Medicine* 9 (1): 37–47.

Marin-Lacarta, Maialen, and Chuan Yu. 2023. "Ethnographic Research in Translation and Interpreting Studies." *The Translator* 29 (2): 147–156.

Moriarty, Erin. 2020. "Filmmaking in a Linguistic Ethnography of Deaf Tourist Encounters." *Sign Language Studies* 20 (4): 572–594.

Morse, Janice, and Linda Niehaus. 2009. *Principles and Procedures of Mixed Methods Design*. Walnut Creek, CA: Left Coast Press.

Napier, Jemina. 2007. "Cooperation in Interpreter-Mediated Monologic Talk." *Discourse and Communication* 1 (4): 407–432.

Napier, Jemina, Audrey Cameron, Lorraine Leeson, Christian Rathmann, Chris Peters, Haaris Sheikh, John Bosco Conama, and Rachel Moiselle. 2020. *Employment for Deaf People in Europe: Research Findings from the DESIGNS Project*. Dublin: Trinity College Dublin.

Napier, Jemina, Andy Carmichael, and Andrew Wiltshire. 2008. "Look-Pause-Nod: A Linguistic Case Study of a Deaf Professional and Interpreters Working Together." In *Deaf Professionals and Designated Interpreters: A New Paradigm*, ed. by Peter C. Hauser, Karen L. Finch, and Angela B. Hauser, 22–42. Washington, DC: Gallaudet University Press.

Napier, Jemina, and Sandra Hale. 2023. "Exploring Mixed Methods in Interpreting Research: An Example from a Series of Studies on Court Interpreting." In *Introducing New Hypertexts on Interpreting (Studies): A Tribute to Franz Pöchhacker*, ed. by Cornelia Zwischenberger, Karin Reithofer, and Sylvi Rennert, 22–43. Amsterdam & Philadelphia: John Benjamins.

Napier, Jemina, and Michael Kidd. 2013. "English Literacy as a Barrier to Healthcare Information for Deaf People Who Use Auslan." *Australian Family Physician* 42 (12): 896–899.

Napier, Jemina, Katherine Lloyd, Robert Skinner, Graham H. Turner, and Mark Wheatley. 2018. "Using Video Technology to Engage Deaf Sign Language Users in Survey Research: An Example from the Insign Project." *International Journal of Translation & Interpreting Research* 10 (2): 101–121.

Napier, Jemina, George Major, and Lindsay Ferrara. 2011. "Medical Signbank: A Cure-All for the Aches and Pains of Medical Sign Language Interpreting?" In *Signed Language Interpreting: Preparation, Practice and Performance*, ed. by Lorraine Leeson, Svenja Wurm, and Myriam Vermeerbergen, 110–137. Manchester: St Jerome.

Napier, Jemina, George Major, Lindsay Ferrara, and Trevor Johnston. 2014b. "Medical Signbank as a Model for Sign Language Planning? A Review of Community Engagement." *Current Issues in Language Planning* 16 (3): 279–295.

Napier, Jemina, and Alastair McEwin. 2015. "Do Deaf People Have the Right to Serve as Jurors in Australia?" *Alternative Law Journal* 40 (1): 23–27.

Napier, Jemina, and Debra Russell. Forthcoming. "The relationship between sign language interpreter positioning and deaf juror participation: An ethnographic case study."

Napier, Jemina, Debra Russell, Sandra Hale, David Spencer, and Mehera San Roque. 2022. "Training Legal Interpreters to Work with Deaf Jurors." In *Legal Interpreting: Teaching, Research, and Practice*, ed. by Jeremy L. Brunson, 246–281. Washington, DC: Gallaudet University Press.

Napier, Jemina, Joseph Sabolcec, Josie Hodgetts, Stef Linder, Gavin Mundy, Marijana Turcinov, and Linda Warby. 2014a. "Direct, Translated or Interpreter-Mediated? A Qualitative Study of Access to Preventative and On-Going Healthcare Information for Australian Deaf People." In *Investigations in Healthcare Interpreting*, ed. by Brenda Nicodemus, and Melanie Metzger, 51–89. Washington, DC: Gallaudet University Press.

Napier, Jemina, Robert Skinner, and Graham H. Turner. 2017. "'It's Good for Them but Not So for Me': Inside the Sign Language Interpreting Call Centre." *International Journal of Translation & Interpreting Research* 9 (2): 1–23.

Napier, Jemina, Robert Skinner, and Graham H. Turner. 2018. "Enabling Political Participation Through Video Remote Interpreting: A Case Study." In *Here or There? Research on Interpreting Via Video Link*, ed. by Jemina Napier, Robert Skinner, and Sabine Braun, 230–263. Washington, DC: Gallaudet University Press.

Napier, Jemina, and David Spencer. 2007. "A Sign of the Times: Deaf Jurors and the Potential for Pioneering Law Reform." *Reform: A Journal of National and International Law Reform* 90: 35–37.

Napier, Jemina, and David Spencer. 2008. "Guilty or not Guilty? An Investigation of Deaf Jurors' Access to Court Proceedings Via Sign Language Interpreting." In *Interpreting in Legal Settings*, ed. by Debra Russell, and Sandra Hale, 71–122. Washington, DC: Gallaudet University Press.

Napier, Jemina, and David Spencer. 2017. "Jury Instructions: Comparing Hearing and Deaf Jurors' Comprehension Via Direct or Interpreter-Mediated Communication." *International Journal of Speech, Language & the Law* 24 (1): 1–29.

Napier, Jemina, David Spencer, Sandra Hale, Mehera San Roque, Gerry Shearim, and Debra Russell. 2019. "Changing the International Justice Landscape: Perspectives on Deaf Citizenship and Jury Service." *Sign Language Studies* 19 (2): 240–266.

Napier, Jemina, David Spencer, and Joe Sabolcec. 2009. "A Shared Responsibility in the Administration of Justice. A Pilot Study of Signed Language Interpretation Access for Deaf Jurors. In *The Critical Link 5. Quality in Interpreting — a Shared Responsibility*, ed. by Sandra Hale, Uldis Ozolins, and Ludmila Stern, 99–118. Amsterdam & Philadelphia: John Benjamins.

Pöchhacker, Franz. 2004. *Introducing Interpreting Studies*. London: Routledge.

Pöchhacker, Franz. 2011. "Researching Interpreting: Approaches to Inquiry." In *Advances in Interpreting Research: Inquiry in Action*, ed. by Brenda Nicodemus, and Laurie Swabey, 5–26. Amsterdam & Philadelphia: John Benjamins.

Puupponen, Anna, Gabrielle Hodge, Benjamin Anible, Juhana Salonen, Tuija Wainio, Jarkko Keränen, Doris Hernández, and Tommi Jantunen. 2025. "Opening up Corpus FinSL: Enriching Corpus Analysis with Linguistic Ethnography in a Study of Constructed Action." *Linguistics*. 63 (1): 277–316.

Rampton, Ben. 2007. "Neo-Hymesian Linguistic Ethnography in the United Kingdom." *Journal of Sociolinguistics* 11 (5): 584–607.

Rampton, Ben, Celia Roberts, Constant Leung, and Roxy Harris. 2002. "Methodology in the Analysis of Classroom Discourse." *Applied Linguistics* 23 (3): 373–392.

Rampton, Ben, Karin Tusting, Janet Maybin, Richard Barwell, Angela Creese, and Vally Lytra. 2004. "UK Linguistic Ethnography: A Discussion Paper." https://www.lancaster.ac.uk/fss/organisations/lingethn/documents/discussion_paper_jan_05.pdf

Roy, Cynthia B. 2000. *Interpreting as a Discourse Process*. New York: Oxford University Press.

Sarangi, Srikant (ed). 2023. *Interpreter Mediated Healthcare Consultations*. Sheffield: Equinox.

Shaw, Sara, Fiona Copland, and Julia Snell. 2015. "An Introduction to Linguistic Ethnography: Interdisciplinary Explorations." In *Linguistic Ethnography: Interdisciplinary Explorations*, ed. by Julia Snell, Sara Shaw, and Fiona Copland, 1–13. Basingstoke: Palgrave.

Sheikh, Haaris, Lorraine Leeson, Jemina Napier, Tobias Haug, and Teresa Lynch. 2021. "Access to Justice for Deaf Signers." In *UNCRPD Implementation in Europe — a Deaf Perspective. Article 9: Access to Information and Communication*, ed. by Goedele De Clerck, 161–175. Brussels: European Union of the Deaf.

Slettebakk Berge, Sigrid. 2018. "How Sign Language Interpreters Use Multimodal Actions to Coordinate Turn-Taking in Group Work Between Deaf and Hearing Upper Secondary School Students." *Interpreting* 20 (1): 96–125.

Slettebakk Berge, Sigrid. 2023. "Interpreters' Use of Environmentally Coupled Gestures to Achieve Mutual Understanding of Speaker Identity in a Deaf and Hearing Classroom." *Lingua* 284: Art. 103486.

Sommer Lindsay, Mette, Audrey Cameron, and Jemina Napier. 2023. "Deaf People in the Workplace." In *Intercultural Issues in Business Management*, ed. by Katerina Strani, and Kerstin Pfeiffer, 241–254. London: Routledge.

Spencer, David, Jemina Napier, Mehera San Roque, and Sandra Hale. 2017b. "Justice is Blind as Long as it Isn't Deaf: Excluding Deaf People from Jury Duty — an Australian Human Rights Breach." *Australian Journal of Human Rights* 23 (3): 332–350.

Spencer, David, Mehera San Roque, Sandra Hale, and Jemina Napier. 2017a. "The High Court Considers Participation of Deaf People in Jury Duty." *Law Society Journal* 33 (May): 80–81.

Starfield, Sue. 2010. "Ethnographies." In *Continuum Companion to Research Methods in Applied Linguistics*, ed. by Brian Paltridge, and Aek Phakiti, 50–65. London: Continuum.

Torkpoor, Rozita, Ingrid Fioretos, Birgitta Essén, and Elisabet Londos. 2022. " 'I Know Hyena. Do you Know Hyena?' Challenges in Interpreter-Mediated Dementia Assessment, Focusing on the Role of the Interpreter." *Journal of Cross-Cultural Gerontology* 37: 45–67.

Turner, Graham H., Jemina Napier, Robert Skinner, and Mark Wheatley. 2016. "Telecommunication Relay Services as a Tool for Deaf Political Participation and Citizenship." *Information, Communication & Society* 20 (10): 1521–1538.

Tusting, Karin, and John Maybin. 2007. "Linguistic Ethnography and Interdisciplinarity: Opening the Discussion." *Journal of Sociolinguistics* 11 (5): 575–583.

Van Hest, Ella, and Marie Jacobs. 2022. "Spaces of Linguistic Non-Understanding in Linguistic Ethnography (and Beyond)." In *Methodological Issues and Challenges in Researching Transculturally*, ed. by Mabel Victoria, 14–38. Newcastle: Cambridge Scholars Publishing.

Wadensjö, Cecilia. 1998. *Interpreting as Interaction*. London: Longman.

Wetherell, Margaret. 2007. "A Step Too Far: Discursive Psychology, Linguistic Ethnography and Questions of Identity." *Journal of Sociolinguistics* 11 (5): 661–681.

Wulff, Helena. 2002. "Yo-Yo Fieldwork: Mobility and Time in a Multi-Local Study of Dance in Ireland." *Anthropological Journal on European Cultures* 11: 117–136.

Yuan, Xiaohui. 2022. "A Symbolic Interactionist Model of Interpreter-Facilitated Communication: Key Communication Issues in Face-To-Face Interpreting." *Frontiers in Communication* 7.

CHAPTER 3

Retrospective ethnography and remembrance
A narrative of UNOG field missions

Lucía Ruiz Rosendo & Alma Barghout
University of Geneva | United Nations Office at Geneva (UNOG)

The present chapter seeks to promote a methodological discussion around the pertinence of drawing on retrospective reflexive ethnography and the notion of 'past presencing' to investigate the practice of interpreting in field missions deployed by the United Nations. The chapter provides an overview of the methodological choices that were made after analysing the implications of the second author's positionality as an insider and after considering the different methods that could be used to make the most of her wide experience as an interpreter who had been deployed to many field missions. After highlighting the particularities of practical issues related to interpreting in said missions, we examine the application of the findings to design and implement interpreter training, which brings about institutional changes at the UN that will eventually have an impact on the interpreters' work.

Keywords: interpreting, reflexive ethnography, retrospective ethnography, past presencing, field missions, international organisation, United Nations, training

1. Introduction: Defining the context

Academic studies about interpreting in the field (see below for a discussion of our specific understanding of this term), which have proliferated particularly in recent decades, have shed new light on the figure of the interpreter in different challenging contexts. Most of the studies about interpreting in the field have focused on the role of interpreters who have been systematically recruited to work alongside armed forces in conflict zones. When interpreters become visible, it is rarely due to the recognition of the crucial role they play as linguistic and cultural mediators, but rather as a result of media coverage of the risks they face, particularly

https://doi.org/10.1075/btl.165.03rui
Available under the CC BY-NC 4.0 license. © 2025 John Benjamins Publishing Company

local interpreters recruited during contemporary conflicts, such as the wars in Afghanistan and Iraq (Salama-Carr 2007; Baker 2014). Moreover, academic interest in the role of interpreters in conflict zones has been sharpened by researchers' interest in the interpreter's positionality and in the political role of language in translation studies (Jones 2014).

This increasing interest from scholars helps to underline the importance of interpreting and translation in the field and to understand the need to develop and adapt ethical principles based on current and available practices. Researchers in this context usually base their studies on surveys and interviews carried out with the interpreters themselves, in which the latter relate the difficulties and challenges they have faced as a result of their complex positionality (e.g. Todorova 2016; Ruiz Rosendo and Persaud 2019; Ruiz Rosendo 2020; Martin and Gómez Amich 2021). However, such investigations rarely involve conference interpreters working for international organisations, in general, and for the United Nations (UN), in particular, despite the fact that they are frequently deployed to the field. This category of interpreters is of interest because they are trained conference interpreters with substantial professional experience whose involvement in missions worldwide has increased in recent decades, especially following the creation of the Office of the High Commissioner for Human Rights (OHCHR) in 1993.

Therefore, there is a scarcity of academic research relating to this category of interpreters and the texts governing their role. It is worth noting that the terms 'interpreting in conflict zones', 'interpreting in war-related scenarios' and 'in conflict-related scenarios' are not universally applicable to UN missions. UN missions can indeed be related to conflict, for example, when a Commission of Inquiry is deployed in the post-conflict phase; when the Secretary General, the High Commissioner for Human Rights or their representatives go on a country visit in a war-related setting; or when they go to refugee camps in countries neighbouring a country in conflict. However, these missions rarely take place *during* armed conflict: to visit any country, UN field missions must obtain prior security clearance from the UN Department of Safety and Security, which is extremely rarely granted during conflict. Moreover, UN field missions are not humanitarian *stricto sensu,* either, unlike missions for other agencies such as the UN High Commissioner for Refugees (UNHCR) or the International Committee of the Red Cross (ICRC). Therefore, the results of studies carried out about interpreting in conflict zones (e.g. Inghilleri 2008; Footitt and Kelly 2012; Gómez Amich 2017; Ruiz Rosendo and Persaud 2019) or on the role of the interpreter in the humanitarian field (e.g. Delgado Luchner and Kherbiche 2018; Moser-Mercer et al. 2021; Tedjouong and Todorova 2022) do not always apply to UN field missions in that the latter are different in nature to military or humanitarian missions carried out by other organisations. Furthermore, the profile of the trained conference interpreters who participate in UN field missions differs from the profile of untrained local interpreters who are usually recruited by the armed forces or by humanitarian organisations.

Our research (Ruiz Rosendo, Barghout, and Martin 2021; Barghout and Ruiz Rosendo 2022) has revealed that the vast majority of UN field missions are serviced by the United Nations Office at Geneva (UNOG). In these missions, interpreters are usually deployed to accompany Special Procedures who conduct country visits, mainly to investigate violations of human rights and ascertain the compliance of member states with their human rights obligations. This probably explains why, prior to the current drafting of Standard Operating Procedures (SOPs) on field missions (internal unpublished document) by UNOG's Interpretation Service, the only available internal guidelines (2010) used the term 'Missions with human rights mechanisms'[1] as 'clients' of interpretation services. They included information on travel arrangements and the working hours and conditions to be taken into account for interpreters accompanying the mission.

Therefore, UN field missions cannot be defined as missions in conflict zones, or in conflict-related zones,[2] inasmuch as they include mandates where there is no link to a conflict. Examples include the missions of the Special Rapporteur on Violence Against Women deployed in European countries; or missions of the Special Rapporteur on the Promotion and Protection of Human Rights and Fundamental Freedoms while countering terrorism visiting the United States or Australia.[3]

---

1. This is a general term that refers to human rights monitoring mechanisms. There are two types of human rights monitoring mechanisms within the UN system: treaty-based bodies and charter-based bodies. The ten human rights Treaty Bodies, made up of committees of independent experts, monitor implementation of the core international human rights treaties. The charter-based bodies include the Human Rights Council (OHCHR), Special Procedures, the Universal Periodic Review and Independent Investigations. OHCHR provides expertise and support to all of the different mechanisms, including interpretation services. However, field missions serviced by UNOG go beyond these mechanisms, since interpreters are also deployed to accompany the Secretary General or his special envoys and representatives. Interpreters also service missions of the Security Council and Special Commissions and Special Committees established by the General Assembly. This is why the new SOPs use the more inclusive term 'field missions'.

2. There is the exception of peacekeeping operations. However, these are serviced by a different category of interpreters. When needed, peacekeeping operations are accompanied by interpreters from troop-contributing countries for their own contingents. These interpreters are a different category from UN staff or freelance interpreters.

3. Special Procedures currently include 45 thematic mandates and 14 country mandates. For a clearer idea of the range of topics that are covered by Special Procedures, please consult the OHCHR website (see https://www.ohchr.org/en/special-procedures-human-rights-council).

Consequently, given these particularities of UN missions, in a previous article we decided to use the more general and better-suited term 'field mission' to define an event where a team of interpreters accompanies a UN mission to locations outside of the four UN duty stations and which does not take place in a conference setting (see Ruiz Rosendo, Barghout, and Martin 2021 for more information about these missions). All further references in this chapter to 'missions' and 'the field' should be understood as referring to 'field missions' as we have defined them here.

We decided to carry out a study to shed more light on the role of interpreters in this very specific setting by answering the following research questions: How can the practice of interpreting be defined in UN field missions? How can the results of the field research serving as the basis for this study be used and applied to training? In this chapter we will focus on the methodological choices and the description of the methodology used to collect the data that informed the training.

The study draws on the notion of 'past presencing', coined by anthropologist Sharon MacDonald (2013), and on Ferreira and Vespeira's (2017) process of 'retrospective ethnography'. In so doing, the chapter will present field work insights by interrogating the various modes whereby the past may be enfolded into the present. Following our reflections, we have adopted an approach which we have entitled 'retrospective reflective ethnography', described in detail below. This approach acknowledges the value of both big and small stories: apart from data collected through interviews, described by Freeman (2006) as big stories, we argue for the relevance of small stories, of casual conversations about events that happen in everyday life (Georgakopoulou 2007). Therefore, our research was based on a dialogue between the two authors of the chapter in which the first author, a conference interpreter and scholar in the field of interpreting studies, acted as interviewer and the second author, a UN conference interpreter, acted as narrator. It also included informal conversations between the second author and other interpreters. The study was further complemented by semi-structured interviews held with all four UN chief interpreters representing the different headquarters (New York, Geneva, Vienna and Nairobi) and a representative of higher management from UNOG to collect their views about the organisational and logistical aspects related to field missions. These complementary activities — the retrospective reflective ethnography, the conversations with interpreters and the semi-structured interviews — enhanced ethnographically-informed knowledge production as a collaborative endeavour.

The chapter also examines the application of these field research findings in a training course to make lasting institutional changes that have a positive impact on the interpreter's work. Therefore, the chapter also deals with the use of the findings to design and implement interpreter training that takes account of the problems encountered on UNOG field missions.

In this discussion of ethnographic field work, we hope to contribute to four ongoing debates. In interpreting studies, this research will offer an account of the challenges faced by *practisearchers,* defined as researchers who work as interpreters during the research period (see also Steinkogler, Chapter 6, this volume). Secondly, it will also describe less-used approaches and processes, such as retrospective reflexive ethnography. Thirdly, it aims to deepen our understanding of current possibilities for applying the findings of field work to training. Finally, the chapter will contribute to current debates about the complexity of doing research when in the employ of international organisations.

2. Ethnographic approach in interpreting studies

In the present chapter, we use 'fieldwork' to refer to fieldwork as carried out in traditional ethnography (Delamont 2009). We will be using the word 'ethnography' to refer to fieldwork as an approach that "establishes a relationship between personal experience and the production of knowledge" (Ferreira and Vespeira 2017: 215).

As Wellin and Fine (2001: 323) posit, "whatever else it may be, ethnography is a form of work". It has, by its very nature, a double meaning: on the one hand, it is an approach based on data collection; a qualitative research method based on obtaining data through direct observation and participant observation, as well as interviews and informal exchanges with interlocutors, as is the case in this study. On the other hand, it is the result of the research, a detailed text written as a first- or third-person account (Clifford and Marcus 1986) within a wider social context. Such a method requires a field presence, allowing the researcher to observe a wide spectrum of interactions at different times and in different circumstances which they analyse in order to draw patterns, values or social schemes.

The ultimate goal of any ethnographic study is, essentially, to present an account of the way in which a social group shares meaning (Geertz 2000). In other words, this method is used to observe and report on the various dynamics that occur between the members of a social group and the interaction these members have with their greater environment. Importantly, ethnography has recently expanded and transformed (Fine and Hancock 2017) and has transcended its initial focus on understanding marginalised groups (Marcus 1986; Ragin 1994) to include other topics.

Ethnography as a method has been increasingly used to shed light on the "everyday practices and implicit knowledge associated with … interpreting settings" (Delgado Luchner 2019: 97). This means that contemporary ethnography has moved away from the traditional assumption of the powerful researcher and the exotic, less powerful, researched group. Furthermore, its aim has evolved to not only focus on the researcher's perspective, but to reproduce the diversity of participants' perspectives. In so doing, the line between the researcher and the researched has become more blurred. It is also worth noting that ethnography has evolved from small-scale studies over lengthy periods of time to projects conducted over shorter periods and several physical sites. In fact, there are some events examined by ethnography, such as UN field missions, that do not take place for a long time — they usually last anywhere from a single day to two weeks — or in one single place. This means that ethnographic studies are, at times, characterised by a compilation of observational periods that are separated through time and space. In the present study, the ethnography was based on 30 missions deployed in different places and times, and within the framework of different UN mandates (see Section 4).

In the field of interpreting studies, we find some examples of ethnographic studies that analyse the practice of interpreting in a given context, time and place, assuming that interpreting is a "socially situated activity" (Flynn 2010:116). Bahadır (2004), in her analogy of the interpreter-researcher as an anthropologist, describes the professional identities of the interpreter-researcher as identities consisting of different social and cultural roles, positions and attitudes. Delgado Luchner (2015, 2019), in her analysis of the 'Nairobi project', aims to deepen our understanding of the challenges associated with interpreter training in Africa by using a participant-observer paradigm. Hokkanen and Koskinen (2016) explore narrated affect using retrospective reflection by reporting on three ethnographic studies negotiating professional identity in different contexts. Hokkanen (2017), in her study on simultaneous interpreting during church services, defines herself as a participant-researcher, and uses autoethnography to contribute to the analysis of embodied somatic and affective field experiences. Duflou (2016) uses her position as a member of the community of practice under observation to explore the skills that conference interpreters working for the European institutions need to acquire in order to cope with their professional tasks, through observation, in-depth interviews and the analysis of institutional documents. Finally, anthropologist Laura Kunreuther (Kunreuther 2020; Kunreuther et al. 2021) focuses on the experiences of interpreters who worked for the UN Office of the High Commissioner for Human Rights (OHCHR) during its mission in Nepal by carrying out a conversation with them. Other authors who have used ethnography as an approach are Angelelli (2000) and Inghilleri (2003) to examine the practice of medical interpreting and of interpreting in asylum seeking procedures, respectively.

However, despite the existence of these works in interpreting studies, which make use of ethnography and which have undoubtedly inspired our work through their use of different methods to collect data (i.e., informal conversations, interviews, autoethnography), to our knowledge no ethnographic studies have been carried out to examine the role of conference interpreters who are deployed to the field by an international organisation, with the noteworthy exception of Haidar and Ruiz Rosendo (2023).

3. Understanding the researcher's positionality

The reason for carrying out an ethnographic study to examine the practice of interpreting in UN field missions was the gap in interpreter training for that specific context, identified by this study's second author: UN interpreters, even if they are fully-fledged conference interpreters, are not necessarily equipped with the skills that they need when deployed in field missions. She remembered how she had to venture into the unknown the first time she went on a mission. Interpreters did not receive any briefing on what to expect and on the challenges of working in the field, meaning that they had no idea of what a field mission was or of how to behave on such missions, not least because there were no guidelines available for interpreters.

In qualitative studies, in general, and in ethnographic studies, in particular, it is essential to be aware of and analyse the researcher's positionality, understood as "the careful consideration of the ways in which researchers' past experiences, points of view, and roles impact these same researchers' interactions with, and interpretations of, the research scene" (Tracy 2013:2). The researcher is confronted with their own positionality regarding the participants and the knowledge they bring with them or help construct in such a collaboration (Flynn 2010). In this context, researchers are human actors who cannot be neutral or objective, in that their mere presence influences and is influenced by the phenomenon under study. Therefore, one may argue that an ethnographer cannot just dispassionately observe events unfolding around them. This is especially true in those cases in which the researcher is also a participant; or, applied to the field of interpreting, when the researcher is also an active interpreter while carrying out the ethnography. In these cases, Bahadır (2004) argues that the interpreter-researcher is caught in the Geertzian dilemma (Geertz 1973) between the 'emic' and the 'etic' perspective, and that when they embody this dual role, interpreter-researchers cannot *not* communicate: communication occurs just by being and behaving. Some degree of subjectivity is therefore unavoidable, because a researcher "never observes the behavioural event which would have taken place in his or her absence, nor hears an account identical with that which the same narrator would have given to another person" (Behar 1996:6).

In the present study, the ethnographer — the second author of the chapter — is an Arabic-booth interpreter who has, since 1997, accumulated experience on 30 missions as a UN staff member; she was an active interpreter in all these field missions, which allowed her to informally speak with interpreters and with other colleagues. Furthermore, from an institutional perspective, she is a staff conference interpreter at an international organisation to which she has pledged allegiance — an insider (Berger 2015). This positionality is not devoid of challenges: the interpreter, while carrying out her work, must abide by the rule of confidentiality (a *sine qua non* condition for interpreters), and by a clear code of conduct (applicable to all officials of and persons under contract with the organisation). These aspects can be very restrictive for research, since professional comments exchanged during a mission, whether interpreted or not, cannot be reported under any circumstances.

4. Choosing the ethnographic method

4.1 Reflexive ethnography

Understanding this positionality was essential in order to decide on the method to collect information. The researcher, in her role as an insider, had privileged access to the phenomenon and to the people involved and had been an active observer-participant herself. This observation allowed her to subsequently reflect on the dilemmas faced by the interpreters, the decisions made, the practical aspects to be considered and the self-care strategies used when confronted with challenging situations. Narrative inquiry seemed to us to be a relevant method, in that it is widely used to focus on stories or storytelling activities (Cihodariu 2012), on life experiences as narrated by those (narrated lives) who live them as a way of "understanding one's own or others' actions, of organising events and objects into a meaningful whole, of connecting and seeing the consequences of actions and events over time" (Chase 2011: 421). As Chase (2011) posits, there are some researchers who use their own stories as a focus of narrative inquiry in an attempt to include their experience of a given topic or research question (see, for example, Behar 2007 or Saukko 2008). Autoethnography or interpretive biography is another version of this approach, in that there is no distinction between the researcher and the researched. It is defined as

> an autobiographical genre of academic writing that draws on and analyses or interprets the lived experience of the author and connects researcher insights to self-identity, cultural rules and resources, communication practices, traditions,

> premises, symbols, rules, shared meanings, emotions, values, and larger social, cultural, and political issues.
>
> (Poulos 2021: 4)

Autoethnography is an increasingly-used method of qualitative research whose aim is to include the researcher's lived experience, recentred as the focus of the research, in the phenomenon under study, a form of self-narrative that places the self within a social context (Campbell 2016; see also Hokkanen, Chapter 4, and Davier, Chapter 7, for examples of autoethnographies in this volume). Delamont (2009) introduces an interesting distinction between reflexive ethnography and autoethnography, according to which, in the latter, the main object of study is the researcher themselves, whereas in the former, the researcher studies a phenomenon, including participants other than themselves, but is very sensitive to the relationships created between themselves and the focus of the research (see, for example, Wolcott's reflexive ethnographies published in 1977 and 1981).

Therefore, whilst we agree with Campbell (2016) that stories of lived experience are needed to gather knowledge of a phenomenon and understand its meanings in a given context, we also consider that we had to go beyond autoethnography to describe the phenomenon under study. Drawing on Delamont's (2009: 58) claim that "the main focus of social science should be analysis of social settings and actors to whom the researcher has had access, not the introspections of the researcher", we also think that it is important to move away from what has been (somewhat controversially) termed autoethnographic self-obsession: the danger of autoethnography is that the personal self is so deeply ingrained in the text that it completely dominates the narrative.

For all these reasons, we wanted to go beyond autoethnography towards an ethnography in which the researcher incorporates her own personal narratives into the ethnographic materials, along the lines of Reed-Danahay's (2001) notion of autobiographical ethnography. Given the importance that we attach to the notion of reflexivity and to the view that the observer is inevitably linked to the observed, we opted for a reflexive ethnography, in which the researcher crafts narratives stemming from her personal experience within a culture, and includes different methods of data collection, such as interviews, participant observation, conversational engagement, archival research, and narrative inquiry, as a procedure of interrogating and integrating the researcher's personal experience into the narratives and experiences of others.

Another important factor to be considered in choosing the method is that we wanted to include the researcher's testimonies about past experiences in the present study, given her wide experience as an interpreter in field missions. Therefore, the retrospective nature of the ethnography also had to be considered: we did not want to ignore the researcher's wealth of experience throughout her 28 years at the UN and in the 30 missions that she had serviced, in the context of different mandates and in different regions. In other words, we did not want to wait for new missions to be organised because we did not know if and when these missions were going to be deployed and if the second author was going to service them. In fact, she did not service any other missions due to her lack of availability and to the fact that local interpreters were increasingly recruited by the UN. The outbreak of the COVID-19 pandemic was also a significant factor resulting in the cancellation of all field missions. Even though missions resumed at the end of 2020, travel restrictions still applied in many places, and the UN continued to mostly recruit local interpreters.

4.2 Retrospective ethnography

Ferreira and Vespeira (2017: 208), in their study on 20th-century pre- and post-revolutionary Portugal, define retrospective ethnography as "a theoretical and methodological process that allows the intensive study of a specific past event and its present reverberations" through different methods, such as interviews, fieldwork, life stories, archive research and observation. The ethnographic participants' narratives of past time allow the researcher to reflect on memory and recollection during the moment of the ethnographic encounter, characterised by the comparison with the present.

These authors focus on the relevance of the dialogical moments stimulated by a retrospective ethnography and inspired by Miller's (2001, 2007) use of mini-analytical portraits for the analysis of the remembrance process. Working by retrogression, diachronically, Ferreira and Vespeira (2017) interviewed two individuals who had experienced the historical episodes and based their study on the two resulting portraits, reviving the past in the present, in order to proceed to a critical analysis of the context they represent. Diachronic ethnography is used to acknowledge the multiple, mutating, polyphonic temporalities of the ethnographic encounter and its multi-timed layers and to move away from an anthropology based in synchronicity and on the "ethnographic present" (Ferreira and Vespeira 2017: 208). As they put it:

> Retrospection and biographic recollection are not linear; there are detours and leaps, (re)creations and silences, periods that are remembered and others that are forgotten. And that moment in time when remembrance is aroused is the terrain par excellence of the ethnographer who maps the past ... making it possible to access information that could not be obtained through daily social interactions.
>
> (Ferreira and Vespeira 2017: 209)

In our present study, careful ethnographic attention had to be directed towards the ways interpreters themselves reflect on events and their involvement in field missions. Taking the lead from Ferreira and Vespeira (2017), we applied retrospective ethnography to recollect past field experiences of the narrator (i.e. the second author). Similarly, our analysis took its cue from anthropologist Sharon MacDonald's (2013:52) notion of 'past presencing', described as "the empirical phenomenon of how people variously experience, understand and produce the past in the present", which examines the multiple modes whereby the past may be enfolded to the present, not only at institutionalised levels but also in everyday practices (Sandberg 2020).

The selected method of *retrospective reflexive ethnography* enabled collaborative knowledge production in that it allowed us to bring together experiences to gain a better understanding of the practice of interpreting in field missions. This method has limitations and risks of biases, 'bias' being defined as "an inclination or tendency in favour of or against one thing, in a way considered to be unfair or not revealing the reality" when what is depicted is "a story or account that the researcher wants to display in order to present a certain impression or conclusion" (Kristi 2021:311–312). Remembered data also comes with certain risks and limitations, in that past occurrences could be mixed up in the absence of specific notes taken during the different missions. Furthermore, we tend to view past events differently the more they are removed and distant from the present. In fact, self-reflection has been criticised for being self-indulgent, narcissistic, introspective, and individualised (Sparkes 2000; Eriksson 2010). For our study to be relevant and methodologically sound, we followed Alvesson's (2003:189) recommendation to avoid 'staying native'. Therefore, intersubjectivity and reflexivity were two essential aspects when carrying out the study. Intersubjectivity referred to exchanging thoughts and feelings between the narrator and the interviewer, while reflexivity entailed the narrator being aware of her positionality and of its impact on the process and outcomes of the research. In practical terms, we decided that there was a need to examine UN documents to identify all references to interpreters (such as internal guidelines), as well as to organise multiple encounters between us — interviewer and narrator — and with the other interpreters. In addition, we designed semi-structured interviews with chief interpreters and a representative from management, which enabled us to triangulate the data, as McIlveen (2008) recommends (see Section 5).

5. The study: Researching the practice of interpreting in UN field missions[4]

5.1 Conversations between the interviewer and the narrator

The study sought to investigate the practice of interpreting in UN field missions by using retrospective reflexive ethnography as a methodology to collect data. Remembrance, in the sense of recalling the past, started *stricto sensu* in 2017, when the two authors of the present chapter decided to design a tailored programme to train UN conference interpreters who were deployed in field missions, as a collaborative endeavour between the University of Geneva's Faculty of Translation and Interpreting and UNOG. After consulting the UN archives and the relevant literature, we identified a lack of documents governing the interpreters' work in field missions, as well as a lack of recorded testimonies of interpreters sharing their experiences in this specific context. We soon realised that in order to firstly fill in these gaps and subsequently design a relevant programme, it was necessary to revisit the past to understand the challenges that interpreters face in this context as well as their needs.

As described above, the second author of this chapter, in her role as researcher and as narrator of the ethnography, falls into the category of the participant-observer, an active member in the phenomenon observed. The narrator was asked to recount, analyse and reconstruct her own past experiences and the context in which she had experienced them in a series of conversations that took place between her and the first author of this chapter, who embodied the role of the interviewer and who took notes during and after these conversations. Similar to Ferreira and Vespeira's (2017) study, the time frame was not completely fixed, and the narrative came and went between multiple missions. More specifically, the missions included 15 UN Special Commissions and Special Committees, 2 Commissions of Inquiry, 5 fact-finding missions, 1 special envoy, and 7 special rapporteurs. These took place in Algeria, Egypt, Iran, Iraq, Israel and the Occupied Palestinian Territory, Jordan, Libya, Syria, Tunisia, and Turkey throughout the interpreter's career as UN staff member. These conversations helped the

---

4. This study is part of an ongoing PhD dissertation carried out at the University of Geneva. It complies with the ethical procedure of the Faculty of Translation and Interpreting of the University of Geneva (Directive relative à l'intégrité dans le domaine de la recherche scientifique et à la procédure à suivre en cas de manquement à l'intégrité) [Guidelines on Scientific Research Integrity and on the Procedure to Follow in the Case of Breach of Integrity]. The study is supported by the Division of Conference Management of UNOG. The study has been granted the Certification of Ethical Compliance by the Commission Universitaire pour une Recherche Ethique à l'Université de Genève (CUREG).

interviewer to understand practices and experiences that could not be lived and observed directly by her given that she would not have the opportunity to go on a field mission. There was a close interaction between the interviewer and the narrator. In this sense, our study focuses on the analysis of a life story (that is elicited by another person) contrary to an autobiography (which is self-initiated). Consequently, the interviewer was an agent of the remembrance process, instigating the remembrance of past experiences and helping the narrator to reconstruct and to analyse them, in "trusted, private encounters" (Schwander-Sievers 2010: 102). In the interviews, the narrator was asked to remember not only her own experiences but also those conversations with the other interpreters that took place in everyday practice throughout all the aforementioned missions. The narrator also relayed her colleagues' experiences (which they shared with her upon their return from the field) of other Special Procedures deployed in 2018 and 2019 in which she had not participated herself.

In this process, the narrator was considered an active player with her own history and story, a storyteller that allowed the interviewer to become immersed in the narrator's personal narratives in order to, vicariously, live through the described experiences. The methodological choice for life stories and oral collection of data was a response to the narrator's positionality, an interpreter-researcher who had experienced her professional life in the field in an undocumented way — without leaving a written trace of these experiences — similarly to her interpreter colleagues who were in the field with her. In addition, the method was chosen to investigate not only what interpreters do in this context, but also what they intended to do, what they believed they were doing and why and what they think they should have done. All these experiences and questions were the basis for a series of case scenarios that were developed with the intention of using them for training interpreters in the future.

The ethnographic encounters between the interviewer and the narrator were characterised by the memory of emotions. The remembrance process was marked by a narrative that shifted between descriptions that emphasised the challenging context in which interpreters work in the field and memories that highlighted the congenial nature of the community of interpreters and the emotional implications of working in this context. The past was compared with the present, highlighting the similarities and the differences, travelling through missions, countries, years, experiences, personal memories, and traumas, to identify commonalities and, more importantly, things that could be done to improve the skills of interpreters who are deployed on missions to the field. In this sense, the future was always present in the ethnographic encounter, as if a continuous past embraced both present and future. As is usually the case in personal stories, some memories were too traumatic to be expressed in words, but the silence surrounding them indicated the emotional implications of a given event, which was essential to really understand the stakes of interpreting in field missions. These passages conveyed through fewer words were even more telling in their silence, particularly because the conversations allowed the interviewer to feel and fill the unsaid, what Gallinat (2006: 355) calls the "heavy silence". Emotions contributed to "the processes of remembering and forgetting, of feeling compelled or unable to speak about the past" (MacDonald 2013: 79). These emotional experiences were usually related to the impact and the psychological toll that the exposure to sensitive or traumatic testimonies of victims of human rights abuses had on the narrator, along the lines of studies carried out in other challenging contexts, for example, humanitarian interpreting (Loutan, Farinelli, and Pampallona 1999; Holmgren, Sondergaard, and Elklit 2003); community interpreting (Hetherington 2011; Bontempo and Malcolm 2012); or interpreting at international criminal tribunals (Ndongo-Keller 2015).

The ethnographic encounters not only triggered an ethnographic narrative on the part of the narrator, they went beyond this to recall the multitude of informal discussions that took place over the years with her interpreter colleagues. Most of these conversations took place during the missions and immediately thereafter. It is worth noting that each mission is unique in its characteristics and multiple challenges, and a very special bond usually forms between the members of the interpretation team, as well as with other UN colleagues accompanying the mission, whether from the OHCHR secretariat or Security. This is due to the fact that the mission team spends all their time together, sharing meals, vehicles and very long working hours. Confidentiality is another reason why those on the same mission share thoughts, feelings, and experiences with one another: colleagues are not permitted to discuss the mission with anyone outside of those assigned to it. Discussions were sometimes of a purely practical nature, such as the interpreter's physical position, the interpreting modality, how and what to prepare but other discussions related to ethical dilemmas or to psychological implications, sharing emotions and even tears at times. These discussions were held in informal debriefing sessions usually at the end of a workday or during the breaks.

During these informal conversations, the need for training and especially for psychological self-care was identified by the interpreters themselves. This led to several initiatives that were supported by management, such as a workshop dedicated to interpreters on 'Mission Readiness and Wellness' with the Staff Counsellor. This workshop included sessions on stress management, meditation and self-care.

5.2 Conversations with other interpreters at UNOG headquarters

In a second stage, other conversations took place with other interpreters at the headquarters to go beyond the narrator's recollection: in 2018 several conversations were held with 3 interpreters from the Arabic and the French booths who shared their experiences about the challenges encountered in the field. The information gathered so far allowed us to organise a first pilot training course in January 2019. After the course, a focus group was organised with the participants in the course (UN staff conference interpreters) to assess the contents of the course and gather their views about the needs and challenges in the field (see Ruiz Rosendo, Barghout, and Martin 2021, as well as Barghout and Ruiz Rosendo 2022 to obtain more information about this course and the results of the focus groups).

More recently, a film entitled 'In Flow of Words' (Bots 2022) was featured at UNOG in the context of the World Day for Safety and Health at Work, an annual UN observance that aims to raise international awareness around the effort to make work environments safe and healthy for all. The film focuses on the experiences of three interpreters who served at The Hague during the International Criminal Tribunal for the former Yugoslavia (ICTY). Born and raised in the former Yugoslavia, and witnesses to the brutal wars of the 1990s, the interpreters were forced to contend with their personal memories and traumas. The screening was followed by a panel discussion on the importance of safeguarding the health and wellbeing of interpreters, whose work can subject them to extraordinarily difficult situations. The success of the event led to a second screening dedicated only to staff and freelance interpreters alike. Over 25 interpreters attended the event, which was a safe space for them to voice many of their experiences and predicaments. Similarly to the narrator and UNOG colleagues, the interpreters in the film recognise the suffering from recurring distressing memories and feelings and the demanding and psychologically degrading working conditions and high level of distress, frustration and powerlessness suffered by interpreters who have to interpret stories of torture and annihilation. The psychological implications were indeed one of the most recurrent narratives shared by both the narrator and the other interpreters.

5.3 Semi-structured interviews with Chief Interpreters and management

In order to complement the information gathered through this process of retrospective reflexive ethnography in which the narrator's own experiences and the experiences of her colleagues were remembered and examined, and the conversations with other interpreters at the headquarters, it was essential to collect the views and needs of the UN Chief Interpreters. Semi-structured interviews were held with all Chief Interpreters at the four Duty Stations, in addition to an interview with a member of higher management. The interview period spanned from December 2020 to February 2022. In addition to organisational needs, some of the Chief Interpreters had serviced field missions themselves and were able to provide substantive input on ethical and other considerations. The same interview questions were sent to all participants in advance of the interview and, due to their physical location and health measures imposed by the COVID pandemic, all interviews were held online. All participants signed informed consent forms and all interviews were recorded and transcribed. The interview protocol was divided into general questions about field missions serviced from the four duty stations, New York, Geneva, Nairobi and Vienna (who the clients are, if they are serviced by staff or freelance interpreters, language combinations, some examples of missions); previous courses and support to interpreters; specific training for UN interpreters who go on field missions (if such specific training is needed, the contents to be included, the skills to be developed); and the feedback received from both users and interpreters about the interpreters' work (main complaints, challenges and needs).

The qualitative analysis of the transcripts confirmed that most UN field missions were serviced by UNOG, a result that is in line with the official statistics (see Ruiz Rosendo, Barghout, and Martin 2021). They also revealed that, apart from peer-to-peer support and occasional briefings with the secretariat organising the mission, there were no institutional measures in place to prepare interpreters for field missions or to debrief them upon their return. Almost all of the participants responded that dedicated training for interpreters was lacking and definitely needed. With regards to the categories of interpreters, the majority of participants confirmed that both staff and freelance interpreters should receive such training since they embark on the same missions and do the same job.

All the resulting stories told during the conversations between the interviewer and the narrator, the conversations with the interpreters at the UNOG headquarters — both codified in notes — and the transcripts of the interviews with UN Chief Interpreters and with the representative of management were then analysed. Data analysis started inductively, with a thorough reading of the notes and interviews, drawing on Corbin and Strauss's (1990) grounded theory. Categories were then identified and were gradually refined and organised hierarchically into higher level themes. These themes were the particular atmosphere of a field mission, very different to a conference setting; the interpreter's distress due to a lack of training in interpreting for field missions and lack of internal guidelines; the interpreter's complex positionality; the importance of the interpreter's physical position; practical aspects to be considered before, during and after going on mission; the ethical implications related to decision-making; security implications in the field; legal and administrative issues; psychological implications; and the importance of self-care. These categories were used to inform the design of the first online self-paced course, backed by the Interpretation Service and the Division of Conference Management, for staff and freelance interpreters who are deployed in field missions which is planned to be launched as soon as possible. The different categories identified during the study allowed us to articulate the contents in the course and to structure it around five main modules:

1. Preparation, both from a logistical and from a contextual perspective.
2. Practical issues, in which a code of conduct for interpreters in the field was identified and described, by using short videos which show what is allowed and what is not allowed in these missions.
3. Ethical implications that could be encountered in the field, drawing on a series of case scenarios that were designed as paradigmatic scenarios based on the experiences shared during the study (real life experiences were used and adapted to preserve confidentiality by changing the subject matter of the title or changing elements that insiders would automatically recognise as belonging to a specific country or mandate).
4. Security and legal implications.
5. Psychological implications and self-care.

6. Conclusion

In this chapter, we present the use of retrospective reflexive ethnography as a relevant method to define a specific interpreting practice. In the many conversations taking place between the interviewer and the narrator, the purpose was to delve into the narrator's thoughts, experiences and emotions not just to understand her role in this context, but also so that knowledge could make a contribution to the field. The contribution was to understand the practice of interpreting in UN field missions and what could be done to improve the performance, working conditions and well-being of those interpreters who are sent to these missions through training that takes into consideration the many different challenges that they face in their work, the dilemmas they are confronted with when making decisions and their needs.

As described in this chapter, understanding the researcher's positionality is essential in choosing the method in qualitative research. In the present study, the researcher's positionality as an insider with many years of experience allowed her the privilege of access to hidden information and lived experiences to which no external researcher would be granted access or allowed to live first hand. Due to

Chapter 3. Retrospective ethnography and remembrance 91

their often sensitive and confidential nature, no researcher would be authorised to accompany such missions. As such, she became a narrator whose past personal narratives were considered as a way to help her make sense of herself and of the context. A central focus was the ways in which the past was configured in the present, what was recalled, when and why, and how the past was used and embedded in everyday life. The presence of the interviewer played an essential role in this remembrance process, as a kind of what Sandberg (2020: 123) calls "midwifery of memory" in which recollections of past events were compelled to be spoken about, which suggest that memory work is the result of collaborative achievement.

In addition to reflection and introspection, the ethnographical encounters of this study triggered a comparison between all the informal conversations held throughout the years with a focus on the needs of the interpreters and the challenges they identified. The past was then compared to the organisational needs as revealed by the semi-structured interviews with the Chief Interpreters and a representative of higher management. In so doing, the past became intertwined with the present with a view to improving the working conditions and well-being of interpreters servicing future UN field missions.

This study is characterised by the convergence between academia and practice. While the interviewer had the methodology and academic experience needed to conduct the study, the narrator had a unique position as a practitioner and researcher. The ethnographic encounters allowed for a valid method of soliciting memory and remembrance in an academic framework that was conducive to elucidating the most pertinent needs and challenges of a UN interpreter on field missions.

7. Disclaimer

The views expressed herein are those of the authors and do not necessarily reflect the views of the United Nations.

References

Alvesson, Mats. 2003. "Methodology for Close Up Studies — Struggling with Closeness and Closure." *Higher Education* 46: 167–193.

Angelelli, Claudia. 2000. "Interpreting as a Communicative Event: A Look through Hymes' Lenses." *Meta* 45 (5): 580–592.

Bahadır, Sebnem. 2004. "Moving In-Between: The Interpreter as Ethnographer and the Interpreting-Researcher as Anthropologist." *Meta* 49 (4): 805–821.

Baker, Mona. 2014. "Interpreters and Translators in the War Zone. Narrated and Narrators." *The Translator* 16 (2): 197–222.

Barghout, Alma, and Lucía Ruiz Rosendo. 2022. "Developing Interpreter Competence: Training Interpreters Servicing UN Field Missions." In *Interpreter Training in Conflict and Post-Conflict Scenarios*, ed. by Lucía Ruiz Rosendo, and Marija Todorova, 63–74. London: Routledge.

Behar, Ruth. 1996. *The Vulnerable Observer*. Boston: Beacon.

Behar, Ruth. 2007. *An Island Called Home: Returning to Jewish Cuba*. New Brunswick: Rutgers University Press.

Berger, Roni. 2015. "Now I See It, Now I Don't: Researcher's Position and Reflexivity in Qualitative Research." *Qualitative Research* 15 (2): 219–234.

Bontempo, Karen, and Karen Malcolm. 2012. "An Ounce of Prevention is Worth a Pound of Cure. Educating Interpreters about the Risk of Vicarious Trauma in Healthcare Settings." In *In Our Hands: Educating Healthcare Interpreters*, ed. by Karen Malcolm, and Laurie Swabey, 105–130. Washington, DC: Gallaudet University Press.

Bots, Eliane E. 2022. "In 'In Flow of Words', War-Crime Interpreters Tell Their Own Stories." *The New Yorker*, November. https://www.newyorker.com/culture/the-new-yorker-documentary/in-in-flow-of-words-war-crime-interpreters-tell-their-own-stories

Campbell, Elaine. 2016. "Exploring Autoethnography as a Method and Methodology in Legal Education Research." *Asian Journal of Legal Education* 3 (1): 95–105.

Chase, Susan E. 2011. "Narrative Enquiry. Still a Field in the Making." In *The SAGE Handbook of Qualitative Research*, ed. by Norman K. Denzin, and Yvonna S. Lincoln, 421–434. Los Angeles: Sage.

Cihodariu, Miriam. 2012. "Narratives as Instrumental Research and as Attempts of Fixing Meaning: The Uses and Misuses of the Concept of 'Narratives.'" *Journal of Comparative Research in Anthropology and Sociology* 3: 27–43.

Clifford, James, and George E. Marcus (eds). 1986. *Writing Culture: The Poetics and Politics of Ethnography*. Berkeley: University of California Press.

Corbin, Juliet M., and Anselm Strauss. 1990. "Grounded Theory Research: Procedures, Canons, and Evaluative Criteria." *Qualitative Sociology* 13 (1): 3–21.

Delamont, Sara. 2009. "The Only Honest Thing: Autoethnography, Reflexivity and Small Crises in Fieldwork." *Ethnography and Education* 4 (1): 51–63.

Delgado Luchner, Carmen. 2015. "Setting up a Master's Programme in Conference Interpreting at the University of Nairobi: An Interdisciplinary Case Study of a Development Project Involving Universities and International Organisations." Unpublished doctoral dissertation, University of Geneva.

Delgado Luchner, Carmen. 2019. "A Beautiful Woman Sitting in the Dark. Three Narratives of Interpreter Training at the University of Nairobi." *Interpreting* 21 (1): 91–114.

Delgado Luchner, Carmen, and Leila Kherbiche. 2018. "Without Fear or Favour? The Positionality of ICRC and UNHCR Interpreters in the Humanitarian Field". *Target* 30 (3): 408–429.

Duflou, Veerle. 2016. *Be(com)ing a Conference Interpreter. An Ethnography of EU Interpreters as a Professional Community*. Amsterdam & Philadelphia: John Benjamins.

Eriksson, Thommy. 2010. "Being Native: Distance, Closeness and Doing Auto/Self-Ethnography." *Art Monitor* 8: 91–100.

Ferreira, Sonia, and Sonia Vespeira. 2017. "Retrospective Ethnography on 20th-Century Portugal: Fieldwork Encounters and its Complicities." *Social Anthropology/Anthropologie Sociale* 25 (2): 206–220.

Fine, Gary A., and Black H. Hancock. 2017. "The New Ethnographer at Work." *Qualitative Research* 17 (2): 260–268.

Flynn, Peter. 2010. "Ethnographic Approaches." In *Handbook of Translation Studies*, ed. by Yves Gambier, and Luc van Doorslaer, 116–119. Amsterdam & Philadelphia: John Benjamins.

Footitt, Hillary, and Michael Kelly. 2012. *Palgrave Studies in Languages at War*. London: Palgrave Macmillan.

Freeman, Mark. 2006. "Life 'on Holiday'? In Defense of Big Stories." *Narrative Inquiry* 16: 131–138.

Gallinat, Anselma. 2006. "Difficult Histories: Public Discourse and Narrative Identity in Eastern Germany." *Ethnos* 71 (3): 343–366.

Geertz, Clifford. 1973. *The Interpretation of Cultures*. New York: Basic Books.

Geertz, Clifford. 2000. *Anthropological Reflections on Philosophical Topics*. Princeton: Princeton University Press.

Georgakopoulou, Alexandra. 2007. "Thinking Big with Small Stories in Narrative and Identity Analysis." In *Narrative — State of the Art*, ed. by Michael Bamberg, 145–154. Amsterdam & Philadelphia: John Benjamins.

Gómez Amich, María. 2017. "Estudio descriptivo de la autopercepción de los intérpretes en zonas de conflicto: estudio de caso en Afganistán." Unpublished doctoral dissertation, University of Granada.

Haidar, Chirine, and Lucía Ruiz Rosendo. 2023. "Negotiating the Challenges of Producing Ethnographic Accounts of Field Missions." *The Translator* 29 (2): 231–246.

Hetherington, Ali. 2011. "A Magical Profession? Causes and Management of Occupational Stress in the Signed Language Interpreting Profession." In *Signed Language Interpreting. Preparation, Practice and Performance*, ed. by Lorraine Leeson, Svenjy Wurm, and Myriam Vermeerbergen, 138–159. Manchester: St. Jerome Publishing.

Hokkanen, Sari. 2017. "Analyzing Personal Embodied Experiences: Autoethnography, Feelings, and Fieldwork." *Translation & Interpreting* 9 (1): 24–35.

Hokkanen, Sari, and Kaisa Koskinen. 2016. "Affect as a Hinge. The Translator's Experiencing Self as a Sociocognitive Interface." *Translation Spaces* 5 (1): 78–96.

Holmgren, Helle, Hanne Sondergaard, and Ask Elklit. 2003. "Stress and Coping in Traumatised Interpreters: A Pilot Study of Refugee Interpreters Working for a Humanitarian Organisation." *Intervention* 1 (3): 22–27.

Inghilleri, Moira. 2003. "Habitus, Field and Discourse. Interpreting as a Socially Situated Activity." *Target* 15 (2): 243–268.

Inghilleri, Moira. 2008. "The Ethical Task of the Translator in the Geopolitical Arena: From Iraq to Guantanamo Bay." *Translation Studies* 1 (2): 212–223.

Jones, Francis R. 2014. "Interpreting the Peace: Peace Operations, Conflict and Language in Bosnia-Herzegovina." *Translation Studies* 7 (3): 360–363.

Kristi, Elizabeth. 2021. "Minimizing Bias and Maximizing the Potential Strengths of Autoethnography as a Narrative Research." *Japanese Psychological Research* 63 (4): 310–323.

Kunreuther, Laura. 2020. "Earwitnesses and Transparent Conduits of Voice: On the Labor of Field Interpreters for UN Missions." *Humanity: An International Journal of Human Rights, Humanitarianism, and Development* 11 (3): 298–316.

Kunreuther, Laura, Shiva Acharya, Ann Hunkins, Sachchi Ghimire Karki, Hikmat Khadka, Loknath Sangroula, Mark Turin, and Laurie Vasily. 2021. "Interpreting the Human Rights Field: A Conversation." *Journal of Human Rights Practice* 2021: 1–21.

Loutan, Louis, Tiziana Farinelli, and Sandro Pampallona. 1999. "Medical Interpreters Have Feelings Too." *Sozial- und Präventivmedizin* 44 (6): 280–282.

MacDonald, Sharon. 2013. *Memory Lands. Heritage and Identity in Europe Today.* London: Routledge.

Marcus, George E. 1986. "Contemporary Problems of Ethnography in the Modern World System." In *Writing Culture: The Poetics and Politics of Ethnography*, ed. by James Clifford, and George E. Marcus, 165–193. Berkeley: University of California Press.

Martin, Anne, and María Gómez Amich. 2021. "Ideology, Positionality and War: Local Interpreters in Afghanistan." *Interpreting* 23 (2): 269–295.

McIlveen, Peter. 2008. "Autoethnography as a Method for Reflexive Research and Practice in Vocational Psychology." *Australian Journal of Career Development* 17: 13–20.

Miller, Daniel. 2001. *Tales from Facebook.* Cambridge: Polity.

Miller, Daniel. 2007. "Very Big and Very Small Societies." In *The Urgency of Theory*, ed. by Antonio Pinto Ribeiro, 79–105. Carcanet: Fundaçao Calouste Gulbenkian.

Moser-Mercer, Barbara, Somia Qudah, Mona Nabeel Ali Malkawi, Jayne Mutiga, and Mohammed Al-Batineh. 2021. "Beyond Aid: Sustainable Responses to Meeting Language Communication Needs in Humanitarian Contexts." *Interpreting and Society: An Interdisciplinary Journal* 1 (1): 5–27.

Ndongo-Keller, Justine. 2015. "Vicarious Trauma (VT) and Stress Management." In *The Routledge Handbook of Interpreting*, ed. by Holly Mikkelson, and Renée Jourdenais, 337–351. London: Routledge.

Poulos, Christopher N. 2021. *Essentials of Autoethnography.* Washington, DC: American Psychological Association.

Ragin, Charles C. 1994. *Constructing Social Research: The Unity and Diversity of Method.* London: Sage.

Reed-Danahay, Deborah. 2001. "Autobiography, Intimacy and Ethnography." In *Handbook of Ethnography*, ed. by Paul Atkinson, Amanda Coffey, Sara Delamont, John Lofland, and Lyn Lofland, 89–107. London: Sage.

Ruiz Rosendo, Lucía. 2020. "Interpreting for the Afghanistan Spanish Force." *War & Society* 39 (1): 42–57.

Ruiz Rosendo, Lucía, Alma Barghout, and Conor Martin. 2021. "Interpreting on UN Field Missions: A Training Programme." *The Interpreter and Translator Trainer* 15 (4): 450–467.

Ruiz Rosendo, Lucía, and Clementina Persaud. 2019. "On the Front Line: Mediating across Languages and Cultures in Peacekeeping Operations." *Armed Forces & Society* 45 (3): 472–490.

Salama-Carr, Myriam. 2007. *Translating and Interpreting Conflict.* Amsterdam: Rodopi.

Sandberg, Marie. 2020. "Retrospective Ethnographies. Twisting Moments of Researching Commemorative Practices among Volunteers after the Refugee Arrivals to Europe 2015." In *Challenges and Solutions in Ethnographic Research*, ed. by Tuuli Lähdesmäki, Eerika Koskinen-Koivisto, Viktorija L.A. Čeginskas, and Aino-Kaisa Koistinen, 117–130. London: Routledge.

Saukko, Paula. 2008. *The Anorexic Self: A Personal, Political Analysis of a Diagnostic Discourse.* Albany: SUNY Press.

Schwander-Sievers, Stephanie. 2010. "Invisible — Inaudible: Albanian Memories of Socialism after the War in Kosovo." In *Post-Communist Nostalgia*, ed. by Marija Todorova, and Zsuzsa Gille, 96–112. Oxford: Berghahn.

Sparkes, Andrew. 2000. "Autoethnography and Narratives of Self: Reflections on Criteria in Action." *Sociology of Sport Journal* 17: 21–43.

Tedjouong, Ebenezer, and Marija Todorova. 2022. "Training Needs of Interpreters in the Refugee Crisis in Africa." In *Interpreter Training in Conflict and Post-Conflict Scenarios*, ed. by Lucía Ruiz Rosendo, and Marija Todorova, 101–113. London: Routledge.

Todorova, Marija. 2016. "Interpreting Conflict Mediation in Kosovo and Macedonia." *Linguistica Antverpiensia* 15: 227–240.

Tracy, Sarah J. 2013. *Qualitative Research Methods.* West Sussex: Blackwell.

Wellin, Christopher, and Gary A. Fine. 2001. "Ethnography as Work: Career Socialization, Settings and Problems." In *Handbook of Ethnography*, ed. by Paul Atkinson, Amanda Coffey, Sara Delamont, John Lofland, and Lyn Lofland, 323–338. London: Sage.

Wolcott, Harry F. 1977. *Teachers versus Technocrats.* Eugene, OT: Center for Educational Policy and Management.

Wolcott, Harry F. 1981. "Confessions of a Trained Observer." In *The Study of Schooling. Field Based Methodologies in Educational Research and Evaluation*, ed. by Thomas S. Popkewitz, and B. Robert Tabachnick, 247–263. New York: Praeger.

PART II

Centering on positionality, reflexivity and ethics

CHAPTER 4

Affective labor in the simultaneous interpreting of prayer
An autoethnographic re-analysis

Sari Hokkanen
Tampere University

This chapter provides a re-analysis of the fieldnotes I gathered in an autoethnographic study of simultaneous church interpreting (Hokkanen 2016). I re-analyzed descriptions of interpreted prayers in the fieldnotes from the perspective of affective labor, understood as the manipulation of one's emotions to achieve organizational goals (Koskinen 2020; Hochschild [1983] 2012). In this paper I also discuss the implications of changes in researcher positionality when re-analyzing past fieldnotes, highlighting the importance of reflexivity. The different social positions I had during fieldwork and during the current re-analysis result in two readings of the affective labor involved in the simultaneous interpreting of prayer. This demonstrates the nature of ethnographic research accounts as constructed representations and the role of the researcher in knowledge production.

Keywords: affective labor, emotions, autoethnography, reflexivity, researcher positionality, church interpreting, faith-based interpreting

1. Introduction

This chapter examines interpreting in a religious setting and discusses the effects of the field researcher's changed positionality over time. I investigate the affective labor carried out by volunteer simultaneous interpreters in a Finnish Pentecostal church as they interpret prayers, using the fieldwork I carried out for my doctoral research (Hokkanen 2016) as a source of data. In the original autoethnographic study, I used my position as a volunteer interpreter and a church member to access the lived and embodied experience of engaging in an interpreting practice embedded in a specific religious environment. In this chapter, I re-analyze my fieldnotes from a new perspective. This new analysis is carried out from a very different researcher positionality than the one in the original study, and this calls

https://doi.org/10.1075/btl.165.04hok
Available under the CC BY-NC 4.0 license. © 2025 John Benjamins Publishing Company

for an increased level of reflexivity. Revisiting the experiences of a past self whose worldview I no longer share demonstrates how "the presupposed linearity" of insider–outsider perspectives and emic–etic accounts does not do justice to "the complexity of the fieldwork experience" (Humonen and Angouri 2023: 88).

The interpreting practice I studied consists of the simultaneous interpreting of weekly services by volunteer members of the church from their native language Finnish into English for non-Finnish-speaking migrants, guests, and visitors. The simultaneous interpreting is carried out with the help of standard conference interpreting equipment, including booths built at the back of the main church auditorium, microphones, and receiver-headphones. Although the services can last up to two hours, the interpreters work without a partner. A service consists of multiple spoken genres that need to be interpreted, including the sermon, songs, and prayers (Hokkanen 2013). The present chapter concentrates on prayers, which in this church are spontaneously produced and may be highly animated and emotional. Given that the interpreters are themselves deeply involved in the religious community and the messages they interpret (Hokkanen 2016), it is worth examining what type of affective labor they engage in when interpreting this affectively laden genre, which plays a spiritually and emotionally significant role in the interpreted event. Here, affective labor refers to the regulation or manipulation of one's emotions in order to meet job-based requirements and to achieve organizational goals (Koskinen 2020; Grandey, Diefendorff, and Rupp 2013: 18; Hochschild [1983] 2012).

The analysis suggests that, in this context, prayer is not only interpreted speech but also a personally meaningful and socially learned devotional practice, and that it is used as a method of emotion regulation. Furthermore, the blended nature of interpreters' private selves and service roles supports the experience of not having to fabricate emotion but simply of allowing existing personal emotion to be displayed (see Ashforth and Humphrey 2012). These elements may contribute to the experience of volunteer interpreters in this church that interpreting prayer feels like a respite during a cognitively laborious task. Given the long stretches that they interpret without breaks, such moments of apparent respite are valuable. On the other hand, it has been suggested that a conflation of private selves and service roles may increase the risk of burnout, and that a perceived authenticity when displaying organizationally expected emotions may be a result of "successfully commercialized" affect (Hochschild [1983] 2012: 136). In this chapter, the concepts of private selves and service roles are mainly seen in the light of affect: an individual's personal emotional life involves a private self, whereas organizationally expected emotions are connected with the service role.

In what follows, I first discuss the analytical framework of affective labor in Section 2 and salient aspects of the social context under study in Section 3.

Then, in Section 4, I elucidate the autoethnographic method used in the analysis and provide a reflexive discussion of my changed positionality in relation to the object of study. Section 5 presents the results of the analysis, blending evocative narratives with analytical perspectives derived from the theoretical framework. Section 6 concludes the chapter with final reflexive notes and a discussion of the main contributions of the present study.

2. Theoretical framework

2.1 Affective labor

The concept of affective labor derives from the work of Hochschild ([1983] 2012) who used the term "emotional labor" to refer to workers' self-regulation of felt and displayed emotions for the benefit of their employer. In this study, I follow Koskinen (2020: 29–33) in using the term affective instead of emotional labor to highlight the socially contingent, embodied, and contextual nature of emotions, rather than the individual, psychological reactions to situational stimuli, even though both aspects are naturally present in almost any examination of the phenomenon. In addition, Hochschild focuses on social interaction rather than the psychological issues related to emotions, which further supports the use of the term affect instead.

A key part of Hochschild's theory is what she names "surface acting" and "deep acting", concepts borrowed from the Soviet Russian theater practitioner Konstantin Stanislavski (Hochschild [1983] 2012: 35–55). Surface acting refers to the conscious management of displayed emotions, with full knowledge of their inauthentic nature. Deep acting, in contrast, refers to a subtler process of cognitive reframing and using trained imagination to induce a desired feeling that is then displayed in a seemingly spontaneous and authentic manner. As Hochschild argues, these subtle processes are often employed for commercial or institutional purposes in such sophisticated ways that people are rarely conscious of them when they are securely embedded in the organization in question (Hochschild [1983] 2012: 75, fn.). Individuals engage in deep and surface acting to manage their emotions so that they are aligned with the expectations of the social context. These expectations or systematic conventions regarding the display of emotions in certain situations are termed "feeling rules" (Hochschild [1983] 2012; Burkitt 2014).

The intellectual roots of Hochschild's work lie partly in Marxist theory, particularly in relation to physical labor and the alienation of the workforce. Her study on flight attendants' affective labor is contextualized in the commercialization of affect, which raises the question of how applicable the concept is for non-commercial, non-profit work, such as volunteer interpreting at church. However, the core mechanisms of affective labor, such as organizational feeling rules and the subtle ways in which organizations place responsibility for displaying the desired affects on the individual, are not necessarily contingent on the capitalist ends of the organization in question. It has also been pointed out that Hochschild's original argument may have distinguished between the commercial sphere and the private sphere at the expense of the social (but non-commercial) sphere (Burkitt 2014).

Hochschild also specifically identifies churches as one of the institutions that "have become very sophisticated in the techniques of deep acting" because "they suggest how to imagine and thus how to feel" (Hochschild [1983] 2012: 49). The intertwined nature of affects and concepts and their subsequent effect on social life has also been taken up in the study of religion. For example, the religious philosopher Mark Wynn (2012: 224) elaborates the phenomenon as follows:

> The spiritual person, we can say, is the person whose creedal affirmations and ideals are rendered in her experience — by virtue of her emotional engagement, by virtue of her capacity to inscribe certain thoughts in the appearances of things, by virtue of her practical stance in the world, where this stance is registered kinaesthetically, and by virtue of the background feeling of reality which provides the context for these more particular commitments. ... Spiritual formation, we might say, is a matter of *cultivating relevant emotions*, thoughts, practical dispositions and background feelings, so that [they] come to be inscribed in the person's lived relationship to the sensory world. (emphasis added)

This is not to say that the process of "spiritual formation" should be conceptualized solely as acting or that it would be experienced as fabricated by the religious person, but an aspect of intentional cultivation is clearly present. Spiritual formation has, indeed, been suggested to involve deep acting, i.e., the regulation of emotion so that the required feelings would occur in a way that feels authentic (Johnston 2021). It is also worth noting that many religious communities actively seek to facilitate "deep-seated and long-lasting emotional transformations" among their adherents through practices that support emotion management, such as prayer (Johnston 2021: 598; see also Section 5.1).

2.2 Affective labor in interpreting

Previous studies on interpreting and affective labor have highlighted questions related to role expectations and role performance. Koskinen (2020) discusses the normative, neutral role of public service interpreters, arguing that neutrality, in fact, requires a constant and intricate process of managing one's felt and performed affects. Being neutral does not, in other words, result from a lack of affects but from a specific kind of affective labor.

A different type of affective labor is required in faith-related interpreting, as demonstrated by Tekgül (2020). Her ethnographic study was carried out in an Armenian Protestant church in Istanbul, where she investigated the simultaneous interpreting of Armenian services into Turkish. She argues that in this volunteer, faith-related interpreting context, the interpreter's affective labor does not consist of suppressing her own emotions as much as it does of amplifying her emotions to meet the expectations of the communicative situation. Furthermore, "not only the message but also the affect is remarkably co-constructed, and the affective mode is instrumental in the conveying of the message" (Tekgül 2020: 53).

From a similar but broader theoretical vantage point, Hild (2017) investigates the affective dimensions of church interpreting. Her study focuses on interpreters' self-regulation, understood as involving behavioral, metacognitive, motivational, and affective dimensions — for example, the ability to direct one's attention or inhibit distracting thoughts or emotions. Hild (2017: 190) concludes that emotional self-regulation among the church interpreters she studied mostly relied on the social support they received (such as immediate help when they could not recall a word) and on the appreciation showed by the other congregants. Thinking that the audience is non-judgmental and appreciative helped the interpreters to mitigate nervousness or other negative emotions. Hild also suggests that the positive emotions and sense of well-being that the interpreters reported having due to their service helped to "modulate the effect of fatigue, which sets in under the conditions of prolonged and intensive work" (2017: 191).

In addition to the work of Koskinen (2020) and Tekgül (2020) mentioned above, Hochschild's theory ([1983] 2012) may help shed light even further on questions related to the interpreter's role. She notes that an overly strong identification with a service role may lead to burnout, due to the lack of a "'healthy' estrangement, a clear separation of self from role" (Hochschild [1983] 2012: 187–188), which would allow the worker to guard their personal emotional life from the emotional demands of the job. A similar need for maintaining emotional distance to the service role has been identified as one of the self-care techniques used by professional community interpreters. In Korpal and Mellinger's (2022) discussion, maintaining distance is seen as a manifestation of practitioners' awareness of the interpreter's role and potential stressors in the work. However, interpreters in religious settings rarely demonstrate awareness of the role of the professional interpreter, nor do they necessarily find it relevant for their practice. Interpreters in these contexts are instead often expected to be personally involved in the community and committed to its beliefs (e.g., Vigouroux 2010; Balcı Tison

2016; Hokkanen 2016), which may also have consequences for the affective labor they carry out.

Also relevant for the interpreter's role in religious settings is Hochschild's argument related to an altruistic "false self" ([1983] 2012:195–196). When a worker's 'true self' is too strongly bonded with the needs and wellbeing of the social group or organization, they may become overly concerned with the needs of others at the expense of their own. This could be understood as a type of pathological altruism, where a person "becomes a victim of his or her own altruistic actions" (Oakley 2016:10408). The argument has interesting parallels with the ethos of Christian service, which creates the overall backdrop to the church interpreting practice I have studied (Hokkanen 2012). As Oakley (2016) argues, the phenomenon of altruism is multifaceted and cannot be easily divided into the morally good and the morally bad. It may even be difficult to distinguish clearly which apparently altruistic actions are either beneficial or harmful for the altruists themselves (Oakley 2016). What is relevant for the present discussion, however, is that a deep sense of altruism may be indicative of a successful conflation of a private self and the service role, and that the individual in question may not experience affective labor in this case as a fabrication of emotion. To adopt Hochschild's vocabulary ([1983] 2012:136): "When feelings are successfully commercialized, the worker does not feel phony or alien; she feels somehow satisfied in how personal her service actually was."

3.   Pentecostal experientiality and prayer

The field in which I collected data and which I analyze here is a Pentecostal church in Finland. Pentecostalism is a branch of the Christian faith that can be defined as either a denomination — represented by churches such as the Assemblies of God — or a wider and more amorphous movement, with adherents in independent churches or in other, more established Christian denominations (Pew Research Center 2006). In the latter case, Pentecostalism is often conflated with Charismatic Christianity, making the estimated numbers of adherents almost 694 million, or one-quarter (27.4%) of all Christians worldwide (Centre for the Study of Global Christianity 2019). Globally, Pentecostalism/Charismatic Christianity is considered as the fastest growing branch of Christianity (Miller 2013:9).

In Finland, however, Pentecostalism (particularly the denomination, not the wider Charismatic movement) is neither as mainstream nor as rapidly growing as on a global scale. Rather, the denomination is characterized by a more marginal status in a country where Evangelical Lutheranism is the most common form of Christianity (with a membership of 65% of the population in 2023; The Evangelical Lutheran Church of Finland 2023) and by stagnation in the number of registered members in Pentecostal churches (with the lowest membership in 25 years recorded in 2021; Tiittanen 2021). Pentecostalism has a long history in the country, however, having found local foothold within a few years of its beginning in the early 20th century in the United States.

Finnish Pentecostalism continues to share key characteristics with the global movement, such as an emphasis on a post-conversion experience of 'being filled with the Holy Spirit', which is often understood to manifest itself in glossolalia, or speaking in unknown (not necessarily naturally existing) languages. Overall, compared to other Christian denominations, Pentecostalism places a stronger emphasis "on the charismatic 'gifts of the spirit', including any combination of healing, exorcism, prophesy, and speaking in tongues, as well as an emphasis on emotional and experiential expressions over and against discursive and doctrinal ones" (Casanova 2001: 435).

Indeed, experientiality is a pervasive feature of the Pentecostal way of life. It is evidenced in the express requirement of personal, emotional engagement with the divine (instead of outward displays of what is perceived as 'empty' religiosity), not only in social gatherings but also in believers' private lives. In the words of Cross (2009: 6), Pentecostals "confess a radical openness to the invasion and intervention of God's Spirit in [their] daily lives", and this is "a central feature of [Pentecostal] communities of faith" (Cross 2009: 6, fn. 5). Furthermore, the "invasion and intervention" of God's Spirit in believers' lives is frequently described in affective terms. Reports on "feeling" the presence of God or being filled with the Spirit are an everyday part of Pentecostal discourse. Sometimes, believers may even describe these experiences as "a mild ecstasy" (Csordas 1987).

This emphasis on the emotional and experiential is also often tangible in Pentecostal prayer. The local understanding of prayer in the social context I studied would define prayer as intimate and spontaneous communication with the Holy Spirit (see also Csordas 1987). Underlying this understanding is the more general conceptualization of Pentecostal worship as "an experience of allowing oneself to feel the presence of God" (Miller and Yamamori 2007: 138). Prayers in the church I studied were frequently interspersed with glossolalia and worship music, often in the background, and sometimes participants singing spontaneously in tongues or in their native language (see also Csordas 1987: 452). The direct addressees of the prayers were, naturally, the triune Christian God (Father, Son, Holy Spirit), but often speakers would address other 'spiritual' entities, such as the devil or a sickness, or the congregants. In the last-mentioned case, speakers would relay prophetic messages or commands believed to originate from the Holy Spirit. Speakers would typically assume a first person singular or plural speaker position, either referring to themselves (e.g., "I ask") or to everyone participating in the prayer ("we pray").

The experientiality emphasized in Pentecostalism as well as the characteristics of Pentecostal prayer discussed here clearly foreground a need for an investigation of affect. Even though emotions or affects were not the main focus of the original doctoral study, I have acknowledged their role in the social setting, the interpreting practice, and in autoethnographic research in previous publications (Hokkanen 2016, 2017; Hokkanen and Koskinen 2016). Here, I broaden the analysis to affective labor, which is presented in Section 5.

4. Autoethnography and the changing researcher positionality

The present study is a continuation of my doctoral research (Hokkanen 2016), which was an autoethnography of simultaneous volunteer interpreting in church. Autoethnography can be described as being "ethnographic in its methodological orientation, cultural in its interpretive orientation, and autobiographical in its content orientation" (Chang 2008: 48). In my doctoral study, I conducted fieldwork in two social contexts: one church where I returned as an ex-member and recorded observations and accounts of others' interpreting experiences, and another church where I was an active member and also took fieldnotes of my personal experiences of interpreting. In this chapter, I return to the field journal I kept in 2011–2014 while doing fieldwork in the latter church, as an active member.[1] Since the completion of my PhD, many parts in my life and my identity have undergone changes, which affects my positionality in the research. Therefore, a careful examination of the implications of this changed positionality is in order (see, e.g., Tracy 2010; Qin 2016; see also Staudinger, Chapter 5, and Steinkogler, Chapter 6, this volume).

My changed positionality is connected to the time that has passed between the fieldwork and the current analysis, but this temporal distance also presents potential challenges in its own right, especially in an analysis focusing on affect. The nine years between the end of fieldwork and the analysis mean that the embodied experiences recorded in fieldnotes are farther removed and are likely more difficult to remember in vivid detail now than they were in the original study concluded in 2016. It has been suggested that one benefit of fieldwork is that the researcher's "[p]hysical and sensuous presence ... allows observation and witness and the use of five-sense channels for recording data relating to social atmosphere,

---

1. The field journal consists of entries on 28 interpreted services and 20 other entries, altogether comprising 55 typed pages.

emotional color and unspoken assumptions" (Willis 2000:xiii). The longer the time between fieldwork and analysis, it may be argued, the more difficult for the researcher to tap into all those channels, especially the ones that may have been difficult to verbalize in field notes.

Despite its fickleness and "homogenizing tendencies" (Emerson, Fretz, and Shaw 2011:17), memory constitutes one source of research data used not only by autoethnographers (Chang 2008; Adams, Holman Jones, and Ellis 2015) but also by ethnographers relying on participants' accounts of past events (see also Ruiz Rosendo and Barghout's discussion of 'remembered data' in Chapter 3, this volume). Furthermore, in classical anthropology, it has been standard practice for fieldwork to take place in the early stage of a research career and for the analysis of those fieldnotes to extend over the following decades, with full acknowledgement of the analytical perspectives changing along with the increased maturity of the researcher, both personally and academically (Ottenberg 1990).

While it is important to be aware of the potential influences of this temporal distance, a more complex methodological issue involves changes in researcher positionality and their effect on the current analysis. After the completion of my PhD, I discontinued the church interpreting activity I had studied as well as my membership in the church. Not only are my worldview and belief system drastically different now, but key parts of my identity have also changed. As a result, some of the life choices I have made to better reflect my understanding of who I am now are the kind I would not have approved of before — and conversely, I currently find it difficult to approve of some of the life choices I made when I was religious. This has created a clear tension between who I was when writing the fieldnotes and who I am now as I was analyzing them for this chapter.

The most prominent example of this tension has to do with my theoretical decisions. In the past, as a fully committed Pentecostal, I would likely not have selected the theory of affective labor to analyze my experiences because it casts them in an ambiguous light, as shown in Sections 5 and 6 below. I would have been reluctant to interpret my affective experiences as anything other than authentic and divinely inspired, even if I had conceded the socially conditioned nature of affect and emotions in general. This reluctance and a sensitivity to what my former self might consider a reductionist explanation of religious phenomena have influenced the present re-analysis, as explained in Section 6.

My initial solution to manage the tension between my conflicting selves was to exclude the discussion of personal issues from this chapter and conduct an "analytical" autoethnographic study (cf. Anderson 2006) that would be more matter-of-fact and less subjective. This solution was partly prompted by a personal need to maintain an emotional distance to my past. It proved to be an untenable solution, however, because it resulted in a research report that had a veneer of quasi-objectivity covering a deep and ethically unsound silence about the influence of the researcher in the construction of knowledge. After all, "people view the world from different embodied locations" (Qin 2016:1), and the way we view the world affects not only what we choose to investigate (Lumsden 2019:70) but also how we choose to investigate it. Interestingly, the initial choice to exclude a personally reflexive account of my current position from this chapter also made it difficult for me to even perceive, at first, this quasi-objectivity and vast silence in an earlier draft of the paper. I find this highly ironic, given that I worked with reflexivity extensively during my PhD and it constitutes one of my main research interests at the moment (Hokkanen and Koskinen, forthcoming). This may, hopefully, be a useful reminder for other field researchers that reflexivity is indeed an ongoing practice and not a box we can tick once in our research careers or even once in a single research project and then forget (see, e.g., Humonen and Angouri 2023).

Rather than try to ignore the tension between my self who wrote the field-notes and the self who re-analyzed them for this chapter, my ultimate solution was, in other words, to engage in reflexivity, or the intensive "scrutiny of 'what I know' and 'how I know it'" (Hertz 1997:vii–viii). This change of direction mirrors Koskinen's (2008:54) experience when she returned to do fieldwork in a social setting where she used to be a member: "Inevitably, my quest for increased objectivity has resulted in an increased understanding of the eternal return to the personal." Practicing reflexivity allowed me to accept the inherent and unresolvable ambiguity in the current analysis: the fieldnotes represent one type of lived experience, the analysis represents an interpretation of that lived experience that is not fully commensurate with the social meanings attached to the practice under study. In this sense, this chapter makes visible the nature of ethnographic research accounts as representation, or "life at least once removed" (Collins and Gallinat 2010:2; see also Clifford and Marcus 1986).

As a practical method of reflexivity in the present study, I wrote reflective memos (Maxwell 1996) and discussed my positionality and its influence with a few close colleagues. When writing reflective memos, I found particularly helpful Cunliffe and Karunanayake's (2013:372) mapping of the complex relationships field researchers may have with participants, of researchers' multiple positionalities, and of their influence in research. The mapping is presented as a method of untangling a researcher's positionality with other participants in the field, but I applied it in an examination of the complex relationship between my current self and my past self. Cunliffe and Karunanayake map these relationships with four dimensions: insiderness–outsiderness; sameness–difference; engagement–distance; and political activism–active neutrality. I found that these dimensions helped untangle the complex ways in which my embodied locations as an autoethnographer were both the same as and also different from what they were in the past.

While it has been crucial to be mindful of my changed analytical footing, it should also be noted that revisiting our past selves is at the core of the tradition of autoethnography (Adams, Holman Jones, and Ellis 2015) and that the methodology does not rest on an understanding of an unchanging and unified self functioning as the subject and the object of research. In fact, many autoethnographers seek to make sense of past experiences from their current vantage points in life, even if the original experiences had taken place decades earlier and even if they had not carried out systematic fieldwork of those experiences (e.g., Fox 2021).

My practical methods of analysis involved re-reading my fieldnotes and identifying in them passages related to prayer. From these passages, I chose two instances that I wrote into full narratives (see Section 5). The first, in Section 5.1, represents a typical occurrence, while the second, in Section 5.2, represents a slightly less frequent occurrence, but one that was deeply significant for me at the time and reflects what I considered to be representative of intense religious experiences in the church in general. When writing the narratives, I employed techniques of emotional recall (Fox 2021) to facilitate the depiction of participant experiences and meanings. In this case, I listened to the music mentioned in Section 5.1 and watched portions of the service mentioned in Section 5.2 that were still available on YouTube. These media products were not analyzed directly, but they helped me relive the "conditions of feeling" (Fox 2021: 66) pertinent to the analysis. Alternating between my current and past positions has highlighted the nature of autoethnography as a dance of closeness and distance and of constant ambivalence when moving from memories of lived experiences to their cultural analysis (Chang 2008).

5. Affective labor in simultaneously interpreted prayer

5.1 Functions of prayer in a church interpreter's work

Narrative 1. (based on fieldnotes from April 23, 2014)
I walk to the car in a foul mood. I'm almost late, my 18-month-old kid had a cranky day, and I'm tired. I nearly wish that no one would need interpreting tonight so I could just come back home. As I start the car, the stereo comes to life blasting a song of worship.

> *here by Your greatness I long to remain*
> *here by Your greatness I'm washed away*
> *in the river of Your love*
> *here by Your glory I lift up my gaze*

> *reach for the One that I long to embrace*
> *I know: You're eternal love*

What an idiot I am! Isn't it so that God can change everything in the blink of an eye? Where is my hope now?

I sigh and shake my head. I start to sing along as I take the 10-minute drive on the highway to the church. I pray and sing in tongues. The music is intense — sustained walls of sound, echoing harmonies, crescendoing drums — and it washes over me as I pray.

By the time I reach the church parking lot, I feel better. At least I'm not focused on myself anymore, but on God and the service I'm here for.

Interpreters in religious settings have reported preparing for their work through spiritual means, often through prayer (e.g., Hokkanen 2017; Friedner 2018: 665). As reported by Friedner (2018: 665), interpreters describe prayer as a way to align themselves with the divine: they "let go" and "open up" to God so that He may work through them in their acts of service (cf. Hokkanen 2012). As illustrated in the narrative above, prayer as a method of preparation emphasizes the other-worldly goals and significance of the interpreting task ahead.

However, the narrative also illustrates how prayer functions as a socially learned method of emotion regulation. Especially in the Pentecostal tradition, what is understood as prayer may include not only direct verbal communication with God but also glossolalia and a mindful awareness of God's presence, frequently facilitated by worship music, as in the narrative. This experience is sometimes referred to as 'soaking', which aptly describes the orientation towards becoming affected by a divine presence without ostensibly doing much. Interaction with an imagined Other has been shown to function as a form of social support that allows individuals to employ specific emotion regulation techniques, such as cognitive reframing, which allows them to reinterpret situations in ways that modulate the related negative emotions (Sharp 2010). Prayer and other religious activities have also been shown to distract individuals from negative emotional stimuli (Sharp 2010; Vishkin, Ben-Nun Bloom, and Tamir 2019).

The function of prayer as a method of preparation for interpreting and as a technique of emotion regulation indicates that the affective labor of the church interpreter extends far beyond the moment of the interpreted event. Prayer helps interpreters generate and maintain affective states that are in line with the organizational goals of the church. In a sense, it could be conceived of as one of Hochschild's ([1983] 2012: 49) "sophisticated … techniques of deep acting" that suggests "how to imagine and thus how to feel". The amount of deep acting required to reach an appropriate state of humility, gratefulness, and 'surrender' to God presumably varies between individual interpreters and from moment to moment even within the same individual. Most likely, however, the feeling rules of the religious community influence even interpreters' self-reported need to prepare for interpreting. Beginning to interpret in church in a negative, self-absorbed mood would feel not only disrespectful towards the perceived spiritual significance of the work but also counterproductive for its believed function of allowing the Holy Spirit to work through the interpreter to reach the listeners.

It should go without saying, however, that prayer is far from being a mere preparatory technique for volunteer church interpreting. It plays a key role in the devotional life of many, if not most, practicing Christians, and it crucially contributes to the everyday experience of Pentecostal Christianity. Nevertheless, prayer also facilitates the cultivation of certain emotions, which is one aspect of spiritual formation (see Section 2.1): "how we feel as Christians is an essential part of authentic Christianity" (Elliott 2012:107). When examined in the light of affective labor, the simultaneous interpreting of prayer cannot be separated from this overall context of spiritual life because the genre to be interpreted is, at the same time, a key method of sustaining this experience of 'being an authentic Christian' through the regulation of situation-appropriate emotions.

5.2   Interpreting prayer through blended roles

Narrative 2. (based on fieldnotes from July 23, 2013)
The sports arena is full of people and sound. I'm sitting in the middle of both, interpreting. On my table is a very basic sound system and a microphone on a small stand. I sit next to the sound engineers, and we are surrounded by hundreds of chairs, most of them occupied. This is the final Sunday morning service of a week-long summer conference organized by my church. People come here from all over the country. The main speaker today is a well-known Finnish preacher, and the worship is led by a world-renowned music team from Brazil.

I've done simultaneous now for over an hour, and I'm exhausted. The sermon is ending, and it's time for the final prayers. The music quiets down, and the preacher closes his eyes for several moments.

"Come Holy Spirit. Now. Give thanks to the Lord in new tongues. Let us give Him room to operate in our lives now. We have some time here. Let us allow the Spirit of God to be poured out, like a quiet breeze. With some of you, a whirlpool of God's power will wash over you. Sweet Spirit of God, thank you for what you are doing."

I render this prayer into English, my eyes closed. I pray together with the preacher and all the others here. When he speaks in tongues, so do I. Sweet Spirit of God, thank you for what you are doing. He turns to prophesize over a Finnish worship leader who is on the stage, and I change to English again.

> *And then something happens. I feel an energy in my entire body, the power of God. I start to cry, almost violently, and I try to keep interpreting. I forget about the people around me. It's easy to find the words now, but hard to speak them clearly.*
> *The Holy Spirit is here. Over me. Now.*

In a discussion of whether translators can be considered authors, Pym (2011) suggests that authors have discursive positioning, beliefs, and commitment, but translators do not. By discursive positioning, Pym refers to the first person, which is typically reserved for authors (or, in the case of interpreting, primary speakers), whereas the translator or interpreter is forced to use the "alien I" (Pym 2011:33). As the narrative above illustrates, this does not apply to the church interpreter when she is interpreting prayer: she speaks not (only) with the "alien I" but from the discursive position of her religious subjectivity. Furthermore, she shares in the beliefs of the speaker, and she is committed to the message (see also Hokkanen 2016). In other words, the interpreted prayer makes visible how the church interpreter's private self and service role are blended in this context.

When regarding these blended roles from the viewpoint of affective labor, it could be argued that the interpreter's personal participation in the prayer supports deep acting in the sense that the interpreter follows the prompt of the speaker to imagine certain things (e.g., the power of God being a whirlpool or a breeze that people can feel) and consequently feels certain situation-appropriate emotions. The experience of "a mild ecstasy" (Csordas 1987:452) depicted in the narrative is aligned with the general feeling rules of the social context. Pentecostal worship has been described as an (ideally) "participatory event within which one loses him or herself" (Alvarado 2012:147; see also Miller and Yamamori 2007, and Section 2 above). In this social context, the sense of ecstasy and of losing oneself are taken as signs of divine influence, of an encounter between believers and the Holy Spirit (see also Cross 2009). The amplification and open display of personal emotions by the interpreter are also in line with Tekgül's (2020) results. Here, too, the interpreter's emotional responses serve the overall goals of the situation, in that they grant increased legitimacy to the perceived spiritual authenticity of the interpreted message and the event.

The blending of a private self and the service role, or more accurately the strong personal identification with the service role, has been shown to influence affective labor in two ways. First, it helps the required affects to occur naturally (Ashforth and Humphrey 2012). When an individual identifies with their service role, they may want to feel as is expected of them, but it may be difficult if they are tired or preoccupied (Ashforth and Humphrey 2012:276). They may, then, embrace surface and deep acting as helpful tools in an effort to "fake it until they make it". Second, identification with the service role also provides a way to express naturally felt emotions (Ashforth and Humphrey 2012:276). In this case, there is no great gap between how the individual is expected to feel in their service role and how they feel irrespective of it. In other words, the individual does not suffer from emotional dissonance (Ashforth and Humphrey 2012:278; cf. Hochschild [1983] 2012:90). This is in contrast with Hochschild's suggestion (Hochschild [1983] 2012:187–188) that strong identification with the service role would more likely lead to burnout and that a sense of ease in generating the expected emotions is a sign of "successfully commercialized" affect (Hochschild [1983] 2012:136). It can also be argued that strong identification with the service role may provide a heightened sense of authenticity because it allows individuals to feel that they are expressing their true selves when enacting their service role (Ashforth and Humphrey 2012:276).

Some of the church interpreters I talked with during fieldwork reported that moments of simultaneously interpreted prayer were felt to be somehow easier and lighter than other parts of the service, even though prayer often occurs at the very end of long stretches of interpreting. I would suggest that one reason for this may be that prayer allows the interpreter to speak, not with the "alien I", but as themselves in a clearer way than any other genre in the service, and that it also allows the display of naturally felt emotions due to the blending of the interpreter's private self and service role. Furthermore, as discussed in Section 5.1, prayer is itself a typical method of emotion regulation in this context, which may alleviate psychological strain, such as fatigue. However, this suggestion would require concentrated research with a different research design than that used in the present study to lend it support. As mentioned in Section 2.2, another channel to alleviate fatigue among church interpreters is the social support they receive from the other participants (Hild 2017). In this context, following Sharp's (2010) argument, imagined social interactions are also worth investigating since they function as a similar technique of emotion regulation.

6. Conclusions

When I had completed the fieldwork and started to analyze my fieldnotes for my doctoral study several years ago (Hokkanen 2016), I felt it was necessary to place a note on the inside of the folder containing the typed and printed notes. The note said, "Remember: who I was then is not (exactly) who I am now!" Awareness of the shifting nature of the self and our positionality as researchers has only become more pronounced as my autoethnographic research project has continued beyond the original study. My aim in this chapter has been not only to provide an analysis of interpreted prayer through the lens of affective labor, but also to make visible the way changes in our identities and social positions have inescapable consequences for field research, especially in research designs making use of the researcher's subjective experiences.

The empirical contribution of this chapter is related to the complex ways in which affective labor is at play in the simultaneous interpreting of prayer in the Pentecostal church I studied. Prayer functions both as a learned technique of emotion regulation that is used to prepare for interpreting and as an outlet for the 'personal I' of the interpreter to surface more clearly in the middle of interpreting a church service. This illustrates how translatorial practices can be deeply enmeshed in social contexts, even in the case of a seemingly clearly delineated genre, as was examined here. In fact, there is a Christian saying that "my life is a prayer", which further highlights the (ideally) ongoing experience of interaction with the divine among Pentecostals. Such phenomena of deep embeddedness of translatorial practices in social contexts and their interwovenness in personally meaningful spiritual practices would be difficult to examine with methods other than field research. Without first-hand, "sensuous presence" (Willis 2000: xiii), it is difficult to gain awareness of all factors potentially relevant to our objects of study.

The chapter does not provide a definite answer to the question of whether the church interpreter's affects are authentic and the service role simply allows her to express them, or whether the experience of authenticity is the result of "successfully commercialized" affect (Hochschild [1983] 2012: 136). By juxtaposing participant narratives written from the perspective of my past self with an analytical discussion written from my current social position as a non-religious ex-Pentecostal, I have tried to include both perspectives and to offer a reflexive account of my current analytical footing in order to leave room for readers to draw their own conclusions. In this way, reflexivity allows us to entertain the notion of multiple realities and "multiple possible readings of data" (Humonen and Angouri 2023: 84–85).

As a final reflexive note on this ambiguity, it should be mentioned that accepting the existence of multiple realities also allowed me to make sense of my own history. My experiences and emotions as a Pentecostal felt authentic at the time. My current non-religious understanding is that much of what I felt can be explained in sociological and psychological terms — which does not make the experiences inauthentic in any way. However, this does not mean that the current analysis was somehow more 'objective' or that I would be less emotionally invested in my object of study. My analysis is differently subjective now and I am differently emotionally invested, but the resulting autoethnographic account is nevertheless a constructed representation of church interpreting, even if differently constructed than the original study in 2016.

References

Adams, Tony E., Stacy Holman Jones, and Carolyn Ellis. 2015. *Autoethnography*. Oxford: Oxford University Press.

Alvarado, Jonathan E. 2012. "Worship in the Spirit: Pentecostal Perspectives on Liturgical Theology and Praxis." *Journal of Pentecostal Theology* 21: 135–151.

Anderson, Leon. 2006. "Analytic Autoethnography." *Journal of Contemporary Ethnography* 35 (4): 373–395.

Ashforth, Blake E., and Ronald H. Humphrey. 2012. "Emotional Labor: Looking Back Nearly 20 Years." In *Emotional Labor in the 21st Century: Diverse Perspectives on Emotion Regulation at Work*, ed. by Alicia A. Grandey, James M. Diefendorff, and Deborah E. Rupp, 276–281. New York & London: Routledge.

Balcı Tison, Alev. 2016. "The Interpreter's Involvement in a Translated Institution: A Case Study of Sermon Interpreting." Doctoral dissertation, Rovira i Virigili University, Tarragona.

Burkitt, Ian. 2014. *Emotions and Social Relations*. Los Angeles, London, New Delhi, Singapore & Washington, DC: Sage.

Casanova, José. 2001. "Religion, the New Millennium, and Globalization." *Sociology of Religion* 62 (4): 415–441.

Centre for the Study of Global Christianity. 2019. "Status of Global Christianity, 2019, in the Context of 1900–2050." https://www.gordonconwell.edu/wp-content/uploads/sites/13/2019/04/StatusofGlobalChristianity20191.pdf

Chang, Heewon. 2008. *Autoethnography as Method*. Walnut Creek: Left Coast Press.

Clifford, James, and George E. Marcus. 1986. *Writing Culture: The Poetics and Politics of Ethnography*. Berkeley, Los Angeles & London: University of California Press.

Collins, Peter, and Anselma Gallinat. 2010. "The Ethnographic Self as Resource: An Introduction." In *The Ethnographic Self as Resource: Writing Memory and Experience into Ethnography*, ed. by Peter Collins, and Anselma Gallinat, 1–24. New York & Oxford: Berghahn Books.

Cross, Terry L. 2009. "The Divine-Human Encounter: Towards a Pentecostal Theology of Experience." *Pneuma* 31: 3–34.

Csordas, Thomas J. 1987. "Genre, Motive, and Metaphor: Conditions for Creativity in Ritual Language." *Cultural Anthropology* 2 (4): 445–469.

Cunliffe, Ann L., and Geetha Karunanayake. 2013. "Working Within Hyphen-Spaces in Ethnographic Research: Implications for Research Identities and Practice." *Organizational Research Methods* 16 (3): 364–392.

Elliott, Matthew. 2012. "The Emotional Core of Love: The Centrality of Emotion in Christian Psychology and Ethics." *Journal of Psychology and Christianity* 31 (2): 105–117.

Emerson, Robert. E., Rachel I. Fretz, and Linda L. Shaw. 2011. *Writing Ethnographic Fieldnotes*. 2nd edition. Chicago & London: The University of Chicago Press.

Fox, Ragan. 2021. "Recalling Emotional Recall: Reflecting on the Methodological Significance of Affective Memory in Autoethnography." *Text and Performance Quarterly* 41 (1–2): 61–80.

Friedner, Michele Ilana. 2018. "Vessel of God/Access to God: American Sign Language Interpreting in American Evangelical Churches." *American Anthropologist* 120 (4): 659–670.

Chapter 4. Affective labor in interpreted prayer **115**

Grandey, Alicia A., James M. Diefendorff, and Deborah E. Rupp. 2013. "Bringing Emotional Labor into Focus: A Review and Integration of Three Research Lenses." In *Emotional Labor in the 21st Century: Diverse Perspectives on Emotion Regulation at Work*, ed. by Alicia A. Grandey, James M. Diefendorff, and Deborah E. Rupp, 3–27. New York & London: Routledge.

Hertz, Rosanna. 1997. *Reflexivity & Voice*. Thousand Oaks: Sage.

Hild, Adelina. 2017. "The Role and Self-Regulation of Non-professional Interpreters in Religious Settings: The VIRS Project." In *Non-professional Interpreting and Translation*, ed. by Rachele Antonini, Letizia Cirillo, Linda Rossato, and Ira Torresi, 177–194. Amsterdam & Philadelphia: John Benjamins.

Hochschild, Arlie. (1983) 2012. *The Managed Heart. Commercialization of Human Feeling.* Berkeley, Los Angeles & London: University of California Press.

Hokkanen, Sari. 2012. "Simultaneous Church Interpreting as Service." *The Translator* 18 (2): 291–309.

Hokkanen, Sari. 2013. "Tulkki keskellä hengellistä kokemusta: Simultaanitulkkaus Tampereen helluntaiseurakunnan kokouksessa [The Interpreter Amidst Spiritual Experience: Simultaneous Interpreting in the Pentecostal Church of Tampere]. In *Tulkattu Tampere*, ed. by Kaisa Koskinen, 273–294. Tampere: Tampere University Press.

Hokkanen, Sari. 2016. "To Serve and to Experience: An Autoethnographic Study on Simultaneous Church Interpreting." Doctoral dissertation, University of Tampere. http://urn.fi/URN:ISBN:978-952-03-0232-0

Hokkanen, Sari. 2017. "Simultaneous Interpreting and Religious Experience: Volunteer Interpreting in a Finnish Pentecostal Church." In *Non-professional Interpreting and Translation*, ed. by Rachele Antonini, Letizia Cirillo, Linda Rossato, and Ira Torresi, 195–212. Amsterdam & Philadelphia: John Benjamins.

Hokkanen, Sari, and Kaisa Koskinen. 2016. "Affect as a Hinge: The Translator's Experiencing Self as a Sociocognitive Interface." *Translation Spaces* 5 (1): 78–96.

Hokkanen, Sari, and Kaisa Koskinen. Forthcoming. "Managing Positionality: Reflexivity as a Key to Robust Research in a Discipline of *Practisearchers*." In *Positionalities of Translation Studies*, ed. by Garda Elsherif, and Joanna Sobesto. London: Bloomsbury.

Humonen, Kristina, and Jo Angouri. 2023. "Revisiting Ethnography and Reflexivity for Language-Sensitive Workplace Research." In *Understanding the Dynamics of Language and Multilingualism in Professional Contexts: Advances in Language-Sensitive Management Research*, ed. by Philippe Lecomte, Mary Vigier, Claudine Gaibrois, and Betty Beeler, 84–101. Cheltenham & Northampton, MA: Edward Elgar.

Johnston, Erin F. 2021. "The Feeling of Enlightenment: Managing Emotions through Yoga and Prayer." *Symbolic Interaction* 44 (3): 576–602.

Korpal, Paweł, and Christopher D. Mellinger. 2022. "Self-Care Strategies of Professional Community Interpreters: An Interview-Based Study." *Translation, Cognition & Behavior* 5 (2): 275–299.

Koskinen, Kaisa. 2008. *Translating Institutions: An Ethnographic Study of EU Translation.* Manchester & Kinderbrook, NY: St. Jerome.

Koskinen, Kaisa. 2020. *Translation and Affect: Essays on Sticky Affects and Translational Affective Labour.* Amsterdam & Philadelphia: John Benjamins.

Lumsden, Karen (with Jan Bradford, and Jackie Goode). 2019. *Reflexivity: Theory, Method, and Practice*. London & New York: Routledge.

Maxwell, Joseph A. 1996. *Qualitative Research Design: An Interactive Approach*. Thousand Oaks: Sage.

Miller, Donald E. 2013. "Introduction: Pentecostalism as a Global Phenomenon." In *Spirit and Power: The Growth and Global Impact of Pentecostalism*, ed. by Donald E. Miller, Kimon H. Sargeant, and Richard Flory, 1–19. Oxford: Oxford University Press.

Miller, Donald E., and Tetsunao Yamamori. 2007. *Global Pentecostalism: The New Face of Christian Social Engagement*. Berkeley, Los Angeles & London: University of California Press.

Oakley, Barbara A. 2016. "Concepts and Implications of Altruism Bias and Pathological Altruism." *PNAS* 110 (Suppl. 2): 10408–10415. www.pnas.org/cgi/doi/10.1073/pnas .1302547110

Ottenberg, Simon. 1990. "Thirty Years of Fieldnotes: Changing Relationships to the Text." In *Fieldnotes: The Makings of Anthropology*, ed. by Roger Sanjek, 139–160. Ithaca & London: Cornell University.

Pew Research Center. 2006. "Spirit and Power: A 10-Country Survey of Pentecostals." https:// www.pewforum.org/2006/10/05/spirit-and-power

Pym, Anthony. 2011. "The Translator as Non-Author, and I Am Sorry About That." In *The Translator as Author: Perspectives on Literary Translation*, ed. by Claudia Buffagni, Beatrice Garzelli, and Serenella Zanotti, 31–44. Berlin: LIT Verlag.

Qin, Dongxiao. 2016. "Positionality." In *The Wiley Blackwell Encyclopedia of Gender and Sexuality Studies*, ed. by Nancy A. Naples, 1–2. Singapore: John Wiley & Sons.

Sharp, Shane. 2010. "How Does Prayer Help Manage Emotions?" *Social Psychology Quarterly* 73 (4): 417–437.

Tekgül, Duygu. 2020. "Faith-Related Interpreting as Emotional Labour: A Case Study at a Protestant Armenian Church in Istanbul." *Perspectives: Studies in Translation Theory and Practice* 28 (1): 43–57.

The Evangelical Lutheran Church of Finland. 2023. "Jäsentilasto 2023 [Membership Statistics 2023]." https://www.kirkontilastot.fi/viz.php?id=246

Tiittanen, Anssi. 2021. "Helluntaiseurakuntien jäsenmäärä pienimmillään 25 vuoteen [The Membership of Pentecostal Churches at its Lowest in 25 Years]." Last modified February 9, 2021. https://suomenhelluntaikirkko.fi/2021/02/09/helluntaiseurakuntien-jasenmaara-pienimmillaan-25-vuoteen

Tracy, Sarah J. 2010. "Qualitative Quality: Eight 'Big-Tent' Criteria for Excellent Qualitative Research." *Qualitative Inquiry* 16 (10): 837–851.

Vigouroux, Cecilia. B. 2010. "Double-Mouthed Discourse: Interpreting, Framing, and Participant Roles." *Journal of Sociolinguistics* 14 (3): 341–369.

Vishkin, Allon, Pazit Ben-Nun Bloom, and Maya Tamir. 2019. "Always Look on the Bright Side of Life: Religiosity, Emotion Regulation and Well-Being in a Jewish and Christian Sample." *Journal of Happiness Studies* 20: 427–447.

Willis, Paul. 2000. *The Ethnographic Imagination*. Cambridge and Malden: Polity.

Wynn, Mark. 2012. "Renewing the Senses: Conversion Experience and the Phenomenology of the Spiritual Life." *International Journal for Philosophy of Religion* 72: 211–226.

CHAPTER 5

'Going native' during field research on multilingual legislation
Methodological and ethical strategies

Cornelia Staudinger
University of Geneva | Swiss Federal Chancellery

Performing in situ research using ethnographic methods can offer new valuable insights into complex phenomena such as the linguistic revision and legal review of multilingual legislative drafts. At the same time, it entails reflections on the type of involvement of the researcher. In this chapter, I describe how my role in the research setting has evolved from outside researcher to partial insider and eventually to full member. In particular, I illustrate the benefits and risks associated with my becoming an insider. To conclude, I challenge the dichotomy of *insider versus outsider*; I argue that it is, first and foremost, crucial for the researcher to be transparent about their positionality and to consciously apply strategies to manage related benefits and risks.

Keywords: multilingual legislation, field research, researcher positionality, insider/outsider, research ethics

1. Introduction

Researching the complex quality assurance procedures in institutions responsible for drafting multilingual legislation calls for methodological approaches providing a holistic view. As Biel (2017: 82) stresses, "some aspects of translations — most notably, quality — cut across all dimensions", i.e., the product, the process, the participants and the context (Saldanha and O'Brien 2014). Thus, phenomena associated with the quality of source and target texts such as the linguistic revision and legal review of multilingual legislative drafts can only be fully explored when also taking into account the different actors involved (participants) as well as the setting in which they are operating (context). Performing in situ research using ethnographic methods can offer new valuable insights and provide rich data regarding these dimensions (Saldanha and O'Brien 2014: 208–209, 232–233).

https://doi.org/10.1075/btl.165.05sta
Available under the CC BY-NC 4.0 license. © 2025 John Benjamins Publishing Company

Collecting data through fieldwork entails reflections on the type of involvement of the researcher in the setting they are studying. In this chapter, I describe my involvement in the setting I am exploring in my research and how it has evolved significantly throughout the research project due to the change of my status from outside researcher to partial insider and eventually to full member. In particular, I illustrate the benefits and risks associated with my becoming a member of the group, using examples from my study. I focus on the strategies I have adopted in order to maximise those benefits while minimising related risks. To conclude, I challenge the dichotomy of *insider versus outsider* with the notion of "the space between" (Corbin Dwyer and Buckle 2009). A researcher may not always be located at one of the extremes of the insider-outsider continuum, and their position along this continuum may change throughout the research cycle. However, it is crucial for the researcher to be transparent about their positionality as well as related benefits and risks.

2. Study objectives and design

The aim of the study is to explore what impact the linguistic revision and legal review of draft legislation have on the original source and target texts. The study sets out to develop a detailed understanding of these quality assurance procedures involving language specialists and legal experts within one specific context.

The research project uses a case study approach. It focuses on Switzerland's federal legislation in German and French at its draft stage in the executive branch and is being carried out in the Swiss Federal Chancellery and the Swiss Federal Office of Justice. It should be emphasised that a case study is not a specific method of data collection, but a focus or strategy that allows for the use of diverse qualitative as well as quantitative methods (Yin 1981:99; Stake 2005:443; Thomas 2011:9). This case study uses a sequential combination of different methods; it is divided into three stages.

Stage 1 consists of an analysis of the official documentation regarding the quality assurance procedures in question. It covers the provisions that constitute the legal basis of the procedures, relevant guidelines as well as texts available on the websites of the federal administration detailing the revision and review procedures. This document analysis is combined with a series of five interviews with experts in the legal and linguistic services concerned. The aim of this stage is to define the procedures in theory, i.e., *how the linguistic revision and legal review should be carried out.*

Stage 2 consists of an analysis of revised and reviewed texts in the source and target languages. During this stage, the changes that have been introduced into the drafts by the linguistic and legal experts are categorised. This text analysis is combined with observations of meetings during which a considerable part of the draft revision and review takes place. These observations are an important complementary tool that allows the reasoning and the process leading to changes being introduced into the drafts to be taken into account during categorisation. The aim of this stage is to define the actual practice, i.e., *how the linguistic revision and legal review are carried out.*

Stage 3 consists of interviews with language specialists and legal experts involved in these procedures. The aim of this stage is to include the perceptions of participants, i.e., *how the language specialists and legal experts experience and perceive the linguistic revision and legal review.*

3.   Role evolution

My role in the setting that I am exploring in my research has evolved significantly since the beginning of the study in 2019 (see Figure 1). This evolution has led to a change in my positionality and perspectives.

3.1   Timeline

I started my research in this field in 2019 when I was employed as a research assistant at the Faculty of Translation and Interpreting (FTI) at the University of Geneva. At that time, I had no experience in working for the Swiss federal institutions, nor did I have any personal contacts within the Swiss Federal Chancellery or the Swiss Federal Office of Justice. During the development of the study's objectives and design, my role was therefore limited to that of an outside researcher.

After a preliminary interview with two employees of the Swiss Federal Chancellery's Central Language Services (CLS) and the preliminary observation of two meetings during which CLS language specialists and Swiss Federal Office of Justice legal experts revised and reviewed a legislative draft, I was offered an internship in the German Section of the Swiss Federal Chancellery's Central Language Services (CLS DE). This was shortly after my project had been approved by the FTI's Board of Professors in October 2019. The submission of my project to the FTI's ethics committee, however, took place in January 2020 after I had been offered the internship. Thus, the information that I would become an intern in the CLS DE was included in the documentation submitted to the ethics committee, which approved the study's approach regarding ethics-related aspects.

My internship contract covered a workload of 60% of a full-time position for a duration of six months (March to August 2020). My workload at the FTI was accordingly reduced to 40% for the duration of the internship, of which approximately half — or 20% of my overall workload — was dedicated to research activities within the Swiss federal administration. To a large extent, the internship covered the tasks that are the subject of my research: I took on the role of a language specialist revising legislative drafts, first in pairs with other language specialists of the CLS DE and subsequently more and more independently.

I started the document analysis and the preparation of the semi-structured interviews of stage 1 of the study before the internship, while still being an outsider. However, I completed both the document analysis and the preparation of the interviews during my time as an intern. My status as an employee allowed me to access additional, internal guidelines that had not been available to me before the internship and that I included in the document analysis. Furthermore, my first experiences in the setting allowed me to make slight adjustments, mostly additions, to the interview guide developed for the five stage 1 interviews. Four interviews were carried out during the second half of my internship, on-site in the federal institutions, and one was conducted shortly after the end of the internship via a conference call. The stage 2 observations also took place during the internship. The stage 2 analysis of the corresponding legislative drafts started during the internship, but was still ongoing when my status changed two more times.

After the internship, I was again exclusively employed by the FTI for a period of five months (September 2020 to January 2021). I then quit my position at the FTI to start a permanent position as legislative drafter and translator in the CLS DE in February 2021. Since then, I have continued my research as a PhD student without an employment contract with the FTI. Therefore, the interviews of stage 3, which have not yet been carried out at the time of writing, will presumably take place while I am a permanent employee in the CLS DE.

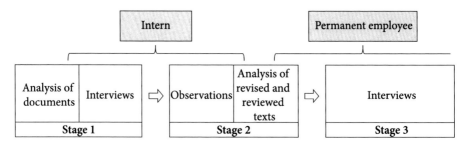

Figure 1. General overview of the 3 stages of the study, the main data collection methods, and my role in the setting beyond being a researcher

3.2 Participation in the setting and membership in the group

Spradley (1980: 58–62), in his work on participant observation, distinguishes five different types of researcher participation according to the degree of their involvement in the setting: nonparticipation, passive participation, moderate participation, active participation and complete participation. On this spectrum, my involvement in the setting during the internship was somewhere between moderate participation, where the researcher keeps a balance between participation and observation, and active participation, where the researcher participates in the group's activities to learn its behaviour. Since the category of complete participation is reserved for researchers who study a setting in which they are already participants, Spradley's spectrum does not comprise a type of participation that can be applied to the role I have taken on since the start of my permanent employment. As the approach of participant observation implies a certain degree of detachment in each type of involvement and does not fully take into account the researcher's self, including their attitudes and perspectives, it provides only a limited framework for discussing my role over the course of the study.

Adler and Adler (1987) in turn propose "membership roles" to categorise a researcher's involvement with their setting and their subjects. They distinguish three types of researchers according to their membership: peripheral-member-researchers, who interact with the group to gain an insider's perspective, but generally do not participate in its core activities; active-member-researchers, who assume a functional role in the setting and participate in the core activities of the group, but only commit partially and temporarily, as their long-term goals are usually different from those of other group members; and complete-member-researchers, who are fully immersed in the group and committed to its goals and values.

The membership role corresponding best to my time as an intern in the CLS DE is that of an active-member-researcher. Although I was actively participating in the service's activities and treated as an equal employee when it came to social interactions, my behaviour was, to a large extent, guided by my initial plans to leave the field after six months. However, in contrast to Adler and Adler's (1987: 57) statement that an active-member-researcher's longer-term plans or life goals are usually different from those of other group members, I did not exclude the possibility of working for the CLS DE at a later time in my career. In my case, it was my short- to medium-term goals and career plans that lay elsewhere. I did not see permanent employment in the CLS DE at that point in my career as an option and I prioritised my role as a researcher during the internship. I therefore held back in certain ways and felt a certain degree of detachment during the duration of the internship. In that regard, my role during the internship also comprised features characteristic of peripheral-member-researchers. Due to my greater commitment to my research, I did not feel like I achieved the status of full insider, but considered myself as a *partial insider* during the internship.

As Adler and Adler (1987:70) state, many researchers who become members of the group they are studying do not have the prior intention of converting to complete membership — a scenario that also applies to me. I can therefore be considered a "convert researcher" (Adler and Adler 1987:68), i.e., a researcher who was not previously involved with the setting, but converts to membership during the course of their research.

As soon as I started my permanent employment in the CLS DE, I became a complete-member-researcher by immersing myself fully in the group. However, even as a complete member committed to the values and goals of the group, I have continued my research in the setting and stayed equally committed to my role as a researcher. Similarly to Koskinen (2008:8), who conducted research in a setting in which she had formerly been involved as an employee, I am "a 'double agent', partially an insider, partially an outsider" in the setting. This partial insiderness and outsiderness should not be interpreted as a specific, clearly determined position in between two extremes, where neither full insiderness is achieved nor full outsiderness maintained. On the contrary, because of my full commitment to both my roles since the start of my permanent employment, I have considered myself *both as an insider and as an outsider*, assuming one of the two roles or (parts of) both of them concurrently depending on the situation.

In the same vein, Spradley (1980:57) argues that "ethnographic fieldwork involves alternating between the insider and outsider experience, and having both simultaneously". A similar point has been made by Yu (2020:27), who introduces the notion of "multiplex persona" as a "perspective that views positionality as a decentred entity that encompasses our multi-faceted characters, roles and aspects of identities, presented to and perceived by others and ourselves in the momentary communicative events".

Along the same lines, Jorgensen (1989:60), in his work on participant observation, points out that a "participant observer may perform a variety of roles over the course of a study". Jorgensen (1989:61) maintains that this is beneficial to a study, as the researcher has access to different viewpoints and perspectives. This, in turn, may contribute to the richness of the data (Lipson 1984:351). Similarly, Adler and Adler (1987:84) conclude that being a complete-member-researcher who gathers data through different roles has a positive impact on the data collection process.

Nonetheless, being an insider is also linked to certain risks, as each advantage usually entails a disadvantage (Hammersley 1993:432–433). Thus, Mercer (2007), who conducted research in educational institutions where she was formerly employed, compares conducting insider research to "wielding a double-edged sword". A detailed description of the benefits and risks identified for my own study and of the strategies applied to wielding my own double-edged sword follows in Sections 4 to 6.

4. Benefits of becoming a member

The main advantages of becoming an insider identified for my study are the ease of access to participants and data, the opportunity to be part of natural social interactions, a larger volume of data, a greater understanding of the phenomena and enhanced self-reflexivity.

4.1 Ease of access to participants and data

Being or becoming an insider may facilitate the access both to participants and to data. Previously established trust between the insider researcher and the other group members may contribute to their acceptance (Corbin Dwyer and Buckle 2009: 58). If the researcher is perceived as a member of the group, there may be greater relational intimacy between them and the participants. Thus, potential benefits — or issues — in terms of access to participants and data are usually related to the existing relationship between the researcher and the participants, particularly the level of trust (Asselin 2003: 101). Consequently, while certain participants may perceive an insider researcher as a threat (cf. Section 5.3), others may feel more comfortable opening up to a researcher who is already a trusted colleague.

As I started my research as an outsider, without any existing personal ties to group members I could build on to negotiate my entry into the setting as a researcher, I went through the common procedure of gaining "overt entrée" into the setting by seeking permission from the heads of the services concerned (Jorgensen 1989: 46). Earning the trust and confidence of these authorities in the setting — who not only granted me access as a researcher, but also invited me to become a member as an intern — likely contributed to other group members' openness to my research (Jorgensen 1989: 46–47); some employees were willing to participate in the study even though I had not yet built a personal relationship with them at the time of the stage 1 interviews or the stage 2 observations.

Being or becoming an insider facilitates not only the first access, but also the completion of missing data at a later stage (Unluer 2012: 5). What proved to be very convenient in my case was the possibility to access the database in which all the documentation of the CLS regarding the revision and review of legislative drafts is stored. This meant that, except during the five months between the end of my internship and the beginning of my permanent employment, I could access any relevant documents by myself without needing to ask the participants to do so for me. This helped keep the administrative burden of participating in the study as low as possible and helped ensure that time constraints would influence their willingness to participate in the study as little as possible.

Another aspect of ease of access is the better reachability of the researcher. A researcher who is also an insider can usually be reached by participants through more channels than an outside researcher (Unluer 2012: 6). In my case, this means that in addition to being reachable by phone or e-mail, I have also regularly been present at the office. This has allowed for spontaneous conversations about my research (Unluer 2012: 5), in particular when participants do not have specific questions about the study, but are nonetheless keen on learning more about it. These spontaneous conversations have become an important tool in establishing trust with the participants. In addition, they have provided me with further insights that have enriched the data (cf. Section 4.3).

4.2 Natural social interactions

Another potential benefit of being an insider researcher is the ability to interact naturally with the participants. An insider researcher's presence may be perceived as less obtrusive and unnatural, which, in turn, may limit the researcher's interference with natural social interactions (Adler and Adler 1994: 380). This view is supported by Jorgensen (1989: 58–59) who maintains that "participant involvement … suggests that what you are able to observe increasingly is what people normally say and do even when an outside observer is not present". Jorgensen (1989: 60) adds that performing a role defined by the setting, i.e., the role of an insider, "offers the distinct advantage of being in all ways a normal part of human interaction and, therefore, fairly unobtrusive".

Another advantage in that regard is the fact that, even if participants alter their behaviour due to the researcher's presence, the researcher may be able to recognise when such changes in the usual pattern of behaviour occur (Bonner and Tolhurst 2002: 4). In my study, this happened during one of the observations, where one of the participants slightly changed their behaviour due to my taking notes while observing them. At the beginning of the observation, the participant seemed a little more reserved than usual when making comments about the draft, as they noticed that I was taking notes after certain statements made by the participants. They also seemed to choose their words more carefully during the first part of the observation. I was only able to recognise this subtle change of behaviour because I had already known that person for several months at the time of the observation and had worked on several drafts with them before. I could therefore take into account that change of behaviour in my analysis of the observation protocol.

4.3 Volume of data

One of the biggest benefits of being an insider researcher is the volume of data the researcher has access to. As an insider, the researcher is immersed in the setting and therefore *surrounded by* or virtually *exposed to data* at any time of their workday, over an extended period of time. This constant exposure to data provides the insider researcher with the possibility of continuous data collection, which would not be available to an outsider and which may contribute to the data being more versatile and complete (Unluer 2012: 5).

As my involvement in the setting has substantially changed since the beginning of the study, I have been exposed to much more data than I had initially planned to collect. Some of the details that have helped me make sense of the data collected during the interviews and observations so far have come to my attention and have been gathered during my daily routine as an insider, in particular during informal conversations with colleagues or during the regular CLS DE team meetings. Furthermore, these informal observations due to my immersion in the setting have enhanced the richness of the data on the collaboration between the different actors involved as well as the context in which they are operating.

4.4 Greater understanding

As an insider, the researcher may also benefit from greater understanding. Being familiar with the processes and the jargon may make it easier for them to understand the phenomena in question, in particular implicit meanings that may be difficult for an outsider to capture (Unluer 2012: 6; Berger 2015: 223). Furthermore, an insider researcher may find it easier to know when and where to gather data, which may contribute to the data being richer, more focused or more diverse (Bonner and Tolhurst 2002: 4).

Being an insider usually means that the researcher knows the routine. While over-familiarisation may cause an emphasis on extreme events rather than the routine (cf. Section 5.2), the opposite may also be true; an insider researcher may be better equipped to judge if something is part of the routine or if it constitutes an extreme event. This may make it easier for them to give the right emphasis to each pattern observed. In my study, I observed certain patterns during the stage 2 formal observations that I identified as atypical and rare based on my growing experience in the setting. For example, during two meetings between CLS language specialists and Federal Office of Justice legal experts, a legal expert took the lead during the whole meeting or a large part of it. This is rather uncommon, as it is usually the language specialist sharing their screen and introducing the modifications and comments directly into the legislative draft that leads such meetings. When this is not the case, interactions between the participants are usually rather balanced. I would not have been able to draw the conclusion that the group dynamics observed did not represent the behavioural routine if my data were limited to formal observations. In general, as Jorgensen (1989:56) argues, there may be less potential for misunderstandings or inaccurate observations when a researcher is involved in the setting and has direct access to participants' perspectives and actions.

4.5 Enhanced self-reflexivity

Another important benefit is the enhanced self-reflexivity required of the insider researcher (Koskinen 2008:9), as they constantly have to explain their role in the setting and will likely be challenged in this regard by the scientific community. Lincoln, Lynham, and Guba (2018:246–247) describe reflexivity as the process of consciously experiencing, critically reflecting on and questioning the multiple identities that are part of the self. When becoming a member of the group in the setting studied during the course of the research, the researcher is faced with decisions regarding their change of status; once an insider, the researcher is continually faced with decisions regarding their dual role. This requires a high level of self-reflexivity which may, in turn, lead to greater awareness of the space the researcher occupies within the research project (Hill and Dao 2021:532) as well as of their own biases. As Breen (2007:169) and Corbin Dwyer and Buckle (2009:59) claim, being an outsider does not automatically entail a complete elimination or even a reduction of personal biases. Greater awareness achieved through enhanced self-reflexivity may thus reduce potential concerns regarding the insider status of the researcher (Corbin Dwyer and Buckle 2009:59; cf. Section 5).

Furthermore, Jorgensen (1989:37) argues that "the methodology of participant observation, more than most scientific approaches, requires the researcher to describe and discuss fully the procedures used to collect information". The reflexivity that is required when employing and discussing ethnographic methods may thus also contribute to increased transparency regarding "the relationship between the procedures employed and the results obtained" (Jorgensen 1989:37).

5. Risks of becoming a member

While becoming an insider comes with certain advantages, there are also potential disadvantages associated with being a member of the group in the setting studied. The main risks identified for my study are role conflicts and confusion, over-familiarisation, bias as well as assumptions about prior knowledge, understanding the culture and similarity (see also Hokkanen, Chapter 4; Steinkogler, Chapter 6; Davier, Chapter 7; and Todorova, Chapter 14, this volume, for discussions of researcher roles and issues of positionality).

5.1 Role conflicts or confusion

According to Adler and Adler (1987:73), a researcher who is a complete member may experience role conflicts due to their dual role. In my case, different kinds of role conflicts occurred in specific situations.

I once was asked in my role as an employee if I could take over a task regarding a draft of a legislative act that I had used for my research at a previous stage of the drafting process. Although this task occurred at a later stage, which is not directly the subject of my study, I handed it over to a colleague in order to avoid any role conflicts or confusion.

Furthermore, there were a few occasions during the stage 2 observations where participants approached me with linguistic questions regarding a draft or made comments about the fact that it would be helpful if I were not solely an observer, but also able to express my thoughts or make suggestions regarding certain aspects of a draft. However, as I was, first and foremost, committed to my research at that time and trying to balance my involvement with a certain degree of detachment, I strove to limit the extent of my influence on the phenomenon I was studying by not interfering during the formal observations, not least because of my limited experience in legislative drafting at that point. In addition, it felt easier to not intervene at all than to have to draw the line at a later point in case the participants expected me to increasingly become involved in working on the draft. Although reiterating the limits of my role as a researcher in those specific situations sometimes felt like refusing a request from someone I would usually be happy to help, apart from this inner conflict or slight feeling of guilt or pressure I put on myself, my prioritising my research was never met with any perceivable negative response by the participants or other colleagues.

In light of these examples, it is important to stress that in other settings where a researcher becomes a complete member and has to deal with divided loyalties towards their role as an employee and their role as a researcher (Koskinen 2008:9), there may be pressure on them to put their role as an employee first.

Furthermore, Asselin (2003:102) draws attention to the "possibility of role confusion during the collection and analysis of data" when a researcher is also a practitioner in their field of research. She describes role confusion as the researcher perceiving or responding to events or analysing data from a perspective that is different from that of a researcher.

In this context, Hammersley and Atkinson (2007:87) point out that one of the dangers of ethnographic research lies in 'going native', an expression that is often used in a sense that implies that a researcher is getting too involved and completely losing their analytical perspective and critical or independent stance towards the phenomena (Adler and Adler 1987:17; Saldanha and O'Brien 2014:188–189).

According to Asselin's definition, role confusion is solely related to the researcher's self. Yet, another important aspect of role confusion is the perception of an insider researcher by participants and colleagues. The people in the setting may not always clearly understand in which role the researcher is addressing them. This kind of role confusion also occurred during my internship. For organisational reasons, for each draft that I worked on I had to communicate whether I was participating as an employee, together with or in place of a colleague, or using it for my research. In a few cases, questions by colleagues came up when they were not sure about which role I was going to assume regarding a specific draft. Since starting my position as a permanent employee, however, no incidents of confusion regarding my role among my colleagues have been brought to my attention.

5.2 Over-familiarisation

When a researcher is a member of the group in the setting studied, there is a risk of over-familiarisation. An insider researcher may miss or overlook subtle details of the routine, as they may take them for granted and thus lose their "'intuition and sensitivity' to familiar and recurrent experiences" (Bonner and Tolhurst 2002:8). This, in turn, may lead the researcher to focus on extreme events or outliers rather than the routine (Bonner and Tolhurst 2002:13).

This was not an issue at the beginning of my own research project, as I started my study as an outsider not previously familiar with the setting. However, as my familiarity has significantly increased over the course of the study in accordance with my growing involvement in the setting, it is essential that I actively foster my awareness of each of the patterns and actions that are part of the phenomena I am studying, whether it be routine behaviour or extreme events.

5.3   Bias

Another issue that is regularly put forward when a researcher is also an insider is bias. The researcher's perceptions may be shaped or affected by their personal perspective and experience (Corbin Dwyer and Buckle 2009:58), a risk that can concern any researcher, but may be heightened or particularly visible when the researcher is also involved in the setting. As Asselin (2003:100) points out, insider researchers tend to believe they know the culture of the group studied. This may influence the data gathering as well as the data analysis. The researcher may make assumptions about the participants' views and issues based on their own experience and not seek clarification, or mostly or exclusively seek confirmation for their own worldview. According to Corbin Dwyer and Buckle (2009:58), in data analysis this may lead to "an emphasis on shared factors between the researcher and the participants and a de-emphasis on factors that are discrepant, or vice versa". Being an insider researcher can therefore increase bias.

Even if an insider researcher is aware of this risk of bias and seeks to mitigate it, participants may still fear that they are not unbiased or impartial. Therefore, it may be easier for certain participants to open up to an outsider and share complex or sensitive professional or personal information with them rather than with an insider who is also a colleague and may be perceived as a threat (Bonner and Tolhurst 2002:9). Until now, I have not observed any behaviour that would lead me to believe that a participant held back due to my being an insider as well. As the first round of interviews and the observations took place while I was an intern who was supposed to be leaving the field, my status as a temporary employee may not have had the same impact on the participants as my complete membership in the group today may have. Consequently, particular attention has to be paid to this aspect during the interviews to be conducted during stage 3 of the project.

5.4   Assumptions about prior knowledge, understanding the culture and similarity

Another risk that has to be taken into account by a researcher who is an insider is that participants may fail to explicitly address certain aspects regarding the phenomena in question or their experience during interviews if they assume similarity (Corbin Dwyer and Buckle 2009:58) and feel the researcher already knows the answers (Breen 2007:164). They may think that it is unnecessary to repeat information on the fundamental features of the culture or the phenomena. Accounts of participants not finishing sentences or referring to the researcher's knowledge and using phrases such as "You know what I mean" during interviews are not uncommon under such circumstances (Lipson 1984:349; Kanuha 2000: 442–443; Berger 2015:223; Chammas 2020:546).

In my study, one of the participants during the stage 1 interviews mentioned an aspect and then also referred to my knowledge of it without giving any further explanation. During the other stage 1 interviews, the participants likely made fewer assumptions, as they were less aware of the knowledge I had gathered as an intern. Again, strategies to mitigate the risk of such assumptions interfering with the information provided during interviews will be of particular relevance during the interviews to be conducted during stage 3 of the project (cf. Section 6).

6. Methodological and ethical strategies

In order to maximise the benefits illustrated in Section 4 while minimising the risks presented in Section 5 associated with 'going native', I made several adjustments to my methodological and ethical strategies after deciding to get involved in the setting I am studying as a member of the group.

First, before deciding whether I would do the internship I was offered, I reviewed the literature on membership roles. This was a crucial step in identifying potential benefits and risks beforehand and in making an informed decision. After I accepted the internship, I reassessed the methodology and the priorities of the project; I concluded that it was essential to introduce supplementary methodological tools to my study and to carry out, or start, certain tasks before I would enter the field, in order to take advantage of my increased involvement while minimising related risks.

I introduced two new methodological tools to my study after accepting the internship: a field diary and an ethics journal (see also Davier, Chapter 7, this volume). The field diary covers classic field notes that consist of descriptions and analytical reflections regarding the phenomena themselves. As an insider, my observations have not, as initially planned, been limited to formal meetings during which a significant part of the revision and review take place and during which I used specific observation protocols; I have also been constantly exposed to people, actions and events in the setting simply by participating in the group's activities myself. In order to make use of this much more comprehensive access to the setting and to enrich the data gathered, I have regularly been taking field notes since the start of my internship. In particular, I tried to use my "initial naiveté" as a "strategic advantage" (Jorgensen 1989:56) by taking extensive field notes in the early stages of the study, before becoming too familiar with the setting and losing the initial sense of strangeness. These notes have proven to be of great value, as they contain my first impressions of the field as well as answers to questions that I had formulated before entering the field from the perspective of an outside researcher.

Similarly to Punch (2012), who used a distinct diary in addition to classic field notes, I have also separated my field notes from more personal records regarding my roles and my relationships, which I have been keeping in the form of a personal journal – or *ethics journal*, as it mainly contains reflections on ethics-related aspects. According to Punch (2012: 91), the main purpose of such a diary is to allow a researcher to release the negative emotions emerging during fieldwork and to enable them to deal with the difficulties encountered. She points out that it is therefore likely for such a diary to mainly contain reflections on difficulties and concerns as well as other negative emotions. My ethics journal, however, contains not only doubts and issues that have arisen, but, more generally, my thoughts and feelings regarding my growing involvement in the setting and the ways in which it has or may have impacted my perceptions and my relationships. As an example, at a certain point I reflected on feeling increasingly like a member of the group. A juxtaposition of the data gathered through field notes and interviews with the entries in the ethics journal showed that that feeling coincided with the moment from which I occasionally began using first-person pronouns during data collection, for example in phrases such as "in *our* service" instead of "in *the CLS DE*". This insight then led me to reflect on the reasons why I referred to the setting in a way that made my membership in the group explicit. While my early entries in the ethics journal suggest a certain hesitation to become a complete insider and to emphasise my membership, the journal provides a record of my journey to a position in which I have felt more comfortable making use of the advantages of being an insider. Tracing back that shift in my perspective has led me to conclude that the use of expressions stressing my membership has also been a cautious attempt, in some situations, to strengthen the connection with a participant by emphasising shared factors without imposing my own view. In that sense, the ethics journal has allowed me to scrutinise my own positionality as well as the ways in which it may have shaped the research process.

Furthermore, I have continually reflected on the benefits and risks associated with my dual role in the ethics journal, in particular when specific events linked to those benefits or risks occurred. The ethics journal has thus contributed to enhancing self-reflexivity and awareness of potential issues. Many insider researchers who reflect on their roles use a similar strategy to foster self-awareness and stress the importance of a tool containing reflections on their actions, thoughts and feelings (Lipson 1984: 349–350; Bonner and Tolhurst 2002: 6; Asselin 2003: 102–103; Le Gallais 2008: 150–153; Berger 2015: 230; Chammas 2020: 548).

Moreover, Punch (2012: 92) argues that such a diary may encourage researchers to be more transparent regarding their positionality as well as issues related to fieldwork. Koch (2006) goes one step further and maintains that the trustworthiness of a qualitative study may be enhanced when a researcher creates a "decision trail" using a journal; providing a record of one's reasoning as well as influences on research decisions may enable the reader to better understand the researcher's interpretation. I would also argue that an open dialogue on factors shaping a research project is, in itself, a measure that increases trustworthiness. While transparency may bring to light flaws in the research, it provides readers with the information they need to judge the study themselves. Just like Koskinen (2008: 54), who included descriptions of her personal experience to allow the reader to form their own opinion about the extent of bias in her study, I have therefore consistently mentioned my dual role, including, if possible, its implications, when presenting details of the study to the scientific community.

Regarding the analysis of the data collected in the field diary and the ethics journal, one of the strategies I have adhered to is the continuous comparison of new and existing data in order to critically examine my perspectives and assumptions and the way they have evolved over the course of the study. Such reflections are crucial in countering or reducing as much as possible the effects of over-familiarisation and bias. As an example, comparing recent field notes with the notes taken during the early stages of the study has helped me to identify aspects that I mentioned exclusively when I first entered the field. This awareness constitutes the foundation necessary in determining their weight in the analysis, according to whether they only attracted my attention at the beginning of the project because they were outliers and have not recurred or because they are part of the routine which I am today familiar with and not mentioning in every single entry in the field diary.

More generally, I have been applying the strategy of "repeated review" (Berger 2015: 230) regarding all the data I have collected, including the interview and observation data. Going back to data analysed in the early stages of the study has allowed me to look at it through a new lens — a lens I acquired through my greater involvement in the setting. Such a review of data from a different perspective at a later time may enable a researcher to uncover nuances that only become apparent as their experience, as well as the perceptions and reflections that are associated with that experience, change (Berger 2015: 226).

Another adjustment I made was in terms of communication. Since I decided to become a member of the group, I have put great emphasis on being transparent about my dual role and on making clear to my colleagues and participants which role I am assuming at any given time. This not only covers the immediate content of oral or written exchanges with people in the setting, but also details that may help avoid role confusion such as the use of different e-mail addresses, signatures and logos for each role.

Moreover, open communication can be an effective strategy to counter potential effects of over-familiarisation, bias and assumptions being made, in particular during the interviewing process. Chammas (2020:546), for example, describes how participants would be startled by her asking questions where it seemed obvious to them that she already knew the answer. In order to prevent such astonishment or incomprehension, the researcher should not only explain their role as a researcher to the participant, but also the fact that it is important for the participant to share their experiences and perspectives in their own words, even when the researcher asks questions where the participant assumes that the researcher already knows the answer or has shared experience with the participant.

A careful review of the stage 1 interviews also helped me become aware of a situation where a participant referred to something without giving any further explanation. They only implied that I already knew what they were talking about. In such cases, the researcher can ask the participant to clarify or elaborate (Kanuha 2000: 443; Asselin 2003:100) or to share their perspectives and feelings on it. Analysing data gradually as the research progresses may therefore also contribute to fostering self-reflexivity and allow the researcher to take into account, during subsequent data collection, certain aspects or issues that came to light.

Lastly, it may be advisable for an insider researcher to put in place a plan of action to follow in case of role conflicts. Koch (2006:97), who conducted research in two elderly care wards in a hospital in the United Kingdom, for example, states that she had not anticipated certain ethical concerns that emerged when she witnessed careless nursing practice during her research, and she regretted not having made a contingency plan beforehand. Even though not all role conflicts entail serious ethical concerns like in Koch's study, there may still be pressure on the researcher to put their role as an employee first if possible conflicts of interest are not discussed and the scope of action of the researcher not defined before they enter the field. In my own project, it has been possible to prevent certain potential incidents of role conflicts due to the great flexibility I have been given since the beginning of the study. During the internship, for example, I could freely decide which drafts I wanted to work on as an employee and which ones I wanted to use for my study, provided that certain conditions, such as participant consent and draft non-confidentiality, were met. In this regard, I never felt any pressure by my employer to prioritise my role as an employee.

7. Conclusion

When a researcher collects data through fieldwork, their involvement is frequently analysed through the binary concept of *insider versus outsider*. However, numerous researchers question or reject the insider/outsider dichotomy. Jorgensen (1989: 56), for example, argues that "supposed competition and conflict between observation and participation have been greatly exaggerated" and that "we routinely perform multiple roles more or less simultaneously". This is consistent with Merton's (1972: 22) view that individuals do not have one single status at a time, but a "status set: a complement of variously interrelated statuses which interact to affect both their behavior and perspectives"; individuals may share certain statuses and not others. This can be applied to researchers who are themselves members of the group they study. Because of their functional role in the group, they may share certain statuses and viewpoints with the other group members, and in those respects, they may be considered as insiders. Yet, as researchers, they may also have statuses that are different from those of other group members, and in those respects, they may be considered as outsiders.

Today, many researchers who are members of the community they study emphasise *both* their *insider and outsider* perspectives. Koskinen (2008: 9), for example, states that in her book on her research in an institution in which she had formerly been employed a dialogue takes place between the insider and outsider viewpoints. Hellawell (2006), Mercer (2007), Le Gallais (2008) and Flores (2018) all use the term "continuum" to describe the scale or range of a researcher's positionality in the research setting. Furthermore, they all stress that the researcher's position may be fluid and that it may fluctuate or shift back and forth along this continuum.

I agree with these viewpoints and join Corbin Dwyer and Buckle (2009) in challenging the dichotomy of insider versus outsider with the notion of the "space between", a third space that bridges the complete outsider and complete insider positions. There are many examples of research projects where the researcher has not been located at one of the extremes of the insider-outsider continuum throughout the whole research cycle. My own journey of becoming a member in the setting I am studying shows that it is not always possible to apply an either/or approach, as positionality and the numerous facets it covers may change or fluctuate over the course of a study. Therefore, I advocate that we move away from binary concepts to categorise a researcher's involvement and positionality and that we embrace an approach of transparency regarding our perspectives, where we foster tools and strategies that contribute to disclosing how they may have shaped the research. Each type of involvement has its own advantages and disadvantages — and the *space between* likely looks different for each individual researcher. It is therefore, first and foremost, crucial for the researcher to be transparent about their positionality throughout the research project and to consciously apply strategies to manage related benefits and risks.

References

Adler, Patricia A., and Peter Adler. 1987. *Membership Roles in Field Research*. Newbury Park: Sage.

Adler, Patricia A., and Peter Adler. 1994. "Observational Techniques." In *Handbook of Qualitative Research*, ed. by Norman K. Denzin, and Yvonna S. Lincoln, 377–392. Thousand Oaks: Sage.

Asselin, Marilyn E. 2003. "Insider Research: Issues to Consider When Doing Qualitative Research in Your Own Setting." *Journal for Nurses in Staff Development* 19 (2): 99–103.

Berger, Roni. 2015. "Now I See It, Now I Don't: Researcher's Position and Reflexivity in Qualitative Research." *Qualitative Research* 15 (2): 219–234.

Biel, Łucja. 2017. "Researching Legal Translation: A Multi-Perspective and Mixed-Method Framework for Legal Translation." *Revista de Llengua i Dret, Journal of Language and Law* 68: 76–88.

Bonner, Ann, and Gerda Tolhurst. 2002. "Insider/Outsider Perspectives of Participant Observation." *Nurse Researcher* 9 (4): 7–19.

Breen, Lauren J. 2007. "The Researcher 'in the Middle': Negotiating the Insider/Outsider Dichotomy." *The Australian Community Psychologist* 19 (1): 163–174.

Chammas, Grace. 2020. "The Insider-Researcher Status: A Challenge for Social Work Practice Research." *The Qualitative Report* 25 (2): 537–552.

Corbin Dwyer, Sonya, and Jennifer L. Buckle. 2009. "The Space Between: On Being an Insider-Outsider in Qualitative Research." *International Journal of Qualitative Methods* 8 (1): 54–63.

Flores, David. 2018. "Standing in the Middle: Insider/Outsider Positionality While Conducting Qualitative Research with Opposing Military Veteran Political Groups." In *Sage Research Methods Cases Part 2*. London: Sage.

Hammersley, Martyn. 1993. "On the Teacher as Researcher." *Educational Action Research* 1 (3): 425–445.

Hammersley, Martyn, and Paul Atkinson. 2007. *Ethnography: Principles in Practice*. 3rd edition. London: Routledge.

Hellawell, David. 2006. "Inside-out: Analysis of the Insider-Outsider Concept as a Heuristic Device to Develop Reflexivity in Students Doing Qualitative Research." *Teaching in Higher Education* 11 (4): 483–494.

Hill, Teresa, and Michael Dao. 2021. "Personal Pasts Become Academic Presents: Engaging Reflexivity and Considering Dual Insider/Outsider Roles in Physical Cultural Fieldwork." *Qualitative Research in Sport, Exercise and Health* 13 (3): 521–535.

Jorgensen, Danny L. 1989. *Participant Observation: A Methodology for Human Studies*. Newbury Park: Sage.

Kanuha, Valli Kalei. 2000. "'Being' Native Versus 'Going Native': Conducting Social Work Research as an Insider." *Social Work* 45 (5): 439–447.

Koch, Tina. 2006. "Establishing Rigour in Qualitative Research: The Decision Trail." *Journal of Advanced Nursing* 53 (1): 91–100.

Koskinen, Kaisa. 2008. *Translating Institutions: An Ethnographic Study of EU Translation*. Manchester: St. Jerome.

Le Gallais, Tricia. 2008. "Wherever I Go There I Am: Reflections on Reflexivity and the Research Stance." *Reflective Practice* 9 (2): 145–155.

Lincoln, Yvonna S., Susan A. Lynham, and Egon G. Guba. 2018. "Paradigmatic Controversies, Contradictions, and Emerging Confluences, Revisited." In *The SAGE Handbook of Qualitative Research*, 5th edition, ed. by Norman K. Denzin, and Yvonna S. Lincoln, 213–263. Los Angeles: Sage.

Lipson, Juliene G. 1984. "Combining Researcher, Clinical and Personal Roles: Enrichment or Confusion?" *Human Organization* 43 (4): 348–352.

Mercer, Justine. 2007. "The Challenges of Insider Research in Educational Institutions: Wielding a Double-edged Sword and Resolving Delicate Dilemmas." *Oxford Review of Education* 33 (1): 1–17.

Merton, Robert K. 1972. "Insiders and Outsiders: A Chapter in the Sociology of Knowledge." *American Journal of Sociology* 78 (1): 9–47.

Punch, Samantha. 2012. "Hidden Struggles of Fieldwork: Exploring the Role and Use of Field Diaries." *Emotion, Space and Society* 5 (2): 86–93.

Saldanha, Gabriela, and Sharon O'Brien. 2014. *Research Methodologies in Translation Studies*. London: Routledge.

Spradley, James P. 1980. *Participant Observation*. New York: Holt, Rinehart and Winston.

Stake, Robert E. 2005. "Qualitative Case Studies." In *The SAGE Handbook of Qualitative Research*, 3rd edition, ed. by Norman K. Denzin, and Yvonna S. Lincoln, 443–466. Thousand Oaks: Sage.

Thomas, Gary. 2011. *How to Do Your Case Study: A Guide for Students and Researchers*. Los Angeles: Sage.

Unluer, Sema. 2012. "Being an Insider Researcher While Conducting Case Study Research." *The Qualitative Report* 17 (29): 1–14. http://nsuworks.nova.edu/tqr/vol17/iss29/2

Yin, Robert K. 1981. "The Case Study as a Serious Research Strategy." *Science Communication* 3 (1): 97–114.

Yu, Chuan. 2020. "Insider, Outsider or Multiplex Persona? Confessions of a Digital Ethnographer's Journey in Translation Studies." *The Journal of Specialised Translation* 34, 9–31.

CHAPTER 6

Practisearcher meets 'non-professionals'
A journey of conducting reflexive translation and interpreting research in an NGO

Vanessa Steinkogler
University of Graz

This chapter discusses the concept of reflexivity, which has increasingly become the focus of research interest in translation and interpreting studies. It is argued that critical reflexive research practices would be particularly beneficial to the field of non-professional interpreting and translation, where so-called non-professional translators and interpreters encounter researchers who are not only translation scholars but also practising translators and/or interpreters themselves. Drawing on experiences from my ethnographic study on interpreting and translation practices in an NGO in Austria, the aim of this chapter is to investigate *boundary work* practices during the fieldwork process. The analysis shows the reciprocal influence between researcher and research participants and how boundaries — if reflected upon — are no obstacle to mutual understanding in fieldwork relationships.

Keywords: ethnographic research, reflexivity, translation practices in NGOs, professional and non-professional interpreting and translation, NPIT, boundary work

1. Introduction

At the heart of ethnographic research is the gaining of rich insights into practices, beliefs and lived experiences through the eyes of a certain group of agents in order to understand the meanings behind them (Hammersley and Atkinson 1983; Koskinen 2008: 36). Alongside the increasingly interdisciplinary nature of translation and interpreting studies (TIS) and the growing focus on agent- and process-oriented approaches in recent years, ethnographic research methods such as interviews, focus groups, participant observations, research diaries and field notes have gained popularity among TIS scholars in the collection, analysis and interpretation of data (see, e.g., Marin-Lacarta and Yu 2023).

https://doi.org/10.1075/btl.165.06ste
Available under the CC BY-NC 4.0 license. © 2025 John Benjamins Publishing Company

Since ethnographic research endeavours are characterised by a high level of personal engagement, they call for a comprehensive critical reflection of the researcher's positionality within their own research projects in order to mitigate possible biases related to the phenomena under study. Contemporary engagements with the concept of (self-)reflexivity are based on the assumption that all research is conditioned by the particular time, place, and context in which the researcher is embedded. Reflexivity includes turning the research process itself into the object of research, revealing preconceived notions and acknowledging the existence of situational dynamics, within which the researcher and the participants jointly produce meaning and knowledge (Soedirgo and Glas 2020:528). Reflexivity has been a part of common research practice in ethnographic studies for decades (cf. Bourdieu and Wacquant 1992; Davies 2008; Denzin and Lincoln 2018; Madison 2019). In TIS, the concept has as yet only rarely been explicitly and systematically applied in empirical studies and hardly been analysed in detail in research reports.

In this chapter, I draw on my experience conducting ethnographic fieldwork in a local office of the Catholic welfare organisation *Caritas Graz-Seckau* in Austria. In this Caritas office, most translation and interpreting practices are performed by multilingual Caritas employees. They are usually categorised as 'non-professional'[1] (Pérez-González and Susam-Saraeva 2012) or 'paraprofessional' (Koskela, Koskinen, and Pilke 2017:466) translators and interpreters as they have no formal TIS training and either translate and interpret in addition to their main job or use translation or interpretation to fulfil their main professional tasks (see also Koskinen, Chapter 1, on the particular importance of field research on paraprofessional T&I). When these translators and interpreters are faced with TIS researchers, who are usually trained and in many cases practising translators and/or interpreters themselves, asymmetrical relationships in terms of education, knowledge, power and status can develop.

All too often, however, the emotional nature of fieldwork as well as the personal and interpersonal dynamics, dilemmas and difficulties remain unaddressed in research narratives. Researchers find themselves navigating their embeddedness in personal, social, cultural, political and academic contexts as well as research traditions that dictate the need to fulfil the expectation of presenting a

---

1. Terminology surrounding the concept of professionalism can be problematic since it is not only extremely simplifying but also has a divisive and evaluative character (see, e.g., Grbić 2023a). When using the terms 'professional' and 'non-professional' in this chapter, these categorisations do not reflect my personal opinion but are classifications from TIS research or classifications made by the research participants.

tidy research account. The latter may lead to a pressure of hiding the sometimes non-linear, messy, and unpredictable ways in which research has evolved.

In this chapter, the concept of reflexivity is used to emphasise the idea that all knowledge is socially co-constructed, recognising that researchers are part of the field they study. This implies that their personal histories, memories and emotions play a crucial part in framing the entire research process (Davies 2008; Denzin and Lincoln 2018). It is therefore the aim of this chapter to critically reflect on my entire fieldwork process; from entering the field and establishing contact with potential research participants, to positioning myself within the field, the perceptions of my research persona and, finally, leaving the field under study. Particular focus is placed on the different roles ascribed to and taken up by myself, in particular my dual role as researcher and practising translator, and the reciprocal influence between myself as a researcher and the participants. As roles are linked to expectations and therefore inherently define symbolic boundaries, I analyse the different types of *boundary work* both the participants of my study and I as a researcher engaged in and I retrace how boundaries are dealt with (Gieryn 1983, 1999).

In what follows, I first provide a short description of my research project and address the aspects of the research process that are usually hidden, deliberately or unconsciously. I then discuss the concept of reflexivity and reflect on my own experiences and positionality in my research study in the field of non-professional interpreting and translation (NPIT). This field calls for a comprehensive reflexive approach given its general invisibility, vulnerable agents, and strong power imbalances between the agents in the field as well as between the researcher and the participants. The chapter concludes by drawing conclusions for further research in the field of NPIT.

2. Setting the scene: Data and methodology

2.1 Professionals, multiprofessionals and everyone in between

The data presented in this chapter is based on a research project on written and spoken translation practices as well as related perception and action patterns in non-governmental organisations (NGOs). Being acquainted with some of the specifics of this research project is crucial to understand under which circumstances and against what background the data referred to in this chapter was gathered. The project focuses on the Catholic welfare organisation Caritas Graz-Seckau in Austria, where translation and interpreting practices are performed in numerous contexts and organisational departments by various agents with different professional backgrounds. This local Caritas office employs a small number of 'professional' interpreters, but mostly multilingual Caritas employees are responsible for language mediation, hence they act as so-called paraprofessionals or multiprofessionals (Pym 1998), who are expected to provide translation services in addition to their primary work activities.

Multilingual Caritas employees apply their language skills in their daily work. Besides translating leaflets, documents and reports as well as performing sight translations, they mostly provide interpreting between their Caritas colleagues and clients or use their first or second language to communicate directly with their clients. The aim of this research project is to analyse different perceptions of translation professionalism and their influence on translators and interpreters, their practices, and their interactions with and perceptions of each other.

At a methodological level, the study is based on an ethnographic qualitative approach consisting of semi-structured interviews, participant observation, a field journal documenting the research process and informal on-site conversations with the agents in the field (Phillippi and Lauderdale 2018; Breuer, Muckel, and Dieris 2019). In this study, I interviewed people who act as interpreters and translators at Caritas, heads of organisational areas who are responsible for the coordination of translational matters, and employees who are not able to communicate with clients due to language barriers and therefore rely on interpreting for their counselling sessions. In total, I carried out 40 interviews from July 2020 to April 2023 in 16 different organisational areas at Caritas. Ideally, it would have been insightful to conduct observations in all those areas, but in view of the sensitivity of many situations, confidentiality issues, and sometimes the participants' reluctance, this data gathering method was feasible only in one organisational area.

2.2 Methodological approach for the chapter

As indicated above, research interactions in the field are always shaped by the personal, conceptual and theoretical lenses of researchers and especially in NPIT, hierarchical imbalances between researchers and participants are apparent when 'non-professionals' interact with trained TIS researchers. This particular profile of TIS scholars is linked not only with benefits such as bridging the professional-academic divide and enabling easier data access (Mellinger 2020: 96) but can also represent a potential challenge in terms of implicit biases (e.g., specific beliefs internalised through education, professional norms etc.). The concept of the so-called "practisearcher" (Gile 1995) implies that scholars often have a prior practical knowledge of the field they study. This circumstance may also entail that current or former colleagues are sources for data collection and in some cases, the researchers' access to the data may have been established only because of their collegial relationship with the participants (Tiselius 2019:748).

The concept of *boundary work* is used in this chapter to analyse how and what boundaries between myself as a researcher and the agents under study are drawn, maintained, blurred, consolidated, shifted and dissolved. Thomas F. Gieryn coined the term *boundary work* in 1983 to describe practices of scientists used to attribute certain qualities to themselves and their methods in order to draw a demarcation between science and non-science. Based on his empirical research, he identifies different reasons why boundaries are established: to expand authority over areas that are claimed by other professionals, to monopolise authority within a specific field and exclude potentially competing professionals, and to protect authority and avoid intervening from other professionals (Gieryn 1983:791–792). Following Gieryn's discussions, Lamont (1992) adopts the concept of *boundary work* to explore how concepts such as gender, nationhood, profession, religion or ideology are used in the construction of societies and social classes and eventually result in the reproduction of inequality. She describes boundaries as "the types of lines that individuals draw when they categorize people" (Lamont 1992:1). On the basis of her data, Lamont extracts three types of boundaries: moral, cultural and socioeconomic. Moral boundaries are based on moral standards such as honesty, integrity, work ethic and solidarity for others. People draw moral boundaries when they aspire to demarcate themselves from others who they believe have lower moral values, are dishonest or selfish. Socioeconomic boundaries are drawn on the basis of assessments regarding a person's social position, which manifests itself in wealth, power and professional success. Specifically, this means that influence, assets or (material) resources are viewed as the primary basis for judgment. Lastly, cultural boundaries refer to qualities such as formal education, intelligence, and sophistication (Lamont 1992:4) and hence emphasise the importance of cultural attainment. In the field of TIS, Grbić (2010, 2023b) encouraged the discussion of boundary practices in her study of professionalisation processes in sign language interpreting in Austria. She argues that the concept of *boundary work* is particularly well suited for TIS, which itself operates on disciplinary boundaries reflected in the many paradigm shifts and turns (Grbić and Kujamäki 2019:116). In the present chapter, the combination of Gieryn's original explanations of the boundary concept and Lamont's extension serve to analyse the relational dynamics between myself as the researcher and the participants.

3. The ethnographic self

As mentioned at the outset of this chapter, there has recently been an increased focus on ethnographic research endeavours within TIS. Defining the concept of ethnography is certainly no straightforward task, but it commonly describes the process of collecting data through fieldwork methods that can include interviews, focus groups, participant observations, research diaries and field notes. Ethnographic researchers immerse themselves as participants and observers in the daily lives of those being studied (Davies 2008: 5). The aim is to understand certain aspects of social lives, relations and interactions, which contains investigating people's actions, viewpoints and beliefs (Hammersley and Atkinson 1983: 3). With a shift in interest from texts to practices, such ethnographic methods have also been incorporated into the repertoire of TIS research methodology, creating a wide ethnographic landscape and an immense diversity of perspectives and settings such as institutional translation (Koskinen 2008), workplace practices in translation companies (Hubscher-Davidson 2011; Ehrensberger-Dow 2014; Milošević and Risku 2020) or conference interpreting in EU institutions (Duflou 2016), to name but a few.[2] Among ethnographic research projects in TIS, there is a growing body of studies whose epistemological claim is not exclusively based on the data gathered but in particular on self-reflective processes (see, e.g., Koskinen 2008; Tipton 2008; Kadiu 2019; Yu 2020).

3.1 'Tales of the field': Reflexivity in qualitative research

It was not until the late twentieth century that scholars of social sciences considered it to be increasingly naïve to assume that research is conducted free of any personal opinions, values and interests. In anthropology and field-based ethnographic research, this critique led to the so-called 'crisis of representation' that emerged against the backdrop that Western scholarship could no longer ignore its role in producing and reproducing colonial and postcolonial power inequalities and oppression (Marcus and Fischer 1986: x). The anthropological discourse at that time revolved around questions of representation of cultures in ethnographic writings, the legitimation of interpretations, and ethnographic authority (Geertz 1973; Clifford 1983). These issues created an awareness for the researcher's moral and ethical duty to represent the multiple voices involved in research and incorporate "tales of the field" (Van Maanen 1988: xiii) into research accounts.

---

2. For a recent overview of ethnographic research projects in TIS see Milošević and Risku (2020).

Against this background, a new ethnographic methodology has been developed which focuses on the researcher's critical self-examination and methodological self-consciousness. The notion of reflexivity as a theoretical concept and methodological strategy assumes that any empirical data that is collected, analysed, and incorporated into a research text is situated and produced in a particular context and from a certain position (Bourdieu and Wacquant 1992; Davies 2008; Denzin and Lincoln 2018; Madison 2019). Reflexive practices aim to make evident how political, cultural, perceptual, intersubjective and disciplinary circumstances can influence the entire research process in an effort to increase credibility and transparency (Davies 2008). This concept has shifted the issue of inevitable and uncontrollable subjectivity in research from a dilemma to a moral and ethical question (Finlay and Gough 2008) and has been focused on and conceptualised from different angles in numerous disciplines and research areas.

In reflective qualitative research, it is assumed that "[a]ll researchers are to some degree connected to, or part of, the object of their research" (Davies 2008:3). Reflexivity can therefore be understood as "a turning back on oneself, a process of self-reference" (Davies 2008:4). It reveals the impossibility of an objective position, as throughout the entire research process the researcher is involved in deciding on what questions to ask, what to observe, what to record and note down, what to ignore and how to describe and interpret what has been observed. Thus, a key assumption underlying reflexive qualitative research is the idea that researchers are not able to genuinely reproduce or represent lived experiences. As Denzin and Lincoln suggest,

> there is no clear window into the inner life of an individual. Any gaze is always filtered through the lenses of language, gender, social class, race, and ethnicity. There are no objective observations, only observations socially situated in the worlds of the observer and the observed.   (Denzin and Lincoln 2018:12)

Especially in critical ethnography, with its increased sensitivity to issues of power and agency, reflexive research practices are an integral part of fieldwork (Madison 2019). Critical ethnography aims at designing democratic research processes in which both the researcher and the participants have an equal say in the production of knowledge. Reflexivity, according to Madison, requires the researcher to take on a moral and ethical responsibility to challenge existing social structures, political inequalities and social power asymmetries in the field. Additionally, a reflexive research approach should counterbalance the 'exploitative' character of fieldwork by addressing issues such as the general imbalance and one-sided researcher-informant relationship, questions regarding participant selection, beneficiaries of the study, risks of the research outcome for the participants, knowledge claims or the selection, interpretation and representation of data (Madison

2019: 5–7). Bourdieu and Wacquant (1992) shift the interest from the individual researcher to the scientific field as a whole and focus on the collective rather than the individualistic nature of reflexivity. In what Bourdieu and Wacquant (1992: 36) call "epistemic reflexivity", the aim is to address not individual biases but unconscious scientific practices of the entire research field that can be attributed, e.g., to presuppositions built into methods of analysis or concepts and practical research activities such as data clearing methods.

Most social scientists and anthropologists share a common understanding about the basic framework of reflexivity and agree on its importance in the academic field. Indeed, *being* reflexive has become a marker of conscious research practice throughout the social sciences. Discussions about the concept often remain, nevertheless, normative and theoretical, and the actual implementation of reflexivity in research practice is rarely discussed, which is why "in practice, *doing* reflexivity is challenging" (Soedirgo and Glas 2020: 528, original emphasis).

3.2 Towards reflexivity in TIS

In TIS, the concept of reflexivity has been discussed both from the perspective of researchers when conducting empirical studies (see, e.g., Pym 1998; Tymoczko 2002; Koskinen 2008; Yu 2020) and from the perspective of interpreters and translators when performing their language practices (see, e.g., Tipton 2008; Kadiu 2019). Since TIS research is often conducted by practising translators and/ or interpreters,[3] these kinds of studies require a particular reflection with respect to the positionality of the researcher (Mellinger 2020: 95–96). One of the first TIS scholars to touch upon reflexive research practices is Pym (1998), who, in his study on translation history, addresses his personal research interests and maintains that "it often helps to ask why you're already looking in one direction rather than another" (Pym 1998: 30). Similarly, Tymoczko (2002) focuses on the researchers' social positioning and their influence on the research programme. She argues that TIS

> may be at an advantage compared to many fields ... because translation studies routinely involve not just inquiry but meta-inquiry [of the intellectual tools of models, theories and paradigms] in the course of research. Hence the field itself encourages the interrogation of frames of reference, including those of the researcher potentially making one's biases more perceptible and making it more possible to enlarge one's frame of reference.   (2002: 22–23)

---

3. Extensive results on the professional background of TIS scholars can be found in Torres-Simón and Pym (2016).

In her research on the Finnish translation unit at the European Commission, Koskinen (2006, 2008) discusses the extent to which ethnographic methods are useful for analysing the field of professional translation and the roles and positions of translators in this field. Against the background that translation scholars who are or have been practising translators and/or interpreters themselves often focus their analysis on a profession, an activity or a field that they themselves are or were part of at some point, Koskinen notes that this dual role as researchers on the one hand and practitioners on the other might lead to "split loyalties" (Koskinen 2008:9). She refers to the problematic distinction between emic and etic or insider and outsider perspectives in ethnography, which is inevitably dissolved when doing research in TIS since "the dividing line is located inside you" (2008:55). Koskinen claims that a transparent research approach enables to make this ambiguity in the researcher position visible and to accept paradoxes, inconsistencies and ambivalences in the data. In the field of interpreting, Tiselius (2019) makes similar observations. Drawing on Gile's concept of 'practisearcher', she argues that this duality forces TIS researchers to "navigate two ethical systems, that of interpreting and that of research" (2019:748), which may result in conflicting positions. In a similar vein, Mellinger (2020) discusses the TIS researchers' distinctive double profile in the context of observational and participatory research in public service interpreting. Thanks to their double role, researchers can "serve as a positive link between the academy, the profession, and consumers of interpreting services" (2020:104) in that they have the agency to help establish codes of ethics in the practice field or raise awareness among the scientific community and society of settings that are in need of interpreting services.

A methodological approach to reflexivity in research on NPIT is provided in the study by Lomeña Galiano (2020). The starting point of her study is the challenge of accessing 'non-professional' interpreters and translators in public service settings. As pointed out by Lomeña Galiano, members of this group and their activities are often unknown to outsiders, or they deliberately keep a low profile because of presumed negative reactions and perceptions. As a result, a major difficulty in the NPIT research field is identifying those very agents practising in the field in the first place; even if identified, they are often reluctant to participate in studies, which has led Lomeña Galiano to conceptualise them as a 'hidden population'. She draws on the notions of reflexivity and rapport between the researcher and research participants and proposes guidelines for the phases of field access and participant recruitment (Lomeña Galiano 2020:81).

One of the most recent discussions of the concept of reflexivity in the field of TIS can be found in Tesseur (2022), who reflects on her intentions with regard to conducting research in international NGOs. Rather than only describing and understanding language and translation policies, Tesseur takes on an empowering research stance and attempts to influence the organisations she collaborated with in order to promote more inclusive translation practices. By being reflective of her own linguistic practices and acknowledging her position as a researcher driven by principles of activism and social justice, her ultimate aim is to ensure research integrity.

As indicated above, the concept of reflexivity has gradually gained ever more popularity in TIS studies in recent years, which is reflected in growing literature on this aspect (see also Hokkanen, Chapter 4; Staudinger, Chapter 5; Davier, Chapter 7; Todorova, Chapter 14, this volume). It is especially in NPIT that complex relational dynamics come into play and incorporating reflective practices becomes crucial.

4. About untold stories of the field

In what follows, I use the theoretical understanding of reflexivity combined with the concept of *boundary work* to critically reflect on the fieldwork process in my research project. I analyse the various types and manifestations of boundaries — socioeconomic, moral and cultural — between me in my roles as researcher and practising translator and the participants.

4.1 Entering and positioning myself in the field

Gaining access to the desired research site or setting often poses one of the greatest challenges in ethnographic research endeavours. Even before gathering data, possible boundaries can become visible. This is especially the case in the present study, where relatively little was known about the field under study prior to the fieldwork and unchallenged boundaries existed between the field of practice and the field of academia. In this context, existing cultural boundaries — that relate to agendas, understandings, approaches and interests — between these two fields were particularly noticeable, raising a number of questions on both sides: Do researchers and practitioners in the field have the same concepts of translation and interpreting? What do researchers and research participants focus on, what research outcome do they hope for and do those interests and expectations coincide? What assumptions does research make about practice and vice versa? Do research-based concepts match actual translation activities in the field? How do scholars and practitioners interact with each other?

The organisation under study is characterised by a strict hierarchical structure which is why permission to enter the field had to be obtained from the management level. Subsequently, I was assigned a Caritas employee as a gatekeeper who, due to his role in the organisation, had a good overview, supposedly knew of all the areas at Caritas that rely on interpreting and translation and whom I expected to familiarise me with the organisation and establish contacts with relevant organisational areas. However, neither this gatekeeper nor any other person in the areas I studied could be identified as having comprehensive knowledge of translation activities in the organisation. Rather, I discovered gradually and often through informal on-site conversations where and when multilingual communication was required.

Before I even conducted actual fieldwork, vertical *boundary work* within the organisation became apparent. I had to go through a hierarchical process from top to bottom, which consequently meant that the perception of my persona was shaped by the way the organisation introduced me to potential research participants. Since the introduction particularly highlighted my role as a researcher and university associate, a certain image of me was created and, above all, socioeconomic and cultural boundaries with regard to our social positions and our educational and professional backgrounds were drawn up or reinforced.

Since I interacted with agents of different levels of professionalism and hierarchical positions, different kinds of boundaries became visible on different levels. Throughout the fieldwork, I presented various selves and emphasised certain aspects of my research depending on who I interacted with, in order to remain approachable and credible. With the heads of departments that regularly rely on translation activities, I discussed the peculiarity of the organisation Caritas as a research object due to its multilingual working environment as well as the relevance and the positive outcomes of research in this field not only for TIS but also for the organisation itself. I aimed to present myself as being capable of bridging the divide between academia and the profession and contributing to a knowledge exchange that can benefit the training of community interpreters. In this case, *boundary work* practices that focused on cultural characteristics such as my education and professional background were important in order to convince the organisation that I have expertise that they do not possess and thereby can add valuable insights.

Identifying and engaging with interpreters and translators as research participants and in particular the hidden population of 'non-professionals' called for a different, particularly sensitive approach, not least because I was aware that I most likely would be confronted with some degree of suspicion. It is often the case that trained practitioners and researchers alike consider 'non-professional' interpreters and translators as a threat to the reputation of the translating profession (Grbić and Kujamäki 2019: 127) and my research project was not intended to come across as yet another measure to criticise them. Thus, I also had to address past and established *boundary work* around the categorisations 'professional' and 'non-professional'. A reflective approach to this dichotomy was an important aspect to avoid excluding agents as research participants simply because they did not fulfil certain criteria concerning their professional background or employment relationship. The first conversations with the agents in the field showed that they had also internalised these categorisations. Such symbolic boundaries became evident, for example, in the fact that multilingual Caritas staff without translation training would never refer to themselves as translators or to their mediating practices as translating and interpreting. I paid great attention to presenting myself as someone who empathises with the possible stresses and strains that they face. I emphasised that I was not aiming to evaluate the quality of interpreting and translation, but rather to illustrate the diversity of such language mediation activities in humanitarian aid organisations. This implied pointing out shared interests in advancing 'non-professional' interpreting and translation, discussing similarities in our cultural and moral standing as well as openly addressing established boundaries. Moreover, it was crucial to demonstrate that I am willing to learn and understand the working reality of translation and interpreting in refugee and humanitarian contexts and that I am not "stuck in an ivory tower at university" (Pole and Hillyard 2016: 41).

In general, the reactions to my research requests differed greatly. As will be shown in the following section, these different field relationships as well as perceptions, roles and positionings have manifested in differences in the scope of data collection.

4.2 Being in the field: Relationships and perceptions

In the process of data collection, researchers develop relationships with their research participants that can shift during the research project and may range from being distant, disengaged and impersonal to close, cooperative and amicable. Such relationships are integral to the disclosure of information and the outcome of the research project. They involve complex role negotiations, reflections on participant recruitment, power dynamics, rapport building as well as external and self-perceptions.

In ethnographic field studies, the so-called insider/outsider debate has long prevailed. Discussions have focused on whether researchers should be "members of specified groups and collectivities or occupants of specified social statuses" (Merton 1972: 21) in order to be capable of fully understanding the group they are studying or whether having an outsider status enables researchers to challenge prevailing assumptions and extend understanding. More recently, however, scholars have emphasised the fluctuating nature of this binary-represented position. They argue that the researchers' positionality can rather be understood as "a continuum with multiple dimensions, and that all researchers constantly move back and forth along a number of axes" (Mercer 2007:1). Similarly, field interactions with research participants as well as the roles and positions that I took on evolved and changed over the course of my research project. For example, I entered the field feeling like a clueless stranger. In the early stages of my fieldwork, I became increasingly aware of the socioeconomic boundaries I felt between myself and the research participants and of my feelings of inappropriateness at investigating a migration-related topic as a Western researcher who has never migrated herself. Since I neither have a migration background nor was familiar with the daily work of employees of humanitarian aid organisations, I was afraid of being unable to relate to the majority of the research participants and of being seen as a hypocritical imposter. Boundary negotiation in this context included processes of understanding the research participants' perspectives in a relational way. Who are they in relation to me? In relation to other research participants? How do we differ? How can we reach a mutual understanding amidst our differences?

As previously indicated, it was primarily the research interactions with those interpreters and translators who provided translation services without specific training and in addition to their main activities in the area of social work that required special sensitivity. I had to be conscious of potential social power asymmetries as well as socioeconomic and cultural boundaries between myself and some of the research participants, who would attribute a double superiority to me. On the one hand, I took on the role as a researcher and, on the other, I was also a member of the 'privileged' group of 'professional' interpreters and translators. Although it should be noted that, strictly speaking, I had only undergone training in the field of translation, not interpreting. However, not all agents in the field without translator and/or interpreter training had concerns about me. Some of those agents quickly warmed up to me as an interested learner, allowed me to gain personal insights into their daily working routines and did not shy away from sharing their frustrations, fears and negative experiences regarding their translation and interpreting practices. On the contrary, with many of them I felt that they appreciated someone showing interest in their usually invisible tasks.

Unsurprisingly, those Caritas interpreters and translators who had undergone translation training often placed me in the role of confidant or ally, which was reinforced by the fact that I was acquainted with a few of them from my studies at a department of TIS. Although our similar professional and/or educational background made it easier to convince these agents to participate in my research project, these circumstances provided a potential for boundary violations by research participants and led to the interviews often digressing from the main research topic and developing into an informal conversation between two old acquaintances. Moreover, in the interviews with 'professional' translators and interpreters, the roles of interviewer and interviewee alternated on several occasions and I myself was asked almost as many questions that even went beyond the research project. Some study participants were enthusiastic about developing a friendly relationship, and my interest in their work life experiences was misinterpreted for friendship. When I got the impression that the boundary between professional and private was blurred, I felt compelled to draw attention to the research-based nature of our relationship as well as our different social positions and roles as researcher and participants. By steering our interactions and relationships, I therefore consolidated the socioeconomic boundaries between us. It was also this group that made several off-the-record remarks and asked me to keep certain information between us (I have of course complied with this request), hence shifting the moral boundaries in terms of solidarity in such a way that put us on the same side. This was especially true when interviewees were telling me about incidents in which they did not behave according to the 'TIS textbook' but felt that a different behaviour was more appropriate. In such moments, the conversations almost took on a confessional character.

In some situations, my perceived role as a confidant actually led me to take on the role of a counsellor. This was especially noticeable in the conversations in which very personal or sensitive issues were shared. Not only was I trusted with very intimate information, but I was even asked for advice and my opinion on whether I felt that interviewees were acting correctly as interpreters.

Those last examples in particular indicate the ethical issues that emerge with close and collegial researcher and research participant relationships. Participants who showed great confidence in me were more likely to disclose very personal accounts while simultaneously and unconsciously shifting and blurring the boundaries between us and reinforcing the already one-sided researcher-informant relationship. While I was aware that building rapport and creating a safe atmosphere for participants is vital to gain research insights, at the same time I was confronted with the constraints of my researcher role. Not only did I struggle with how to respond to deeply emotional revelations and sometimes even felt obliged to 'return the favour' by opening up myself, I also felt a strong ethical responsibility. After all, research ownership and authority lay in my hands, and I would be the one to share those intimate matters with the scientific community, possibly leading to feelings of betrayal or disloyalty on the part of the research participants.[4] However, contrary to what I initially assumed, it is not only researchers who have power, but also participants. Researchers are of course the ones who set the parameters of the study, but it is mostly the participants

---

4. For a detailed discussion on the ethical responsibility in TIS research see Mellinger and Baer (2020).

who direct the fieldwork process and determine the interpersonal relationships on which fieldwork is dependent. Additionally, some participants seemed to consider me as a kind of resource and developed high expectations for the research findings in terms of positive impact on their daily work. This made it even more important to mark the boundaries of my role as a researcher and clarify the limitations and the scope of my research project.

The research experience described above shows that my perceived role in the field under study was not static but subject to ongoing change from one person to another, from one interaction to another, and even from one conversation topic to another. I had to juggle multiple roles and selves throughout my project and had to decide when to act as a researcher and when to (additionally) take on the role of ally, problem solver, trained translator, ethicist or advocate, which in turn led to shifting boundaries between me and the research participants.

4.3 Exiting the field and leaving behind footprints

During my fieldwork activities, it quickly became evident how deeply involved I would become in the very processes and practices that I was studying. Whether intentionally or not, whether consciously or not, at no point during my research project was I a mere observer, but rather a participant in and even co-creator of the field, and, most importantly, an agent that facilitated bridging boundaries between the research field and the field of practice, between different concepts of translation and interpreting, and between the established categories of 'non-professional' and 'professional'.

From the interviews and participant observation in the field, I became aware that within Caritas there is relatively little to no communication and exchange of experiences between interpreters and translators. These mostly cultural boundaries, as indicated by the different employment relationships as well as educational and professional backgrounds, existed both across and within organisational areas as well as across different levels of translational professionalism. For multilingual Caritas employees, interpreting and translating was simply part of their employment profile and often these tasks were perceived not to be worth talking about with their colleagues. Those interpreters and translators who had had specific training were employed on a freelance basis and only stayed in the various Caritas facilities for the duration of their appointments, which is why they hardly ever met their translation and interpreting colleagues. After my first few visits to the organisation, however, I noticed increased communication between Caritas staff. In the later interviews, I was surprised to discover that several interviewees had already been informed about some of the research-related topics by colleagues I had already spoken to or accompanied in their work. In addition, during my repeated visits I often happened to meet participants who had already been interviewed, and we talked about the progress of my study. Some of them admitted that since our conversation they became more aware of certain action patterns in their daily interpreting and translation practices. But it was not only the boundaries within the organisation that could be dissolved at least to some extent. Since the beginning of my research project, the boundaries between Caritas and our department at the university became more permeable with Caritas social workers visiting interpreting classes to foster knowledge exchange.

Finally, the way in which I exited the study site was especially delicate to deal with since by the end of my research stay concerns of the study participants became more apparent. My approaching exit of the organisation caused participants to reassess their comments and behaviour and several communicated their fear of how I would represent them. Moreover, since I was their only chance to talk openly about frustrations, fears and experiences, some suggested staying in contact after the fieldwork process had ended. These circumstances caused me to keep undertaking field research for longer than planned and almost out of a sense of duty, even though I noticed that the data I was gathering was no longer adding new insights.

5. Concluding remarks

It is especially in the context of NGOs that, due to limited financial resources, trained translators and interpreters are scarce and so-called 'non-professionals' or 'paraprofessionals' have to provide translation and interpreting practices. In this chapter, I have presented a reflexive analysis of my experience conducting ethnographic research in an Austrian local office of Caritas. My reflections covered the entire fieldwork process starting with entering the field and establishing contact with potential participants, positioning myself in the field, the perceptions of my research persona, the roles I was ascribed and took on and, finally, the impact of my research practice on the field. The aim was to shed light on those aspects in ethnographic research endeavours in TIS that are usually not included into research accounts and remain hidden not only from the readership, but often from the researchers themselves.

The results of the analysis show that in order to gain access to the research site, it was crucial to present and play out a number of different selves to the agents with whom I have come into contact. This was supposed to help lay the foundation for fruitful and mutually beneficial fieldwork relationships, to establish rapport and to build trust. Once access to the field was established, I was assigned and took on various roles that ranged from an ignorant university member to a 'professional' translator, from an interested learner and a trusting confidant to a counsellor. These different perceptions, presuppositions and attributions had significant implications for the data collection and the extent to which insights were provided. Moreover, as I repeatedly returned to the same Caritas facilities in the course of my research activities and frequently chanced to meet field agents who had already participated in my study, I was able to identify how my physical presence in the field, our conversations, and interactions have left an imprint, thus altering the very field of study.

This chapter analysed *boundary work* practices (Gieryn 1983) that I as a researcher and the participants performed implicitly and explicitly, consciously and unconsciously for navigating interpersonal fieldwork relationships. I illustrated how the ambiguity and flexibility of boundaries surrounding researchers and research participants become a paramount part of the research process. Researchers and participants use *boundary work* to navigate similarities and differences, closeness and distance, and come to understand each other both as individuals as well as representatives of social categories. Analysing how and why boundaries are established, negotiated, demolished or shifted helps to understand researcher-participant relationships and also enables us to do research with agents we cannot relate to, we disagree with or we even dislike, without this being considered an obstacle to mutual understanding. In the present study it became evident that, especially in the research field of NPIT, interpersonal research relationships and associated role assignments, perceptions and categorisations are a central element. This makes it essential to incorporate reflexivity into the research practice.

However, the analysis in this chapter has its limitations. While it focused on incorporating the concept of reflexivity in the fieldwork process and its direct aftermath, it can also be applied at an earlier or later stage in empirically based studies, e.g., in the selection of the research topic, the formulation of the hypothesis, the choice of the method of data collection or the interpretation and analysis of data. More research studies applying reflexivity as an analytical tool are needed in order to contribute to a critical production of scientific knowledge, i.e., generating research that is not only rigorous and methodologically sound but also ethically grounded and inclusive of diverse perspectives.

References

Bourdieu, Pierre, and Loïc J. D. Wacquant. 1992. *An Invitation to Reflexive Sociology.* Chicago: University of Chicago Press.

Breuer, Franz, Petra Muckel, and Barbara Dieris. 2019. *Reflexive Grounded Theory: Eine Einführung für die Forschungspraxis* [*Reflexive Grounded Theory: An Introduction for Research Practice*], 4th edition. Wiesbaden: Springer VS.

Clifford, James. 1983. "On Ethnographic Authority." *Representations* 2: 118–146.

Davies, Charlotte Aull. 2008. *Reflexive Ethnography: A Guide to Researching Selves and Others*, 2nd edition. London: Routledge.

Denzin, Norman K., and Yvonna S. Lincoln. 2018. "Introduction. Entering the Field of Qualitative Research." In *The Sage Handbook of Qualitative Research*, 5th edition, ed. by Yvonna S. Lincoln, and Norman K. Denzin, 1–17. Thousand Oaks: Sage.

Duflou, Veerle. 2016. *Be(com)ing a Conference Interpreter: An Ethnography of EU Interpreters as a Professional Community*. Amsterdam & Philadelphia: John Benjamins.

Ehrensberger-Dow, Maureen. 2014. "Challenges of Translation Process Research at the Workplace." *MonTI Special Issue 1 — Minding Translation*: 355–383.

Finlay, Linda, and Brendan Gough. 2008. *Reflexivity: A Practical Guide for Researchers in Health and Social Sciences*. Oxford: Blackwell.

Geertz, Clifford. 1973. *The Interpretation of Cultures. Selected Essays by Clifford Geertz*. New York: Basic Books.

Gieryn, Thomas F. 1983. "Boundary-Work and the Demarcation of Science from Non-Science. Strains and Interests in Professional Ideologies of Scientists." *American Sociological Association* 48 (6): 781–795.

Gieryn, Thomas F. 1999. *Cultural Boundaries of Science: Credibility on the Line*. Chicago & London: University of Chicago Press.

Gile, Daniel. 1995. "Interpretation Research: A New Impetus." *Hermes: Journal of Linguistics* 14: 15–31.

Grbić, Nadja. 2010. "'Boundary Work' as a Concept for Studying Professionalization Processes in the Interpreting Field." *Translation and Interpreting Studies* 5 (1): 109–123.

Grbić, Nadja. 2023a. "Who is an Interpreter? Introducing a Flexible Map of Translation and Interpreting Phenomena." In *Introducing New Hypertexts on Interpreting (Studies)*, ed. by Cornelia Zwischenberger, Karin Reithofer, and Sylvi Rennert, 147–166. Amsterdam & Philadelphia: John Benjamins.

Grbić, Nadja. 2023b. *Gebärdensprachdolmetschen als Beruf. Professionalisierung als Grenzziehungsarbeit. Eine historische Fallstudie in Österreich* [*Sign Language Interpreting as a Profession. Professionalisation as Boundary Work. A Historical Case Study in Austria*]. Bielefeld: transcript.

Grbić, Nadja, and Pekka Kujamäki. 2019. "Professional vs Non-Professional? How Boundary Work Shapes Research Agendas in Translation and Interpreting Studies." In *Moving Boundaries in Translation Studies*, ed. by Helle V. Dam, Matilde Nisbeth Brøgger, and Karen Korning Zethsen, 113–131. London: Taylor & Francis.

Hammersley, Martyn, and Paul Atkinson. 1983. *Ethnography. Principles in Practice*. London & New York: Tavistock Publications.

Hubscher-Davidson, Severine. 2011. "A Discussion of Ethnographic Research Methods and Their Relevance for Translation Process Research." *Across Languages and Cultures* 12 (1): 1–18.

Kadiu, Silvia. 2019. *Reflexive Translation Studies: Translation as Critical Reflection*. London: UCL Press.

Koskela, Merja, Kaisa Koskinen, and Nina Pilke. 2017. "Bilingual Formal Meeting as a Context of Translatoriality." *Target* 29 (3): 464–485.

Koskinen, Kaisa. 2006. "Going into the Field: Ethnographic Methods in Translation Studies." In *Übersetzen — Translating — Traduire: Towards a 'Social Turn'?*, ed. by Michaela Wolf, 109–118. Münster, Hamburg, Berlin, Wien & London: LIT-Verlag.

Koskinen, Kaisa. 2008. *Translating Institutions: An Ethnographic Study of EU Translation.* Manchester: St. Jerome.

Lamont, Michèle. 1992. *Money, Morals, and Manners: The Culture of the French and American Upper-Middle Class.* Chicago: The University of Chicago Press.

Lomeña Galiano, María. 2020. "Finding Hidden Populations in the Field of Translating and Interpreting: A Methodological Model for Improving Access to Non-Professional Translators and Interpreters Working in Public Service Settings." *FITISPos International Journal* 7 (1): 72–91.

Madison, D. Soyini. 2019. *Critical Ethnography: Method, Ethics and Performance*, 3rd edition. Los Angeles: Sage.

Marcus, George E. E., and Michael M. J. Fischer. 1986. *Anthropology as Cultural Critique.* Chicago: Chicago University Press.

Marin-Lacarta, Maialen, and Chuan Yu (eds). 2023. "Ethnographic Research in Translation and Interpreting Studies." Special Issue, *The Translator* 29 (2).

Mellinger, Christopher D. 2020. "Positionality in Public Service Interpreting Research." *FITISPos International Journal* 7 (1): 92–109.

Mellinger, Christopher D., and Brian James Baer. 2020. "Research Ethics in Translation and Interpreting Studies." In *The Routledge Handbook of Translation and Ethics*, ed. by Kaisa Koskinen, and Nike K. Pokorn, 365–380. London & New York: Routledge.

Mercer, Justine. 2007. "The Challenges of Insider Research in Educational Institutions: Wielding a Double-Edged Sword and Resolving Delicate Dilemmas." *Oxford Review of Education* 33: 1–17.

Merton, Robert K. 1972. "Insiders and Outsiders: A Chapter in the Sociology of Knowledge." *American Journal of Sociology* 78 (1): 9–47.

Milošević, Jelena, and Hanna Risku. 2020. "Situated Cognition and the Ethnographic Study of Translation Processes: Translation Scholars as Outsiders, Consultants and Passionate Participants." *Linguistica Antverpiensia* 19: 111–131.

Pérez-González, Luis, and Şebnem Susam-Saraeva. 2012. "Non-Professionals Translating and Interpreting. Participatory and Engaged Perspectives." *The Translator* 18 (2): 149–165.

Phillippi, Julia, and Jane Lauderdale. 2018. "A Guide to Field Notes for Qualitative Research: Context and Conversation." *Qualitative Health Research* 28 (3): 381–388.

Pole, Christopher, and Sam Hillyard. 2016. *Doing Fieldwork.* London: Sage.

Pym, Anthony. 1998. *Method in Translation History.* Manchester: St. Jerome.

Soedirgo, Jessica, and Aarie Glas. 2020. "Toward Active Reflexivity: Positionality and Practice in the Production of Knowledge." *PS: Political Science & Politics* 53 (3): 527–531.

Tesseur, Wine. 2022. *Translation as Social Justice. Translation Policies and Practices in Non-Governmental Organisations.* New York: Routledge.

Tipton, Rebecca. 2008. "Reflexivity and the Social Construction of Identity in Interpreter-Mediated Asylum Interviews." *The Translator* 14 (1): 1–19.

Tiselius, Elisabet. 2019. "The (Un-)Ethical Interpreting Researcher: Ethics, Voice and Discretionary Power in Interpreting Research." *Perspectives* 27 (5): 747–760.

Torres-Simón, Esther, and Anthony Pym. 2016. "The Professional Backgrounds of Translation Scholars. Report on a Survey." *Target* 28 (1): 110–131.

Tymoczko, Maria. 2002. "Connecting the Two Infinite Orders: Research Methods in Translation Studies." In *Crosscultural Transgressions: Research Models in Translation Studies II. Historical and Ideological Issues*, ed. by Theo Hermans, 9–25. Manchester, UK & Northampton, MA: St. Jerome.

Van Maanen, John. 1988. *Tales of the Field*. Chicago: University of Chicago Press.

Yu, Chuan. 2020. "Insider, Outsider or Multiplex Persona? Confessions of a Digital Ethnographer's Journey in Translation Studies." *Journal of Specialised Translation* 34: 9–31.

CHAPTER 7

The field diary as a resource for (auto)ethnographies of translation and interpreting

Lucile Davier
University of Geneva

Although many ethnography handbooks recommend keeping fieldnotes, very few publications have concretely discussed the form and role of a field diary. What can keeping a research diary in (auto)ethnographies of translation teach translation scholars about their research? In this chapter, I present examples drawn from the diary I kept as part of an autoethnographic study of volunteer translation in an organization that promotes vegetarianism and veganism in Switzerland. The examples show that field diaries can be complementary sources of data. They can improve the quality of data collection and provide a space for ongoing ethical appraisal. Research journals also create space for self-reflexivity and theoretical production. Furthermore, they can function as therapeutic tools and fuel academic creativity.

Keywords: field diary, research journal, autoethnography, translation ethnography, committed approaches, volunteer translation, fieldwork

1. Introduction

In this chapter, I address the role that field diaries can play in autoethnographies or ethnographies of translation, particularly if the ethnographer is socially engaged in their research. When I started taking notes about the first contacts that I established in my potential field in September 2020, I did not imagine that the notes themselves would become the subject of a scholarly chapter. As I read about the importance of the self in autoethnography (see also Hokkanen, Chapter 4, and Ruiz Rosendo & Barghout, Chapter 3, this volume), I felt a need to systematize the way that I documented my research involvement. I realized the importance of keeping field notes that left space for the researcher's emotions. From one reading to the next, I discovered the concept of the field diary, although the

https://doi.org/10.1075/btl.165.07dav
Available under the CC BY-NC 4.0 license. © 2025 John Benjamins Publishing Company

literature about such diaries is practically non-existent in translation studies. In this chapter, I discuss my findings through excerpts from a research journal that I continue to keep as part of an autoethnography of committed translation. This research project went on from March 2021 to March 2023; I conducted interviews and observed translational practices as a researcher and volunteer translator (or proofreader) at an organization that supports veganism in Switzerland.

2. Definitions

This chapter uses terms that are not widely known or whose definitions are debated in translation studies. Therefore, this section defines the terms *field diary, autoethnography*, and *committed approaches to translation*.

2.1 What do I mean by *field diary*?

I became aware of the concept of field diaries in my search for methodological recommendations about field notes in autoethnography (Punch 2012). Subsequently, I discovered that field diaries had not been extensively discussed in research and observed terminological instability. That is, different authors have referred to the concept using various terms: 'field diary', 'research diary', 'field journal', and 'research journal'. Smith-Sullivan distinguishes between "diaries", which are generally used to record "daily activities and objective experiences", and "journals", which are used to capture "emotion, introspection, and self-reflection" (2008: np). However, not all authors make these same distinctions; for example, Punch (2012) uses the term "field diary", even though, from her perspective, field diaries should have an introspective component. Given this instability, I use the terms *diary* and *journal* interchangeably in this chapter, similar to Janesick (1999: 518). Moreover, I use the term *research diary* or *research journal* in reference to considerations about the research that do not necessarily imply a field, while the terms *field diary* or *field journal* designate uses related to fieldwork.

Furthermore, publications that discuss field diaries are scattered across the social sciences, including geography (Anderson 2012), human rights (Browne 2013), ethnography (Ventsel 2019; Fort 2022), other qualitative methods (Janesick 1999; Smith-Sullivan 2008), and photography (Newbury 2001). The bulk of the literature on the importance of keeping a reflexive journal comes from educational sciences (Browne 2013: 422). However, these studies (Altrichter, Posch, and Somekh 1993; Glaze 2002; Gleaves, Walker, and Grey 2007; Engin 2011) have focused on *reflective* journals for students and teachers rather than researchers (Borg 2001: 157). One publication investigates the advantages and disadvantages of participant diaries to assess the factors motivating and demotivating translators (Mossop 2014).

Authors across academic fields agree that 'notes' and 'diary' or 'journal' refer to different realities. On the one hand, field notes (or fieldwork notes) are defined as a "record of observations" made in the field or after interviews (Newbury 2001: 3) or "the recounting of observations ... in a methodological perspective" (Fort 2022: 350). Field notes can also include analytical and theoretical reflections (Newbury 2001; Punch 2012; Stephens Griffin and Griffin 2019). On the other hand, field diaries focus on researchers as people and record their emotions and thoughts about the research process and its difficulties (Newbury 2001; Punch 2012; Fort 2022).

While Punch (2012) found it important to distinguish field notes from field diaries, I agree with Burgess (1981), Newbury (2001), and Fort (2022) that these may be difficult to practically separate because they likely consist of a continuum of writing practices that range from observational notes written in bullet points to more elaborate methodological or theoretical notes. Whereas Punch (2012) and Browne (2013) have highlighted the value of keeping a journal when conducting fieldwork in difficult material conditions (e.g. in rural areas without facilities, such as running water and electricity [Punch 2012] or in a conflict zone [Browne 2013]), I argue that their findings may also be applicable in less stressful contexts.

2.2 What do I mean by *autoethnography*?

I broadly define the term *autoethnography* as studies that combine characteristics of autobiography and ethnography (Ellis, Adams, and Bochner 2011: Section 2) rather than investigations of a community in which the researcher was a committed member before the beginning of the study (Anderson 2006: 373). Autoethnographies are sometimes restricted to the definition popularized by Hayano (1982), a scholar who wrote about poker as a semi-professional poker player and characterized this kind of text as an ethnography of one's own people. However, I agree with Ellis' intention "to keep the boundaries blurry and inclusive" (2003: 39). Although I am not a full member of the professional community that I explore (see Section 2), I incorporate my own feelings and reflections into this project and consider them "vital data" through which to understand the people and phenomena that I observe (Anderson 2006: 384). My process is one of analytical autoethnography (as opposed to evocative autoethnography, which replaces social science prose with storytelling), which implies reflexivity (i.e., awareness of my positionality) and "commitment to theoretical analysis", in addition to my own visibility in the text (Anderson 2006: 378).

Autoethnographic texts are written in the first person and can take a variety of forms, such as social science prose, photographic essays, and poetry (Ellis 2003:38). Their validity stems from a comparison of "personal experience against existing research" and the study of interactions between the researcher and their informants (Ellis, Adams, and Bochner 2011: Section 2).

To date, few scholars have used autoethnography in translation studies. Three translation scholars, Hensley (2016), Tison (2016), and Hokkanen (2017a) have adopted a more restrictive definition of autoethnography by studying interpreting as interpreters themselves. However, Tison's research (2016) is likely grounded in a postpositivist framework since he applied a multimethod design to collect both qualitative and quantitative data and attempted to distance himself from his research site. By contrast, Hensley (2016), Hokkanen (2017a), and Voinova (2024) worked within a postmodern paradigm by investigating their multiple roles, among other elements. In particular, Hokkanen (2017a) acknowledged her interest in exploring her subjective experience as a volunteer church interpreter and noted that she conceived of writing (field notes or ethnographies) as "a method of discovery and analysis", to cite Richardson (1994:516). Tison (2016), Borg (2024), and Pálušová (2024) relied on field notes without giving further detail about them, whereas Hokkanen transformed her field notes from an earlier study (2012) into a "field journal proper" (2017a:27) and quoted long excerpts from it in more recent publications (e.g., Hokkanen and Koskinen 2016; Hokkanen 2017a, b, and this volume). Voinova (2024) drafted a 7,000-word account based on her memory of former interpreting tasks. Eventually, although she did not use the term *autoethnography*, Yu (2020) reflected on her relationships with participants in a "confessional tale" — an ethnographic genre that is close to autoethnographies (Ellis and Bochner 2000).

There is a fine line between these autoethnographies and other ethnographies in which translation studies scholars engaged in participant observations (Olohan and Davitti 2017; Marin-Lacarta and Vargas-Urpí 2019, 2020; Yu 2019, 2020). Yu (2019, 2020) also discussed how she and her participants negotiated their identity roles and her "multiplex persona" in her virtual ethnography of the Chinese online collaborative platform Yeeyan. Nonetheless, she did not fully embrace subjectivity and local meanings as sufficient means of establishing validity in her 2019 article, as she attempted to "keep a distance from the studied field and [her] 'friends'" (Yu 2019:237). In their ethnography-inspired sociology of a self-publishing initiative led by literary translators, Marin-Lacarta and Vargas-Urpí (2020:463) pursued the same objective of distancing themselves from their data. In terms of data collection, all of the aforementioned researchers describe the use of field notes (Olohan and Davitti 2017), reflective diaries based on field notes (Marin-Lacarta and Vargas-Urpí 2019), and field journals that include "feelings and reflections" (Yu 2019: 237); however, none provided details about how they collected this personal data and how their personal reflections benefitted their research.

In this chapter, I aim to fill this lacuna. Given the researcher's centrality in autoethnographic analysis and writing, I argue that a field diary can serve as a resource that yields "analytical benefits" (Hokkanen 2017a: 32) and tells "a personal tale of what went on in the backstage of doing a research project" (Ellis 2003: 50).

2.3 What do I mean by *committed approaches*?

The term *committed* or *activist approaches* derives from the School of Manipulation, critical descriptive approaches (Assis Rosa 2010), and the cultural turn (Brownlie 2009) – approaches that all challenge the traditional divide between descriptive and prescriptive (Brownlie 2009). Wolf (2014) even spoke of an "activist turn" and the need to increase the visibility of translators and translation scholars in the public space. Activist approaches include a commitment to effect social, political, cultural, or linguistic change (Brownlie [2010] 2016; Boéri 2019; Boéri and Delgado Luchner 2020; and Pálušová 2024), which poses particular ethical questions (Boéri and Delgado Luchner 2020). Scholars have acknowledged the numerous overlaps between non-professional translation, volunteer translation, committed approaches and activist translation, all of which are generally applied in practice outside of the translation industry (Boéri and Delgado Luchner 2020). A wide array of actors other than trained translators are involved in committed or activist translation (Boéri and Delgado Luchner 2020). Translation activism can be observed in wars, conflict situations, human rights organizations, feminist and LGBTQIA+ movements, etc. (Wolf 2014; Gould and Tahmasebian 2020).

Committed approaches may involve activist translators or interpreters, as well as activist scholars (Brownlie 2009; Wolf 2014; Boéri and Delgado Luchner 2020; Gould and Tahmasebian 2020; and Pálušová 2024), whose positionality is as central to the research as in autoethnography. I wish to anchor my research in committed approaches because of my personal belief in the importance of the values shared in the organization that I study: namely, the ethical and ecological necessity of stopping the exploitation of animals for food, work, and entertainment. Contrary to Hermans' (1999: 149–150) argument, I believe that authors who are writing committed studies can question their presuppositions through self-reflexivity (Brownlie 2009: 80), especially within the framework of autoethnography.

3. My field and I

I chose autoethnography as my study approach because this method is particularly suited to producing academic accounts of "marginal and non-normative group[s]", such as punks and vegans (Stephens Griffin and Griffin 2019:8). The organization that I study — which I refer to as *Vego* in this publication — supports vegetarians and vegans in Switzerland. As of January 2023, it employed 19 staff members, including two translators, and worked with volunteers, some of whom also translated.

At this stage, it may be useful to introduce some definitions. The term 'vegetarianism' describes the principle of excluding all meat and fish from one's diet, whereas the term 'veganism' more broadly refers to "a way of living which seeks to exclude, as far as is possible and practicable, all forms of exploitation of, and cruelty to, animals for food, clothing or any other purpose" (The Vegan Society 2025). Scholars have described veganism as a form of everyday animal advocacy (Stephens Griffin 2017:5), a lifestyle movement, and a cultural movement (Cherry 2006, 2015). To the best of my knowledge, veganism has not yet been explored from a translational perspective, although Cronin criticizes "human exceptionalism" (2017:5) and advocates for overcoming the dichotomy between animal and human (Cronin 2017:113; see also Jansen van Vuuren, Chapter 15, this volume, for an empirical application in a translation studies context).

My research project was approved by the ethics board of the Faculty of Translation and Interpreting (University of Geneva, Switzerland) on March 1, 2021, which means that I began to collect data at a time when coronavirus-related restrictions in Switzerland limited non-essential professional contact. Therefore, I conducted my participant observations and most interviews remotely. Under more ordinary circumstances, I would have traveled to meet the team at least once and interviewed my participants face to face. When the restrictions were lifted, I discovered that most of the staff and all volunteers at Vego continued to work from home. At least one employee is a digital nomad. That is, she travels to different countries and works from locales with a good Internet connection; she only meets the rest of the staff for teambuilding events.

There were two exceptions to remote data collection: the first was a face-to-face interview with a committee member in the city from which she was working remotely in October 2021 and the second was my volunteer stint at a stand that the organization ran at a sustainability festival in September 2022 (4 hours). The remainder of my contact with the team as a participant observer took place over videoconferencing software (4 one-hour sessions) or via e-mail (96 emails received from the team) from March 2021 to March 2023.

Nevertheless, I wondered whether my research qualified as a netnography (Kozinets 2010). Vego manages accounts on various social networks, but the volunteers do not use these channels to interact with the organization. As volunteers, our exchanges with the organization are computer-mediated but only one-to-one (Hine 2003). There was no data to be collected online. If I apply the criteria that Kozinets (2010) borrows from Rheingold (1993), the volunteers that I studied did not form a "virtual community", as they did not share a culture or "carry on ... public discussions long enough" (Rheingold 1993:5). I was therefore left with remote fieldwork and participants who maintained loose relationships with the organization that they served — and thus no possibility of conducting a proper netnography (see also Tekgül-Akın's experience with virtual fieldwork in a different setting, Chapter 12, this volume). Was this reason strong enough to abandon the study? Did these constraints prevent me from conducting an autoethnography?

In line with Hine, I argue that this situation eventually helped me to have "similar experiences to those of [my] informants" (2003:10) — at least, to the volunteer translators and proofreaders, who regularly stay in touch with Vego employees only via email. In this sense, my ethnography was adapted to the conditions in which I and the other participants found ourselves (Hine 2003:65). In other words, my research does not qualify as a netnography (Kozinets 2010) but could be seen as a virtual ethnography according to Hine's (2003) definition.

However, I must confess that I was disappointed and felt the need to reflect on my experiences and emotions to compensate for this disembodied fieldwork. I spent time pondering these questions in my research journal, which included 28,177 words and 96 entries up until the end of March 2023. I started the journal in paper format but moved to an electronic format on 25 March 2021 to simplify coding and analysis. Based on suggestions made by scholars who presented their own research diaries (Borg 2001; Browne 2013), I thematically coded the entries using the qualitative data analysis software QDA Miner Lite (Provalis Research 2025). Multiple codes can be attributed to the same segment (Saldaña 2011).

4. Findings from the inclusion of a field diary in a translation autoethnography

As I would later discover, my disappointment upon realizing in the autumn of 2020 that my fieldwork would be mediated through computer screens was the first of many frustrations. Shortly after I obtained ethical clearance from the ethics board of my university, Chloé,[1] my gatekeeper at Vego, told me that she and her colleague Zoé did not need my help with translations. Since I offered to volunteer in other ways, Chloé — a bilingual communications manager — entrusted me with the creation of German-French terminology records on the topic of veganism, the elaboration of guidelines on inclusive language in French, and the identification of a cost-effective computer-assisted translation (CAT) tool for Vego. These tasks kept me happily busy from March to June 2021, when Chloé and Zoé started to send me German source texts for translation into French. However, this honeymoon phase abruptly ended when Chloé left Vego in September 2021 and was replaced by Manon, a translator who worked so efficiently that she no longer needed my assistance, except to proofread the French version of Vego's quarterly magazine with another volunteer. Within a year, my high hopes had faded and my participation as a volunteer translator vanished into thin air. I wrote in my field diary:

(1) My participation is shrinking away; my volunteer engagement is fading; my veganism is less and less embodied. Can I still justify an autoethnographic approach? (2 November 2021)

At this point, I focused on ethnographic interviews and logging what had become more of a research diary than a field diary, in the absence of a material or netnographic field. Thus, the research question that I want to address in this publication is as follows: What can keeping a research diary in autoethnographies of translation teach translation scholars about their research?

4.1 Another set of data

First, I argue that research diaries offer analyzable data that can save research projects in which negotiations to access the field fail (Darmon 2005), a given type of collection method proves impossible, or the field turns out to be completely different from the researcher's expectations, as was the case in my study. For instance, they can provide a space to ponder the reasons why access was refused. In the following excerpt, I reflect on my role as an informant in my own research:

(2) Lucile Davier produces data just like her other research participants... It seems rather comical to put it this way, but I am very much looking forward to this experience, which will, at the very least, be an enriching personal experience, even if it isn't very productive on a scientific level. (April 12, 2021)[2]

---

1. I chose French and feminine pseudonyms to conceal the identity of my participants.

2. My own translations of passages I originally drafted in French and that can be found at this URL: https://archive-ouverte.unige.ch/unige:172452

In my research diary, I expressed doubts about the feasibility of the research project, which I then counterbalanced by emphasizing that I will benefit from this scientific experience on a personal level. Nearly two years after writing this diary entry, I am impressed by the major role that my diary has played in my research, which provides an autobiographical and methodological twist that I had not envisaged at the beginning of this study.

Furthermore, in my remote participant observations, my field diary helped to materialize the exchange of digital documents, as is apparent in the following excerpt:

(3) Zoé assigned me two new articles in the CAT tool: one about avocados and the other about the connection between animal agriculture and world hunger. I had so much fun! I loved translating, improving the style of text and its reasoning, looking up information and working with the translation memory.

(June 21, 2021)

I had collected source texts and target texts, but all traces of revision and marginal comments were erased in the free CAT tool that the organization has been using since June 2021. The only way that I was able to comment on my experience as a volunteer translator was through descriptions of my subjective experiences in my journal.

4.2 Recording emotions

Moreover, keeping a reflective research diary created space to record embodied experiences that might otherwise be lost to memory (Hokkanen 2017a; Stephens Griffin and Griffin 2019: 12). In one instance, I had a strong bodily reaction while reading an autoethnographic article about vegan activism in dairy farms:

(4) When I read about her story as a mother, I get a knot in my stomach. She witnesses a cow calling desperately for her baby. Now that I am a mother myself, reading it is completely unbearable. I imagine my daughters being taken away from me.

On page 191, I'm starting to feel nauseous. ... I read an interview that the author conducted with an activist whose child asked if the calf cried when it was taken away from its mother. I can't take it anymore: I cry.   (March 8, 2021)

Without a research diary, these strong reactions might have faded away over time. My journal bears evidence of the feelings that can be elicited by reading and practicing autoethnography. Since committed researchers are likely to be blamed for their lack of self-criticism (Brownlie 2009), journaling is an honest way of documenting the emotions that may have influenced the research throughout a study.

4.3 A cathartic role

My research journal also played a cathartic role. It helped me to purge the negative emotions provoked by the unfavorable turn of events and identify solutions. For example, after I read that diary keeping could be used as a resource to rationalize a stressful situation and create a path "to positive thinking and action" (Borg 2001: 163), I wrote about how I negotiated interviews:

> (5) I wrote an initial introductory email, which remained in my draft folder. The official explanation to myself: I needed to have enough time to carefully proofread the message in German to make a good impression. Strangely enough, this email remained abandoned for a week. Until I read an article on the benefits of a field diary, in which the author talks about how he had to deal with mental blocks when contacting potential participants and explains how keeping a log helped him get over it. In a flash, I reopened my draft folder, read through the invitation, and sent it off with only a few minor improvements.
>
> (November 16, 2021)

Writing about my anticipated fear of receiving a negative reply motivated me to act, providing a way of resolving fieldwork anxiety, as described by Borg (2001). Just as negative emotions can block action, creating a written space for them can spark action.

In other entries, logging gave me the opportunity to write about two emotions that are often considered taboo among scholars of translation studies: shame about one's lack of fresh experience in translation and apprehension about one's inadequate language skills:

> (6a) It questions my legitimacy as a professional since I have barely translated for more than six years. It questions my ability to translate, which I have more and more doubts about. (October 14, 2021)

> (6b) Apprehensions. ... The fear of not feeling up to the task, linguistically speaking. The shame over my German skills, which have melted away in 15 years like snow under the sun. (November 16, 2021)

Ruminating on these feelings prevented me from contacting potential participants, while reflecting on them liberated mental space for academic work and experimenting with a new method of preparing for interviews in a passive language (German, in my case):

> (7) I found her [this influencer] when I was looking up YouTube videos on veganism in German. I thought that immersing myself in German and veganism before an interview could help me reactivate my language skills. And it worked:

Chapter 7. The field diary as a resource **167**

> after half an hour of full video immersion, I felt more comfortable asking questions, despite drawing of a few blanks .... I will definitely do this again before my next interviews in German. (December 7, 2021)

Instead of fixating on the shame of my diminished language skills in isolation, I wrote about this issue, which helped me to identify, evaluate, and apply a solution to later interviews.

Journal writing can also be experienced as a creative activity that fuels motivation when researchers feel alienated from their work (Janesick 1999: 512–513). I describe my own powerful experience with this aspect of journal writing in the following passage:

(8)   It's amazing how writing helps me to channel my energy, which would otherwise have been wasted on compulsively checking my phone, and refocus on my work instead of trying to distract myself by all means possible.
(November 23, 2021)

Motivation can also be increased by practicing creative forms of journaling, such as scribbling and doodling. In the following excerpt, I observe that scribbling helped me to overcome a morning blockage:

(9)   There you go, a bit of liberating scribbling in my journal and I'm off!
(October 14, 2021)

4.4   Improving data collection and ethical considerations

The research journal enabled me to learn from an unexpected change in my data collection. A potential participant asked if she could answer my questions via e-mail. Her request forced me to formulate questions instead of following Kaufmann's (2008) recommendation to prepare a flexible list of themes to be addressed at the most appropriate moment in the interview:

(10)   It's funny. I'm the one who's always teaching my supervisees to prepare a list of interview topics, instead of formulating questions ahead of time, and yet I'm surprised by the new elements that emerge when writing down questions. Is it because I'm writing in complete sentences and making connections? I can see new ideas blooming before me, which, I hope, will nourish my live interviews.
(April 12, 2022)

Thus, the participant's request for an e-mail interview suddenly challenged the way that I practice and teach master's students about data collection in methodology classes or during thesis supervision. Keeping a research diary gave me the space to reflect on the usefulness of my principles and the new possibilities that arise from a different experience.

In other entries, I reflected on ethical issues that emerged after I obtained ethical clearance. For example, in my second year of research, I thought about introducing more restrictive confidentiality measures than those imposed by the ethics board of my institution (see also Riondel, Chapter 8, for a critical reflection on ethical clearance practices):

(11)   This makes me wonder if
  –   I should create a new table linking the pseudonyms made up by participants with new pseudonyms to completely safeguard their confidentiality,
  –   I should only use feminine pronouns and pseudonyms to refer to my participants so that they cannot be identified,
  –   I should only use translations and paraphrases of the interviews in English so that they cannot be identified by their native language,
  –   I should refrain from naming the organization.   (June 14, 2022)

Although I believe that most of the participants would not mind being recognized by their colleagues, I know that one of them in particular wished me to protect her identity. Keeping a field journal creates a space for a self-dialogue on ethical considerations that go beyond the initial expectations of ethics boards, but are necessary to ensure that a project remains ethical for its entire duration.

Self-reflexivity is an ethical requirement in engaged research projects such as my own: readers must know who I am and how I perceive myself to understand and evaluate my interpretations. I realized that the topic of guilt recurred 12 times in my field diary, as illustrated by the following excerpt:

(12)   Nevertheless, as I read the vegan biographies presented in this book, I can feel my guilt returning through the back door: who am I to claim a vegan identity? I definitely don't measure up to Claire, a young disabled woman who, in spite of her pain, refuses to take painkillers that have been tested on animals.
                                                                    (June 1, 2021)

This guilt is related to my identity as an engaged scholar who researches veganism without being a perfect vegan myself. Other entries focus on my 'in-between' status, stuck between my relatives' resistance to veganism and the inspiring examples in my research interviews or the literature on veganism.

4.5   Commitment and rapport

My research journal also provided an opportunity to observe variations in my engagement during the fieldwork. My field diary reveals the flow of vegan topics into my personal life as I became increasingly involved with vegan texts through translation or proofreading:

(13) When it comes to identity, I am able to strengthen my convictions when I translate. On Thursday, I started a discussion with a friend on eggs and chicken.
(August 30, 2021)

Different aspects of my identity were highlighted, depending on the people that I met, and my journal records these transformations.

For example, I told one participant that my sensitivity to the vegan cause increased as I worked on my project. She replied that she had had a similar experience. While she had been trying to become completely vegan for some time, her first months of work at Vego had empowered her to succeed:

(14) … your brain is uh continuously stimulated by all this information, so it's lingering in your mind, no matter what you do [L: Absolutely!], and for me, it's when I started working in this business, and, well, it really would have been hypocritical on my part to write things about uh, well about it [veganism], and to, to consume certain products at the same time.   (Interview with Manon)

Undergoing a similar experience (despite not becoming vegan for other reasons) helped me to understand that engaging with background information about veganism can reinforce one's convictions. This experience I shared with one of my participants shows that it is a research track worth pursuing, perhaps with a different methodology, as it seems that sustained engagement with an ideology through translation or proofreading can empower one to make committed decisions.

Other diary entries focused on my emotional responses to interviews. For example, the following passage expresses the emotional proximity that I felt to one participant:

(15) I actually think my feelings are quite similar to her idea of a 'soft', non-vindictive activism that takes advantage of personal skills and pleasures. (August 30, 2021)

This closeness laid the foundation for empathy and self-projection. By contrast, I felt very uncomfortable after an interview with another participant. These emotions constitute material that can be used to analyze the different meanings that the participant and I assigned to veganism and activism.

4.6 Supporting academic production

I also experienced the research journal as a particularly powerful tool for clarifying emerging ideas. For example, when I understood that I needed to deepen my knowledge about ethnographic diaries, I wrote:

(16a)   End of the day: I need literature on the ethnographic diary.   (March 8, 2021)

A few weeks later, I immediately applied the new distinction between field notes and field diaries that I discovered in Punch (2012):

(16b)   A field diary it will be, then! After reading this publication on March 25, I feel as if I've grown editorial wings — and in French!   (April 12, 2021)

I also used my diary to produce theoretical reflections during the interview transcription stage. In these entries, I often quoted or paraphrased passages from the interviews that I was transcribing and used these as a basis for future interpretations. For example, in the excerpt below, I discuss the meaning that a participant ascribed to volunteer work and commitment:

(17)   It sounds like Élodie would like to consider herself as "engaged" but is embarrassed to admit that she never worked as a volunteer before being hired by Vego. She talks about her day-to-day but soft engagement, for instance, when doing presentations about vegetarianism/veganism at school. Here, autoethnography starts to make sense, because my "engagement" through scholarship seems comparable to Élodie's engagement at school with her former classmates.   (September 29, 2022)

There seems to be a discrepancy between this participant's ideal representation of commitment (probably someone who volunteers for the vegan cause) and her self-representation as an individual who 'only' engages through school presentations. According to her representation, I could probably describe myself as 'engaged' through my volunteer work for Vego but not through my research about commitment to the vegan cause.

Moreover, a journal can help researchers to describe and evaluate progress. I used my field diary in this way three times, as illustrated by the following example:

(18)   There was anxiety at the end of 2020, when I knew that Chloé was presenting my project to the committee, and I was having doubts about my connection to veganism. There was overexcitement on December 15, 2020 when I received an acceptance from the president of the committee; there was productive fever as I read and prepared my application to obtain ethical clearance. Then I learned

to roll with the punches when Chloé told me that she didn't really need translations, but my enthusiasm picked up again when she gave me a new task ....

(April 12, 2021)

In this excerpt, I retrospectively revise the initial steps of my project and explain
how my mood varied during this process.

Excerpts from my research journal illustrate some of the numerous benefits I
have gained from journaling, such as creating analyzable data in a dematerialized
field, remotivating me in difficult moments and developing self-reflexivity, just to
name a few. In the following section, I discuss how these advantages are reflected
in the literature.

5. Discussion

As illustrated in the previous section, journaling has been instrumental in overcoming setbacks with my fieldwork. However, the more I log, the more I am convinced that these insights can inform other (auto)ethnographies of translation, as
I am not the only scholar whose conditions of access have changed or who has
been refused access to her field.

Keeping a research journal creates a "data set of the researcher's reflections on
the research act" (Janesick 1999:505) and provides a memory support for ethnographers (Punch 2012:90; Hokkanen 2017a:33) that can be retrospectively analyzed (Richardson 1994:526; Borg 2001:161). It is particularly important to record
embodiment or fleeting impressions (see also Hokkanen, Chapter 4, this volume).
In my case, the data set compensated for the virtualization of my field and the fact
that my participant observation was much less sustained than expected.

Authors who have written about autoethnography (Ellis, Adams, and Bochner
2011; Stephens Griffin and Griffin 2019) and field diaries in particular (Janesick
1999:511; Borg 2001:163; Punch 2012; Browne 2013) agree that field diaries can
play a cathartic role. Janesick describes their function as "a way of getting in touch
with yourself in terms of reflection, catharsis, remembrance, creation, exploration, problem solving, problem posing, and personal growth" (1999:511). This
description has been supported by Pennebaker and Smyth ([1990] 2016), two psychologists who investigated the overwhelmingly positive effects of expressive writing about hidden emotions, such as guilt, on the immune system.

Beyond this therapeutic role, research journals are central methods of data
collection under a paradigm in which the researcher is the research instrument
(Richardson 1994; Janesick 1999). They improve the precision of qualitative
research by developing researchers' self-consciousness and critical self-reflexivity

(Progoff 1992; Janesick 1999:506; Borg 2001:170; Ellis 2003:37–38). In autoethnography in particular, researchers are expected to include reflections on their personal experiences and feelings in their analyses (Anderson 2006:384; Collins and Gallinat 2010:17).

The relationship between researcher and informants must be analyzed to guarantee the authenticity of data collection, as (auto)ethnographic fieldwork involves "relational work of a unique and intense kind" between these actors (Coffey 1999:39). My examples show that field diaries can be used to record one's emotional response to an interview (Ellis, Adams, and Bochner 2011:Section 4.1). Laying bare their own emotions helps the researchers comprehend participants' emotions (Janesick 1999:506), build rapport (Punch 2012:89), and amplify their emotions to meet the expectations of the communicative situation (see also Hokkanen, Chapter 4, this volume). Field diaries can also be used to report the "ways in which the interviewer may have been changed by the process of interviewing" (Punch 2012:89) and the personal transformation of the researcher during fieldwork (Browne 2013:422).

Since they create space for reflexivity (Janesick 1999; Punch 2012; Stephens Griffin and Griffin 2019), field diaries can directly influence the ethical quality of a research project. Furthermore, through autoethnography and journal writing, researchers become acutely aware of what it means to reveal one's inner self. Therefore, they develop increased empathy toward participants who share their personal stories for the research, even if they are in anonymized form (Janesick 1999:507; Punch 2012:91; Stephens Griffin and Griffin 2019:Section 3.1.1). Reflexive writing encourages "continual ethical appraisal ... throughout a project's duration" to address numerous "unanticipated ethical situations and dilemmas encountered in fieldwork" (Stephens Griffin and Griffin 2019:Section 3.1.1), well beyond the approval of ethics boards (Silverman 2011:100; Miles, Huberman, and Saldaña 2014:68).

As shown in the examples presented in the present chapter, research diaries can improve practical decisions about data collection and help "refine one's thoughts about qualitative research techniques" (Janesick 1999:506) and techniques for preparing for and conducting interviews (Browne 2013).

Beyond autoethnographies and ethnographies, field diaries can be a productive tool for knowledge development (Altrichter, Posch, and Somekh 1993; Engin 2011; Browne 2013:422). They can help researchers to generate ideas (Borg 2001:160) and clarify their thoughts by writing them down (Richardson 1994:516; Janesick 1999:514; Newbury 2001:9; Pennebaker and Smyth ([1990] 2016:67). The excerpts presented in the previous section illustrate how journaling can be used to clarify concepts and evaluate progress.

Beyond knowledge development, field diaries can add value by "provid[ing] other researchers — novice and experienced — with insight into 'doing research'" (Borg 2001:160). The depiction of real-life experiences in research diaries may be a useful complement to methods handbooks, which often depict ideal situations, whereas fieldwork is "difficult and awkward ..., messy and complex" (Punch 2012:90). Idealized models may encourage novice researchers to interpret their own difficulties as "personal deficiencies arising from insufficient preparation, knowledge, or experience" (Borg 2001:174), while direct excerpts from field diaries "may reassure others that their guilt, apprehension, fears and worries are legitimate, common and even useful experiences" (Punch 2012:91). Field diaries demonstrate that research does not occur in a "linear fashion"; by contrast, scientific publications offer a reconstructed view of the logic of science (Newbury 2001:2). Indeed, the passages from my research journal show that fieldwork often does not go according to plan.

Creativity and pleasure can also be integral parts of the field diary (Janesick 1999:516; Borg 2001:171). This is unsurprising, as autoethnography also seeks to explore creative and artistic avenues (Ellis 2003:42). Personal growth is a natural byproduct of keeping a research diary (Janesick 1999:511), and directly impacts the quality of research (Borg 2001:171), which I can attest to myself.

However, all of these benefits should not conceal the drawbacks of diary keeping in relation to autoethnography. Ellis and Bochner (2000:738) remind researchers that revealing themselves in their publications makes them vulnerable and can generate emotional pain, a difficulty that I experienced when I began to leave the comfort of neutral academic prose and expose my inner self. Using passages from one's research journal also raises almost as many ethical questions as it solves when, for example, writing about loved ones (Ellis and Bochner 2000:738). For now, I have only addressed this issue by excluding quotations that involve family members.

Research diaries report on the researcher's self; therefore, language plays an important role. Ellis and Bochner (2000:738) criticize many social scientists for not writing well enough to achieve introspective writing — a problem that I indirectly struggled with when I had to translate my own quotations from French into English, the language of science. Limited mastery of a passive language can transform logging into an alienating and unpleasurable experience, as described by Ventsel (2019:5), who was obliged to keep a research journal in English to share with his team.

In addition, autoethnography has been criticized in academia as navel gazing (Fine 1999; Bradley and Nash 2011). Pennebaker and Smyth ([1990] 2016:78–19) acknowledged that self-absorption is a possible risk in diary keeping; however, this risk can be minimized through the practice of critical and analytical self-reflection (as opposed to obsessive disclosure). Fine also accused autoethnography of "transforming the intensive labor of field research into the armchair pleasures of 'me-search'" (Fine 1999:534), thereby wrongly invoking postmodernism. This accusation refers to the debate about the emergence of autoethnography, which marks a shift from an emphasis on participant observation to the "observation of participation" (Tedlock 1991) and the process of writing (Ellis and Bochner 2000:741). Indeed, affirming the centrality of the self subverts the "scientific default position of standing outside" (Anderson 2012:617). For Richardson (1994:518), "knowing the Self and knowing 'about'" a subject are inseparable. Consequently, authors should no longer separate formal ethnographies from personal narratives (Richardson 1994:520). In addition, the form of writing influences its content, which is why Clifford (1986) and Richardson (1994) argued that ethnographies should welcome creative and experimental forms of writing that were excluded from universities in the 17th, 18th and 19th centuries. Far from representations of objectivity, meaning-making involves the individual's self (Hokkanen and Koskinen 2016:92) and is partial, local, and contingent (Clifford 1986; Richardson 1994).

While writing entries about the constraints of remote observation and the gradual disappearance of my participation, I did not imagine that this apparent failure would transform into an opportunity to explore a powerful data collection tool. I did not foresee how much I would experiment with myself as a research instrument, nor how central journaling would become in my research practice. Two years after the beginning of this research project, I would not consider conducting another project without a research diary; I recommend keeping a diary to all students whose dissertation I supervise. I hope that this chapter illustrates the need to develop writing about the researcher in the field of translation studies, whether in the form of confessional tales (Yu 2020) or autoethnography (i.a., Hokkanen 2017a) and that this work will inspire scholars to use field diaries or research journals to share their doubts and increase the rigor of their research.

Acknowledgements

I am deeply indebted to the editors of this volume and the anonymous referees who challenged me and pushed me to do my best. I am also very grateful to Danielle Thien for revising my own translations of excerpts from my research journal and making them more colorful. All remaining mistakes and approximations are my own.

References

Altrichter, Herbert, Peter Posch, and Bridget Somekh. 1993. *Teachers Investigate Their Work: An Introduction to the Methods of Action Research*. London: Routledge.

Anderson, Jon. 2012. "Reflective Journals as a Tool for Auto-Ethnographic Learning: A Case Study of Student Experiences with Individualized Sustainability." *Journal of Geography in Higher Education* 36 (4): 613–623.

Anderson, Leon. 2006. "Analytic Autoethnography." *Journal of Contemporary Ethnography* 35 (4): 373–395.

Assis Rosa, Alexandra. 2010. "Descriptive Translation Studies (DTS)." In *Handbook of Translation Studies*, ed. by Yves Gambier, and Luc van Doorslaer, 94–104. Amsterdam & Philadelphia: John Benjamins.

Boéri, Julie. 2019. "Activism." In *Routledge Encyclopedia of Translation Studies*, ed. by Mona Baker, and Gabriela Saldanha, 1–5. London: Routledge.

Boéri, Julie, and Carmen Delgado Luchner. 2020. "Ethics of Activist Translation and Interpreting." In *The Routledge Handbook of Translation and Ethics*, ed. by Kaisa Koskinen, and Nike Kocijančič Pokorn, 245–261. London: Routledge.

Borg, Claudine. 2024. *"Revising a Literary Translation for Publication." Translation Spaces* 13 (2): 225–243.

Borg, Simon. 2001. "The Research Journal: A Tool for Promoting and Understanding Researcher Development." *Language Teaching Research* 5 (2): 156–177.

Bradley, DeMethra L., and Robert Nash. 2011. *Mesearch and Research: A Guide for Writing Scholarly Personal Narrative Manuscripts*. Charlotte, NC: Information Age Publishing.

Browne, Brendan Ciaran. 2013. "Recording the Personal: The Benefits in Maintaining Research Diaries for Documenting the Emotional and Practical Challenges of Fieldwork in Unfamiliar Settings." *International Journal of Qualitative Methods* 12 (1): 420–435.

Brownlie, Siobhan. 2009. "Descriptive vs. Committed Approaches." In *Routledge Encyclopedia of Translation Studies*, ed. by Mona Baker, and Gabriela Saldanha, 77–81. Manchester: St. Jerome.

Brownlie, Siobhan. (2010) 2016. "Committed Approaches and Activism." In *Handbook of Translation Studies*, ed. by Yves Gambier, and Luc van Doorslaer, 45–48. Amsterdam & Philadelphia: John Benjamins.

Burgess, Robert G. 1981. "Keeping a Research Diary." *Cambridge Journal of Education* 11 (1): 75–83.

Cherry, Elizabeth. 2006. "Veganism as a Cultural Movement: A Relational Approach." *Social Movement Studies* 5 (2): 155–170.

Cherry, Elizabeth. 2015. "I Was a Teenage Vegan: Motivation and Maintenance of Lifestyle Movements." *Sociological Inquiry* 85 (1): 55–74.

Clifford, James. 1986. "Introduction: Partial Truths." In *Writing Culture: The Poetics and Politics of Ethnography*, ed. by James Clifford, and George E. Marcus, 1–26. Berkeley: University of California Press.

Coffey, Amanda. 1999. *The Ethnographic Self*. London: Sage.

Collins, Peter, and Anselma Gallinat. 2010. "The Ethnographic Self as Resource: An Introduction." In *The Ethnographic Self as Resource: Writing Memory and Experience into Ethnography*, ed. by Peter Collins, and Anselma Gallinat, 1–24. New York: Berghahn Books.

Cronin, Michael. 2017. *Eco-Translation: Translation and Ecology in the Age of the Anthropocene*. London: Routledge.

Darmon, Muriel. 2005. "Le psychiatre, la sociologue et la boulangère : Analyse d'un refus de terrain [The Psychiatrist, the Sociologist, and the Baker: Analysis of the Reasons Why Access to the Field Was Refused]." *Genèses* 58 (1): 98–112.

Ellis, Carolyn. 2003. *The Ethnographic I: A Methodological Novel About Autoethnography*. California: AltaMira Press.

Ellis, Carolyn, Tony E. Adams, and Arthur P. Bochner. 2011. "Autoethnography: An Overview." *Forum: Qualitative Social Research* 12 (1): Art. 10.

Ellis, Carolyn, and Arthur P. Bochner. 2000. "Autoethnography, Personal Narrative, Reflexivity: Research as Subject." In *Handbook of Qualitative Research*, ed. by Norman K. Denzin, and Yvonna S. Lincoln, 733–768. Thousand Oaks: Sage.

Engin, Marion. 2011. "Research Diary: A Tool for Scaffolding." *International Journal of Qualitative Methods* 10 (3): 296–306.

Fine, Gary Alan. 1999. "Field Labor and Ethnographic Reality." *Journal of Contemporary Ethnography* 28 (5): 532–539.

Fort, Emilie. 2022. "Managing Our Personal Traits in the Field: Exploring the Methodological and Analytical Benefits of Mobilizing Field Diaries." *International Journal of Social Research Methodology* 25 (3): 345–356.

Glaze, Jane. 2002. "Ph.D. Study and the Use of a Reflective Diary: A Dialogue with Self." *Reflective Practice* 3 (2): 153–166.

Gleaves, Alan, Caroline Walker, and John Grey. 2007. "Using Digital and Paper Diaries for Learning and Assessment Purposes in Higher Education: A Comparative Study of Feasibility and Reliability." *Assessment and Evaluation in Higher Education* 32 (6): 631–643.

Gould, Rebecca Ruth, and Kayvan Tahmasebian. 2020. "Introduction: Translation and Activism in the Time of the Now." In *The Routledge Handbook of Translation and Activism*, ed. by Rebecca Ruth Gould, and Kayvan Tahmasebian, 1–9. Abingdon: Routledge.

Hayano, David M. 1982. *Poker Faces: The Life and Work of Professional Card Players*. Berkeley: University of California Press.

Hensley, Jennifer S. 2016. "Blurred Boundaries: Interpreters as Researchers in Cross-Cultural Settings." *Journal of Interpretation* 25 (1): Art. 5. https://digitalcommons.unf.edu/joi/vol25/iss1/5

Hermans, Theo. 1999. *Translation in Systems: Descriptive and Systemic Approaches Explained*. Manchester: St. Jerome.

Hine, Christine. 2003. *Virtual Ethnography*. London: Sage.

Hokkanen, Sari. 2012. "Simultaneous Church Interpreting as Service." *The Translator: Studies in Intercultural Communication* 18 (2): 291–309.

Hokkanen, Sari. 2017a. "Analyzing Personal Embodied Experiences: Autoethnography, Feelings, and Fieldwork." *Translation and Interpreting* 9 (1): 24–35.

Hokkanen, Sari. 2017b. "Experiencing the Interpreter's Role: Emotions of Involvement and Detachment in Simultaneous Church Interpreting." *Translation Spaces* 6 (1): 62–78.

Hokkanen, Sari, and Kaisa Koskinen. 2016. "Affect as a Hinge: The Translator's Experiencing Self as a Sociocognitive Interface." *Translation Spaces* 5 (1): 78–96.

Janesick, Valerie J. 1999. "A Journal About Journal Writing as a Qualitative Research Technique: History, Issues and Reflections." *Qualitative Inquiry* 5 (4): 505–524.

Kaufmann, Jean-Claude. 2008. *L'entretien compréhensif [Empathic interviewing]*. Paris: Armand Colin.

Kozinets, Robert V. 2010. *Netnography: Doing Ethnographic Research Online*. Los Angeles: Sage.

Marin-Lacarta, Maialen, and Mireia Vargas-Urpí. 2019. "Translators Revising Translators: A Fruitful Alliance." *Perspectives: Studies in Translation Theory and Practice* 27 (3): 404–418.

Marin-Lacarta, Maialen, and Mireia Vargas-Urpí. 2020. "Translators as Publishers: Exploring the Motivations for Non-Profit Literary Translation in a Digital Initiative." *Meta: Translators' Journal* 65 (2): 459–478.

Miles, Matthew B., Michael A. Huberman, and Johnny Saldaña. 2014. *Qualitative Data Analysis: A Methods Sourcebook*. Los Angeles: Sage.

Mossop, Brian. 2014. "Motivation and De-Motivation in a Government Translation Service: A Diary-Based Approach." *Perspectives: Studies in Translation Theory and Practice* 22 (4): 581–591.

Newbury, Darren. 2001. "Diaries and Fieldnotes in the Research Process." *Research Issues in Art, Design, and Media* 1: 1–17.

Olohan, Maeve, and Elena Davitti. 2017. "Dynamics of Trusting in Translation Project Management: Leaps of Faith and Balancing Acts." *Journal of Contemporary Ethnography* 46 (4): 391–416.

Pálušová, Martina. 2024. "The Translator as a Social Activist in the Digital Age: An Autoethnographic Study of Translating *Insulted. Belarus* as Part of the Worldwide Readings Project ." *Translation in Society* 3 (1): 17–39.

Pennebaker, James W., and Joshua M. Smyth. (1990) 2016. *Opening up by Writing It Down: How Expressive Writing Improves Health and Eases Emotional Pain*. 3rd edition. New York: The Guilford Press.

Progoff, Ira. 1992. *At a Journal Workshop: Writing to Access the Power of the Unconscious and Evoke Creative Ability*. Los Angeles: J. P. Tarcher.

Provalis Research, QDA Miner. 2025. "QDA Miner Lite: Free Qualitative Data Analysis Software." https://provalisresearch.com/products/qualitative-data-analysis-software/freeware/

Punch, Samantha. 2012. "Hidden Struggles of Fieldwork: Exploring the Role and Use of Field Diaries." *Emotion, Space and Society* 5 (2): 86–93.

Rheingold, Howard. 1993. *The Virtual Community: Homesteading on the Electronic Frontier*. Reading, MA: Addison-Wesley.

Richardson, Laurel. 1994. "Writing: A Method of Inquiry." In *The Sage Handbook of Qualitative Research*, ed. by Norman K. Denzin, and Yvonna S. Lincoln, 516–529. Thousand Oaks: Sage.

Saldaña, Johnny. 2011. *Fundamentals of Qualitative Research: Understanding Qualitative Research*. Oxford: Oxford University Press.

Silverman, David. 2011. *Interpreting Qualitative Data*. Los Angeles: Sage.

Smith-Sullivan, Kendall. 2008. Diaries and Journals. In *The SAGE Encyclopedia of Qualitative Research Methods*, ed. by Lisa M. Given. Thousand Oaks: Sage.

Stephens Griffin, Nathan. 2017. *Understanding Veganism: Biography and Identity*. Cham: Palgrave Macmillan.

Stephens Griffin, Nathan David, and Naomi Christina Griffin. 2019. "A Millennial Methodology? Autoethnographic Research in Do-It-Yourself (DIY) Punk and Activist Communities." *Forum: Qualitative Social Research* 20 (3): Art. 3.

Tedlock, Barbara. 1991. "From Participant Observation to the Observation of Participation: The Emergence of Narrative Ethnography." *Journal of Anthropological Research* 47 (1): 69–94.

The Vegan Society. 2025. "Definition of Veganism." https://www.vegansociety.com/go-vegan/definition-veganism

Tison, Alev Balci. 2016. "The Interpreter's Involvement in a Translated Institution: A Case Study of Sermon Interpreting." PhD diss., Universitat Rovira i Virgili.

Ventsel, Aimar. 2019. "Notes de terrain et histoire cachée [Field notes and hidden story]." *Études finno-ougriennes [Finno-Ugric studies]* 49–50:1–9.

Voinova, Tanya. 2024. ""Who Are You Standing With?": Cultural (Self-Re)Translation of a Russian-Speaking Conference Immigrant-Interpreter in Israel During the War in Ukraine." *Multilingua: Journal of Cross-Cultural and Interlanguage Communication* 43 (1): 63–90.

Wolf, Michaela. 2014. "The Sociology of Translation and Its 'Activist Turn'." In *The Sociological Turn in Translation and Interpreting Studies*, ed. by Claudia Angelelli, 7–21. Amsterdam & Philadelphia: John Benjamins.

Yu, Chuan. 2019. "Negotiating Identity Roles During the Process of Online Collaborative Translation: An Ethnographic Approach." *Translation Studies* 12 (2): 231–252.

Yu, Chuan. 2020. "Insider, Outsider or Multiplex Persona? Confessions of a Digital Ethnographer's Journey in Translation Studies." *Journal of Specialised Translation* 34: 9–31.

CHAPTER 8

Beyond ethical clearance in field research

In search of situated and reflexive ethics

Aurélien Riondel
University of Geneva | University of Antwerp

Research ethics has gained much attention in the social sciences and
translation and interpreting studies. Researchers are expected to pay greater
attention to ethical issues when researching human beings, which
increasingly means obtaining authorisation from a research ethics
committee. While this rise of ethics can be seen as positive, ethical clearance
entails risks for field researchers because it is prospective, standardised, and
based on a utilitarian approach. In this chapter, I argue for an approach to
research ethics that is situated and reflexive, and improves something for
the participants and context studied. Based on an interview study on
revision in translation teams, the chapter addresses the topics of
confidentiality in field research and involvement in interview studies.

Keywords: ethics, research ethics committee (REC), confidentiality,
interviews, revision

1. Introduction

Ethics has long been a topic of interest in translation and interpreting studies
(TIS), but more in terms of translator ethics (see seminal works by Pym 1997 and
Koskinen 2000, and for an up-to-date overview and discussion, Koskinen and
Pokorn 2021). Research ethics, on the other hand, has rarely been taken up as such
in TIS (see Hekkanen 2007 for an exception). This is probably due to the fact that
TIS has adopted methods from other disciplines, including ethical considerations
and practices (Mellinger and Baer 2021: 365).

Since the turn of the century, social research has witnessed a rise in ethics,
manifested by growing scholarly interest, increasing consideration by researchers,
and, above all, the advent of ethical regulations: codes of professional conduct,
law, and research ethics committees (RECs). These regulations notably originate
in problems observed in the past and seek to remedy detrimental research prac-

https://doi.org/10.1075/btl.165.08rio
Available under the CC BY-NC 4.0 license. © 2025 John Benjamins Publishing Company

tices such as — in the humanities and social sciences — misuse of personal data, damage to reputations and betrayal of confidentiality. RECs are migrating from experimental and medical sciences to the humanities and social sciences, and from North America to the rest of the world, including Europe. As TIS is usually seen as part of the humanities and social sciences, this trend also applies to our discipline in a context in which ethical clearance and data management planning are becoming a standard in many countries.

Research ethics is a wide-ranging topic, from ethics of studies involving animals (see also Jansen van Vuuren, Chapter 15, this volume) or humans to data management, through scientific integrity (Larouche 2019:482). It concerns all steps of a research project: research design, data production, data management, reporting and publication of the results (Mellinger and Baer 2021:376). In other terms, ethics is as much about ethical validation as it is about behaviour during the study and beyond. This prompts several observations. Ethics relates to administrative tasks as well as to social aspects. It involves many actors (people and institutions). For a researcher, it not only encompasses relationships with participants, but also with funding institutions and peers, e.g., a co-author or the scientific community. When it comes to relationships, it is a combination of formal rules and general attitudes or values, such as honesty, respect and integrity. More specifically, research ethics consists of concrete decisions embedded in a larger context; in other words, it concerns both the micro and macro levels. Finally, it takes place on different time scales. It is a combination of rules or principles that are defined beforehand and decisions that are taken on the spot.

In this chapter, I will advocate for a situated and reflexive approach to ethics, as well as an encompassing view of ethics that entails not only doing no harm, but also doing good by improving something in the environment under scrutiny. I will illustrate this vision with an interview study I conducted in translation departments on translation revision with a focus on the translator-reviser relationship (see also Korhonen, Chapter 10, this volume, on translator-reviser interactions). More specifically, I will discuss two topics: confidentiality in field research and relationships with participants in interview studies. In this chapter, field research is used as an umbrella term to refer to all qualitative studies that take place in the field with the agents. It encompasses different kind of studies, for example ethnographic studies, which entail long-term involvement in the field (Beaud and Weber 2010:274–278) and generally require a combination of methods (Olivier de Sardan 2008:46–76), and interview studies, in which participants are generally met once and an interview is the lone method for producing data (for interview research, see e.g., Gubrium et al. 2012).

The chapter first addresses main issues related to present ethical challenges in field research. Section 2 outlines the vision of RECs and its implication for field research, while Section 3 describes an approach to ethics that would better suit qualitative social sciences. Section 4 presents the study that gave rise to the empirical component of this chapter. Section 5 applies the concept of situated and reflexive ethics to the issue of confidentiality in qualitative research in general. Finally, Section 6 shows how the concept of involvement can foster ethical interview research.

2. Research ethics committees and qualitative research: A treacherous path

North American countries have a fairly long tradition of research ethics committees (RECs) endorsing social research: American Institutional Review Boards (IRBs) have existed since 1981 (Haggerty 2004: 393), while Canadian Research Ethics Boards (REBs) were implemented in the 1970's before being generalised and standardised after the *Tri-Council Policy Statement: Ethical Conduct for Research Involving Humans* was issued in 1998 (Haggerty 2004: 392; Larouche 2019: 480; Taylor, Taylor-Neu, and Butterwick 2020: 60–61). By contrast, research ethics committees for the social sciences seem fairly new in Europe.[1]

Ethical regulation through RECs has drawn harsh criticism in the social sciences (for a brief overview, see Taylor, Taylor-Neu, and Butterwick 2020: 58). Hunter (2018: 289) sums up this criticism in four points: little knowledge of the social sciences among committee members, a focus on issues more relevant to biomedical research, the infringement of academic freedom, and the undemocratic nature of these committees. Furthermore, Gillam and Guillemin (2018: 263) point out that scientists conducting qualitative research tend to be distrustful of these committees and have the impression that these bodies do not understand or trust them. The resistance to regulatory bodies is embodied by strong terms like "ethical imperialism" (Schrag 2010), which alludes to ethical rules that are imposed upon biomedical and behavioural research in the social sciences, and "ethicocracy"[2] (Larouche 2019, my translation), a term that suggests that RECs have absolute power. The rise of ethics is to be welcomed in and of itself, and yet, this rise should be scrutinised in order to analyse the changes it brings (including negative ones) and the challenges it poses to field researchers.

Ethical regulation, such as approval by a REC, is a means of managing risks posed by scientific research (Haggerty 2004: 392). Multiple factors are at its origin,

---

1. For example, at the University of Geneva, ethical committees were implemented in the Geneva School of Social Sciences and the Faculty of Translation and Interpreting in 2015 and 2016, respectively (Burton-Jeangros 2017: 11).

2. "éthicocratie".

including manifest abuse in the past; lack of objectivity when it comes to assessing our own situation; potential conflict of interest between researchers and participants; the complexity and unpredictability of research (which make ethical decisions difficult for a single researcher); and the external legitimacy ensured by having risks verified and minimised by an external body (Hunter 2018: 291–292).

RECs can prove to be controversial for field research, due to three characteristics that I will describe below: (1) ethical clearance is prospective; (2) RECs have a utilitarian view; and (3) they tend to act in a standardised way. They are prospective, in the sense that they examine ethical issues at the planning stage in order to establish how the research project must be carried out later on (Haggerty 2004: 396; Hunter 2018: 290). This is a challenge for field research, because qualitative studies are evolutionary by nature; they typically have an emergent design (Maxwell 2013; Creswell 2013: 47) and it is virtually impossible to anticipate everything that will or might happen in the field, notably because participants are not *subjects* in experiments, but *agents* (Gagnon 2010: 303–304).

RECs generally adopt a utilitarian approach to research, weighing the harm and benefits (Haggerty 2004: 395–396; Dawson 2006: 114; Mellinger and Baer 2021: 369). More specifically, they assess whether the risk of harmful consequences is mitigated through appropriate procedures (and what is intended to alleviate harm if the risk materialises), then consider whether it is worth taking the remaining risk, given the expected benefit to be gained by the study. This utilitarian approach can be rejected on principle. This is the case with Gagnon (2010: 304), who considers that balancing risks and benefits makes no sense in the social sciences because a study can only produce harm that is impossible to measure (like reputational issues or discomfort generated by the memory of a painful experience) and brings no greater benefit than changing the perception of a situation or deepening knowledge of a phenomenon. Moreover, concepts on both sides of the balance, i.e., risk and harm, can be problematic in the humanities and social sciences. Ostensibly, the notion of harm is quite different in these disciplines than, for example, the natural sciences or a medical trial: in the former, it is mostly reputational, emotional, related to social relationships or economical, while in the latter, it is primarily material or physiological. In addition, Haggerty (2004: 400) and Taylor, Taylor-Neu, and Butterwick (2020: 66) indicate that Canadian Research Ethics Boards maintain a flawed definition of harm, as every change in personal life is potentially harmful. On the other hand, benefits can be challenging for field researchers. As qualitative researchers are not accustomed to viewing their work with a utilitarian eye, they sometimes fail to describe and put forth the potential benefits of their studies (Dawson 2006: 114). As a result, every study that may cause harm can be considered not to be worth the effort, because, as there is no expected benefit, the scale is tipped in favour of risks.

As for the third controversial characteristic, i.e., standardisation, RECs tend (1) to define rules rather than principles and (2) to apply the same standard to all kinds of research (e.g., written informed consent) or to all studies that feature the same type of research (e.g., sending the transcript to the participant in an interview study). In the Canadian context, Gagnon (2010: 301–302) points out that the desire of RECs to subject all researchers to the same rules results in the standards being applied indiscriminately, in a somewhat mechanical manner. Haggerty (2004) even refers to a "fetishization of rules" (2004: 410–411), which he describes as the desire of RECs to achieve a "form of legal consistency" for equality, in the manner that a court takes into account previous judgments (2004: 412). This is why Dawson (2006: 116), a proponent of RECs, calls for the rules to be applied in a differentiated way in order to take into consideration the level of risk and severity of possible harm.

This "'one size fits all' approach" criticised by Dawson (2006: 116) and Taylor, Taylor-Neu, and Butterwick (2020) is detrimental for qualitative researchers for two reasons. First, as researchers with background in experimental research such as psychologists tend to be over-represented in the composition and chairmanship of RECs (van den Hoonaard 2011: 77–78, 82–84), and REC members may have little knowledge of qualitative research (Dawson 2006: 115), there is a risk that the standards imposed on field researchers are imported from or inspired by the experimental-quantitative paradigm. Second, while following best practices is a guarantee of quality in hypothesis-driven research, in the qualitative paradigm, quality is more of a dynamic notion (Flick 2018: 11–13) that must be addressed throughout the research project. A quantitative mental framework of RECs would explain why such committees tend to set rules, as well as why such rules may not be that relevant to field researchers (e.g., obtaining written consent from anyone who enters the situation being observed by the researcher in a real example from a colleague).

The prospective character of RECs and their adjudicative capacity can have unwarranted and detrimental effects (Haggerty 2004: 410; Gagnon 2010; Genard and Roca i Escoda 2019: 148, 150; Larouche 2019). During fieldwork, researchers may no longer question whether their actions are appropriate, but instead focus on whether or not they are complying with the rules defined beforehand. Moreover, when they adapt or deviate from the rule, they may be inclined to conceal what they have done, even though ethics should promote transparency with regard to what occurs in the field. Another troubling effect is that after getting approval from a REC, researchers may have the impression that ethical concerns are over once field work begins, which is anything but true (Genard and Roca i Escoda 2019: 150).

That being said, RECs have clear advantages. They provide legitimacy to studies and can protect researchers against public reaction (Gillam and Guillemin 2018:265; Hunter 2018:292). Furthermore, getting ethical clearance gives researchers the opportunity to reflect upon ethical issues, and, hence, enter the field better prepared (Gillam and Guillemin 2018:265; Hunter 2018:292; Genard and Roca i Escoda 2019:153).

To sum up, research ethics approval through a REC, which is increasingly emerging as a requirement, has attracted harsh criticism from some qualitative social scientists. It may indeed be challenging — or even hampering — for field researchers for the reasons described above. In the next section, I will describe a view of ethics that better suits field research.

3. Beyond the prospective and standardised approach: A plea for situated and reflexive research ethics

One way to overcome the disadvantages described in the previous section is to adopt a situated and reflexive view of research ethics (Burton-Jeangros 2017). 'Situated' means that ethics should be defined on a case-by-case basis and anchored in each step of specific projects; 'reflexive' involves thinking about ethics, documenting the considerations and making ethical decisions throughout the research project. These two attributes are important, because (1) each study has its own ethical challenges (it would be inappropriate to apply the same standards to all research projects), and (2) ethics is multi-faceted and (3) difficult to formalise. As Genard and Roca i Escoda (2019:12, my translation) observe, "ethics … is everywhere in practice".[3] In other words, ethical regulations do not exempt researchers from making ethical decisions while conducting research (Flick 2018:113), and doing ethical research means more than simply complying with the rules set by a regulatory body (Rubin and Rubin 2012:93).

Furthermore, ethical research should contribute to building a better world. Thus, research ethics should not put too much emphasis on merely doing no harm, as is sometimes the case with ethical regulations (Genard and Roca i Escoda 2019:160–161; see also Haggerty 2004 and Taylor, Taylor-Neu, and Butterwick 2020). Simply not causing harm is akin to "ethical abandonment or defection" (Genard and Roca i Escoda 2019:160, my translation).[4] Without going so far, it is clear that avoiding harm constitutes a minimalist approach to ethics, as there ought to be a legitimate expectation that research will improve some-

---

3. "l'éthique … se loge partout dans la pratique".
4. "un abandon ou une défection éthique".

Chapter 8. Beyond ethical clearance in field research **185**

thing. Flick (2018:108–109) states that the inconvenience posed by any kind of research is only justified if there is a direct or indirect benefit for the environment under investigation, such as improving knowledge of an issue or helping to solve a problem. Rubin and Rubin (2012:89) discuss this issue in terms of reciprocity: for them, a study should serve not only the researcher, but also participants, for example by highlighting the issues that concern them. Yet, it does not mean that the intended positive consequences are measurable benefits that can be estimated and compared to the possible harm, as a utilitarian view of ethics would entail. When adopting an approach to research ethics that strives to do good instead of doing no harm, a study must also be (1) relevant (Flick 2018:109) and (2) of good quality (Flick 2018:111–113). In addition, results must be (3) disseminated effectively to maximise potential benefits for participants. These three criteria ensure that both the time spent by the participants and the resources invested in the research project are being used as efficiently as possible.

In this section, I have argued for (1) a situated and reflexive approach to ethics, i.e., an ethical reflection specific to the study, which should take place before, during and after the completion of the project and (2) an encompassing view of ethics that involves doing good (instead of doing no harm) by conducting relevant, high-quality research, then disseminating results. The potential significance of a situated and reflexive approach will be illustrated in Section 5, along with a description of how confidentiality was dealt with in my research. Section 6 will present ideas on how to conduct interview studies that have a positive impact. Prior to that, the next short section presents the study upon which the empirical part of this chapter is based.

4. Studying revision policies and translator-reviser relationships with an interview study

For my PhD thesis, I carried out an interview study in Switzerland on revision and, more specifically, on the translator-reviser relationship (Riondel 2023).[5] I conducted 45 in-depth interviews with department heads, translators and revisers, as well as with one proof-reader and two project managers. The study mainly took place in translation departments and covered four areas: the Swiss Con-

---

5. The study received ethical clearance from the Ethical Review Board of the Faculty of Translation and Interpreting of the University of Geneva. The participants were given an Information and Consent Form, which they had to sign before the start of the interview. They could choose not to be recorded and it was clearly stated that they had the right to withdraw from the study without providing any justification and with no penalty or negative consequences.

federation ($n=20$), the international organisations based in Geneva ($n=12$), private companies with in-house translation departments ($n=8$) and the translation industry ($n=5$, three agency employees, plus two freelance translators working with agencies). The study looks at the organisation of revision (what texts are revised and by whom), revision practices (how translations are revised) and revision beliefs (how revision is perceived and what revision means for professionals). These three levels were first defined by Spolsky (2004) for language policy, then introduced to TIS by González Núñez (2016) for translation policy. I have adapted them for revision policy.

The topics covered in the interviews were quite broad: they range from general topics, such as the interviewees' professional background and job description, to questions about revision practices and perceptions of the activity. The interviews also included more specific issues like translator-reviser communication. They were conducted in line with the "responsive interviewing" approach, as defined by Rubin and Rubin (2012, see Section 6).

5. The concept of situated and reflexive ethics applied to confidentiality

The kinds of negative consequences that a field study (in TIS) can have include damaging participants' reputation, having negative repercussions on their careers, provoking conflicts among participants and unveiling information that can jeopardise businesses (unless the study deals with illegal behaviour, in which case the potential fallout is evidently more severe). These risks mainly exist when participants or companies are identified, i.e., when confidentiality is breached. Confidentiality can be defined as "guaranteeing respondents a dissociation between their words — sometimes also their actions — and their identity" (Béliard and Eideliman 2008:124, my translation).[6] It is one of the main ethical concerns in the social sciences and, as such, one of the preferred topics of RECs (Haggerty 2004:407–409). In field research, confidentiality is complex because the analysis aims at describing a human phenomenon in detail in order to advance our understanding of it. In other words, people are at its centre and situations are described at length. Furthermore, confidentiality comes in many forms: it not only applies to people, but also to institutions, companies, associations, or the specific context in which the study is being conducted, which is generally referred to as a case (on cases in general, see Dumez 2015; on cases in TIS, see Susam-Sarajeva 2009).

---

6. "garantir aux enquêtés une dissociation entre leurs paroles — parfois aussi leurs actes — et leur identité".

There are several types of identification, which concern both contexts and people. If we take people, for example:

1. a participant can recognise themselves;
2. a participant or another member of the group being studied (e.g., a colleague or a superior who did not take part in the study) can recognise one or more participants;
3. a person outside of the study can recognise one or more participants.

The first type of identification is inevitable, at least according to Beaud and Weber (2010: 255), as people are bound to recognise their own words when interview excerpts are reproduced in reports. The second type is the thorniest. Avoiding this type of identification means ensuring "internal confidentiality" (Tolich 2004) or simply "confidentiality" (Béliard and Eideliman 2008). The third type relates to a breach of "external confidentiality" (Tolich 2004) or "anonymity" (Béliard and Eideliman 2008). "Anonymity" (or external confidentiality) can be quite easily achieved if readers are not familiar with the case being described. Replacing the person's name by a pseudonym or an alphanumeric code, as is oftentimes the case today, is usually sufficient, in addition to abstaining from giving (too much) personal information. "Confidentiality" (or internal confidentiality) is a more complex issue. It often is not sufficient to use pseudonyms or codes to safeguard confidentiality. For example, if you reproduce several quotes from the same person, the risk of identification can be high, through what is called "jigsaw identification" (Saunders, Kitzinger, and Kitzinger 2015: 627). In some cases, researchers use complex confidentiality strategies, like mixing information from different people or substituting one piece of information for another that is close to it (Béliard and Eideliman 2008: 132, 138–139; Saunders, Kitzinger, and Kitzinger 2015: 627). In TIS, the second strategy may involve substituting one language for another when an interviewee's language combination is referred to.

The identification of the context (typically an institution, company or association) is both less sensitive and more difficult to deal with. On the one hand, it is less sensitive because it does not concern individuals. On the other hand, it is more complicated because qualitative research aims at describing a situation in detail in order to provide a holistic report. This means contextualising the phenomenon under study, which, in turn, implies providing information about the case that is being studied. Ultimately, the confidentiality of people and that of organisations are closely linked: if the context is identified, there is a higher chance that people will also be recognised.

Beyond obeying the legal or regulatory framework, e.g., rules established by a REC, researchers generally have some degree of freedom when it comes to deciding how to ensure confidentiality. They can choose a restrictive approach, as I did for my own study (see below), or a more open approach. The latter could mean providing the name of the settings studied, supplying pseudonyms or codes after the quotes, or being generous about the information provided about the participants (life stories, career or profiles). I believe that four elements must be taken into account in order to select the right approach: the size of the group being studied, the sensitivity of the topic, the analytical position of the researcher and usual practices in similar studies (see Figure 1). The first dimension hinges on the object of study: the smaller the group, the greater the risk of identification. Here, 'group' does not mean sample size, but the population under study. The second dimension concerns the sensitivity of the topic (or data) and the vulnerability of participants. Sensitive topics typically include health, illegal behaviour, religious beliefs and political opinion; people who are considered to be particularly vulnerable include minors, detainees and people with disabilities. The third element that I would suggest needs to be taken into account is the analytical stance of the researcher: the more critical the analysis, the higher the risk of inciting a negative reaction from identified individuals or entities. Finally, the fourth aspect that can influence a confidentiality strategy is the choices made in similar studies, since it is advisable to draw from the (best) practices of peers. For example, if recognised works in the same field adopt a strict approach to confidentiality, then confidentiality choices might be more restrictive.

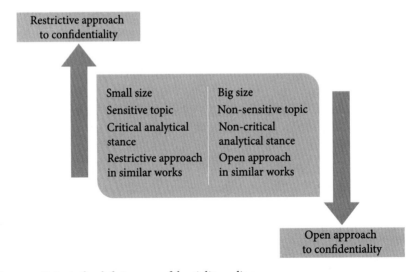

Figure 1. Criteria for defining a confidentiality policy

The four suggested criteria — the first two being more conventional, and the last two more subjective — show that there is no one-size-fits-all solution when defining a confidentiality policy. In other words, confidentiality must be situated, i.e., specific to a single research project.

I will now discuss how these criteria have influenced the confidentiality strategy I adopted for my study. The first criterion was not decisive, since the size of the group I studied can be characterised as medium, thereby providing more options for the confidentiality policy. The second criterion, by contrast, was crucial. My study deals with the professional environment, which can be seen as quite sensitive. Just as in the family sphere, relationships in the workplace are relatively extensive and long-term; they are imposed upon people and involve all members of the group, i.e., everyone knows everyone else. Moreover, work is an important and necessary part of life as it ensures subsistence. On top of that, revision and the translator-reviser relationship are sensitive topics. Revision has two facets, revising and being revised, and both positions can induce strong emotions. As a reviser, it is easy to get angry at the translator; as a revisee, it can be highly demoralising to have one's text revised (Riondel 2023). In interviews on revision, participants discuss both themselves and their colleagues, which is a sensitive matter. The sensitivity of the subject became apparent several times during the interviews. First, the meetings made it clear that being revised involves a kind of violence that some participants voiced in very strong terms. Second, revision involves judging a translation, and therefore the work of one's colleagues. Participants sometimes said they were embarrassed to talk about their colleagues if it was not to praise them. Finally, before expressing an opinion that could make them look arrogant, one person explicitly told me that what they had to tell me really had to be kept between us, which highlights the particular importance they place on confidentiality.

The third criterion, i.e., the analytical stance, shaped the confidentiality strategy inasmuch as I wanted to feel free in my analyses and have the opportunity to express a critical point of view. As for the fourth suggested criterion, I drew mainly on similar studies to determine the right attitude to adopt with regard to the (non-)disclosure of the names of the contexts studied. As far as institutions are concerned, usages differ in TIS: LeBlanc (2021) does not mention the names of the institutions he has been to, while Koskinen (2008) and Duflou (2016) overtly work in the context of EU institutions. As for companies (translation agencies), researchers do not generally disclose the names of companies (see, e.g., Drugan 2013; Risku 2016; Olohan 2021). I therefore decided not to name the contexts under study, as is the norm when working with translation agencies, and sometimes the case when dealing with institutions. This ensures some form of homogeneity across all contexts, and improves confidentiality with regard to people, as people are more likely to be recognised when the context is specified.

Taking the above into account, I used quite a restrictive approach to confidentiality for my study. As far as contexts are concerned, the goal was that outsiders should not be able to recognise them (Beaud and Weber 2010:255), although insiders, e.g., team members or partners, certainly would. As for participants, I strived for both external and internal confidentiality. The codes used to identify people in the raw data and for data storage have not been reproduced in reports, especially after a quote. Avoiding codes is a strategy for preventing jigsaw identification (Saunders, Kitzinger, and Kitzinger 2015:627), although it entails the risk of not informing the reader that several related quotes stem from the same participant — a problem that can be partly solved by giving the information in the body of the text when it is meaningful. In addition, quotes are contextualised, but information like sex, age and other classical socio-demographic variables are not used before or after a quote. This approach complies with the principle that personal information should not be disclosed unless it is necessary (Flick 2018:111), and it also helps avoid narrowing down the reader's interpretation by putting forward a few characteristics out of the infinite possibilities when describing a person's identity (Silverman 2017:151–152). That being said, information that is necessary to understand the situation is provided, including the case in which a participant is working, their function (translator, reviser, head) and work experience, if relevant.

Confidentiality strategies are complex not only because they are multifactorial, as seen above, but also because they cannot be defined upstream or left until last. Instead, they must be established prior to the fieldwork, then reflexively reassessed throughout the whole research project (Béliard and Eideliman 2008:131–132). This clearly highlights why ethics must be reflexive. In the study described here, not all decisions regarding confidentiality were taken at the planning stage. In particular, the final decision to keep the names of the institutions and companies secret was taken near the end, when writing the report. More specifically, as I was progressing with the data production and analysis, I felt more and more strongly that it would be preferable not to disclose names in order to protect the services, because there were a few negative aspects that had to be reported, the most notable being the pressure that junior translators feel with regard to revision (participants mentioned young translators — themselves or colleagues — crying after receiving a revised text).

In qualitative research, confidentiality involves a tension between protecting participants and ensuring the validity of the study (or its interest to the public). Indeed, confidentiality strategies must always strike a balance between confidentiality and integrity of the data (Saunders, Kitzinger, and Kitzinger 2015:627–628), or between protecting participants and maintaining accuracy (Rubin and Rubin 2012:89–90). In concrete terms, the more limited the information, the greater the harm to data, since their value lies in their details and richness. Conversely, the more information is provided, the more participants' protection is put at risk. As there often is no perfect solution, the goal is to arrive at the "'best possible', or 'least worst', option" (Saunders, Kitzinger, and Kitzinger 2015: 628). I would suggest that applying a situated and reflexive approach to research ethics helps attain a compromise that gives participants a sufficient level of protection while providing the scientific community with valuable research.

6. Involvement of researcher and participants as a means of producing ethical interview research

While the previous sections addressed field research as a whole, this section focuses on interviews and interview studies, a common type of method and research. It aims to show how methodological and organisational choices can foster ethical research. As explained in Section 3, ethics not only should mean causing no harm but should also entail having a positive impact on the group being studied or society at large. In my view, this is possible when two conditions are met: (1) the existence of a good relationship between the researcher(s) and the participants, (2) research of high quality, disseminated in an effective way, in academic venues and beyond. In interview research, these two goals — maintaining a good relationship and producing high-quality research — are closely connected to the concept of involvement: first, involvement of the researcher in the interview (as well as in the research project at large), and second, involvement of participants throughout the research project.

Different approaches to interviewing have been put forward in which interviewers position themselves differently in the interaction. Some authors champion a detached approach in order to avoid influencing the responses of the interviewee (see, for instance, the volume edited by Bréchon 2011). Other authors advocate for the researcher's involvement in the conversation in order to mitigate the artificiality of communication and bring the interview closer to a normal conversation. Examples of this perspective are textbooks by Kaufmann (2016), a French sociologist, and, in English, by Rubin and Rubin (2012). Rubin and Rubin (2012) have developed their own method of in-depth interviewing, which they call "responsive interviewing", a model where "researchers respond to and then ask further questions about what they hear from the interviewees" (Rubin and Rubin 2012: xv). Under this approach, interviewees are viewed as "conversational partners", with whom researchers must strive to "develo[p] and maintai[n] an ongoing relationship" (Rubin and Rubin 2012: xv). In an interview, openness and trust of participants, i.e., the involvement of the interviewee, are key to producing good data. The involvement of the researcher in the conversation is a way to foster this involvement (as well as a natural response to it). Furthermore, it brings reciprocity to both conversational partners, which can be viewed as an ethical attitude.

On one occasion, this openness and reciprocity led to an ethically challenging situation in my own study. Towards the end of an interview, I asked a participant if he wished to add anything, as I always did. He then asked me whether what he said corresponded to what his colleagues had told me. I was disconcerted, but I managed to do two things: first, I said that it was difficult to answer the question since I had not analysed the data yet, and second, I mentioned two phenomena that I had noticed at previous meetings, presenting them in a general way. The participant's question may be understood in different ways. It may express a need for validation: the participant may want to know the opinion of colleagues in order to be reassured, or receive validation for what he said. It could also be the result of a form of curiosity, whether sincere or unhealthy. It could also be a way — admittedly, a little tactless — of enquiring about the results of the study. In retrospect, I think the situation was much more banal than how I experienced it at the time. I think that the two reactions I had, both instinctive and clumsy, provide keys to dealing with this kind of situation. My first reaction was more or less to avoid the issue. Contrary to what one might think, giving a general or a somewhat irrelevant answer is an option for researchers, just as it is always an option for interviewees. Secondly, I think that the way in which results are reported on the spot should be inspired by what is done in reports. Thus, it is possible to provide information anonymously or in a generalised way, as we do in publications. All in all, this situation arose from a relationship between equals, which I had sought to establish; as uncomfortable as it may have made me at the time, this example is also proof that I was successful in doing so.

The second type of involvement — that of the participants in the research project — is not straightforward in interview research, i.e., studies where interviews are the only method of producing data (see introduction). The researcher and participant rarely have a long-term relationship. On the contrary, they often get to know each other on the day of the interview and do not have any further contact until participants receive a summary sheet at the end of the project (if any). It is therefore difficult for the researcher to build a relationship with participants that can allow them to avoid conflict and ensure that there is no discomfort on the participants' end — two goals that can be described as ethical.

There are two moments in a research project that are well-suited for further involving the participants in a study: the first is when the transcript is produced and the second is at the end of the project, when results are ready. Sending the transcript to participants has become a standard in qualitative research. It may be required by RECs (as was the case in the present study) and can also be used as a way to implement the validity strategy known as member checking (synonyms are: communicative validation, informant feedback, respondent validation, member validation and dependability checking, see Maxwell 2013:126–127; Varpio et al. 2017:46–47; Flick 2018:33, 88–90). Member checking can be traced back to Lincoln and Guba (1985:314) and refers to soliciting feedback from the participants on data or interpretation. Sending the transcript to participants is also a matter of courtesy and openness — an aspect that is less frequently emphasised — and it helps maintain contact. In addition, it is an opportunity for participants to voice their thoughts more easily than if they had had to write an e-mail on their own initiative.

As far as the presentation of the results is concerned, it is quite common to draw up a summary sheet and send it to participants. When a study takes place in a group in which members know each other, as is often the case in field research, researchers may organise a meeting to present and discuss their results. This may be seen as a form of compensation for participants for their time. For the researcher, it is an opportunity to give back to participants and show respect by preparing a good presentation. These meetings also provide an occasion to discuss results with the people who are primarily concerned by the study, which can be very valuable when developing an interpretation of the data.

Involving participants throughout the research project is a way to create reciprocity, as is involving the researcher in the conversation. By maintaining contact, researchers show that they have invested time and effort in the study, for example, by producing an accurate transcript, writing a clear summary of the results and/or putting together a coherent oral presentation. It lends equilibrium to the relationship and stands in contrast to the classic relationship in which the researcher receives all the benefits. Keeping interviewees updated is also a way of showing openness, which is an ethical value. In this section, I have argued that getting involved as a researcher and involving the participants throughout the research project is a suitable way of conducting an ethical interview study, i.e., a means for conducting quality research that maintains a good researcher-participant relationship and has positive effects for the participants and, more generally, the community being studied.

7.   Conclusion: Risks of ethical regulation vs. promotion of ethical reflexion

In this chapter, I have tried to emphasise that ethics is a far-reaching and complex topic. In order to do so, I have provided background information on ethics in the social sciences and gone into the detail on two particular aspects: confidentiality in field research and relationships with participants in interview studies. Concurrently, I have argued for a positive approach to ethics that promotes beneficial change in society and puts human beings centre stage. Indeed, an ethical vision should be neither too restrictive nor too negative: ethics is not just a matter of getting people to sign a consent form, deleting names from files or avoiding harm. Even if it is important to avoid causing conflict or inflicting other negative consequences on participants, ethics is also about showing respect, having a good relationship with participants and trying to improve their environment. To conclude, I would like to summarise and discuss challenges and risks associated with ethical regulation and to promote ethical reflection.

There are advantages to ethical regulation and RECs, particularly when it comes to legitimising research and giving researchers the opportunity to reflect on ethical issues before the study begins. However, they pose several challenges for field research. First, ethical clearance is prospective, which obliges the researcher to establish the ethical framework before going to the field, even though adjustments are vital to take into account the evolutionary nature of qualitative research. In addition, the prospective dimension may contradict the reflexive dimension of ethics. Furthermore, RECs tend to put too much emphasis on harm (Haggerty 2004; Taylor, Taylor-Neu, and Butterwick 2020), to act in too standardised a way (Dawson 2006; Gagnon 2010; Taylor, Taylor-Neu, and Butterwick 2020), and to impose standards that are not suited to the qualitative paradigm or do not take into account the specificities of field research (Gagnon 2010:303; Larouche 2019:492, 494–495; for an example of how methodological choices imposed by REC can impair the quality of research, see Leisey 2008).

Ethical regulation entails broader risks: it may lead researchers to use standard research methods or designs, resulting in limited creativity in research or the abandonment of some studies (Haggerty 2004:412; Larouche 2019:481, 491; Taylor, Taylor-Neu, and Butterwick 2020:61, 69; van den Hoonaard 2011:3, 239–246). Even if the abandoning of some projects may be justified, I would find it unfortunate if ethical reviews lead to the promotion of a conservative ideology, the view championed by Taylor, Taylor-Neu, and Butterwick (2020), who observe that RECs are reluctant about any change, including social change.

Applying the same rules to all field studies means denying the situated nature of ethics. A concrete example could illustrate the detrimental effect of standardised policy. Requiring written consent has several consequences: it is difficult to use in contexts where people act under pseudonyms, notably online; it can arouse suspicion, and thus affect the quality of the data (Fassin 2008:125–126); and it makes it almost impossible to study deviant, dysfunctional or illegal behaviour (Gagnon 2010:303; Genard and Roca i Escoda 2019:149–150). In TIS, it may lead to dropping or avoiding doing studies on illegal or dangerous behaviour, like fansubbing or activist translation (be it political texts in regimes that do not tolerate dissent or texts calling for illegal action in any regime).

Ideally, there should be no taboos in ethics. There should be the possibility of doing away with written consent in some cases. The same applies to confidentiality: some people want to be acknowledged, for example, if it can afford them some kind of status or recognition; furthermore, in some cases, the essence of what is being said is lost through anonymity, as is the case with public figures, such as politicians or business leaders (Béliard and Eideliman 2008: 134; Bréchon 2011: 69) or, in TIS, literary translators.

Another risk is that "ethical review drives out ethical reflection"[7] (Gagnon 2010: 305, my translation), despite the fact that ethical reflection is exactly what should be pursued. Researchers need to engage with ethics throughout the project. This begins by taking into consideration the ethical issues before the study is carried out. The process of getting approval from a REC should therefore be seen as an opportunity to reflect on ethical issues (Hunter 2018: 292). Reflections on ethics can also include discussions with RECs in order to explain the theoretical basis of the proposed procedures. Another way to be even more involved would be to serve on an ethics committee. Finally, ethical reflections should also lead to more intense debate in academic circles. Ideally, these discussions should be both specific to TIS and part of the debates in related disciplines (e.g., linguistics, psychology, sociology and anthropology).

Funding

This research was supported in part by the Swiss National Science Foundation (Grant No. P1GEP1_195089).

Acknowledgements

I would like to thank all participants for their precious time. I am especially indebted to the department heads for their trust and warm welcome.

---

7. "l'évaluation éthique chasse la réflexion éthique".

References

Beaud, Stéphane, and Florence Weber. 2010. *Guide de l'enquête de terrain : produire et analyser des données ethnographiques.* 4th edition. Paris: La Découverte.

Béliard, Aude, and Jean-Sébastien Eideliman. 2008. "Au-delà de la déontologie. Anonymat et confidentialité dans le travail ethnographique." In *Les politiques de l'enquête. Épreuves ethnographiques,* ed. by Didier Fassin, and Alban Bensa, 123–141. Paris: La Découverte.

Bréchon, Pierre (ed). 2011. *Enquêtes qualitatives, enquêtes quantitatives.* Grenoble: Presses universitaires de Grenoble.

Burton-Jeangros, Claudine (ed). 2017. *L'éthique (en) pratique : la recherche en sciences sociales.* Genève: Université de Genève.

Creswell, John W. 2013. *Qualitative Inquiry & Research Design: Choosing Among Five Approaches.* 3rd edition. Los Angeles & London: Sage.

Dawson, Angus J. 2006. "A Messy Business: Qualitative Research and Ethical Review." *Clinical Ethics* 1 (2): 114–116.

Drugan, Joanna. 2013. *Quality in Professional Translation: Assessment and Improvement.* London: Bloomsbury.

Duflou, Veerle. 2016. *Be(com)ing a Conference Interpreter: An Ethnography of EU Interpreters as a Professional Community.* Amsterdam & Philadelphia: John Benjamins.

Dumez, Hervé. 2015. "What Is a Case, and What Is a Case Study?" *BMS: Bulletin of Sociological Methodology* 127: 43–57.

Fassin, Didier. 2008. "L'éthique, au-delà de la règle. Réflexions autour d'une enquête ethnographique sur les pratiques de soins en Afrique du Sud." *Sociétés contemporaines* 71: 117–135.

Flick, Uwe. 2018. *Managing Quality in Qualitative Research.* 2nd edition. Los Angeles & London: Sage.

Gagnon, Éric. 2010. "Le comité d'éthique de la recherche, et au-delà." *Éthique publique* 12 (1): 299–308.

Genard, Jean-Louis, and Marta Roca i Escoda. 2019. *Ethique de la recherche en sociologie.* Louvain-La-Neuve: De Boeck Supérieur.

Gillam, Lynn, and Marilys Guillemin. 2018. "Reflexivity: Overcoming Mistrust Between Research Ethics Committees and Researchers." In *The SAGE Handbook of Qualitative Research Ethics,* ed. by Ron Iphofen, and Martin Tolich, 263–275. London: Sage.

González Núñez, Gabriel. 2016. "On Translation Policy." *Target* 28 (1): 87–109.

Gubrium, Jaber F., James A. Holstein, Amir Marvasti, and Karyn D. McKinney (eds). 2012. *The SAGE Handbook of Interview Research: The Complexity of the Craft.* 2nd edition. Los Angeles & London: Sage.

Haggerty, Kevin D. 2004. "Ethics Creep: Governing Social Science Research in the Name of Ethics." *Qualitative Sociology* 27 (4): 391–414.

Hekkanen, Raila. 2007. "The Role of Ethics in Translation and in Translation Studies Research." *Across Languages and Cultures* 8 (2): 231–247.

Hunter, David. 2018. "Research Ethics Committees — What Are They Good For?" In *The SAGE Handbook of Qualitative Research Ethics,* ed. by Ron Iphofen, and Martin Tolich, 289–300. London: Sage.

Kaufmann, Jean-Claude. 2016. *L'entretien compréhensif.* 4th edition. Paris: Armand Colin.

Koskinen, Kaisa. 2000. Beyond Ambivalence: Postmodernity and the Ethics of Translation. PhD Thesis, University of Tampere.

Koskinen, Kaisa. 2008. *Translating Institutions: An Ethnographic Study of EU Translation.* Manchester: St. Jerome.

Koskinen, Kaisa, and Nike K. Pokorn (eds). 2021. *The Routledge Handbook of Translation and Ethics.* Abingdon & New York: Routledge.

Larouche, Jean-Marc. 2019. "Les sciences sociales et l'éthique en recherche en contexte canadien. Régulation imposée ou approche réflexive?" *Revue d'anthropologie des connaissances* 13 (2): 479–501.

LeBlanc, Matthieu. 2021. "Non-Professional Editing in the Workplace. Examples from the Canadian Context." In *Translation Revision and Post-editing: Industry Practices and Cognitive Processes*, ed. by Maarit Koponen, Brian Mossop, Isabelle S. Robert, and Giovanna Scocchera, 73–88. Abingdon & New York: Routledge.

Leisey, Monica. 2008. "Qualitative Inquiry and the IRB: Protection at all Costs?" *Qualitative Social Work* 7 (4): 415–426.

Lincoln, Yvonna S., and Egon G. Guba. 1985. *Naturalistic Inquiry.* Newbury Park & London: Sage.

Maxwell, Joseph A. 2013. *Qualitative Research Design: An Interactive Approach.* 3rd edition. Los Angeles & London: Sage.

Mellinger, Christopher D., and Brian James Baer. 2021. "Research Ethics in Translation and Interpreting Studies." In *The Routledge Handbook of Translation and Ethics*, ed. by Kaisa Koskinen, and Nike K. Pokorn, 365–380. Abingdon & New York: Routledge.

Olivier de Sardan, Jean-Pierre. 2008. *La rigueur du qualitatif. Les contraintes empiriques de l'interprétation socio-anthropologique.* Louvain-la-Neuve: Academia-Bruylant.

Olohan, Maeve. 2021. *Translation and Practice Theory.* Abingdon & New York: Routledge.

Pym, Anthony. 1997. *Pour une éthique du traducteur.* Arras & Ottawa: Artois Presses Université/Presses de l'Université d'Ottawa.

Riondel, Aurélien. 2023. "Le grand écart de la révision. Étude par entretien des politiques de révision et des relations traducteurs-réviseurs." Unpublished PhD thesis, University of Geneva.

Risku, Hanna. 2016. *Translationsmanagement: Interkulturelle Fachkommunikation im Informationszeitalter.* 3rd edition. Tübingen: Gunter Narr.

Rubin, Herbert J., and Irene S. Rubin. 2012. *Qualitative Interviewing: The Art of Hearing Data.* 3rd edition. Los Angeles & London: Sage.

Saunders, Benjamin, Jenny Kitzinger, and Celia Kitzinger. 2015. "Anonymising Interview Data: Challenges and Compromise in Practice." *Qualitative Research* 15 (5): 616–632.

Schrag, Zachary M. 2010. *Ethical Imperialism: Institutional Review Boards and the Social Sciences, 1965–2009.* Baltimore: Johns Hopkins University Press.

Silverman, David. 2017. "How Was It for You? The Interview Society and the Irresistible Rise of the (Poorly Analyzed) Interview." *Qualitative Research* 17 (2): 144–158.

Spolsky, Bernard. 2004. *Language Policy.* Cambridge: Cambridge University Press.

Susam-Sarajeva, Şebnem. 2009. "The Case Study Research Method in Translation Studies." *The Interpreter and Translator Trainer* 3 (1): 37–56.

Taylor, Alison, Robyn Taylor-Neu, and Shauna Butterwick. 2020. "'Trying to Square the Circle': Research Ethics and Canadian Higher Education." *European Educational Research Journal* 19 (1): 56–71.

Tolich, Martin. 2004. "Internal Confidentiality: When Confidentiality Assurances Fail Relational Informants." *Qualitative Sociology* 27 (1): 101–106.

van den Hoonaard, Will C. 2011. *The Seduction of Ethics: Transforming the Social Sciences.* Toronto: University of Toronto Press.

Varpio, Lara, Rola Ajjawi, Lynn V. Monrouxe, Bridget C. O'Brien, and Charlotte E. Rees. 2017. "Shedding the Cobra Effect: Problematising Thematic Emergence, Triangulation, Saturation and Member Checking." *Medical Education* 51 (1): 40–50.

PART III

Zooming in on processes and materiality

CHAPTER 9

Co-constructing cognitive artifacts in the translation workplace

Raphael Sannholm
Stockholm University

This chapter concerns collaboration in the translation workplace, specifically the joint construction of a central workplace resource, a client guidelines document, by two translators. Using conversation analysis, the moment-to-moment interaction between the translators is analysed as they engage in decision making with regard to the contents of the document. Considered from the perspective of distributed cognition, the decision-making process is distributed between the participants through their interaction with each other and with material artifacts. The analysis shows how decisions about how to resolve epistemic uncertainty emerge interactively, how material resources are made relevant in the decision-making process, and how authority is jointly constructed. The chapter also discusses how the collaborative document revision contributes to the development of the cultural-cognitive ecosystem of the workplace.

Keywords: distributed cognition, conversation analysis, cognitive artifact, workplace ethnography, cultural-cognitive ecosystem

1. Introduction

There is now a fairly solid body of research on translators' use of technological tools and other resources (e.g., Dragsted 2008; Bundgaard 2017; Christensen, Flanagan, and Schjoldager 2017; Hvelplund 2017; Bundgaard and Christensen 2019; O'Hagan 2019; Bowker 2022; Rothwell et al. 2023). Research into the interface between cognition and ergonomics in translation settings has also contributed to the knowledge of how the physical and technological environments of translators are perceived and organised (Ehrensberger-Dow 2021:149). However, less attention has been paid to the ways in which resources of different kinds are constructed and maintained in translation settings (however, see Karamanis, Luz and Doherty 2011), in particular from a socio-cognitive theoretical viewpoint.

https://doi.org/10.1075/btl.165.09san
Available under the CC BY-NC 4.0 license. © 2025 John Benjamins Publishing Company

Based on interaction data collected as part of an ethnographic workplace study in the Swedish translation office of a global language service provider (LSP), the present chapter investigates the collective construction of digital resources in a translation workplace. The aim is to demonstrate how particular resources, which may be considered as cognitive artifacts (Hutchins 1999; see Section 3.2), are jointly constructed in the translation workplace, and to discuss how their construction reflects and contributes to the cultural-cognitive ecosystem of the workplace.

The study reported in this chapter examines the interaction of two translators involved in the joint assessment and revision of a central workplace document which outlines procedures, tools, social networks etc., for the LSP's clients. I will refer to this document as *client-specific guidelines* (CSG) (see Section 4.2.3). The chapter contributes to the knowledge of the role of social interaction and use of artifacts in the translation workplace in two main respects. First, it considers the interaction and the artifact in question from a socio-cognitive theoretical perspective which emphasises the relationship between cultural practices and cognitive processes in the translation workplace. It thus aligns with socio-cognitive approaches to translation, particularly extended translation (Risku and Windhager 2015) and cognitive translatology (Muñoz 2010, 2016, 2017). In terms of the broader theoretical framing, the study can be seen to adopt what Alves and Jakobsen (2021: 550) have termed "a SDE (situated, distributed and extended) approach to cognition within CTS" (cognitive translation studies, see Halverson 2010), with a particular emphasis on the distributed aspect, as put forward by the framework of distributed cognition (Hutchins 1995a, 1995b, 2006, 2008, 2010, 2013; see also Korhonen, Chapter 10, this volume). Second, similarly to Hirvonen (2025), the study uses conversation analysis (CA) to investigate cognition in real-life settings. Using CA, the social actions performed by the translators in the process of jointly assessing and revising a workplace document are described and analysed in detail, including the mobilisation of material resources and social support. In the analysis, I pay attention to manifestations of knowledge, or lack thereof, on the part of the participants, as well as of their respective mandates to propose courses of action with regard to the CSG document. To this end, the concepts of epistemic status and stance (Heritage 2012) and deontic authority (Stevanovic and Peräkylä 2012) are used to examine the interaction (see Section 4.1.2).

The remainder of this chapter is organised as follows. Section 2 summarises relevant previous research, and Section 3 introduces the theoretical framework used in the chapter. Section 4 explains the methodology and describes the data. Sections 5 and 6 present the analysis and discussion, respectively. Finally, conclusions are presented in Section 7.

2. Previous research

Empirical and conceptual research on the role of tools and environments as well as cooperation in authentic work settings of translators have opened up new research avenues and broadened our understanding of how translators interact with their social and material environments in the translation process. A thorough review is beyond the scope of this chapter, but core conceptual groundwork has been presented by Risku and colleagues in a number of publications (e.g., Risku 2002, 2010; Risku, Windhager, and Apfelthaler 2013; Risku and Windhager 2015; Risku and Rogl 2021). A central assumption put forward already two decades ago by Risku (2002: 530) is that "[t]ranslation is done not only by the brain, but also by complex systems, systems which include people, their specific social and physical environments and all their cultural artefacts" (see also Risku 2010: 102–103). Sannholm and Risku (2024) probe further into central cognitive science conceptualisations relevant to analyses of interactions in translation work, and point to the potential added value of applying a distributed perspective on team collaborations.

In turn, particularly relevant empirical research focusing on cooperation in translation work (with situated approaches as more or less explicit theoretical frames of reference), is presented by Karamanis, Luz and Doherty (2011), who explore not only the use of resources but also their construction and maintenance in translation settings. They note how translators working in a LSP jointly create term lists to ensure terminological consistency in translation projects that involve several translators. Terms were entered into a spreadsheet after having been discussed among the translators, and the spreadsheet was continuously updated. In a similar vein, Sannholm (2021) demonstrates how translators in a LSP workplace actively maintain and manipulate shared material resources, specifically TM systems. The translators evaluate the importance of adding the content of certain translation jobs to TM systems, which entails decisions on their part about what translation tool to use in certain situations. Moreover, translators refrain from actions that would lead to the storage of faulty content in TM resources, e.g., when misalignments between future source text content and TM content are anticipated. Such actions and non-actions thus serve to maintain the usefulness of common material resources in the workplace. Collaboration in translation workplace settings is also investigated by Korhonen and Hirvonen (2021), and Hirvonen (2025). Focusing on teamwork in audio-description, Hirvonen (2025) shows how phenomena such as problem solving and decision making unfold collaboratively as translation problems are jointly addressed by different actors. Korhonen and Hirvonen (2021) compare teamwork in audio-description and commercial specialised translation, focusing on the co-creation of translated texts.

Of particular interest to the present chapter is their observation that, in commercial specialised translation, draft translations function as cognitive artifacts that allow for the involvement of different actors in the co-creation of the texts in question (Korhonen and Hirvonen 2021: 270–271).

Common to the abovementioned studies is the use of theoretical frameworks that consider cognition as culturally and socially embedded. This is also the case for the present chapter, and the theoretical framework is presented next.

3. Theoretical framework

3.1 Distributed cognition

The analysis presented in this chapter is theoretically informed by the distributed cognition framework (Hutchins 1995a, 1995b, 2001, 2006) because of its emphasis on the cultural framing of cognition and the relationship between interaction and the distribution of cognitive processes among human actors and artifacts (Hutchins 2006: 376). The central tenets of distributed cognition (DC) hold that "cognition is distributed through time, between person and culturally constructed environment, and among persons in socially organized settings" (Hutchins 2006: 377). Therefore, approaching an understanding of how the distribution of cognitive processes may emerge and unfold, requires paying attention to interactions of different sorts, including how such interactions unfold over longer periods of time. As Hutchins (2006: 376) puts it, "the distributed cognition perspective directs our attention to particular classes of interactions", namely "[i]nteraction with social others" (2006: 377, italics removed), with the "material environment" (Hutchins 2006: 378), as well as "of the [p]resent with the [p]ast" (2006: 379, italics removed). The attention to the local context and long-term development of such interactions also explains why DC scholars advocate the use of ethnographic field research as one of the preferred methodological approaches (see Hollan, Hutchins, and Kirsh 2000: 179–180).

DC shares many assumptions with perspectives such as extended, embodied, and enacted cognition, which are often gathered under the umbrella term "situated cognition" (Robbins and Aydede 2009) or "situated approaches" (Risku and Rogl 2021: 478), including the emphasis on the central role of environments and artifacts. Teasing out the differences and similarities of different perspectives is beyond the scope of this chapter (this is done, e.g., by Risku and Rogl 2021, and Sannholm and Risku 2024). However, one point that needs to be made clear here is that DC posits that constellations of human actors, often using material artifacts, may display different cognitive properties than the sum of the individual actors alone. Thus, from the perspective of DC, cognitive processes, such as remembering, are taken to unfold within cognitive systems that extend beyond individual actors (Hutchins 1995a, 1995b, 2001, 2006, 2008, 2013).

3.2 Cognitive artifacts and ecosystems

In line with previous CTS research (Risku 2010; Rogl and Risku 2024; Sannholm and Risku 2024), I will use the concept of *cognitive artifact* to consider and conceptualise the potential role of digital and physical resources in the translation workplace. The term appears to have been coined by Norman (1993), who also develops theoretical accounts of the role of different sorts of cognitive artifacts. As this chapter takes as its overarching theoretical orientation the framework of distributed cognition as developed by Hutchins (1995a, 1995b, 2006), I refrain here from elaborating further on Norman's ideas, and adopt the perspective of cognitive artifacts found in Hutchins' approach of distributed cognition. In fact, it has also been suggested that Hutchins' work builds on Norman (Garbis 2002:50). Cognitive artifacts, according to Hutchins (1999:126), "are physical objects made by humans for the purpose of aiding, enhancing, or improving cognition. Examples of cognitive artifacts include a string tied around the finger as a reminder, a calendar, a shopping list, and a computer". Highly pertinent to the present study is Hutchins' specification that "[l]ists of various kinds support not only memory, but also reasoning about classification and comparison" (1999:126, emphasis removed from original). Now, the view that cognitive abilities are amplified in any actual sense is rejected by many scholars (see Hutchins 1999:127; Garbis 2002:64–65). What cognitive artifacts are rather taken to do is that they change the organisation of cognitive processes. Thus, from this view, when translators use, say, translation memory systems (TMS), it is not their ability to remember that is amplified. Rather, the cognitive artifact, the TMS in this case, re-structures certain parts of the cognitive process. Instead of remembering which particular target language items have previously been used for particular source text items from particular clients, the task is restructured to searching for, and (possibly) choosing between, competing solutions.

Importantly, Hutchins (1999:127) also points out that "[c]ognitive artifacts are always embedded in larger socio-cultural systems that organize the practices in which they are used. The utility of a cognitive artifact depends on other processes that create the conditions and exploit the consequences of its use". Recently, a similar view, i.e., that cognitive artifacts form part of particular cultural settings and that their use is dependent on culturally constituted knowledge about how to use them, has been developed by Menary and Gillet (2022). Connecting the use of cognitive artifacts (actually, Menary and Gillet use the term "cognitive tool") to cultural learning, they argue that approaches to cognitive artifacts that stress their role as amplifiers of cognitive abilities or temporary scaffolds for learning fail to take into account how the use of artifacts is intrinsically intertwined with what they term "cognitive practices" (Menary and Gillet 2022:366). Practices refer here to "repeatable actions that can be spread out across a population, [and] are acquired through social or specific cultural learning". Through a process labelled "enculturation" (Menary and Gillet 2022:367), cognitive artifacts become integrated components of cognition, rather than functioning as temporary 'external' aids for 'internal' cognition. Hutchins (2006:379) makes a similar proposal with regard to what he calls "cultural cognitive ecology". As this has particular relevance for the way in which the use of guideline documents can be understood, I quote him at length here:

> The development of cultural cognitive ecology is itself a cognitive process. It is a kind of learning process. Culture is a process that, among other things, accumulates partial solutions to frequently encountered problems. *Artifacts and practices have historically contingent cultural development trajectories. As cultural creatures, we need not discover the solutions to most of the problems we face.* Both the framing of problems and their solutions are already available for learning as part of our cultural heritage. (Hutchins 2006:379, my emphasis)

Moreover, Hutchins (1995a) argues that the environments in which humans operate are constructed by humans for the purpose of performing the activities at hand: "The environments of human thinking are not 'natural' environments. They are artificial through and through. Humans create their cognitive powers by creating the environments in which they exercise those powers" (Hutchins 1995a:169). This observation is of particular interest to the present study, as the artifact of interest — the CSG document — clearly forms part of the environment in which the LSP translators operate on a daily basis.

The interpretation of culture coming across here resonates clearly with the notion of culture advocated by Risku and Windhager (2015:37), namely an "interactive and dynamic concept ... that includes aspects like how artefacts (e.g., texts) are cultivated, the tools and technologies used in the process and the way things are done and achieved collectively". The present chapter attends to all of these aspects in a specific setting and situation.

4. Method and data

This section starts by presenting the general methodology, the method of analysis, and features of institutional interaction (Section 4.1). Section 4.2 presents the data, the participants, and the empirical setting.

4.1 Methodology

The overarching methodology used as the empirical data were collected was ethnographic fieldwork. For a period of close to one year (March 2017–February 2018), I collected and elicited data in the Swedish translation office of a global LSP. The data encompass fieldnotes, interviews, logs from digital interaction, photographs, workplace documents, and audio recordings of naturally occurring interaction. This chapter focuses on the latter two types of data: documents and audio recordings. In total, 22 documents of the sort attended to here — client specific guidelines — were collected throughout the fieldwork. In this chapter, a face-to-face interaction relating to one of these documents is analysed. The transcription, which uses Jeffersonian transcription conventions, as specified by ten Have (2007; cf. also Appendix 1), amounts to close to 4,800 words in total. Further details about the data are given in Section 4.2.4.

4.1.1 Conversation analysis

This study uses conversation analysis (CA) as its method of data analysis. The disciplinary roots of CA are found in sociology, specifically in the pioneering work of Schegloff and Sacks (e.g., 1973). The focus of CA is on investigating how *social order* is created and maintained in society by analysing *social action(s)* (see, e.g., Broth and Keevallik 2020:19). A central assumption underlying CA research is thus that a social order exists (or, rather, multiple social orders), and consequently that the actions that people perform in social settings are not haphazard (Broth and Keevallik 2020:24) but orient towards the parameters of the social practice at hand, be it a job interview, a dinner conversation, or joint problem solving in a workplace setting. Importantly, from a CA perspective, actions are not merely performed by means of speech, but rather through the use of different "communicative resources", including gaze, gesture, the use of artifacts, etc. (Broth and Keevallik 2020:23, italics removed). Broth and Keevallik (2020:24) also point to the role of context (epistemic, spatial, institutional, interpersonal, etc.) for intersubjective meaning making in interaction, concluding that both multimodal resources and context come into play when interpersonal intersubjectivity is established.

CA has found its way into several academic disciplines that have acknowledged its potential to lay bare minute details of interactions in different settings, including cognitive science (e.g., Hutchins 2006; Arvola 2020) and TIS, in particular in research on interpreting (e.g., Wadensjö 1998; Angelelli 2004; see also Gavioli 2015). However, with the notable exception of studies such as Hirvonen and Tiittula (2018), who use multimodal interaction analysis to investigate cooperation in audio description, activities in translation workplaces have not yet been extensively investigated using CA.

Traditionally, CA emphasised that interpretations be grounded solely in the observable interaction, and specifically in what can reliably be shown as relevant to the participants themselves. However, nowadays CA researchers often acknowledge the relevance and importance of the ethnographic knowledge acquired by the researcher during the fieldwork (see Norrthon 2020: 21). In the present analysis, I generally ground interpretations in the participants' actions, as they go about the joint assessment of the CSG document. However, I also draw on ethnographic knowledge gathered through fieldwork as well as on my own experience from professional translation work. This becomes relevant for laying bare industry jargon, which is not otherwise easily understood solely from the interaction.

4.1.2 *Institutional interaction*

CA research often investigates settings where representatives of an institution, say, healthcare services, come into contact with laypeople that for one reason or another seek the services of said institution (Heritage 2004). In the case at hand, however, the interaction does not take place between professionals and laypeople, but is rather of an "intra-professional" kind (Linell 2011: 102, my translation) and can be characterised as "workplace discourse" (Koester 2006: 3). Nevertheless, the fact that the interaction concerns professional matters and takes place in a workplace makes certain observations with regard to institutional interaction relevant. According to Heritage's (2004: 224–225) well-known outline, institutional interaction is characterised by (1) "specific goal orientations which are tied to [the participants'] institution-relevant identities", (2) "special constraints on what will be treated as allowable contributions to the business at hand", and that institutional interaction is (3) "associated with inferential frameworks and procedures that are particular to specific institutional contexts".

Two additional aspects of institutional interaction that have proven particularly relevant for examining the co-construction of cognitive artifacts concern knowledge and authority. With regard to knowledge, Heritage (2012, 2013) discusses the concepts of *epistemic status* and *epistemic stance*, and their significance and role in human interaction. Epistemic status concerns interacting "parties' joint recognition of their comparable access, knowledgeability, and rights relative to some domain of knowledge" (Heritage 2013:376). Epistemic stance, on the other hand, "concerns how speakers position themselves in terms of epistemic status in and through the designs of turns at talk" (Heritage 2012:33). When interacting, participants thus display preconceptions about others' epistemic status, e.g., by stating information in a way that suggests that the other parties are previously unaware of the information. Epistemic stance, in turn, becomes manifest, e.g., in how questions are formulated, signalling more or less certainty of some state-of-affairs (Heritage 2013:377). As to the role of authority, Stevanovic and Peräkylä (2012:297) use the concept of "deontic authority" to refer to an actor's "right to determine others' future actions" in a given interactional situation. They maintain that a person's deontic authority is connected to the level of knowledge that he or she has in relation to a particular domain, and that the "deontic rights of a person vary from domain to domain" (Stevanovic and Peräkylä 2012:298). In other words, people may "have more rights to decide about future actions in some areas of action than in others" (Stevanovic and Peräkylä 2012:298). The concepts of epistemic status and stance and deontic authority will be used in the analysis to discuss how manifestations of knowledge and authority come into play in the assessment and joint construction of the CSG document.

4.2 Data

This study presents a "single case analysis" (Broth, Musk, and Persson 2020:52) of interaction, which concerns the examination of a single instance of interaction rather than compiling a collection of cases. Broth, Musk, and Persson (2020:52) maintain that analyses of single cases may be sufficient when the purpose is to investigate a phenomenon which has so far remained unexamined, such as the use of a particular resource. This corresponds well to the present study which enters into a previously unexplored territory in its detailed examination of the joint assessment and revision of a central digital resource in a translation workplace.[1]

Before describing the data in greater detail, some background is provided. First, I briefly describe some general features of the workplace. Then, I give a brief account of the translators participating in the interaction, their tasks, relationship, and spatial positioning in the workplace. I also describe the situation in which the recording was made, and the goals of the joint activity. Lastly, an overview of CSG documents is given, with brief descriptions of the sections and topics that are typically included.

---

1. However, Broth, Musk, and Persson (2020) maintain that several cases are necessary if the purpose is, for example, to examine a particular linguistic interactional feature.

4.2.1 The workplace

The workplace where the data was recorded is the Swedish translation office of an international LSP, with offices and co-workers across the globe. At the time of the fieldwork (2017–2018), the staff in the translation office consisted of about 30 translators and a smaller number of staff in other roles, such as managers and technical staff. The translators, who all translated into Swedish, mainly from English but also from other European languages, were divided into three teams. Each team had a team leader, who was responsible for the overall organisation of work, and each team focused on a particular subject area: information technology, general technology, and medical technology. The translators were loosely grouped together with the other members of their team in the office space.

4.2.2 Participants and activity

The participants in this study — referred to here as Maud and Linn — both formed part of the general technology team. At the time of the fieldwork, Maud had been working as a translator for about 3 years in total and 1.5 years in the LSP, whereas Linn had 1.5 years of experience as a translator, 10 months of which in the LSP. They were of similar age, between 25 and 30 years old. In the office space, they were seated close to each other together with other members of their team. Interactions within the team took place frequently, as the translators often consulted each other about translation-related and technical issues. However, most such interactions were brief, typically not planned in advance, and concerned requests for assistance with term questions, reviews, etc. The interaction analysed in this study, in contrast, was planned beforehand, and prompted by the fact that Linn had taken over two clients for which Maud was previously the primary translator. As part of the hand-over process, they jointly go through and assess the contents of two different CSG documents for the two clients in question. In other words, the assessment of the documents could reliably be constructed as a goal of the two interactions of interest (cf. Heritage 2004: 224). Both these interactions took place the same day, and both were audio recorded. For the purposes of the present chapter, I have limited the analysis to the interaction that concerned the *first* of the two documents and lasted close to 21 minutes. During the interaction, both participants are seated in front of Linn's computer, looking at the same screen, which means they share a visual space. Linn is at the keyboard, doing the writing as well as navigating different online resources.

4.2.3 CSG documents

CSG documents are created for regular clients in order to keep track of specific details for each client. Due to lack of space, a detailed description is not provided here, but some general characteristics are presented. Each document starts with a section summarising the most important information about the client (see Figure 1). The summary typically informs about central tools to be or not to be used, rates, instructions regarding TM management, etc. The interaction in all of the excerpts analysed in this chapter concerns the summary section displayed in Figure 1. In this particular summary, the last sentence is highlighted in yellow. This was done by Linn during the interaction, as a reminder to herself to ask the project manager whether so called SA files were available. It is clear from the recording that the participants were not sure about the meaning of SA, but they assume it refers to 'source analysis'.

In the section following the summary, more detailed information about the client is given, e.g., about the products and/or services provided by the client, typical text types, as well as the typical size and frequency of translation jobs. Then a section follows that specifies which actors are involved in the client account, such as the primary and backup translators and project managers. After that, the workflow is outlined, and tasks are specified for the whole translation process, followed by a section specifying whether translation or post-editing is used. Lastly, instructions for the use of specific tools are given, such as TM, checklists, quality assessment tools, as well as instructions for working with freelance translators.

Sammanfattning

Uppdaterad 2017-01-24

- Görs i GroupShare i Studio.
- Alltid ▮▮▮▮ rate
- ▮▮▮▮ får EJ användas
- Våra egna 100 %-ingar måste bekräftas i Studio i korret, men de betalar bara/inte alls? för Spotcheck av 100 %
- Ofta tillkommer referensfiler, går att ladda ner i TMS samtidigt som xliffarna.
- Ibland tillkommer även så kallade SA-filer, som innehåller kommentarer och förklaringar.

Figure 1. Summary section of the CSG document

In what follows, the contents of the CSG will be discussed using translations into English.

4.2.4 *The audio data*

As previously specified, the audio recording from which the empirical excerpts are retrieved was made as part of extended ethnographic fieldwork (March 2017–February 2018). Whereas the main body of empirical data elicited and gathered during the fieldwork consists of fieldnotes, interviews, digital interaction logs, and documents, a couple of audio recordings were made of interactions between translators in the workplace. The recording used in this chapter amounts to close to 21 minutes in total, and for the analysis presented here, 1 minute and 33.5 seconds are used (Table 1).

Table 1. Data excerpts

Excerpt number	Occurrence in the recording	Excerpt length
1	(2.05–2.15)	10 seconds
2	(2.39–2.53)	13.5 seconds
3	(4.22–4.50)	28 seconds
4	(5.01–5.43)	42 seconds

5. Analysis

In this section, a detailed analysis is presented of actions performed by the translators as they jointly assess and edit the contents of the cognitive artifact – the CSG document. First, however, some general characteristics of the interactions are described. As mentioned above, an overall goal of the interaction is to assess the contents of the CSG (cf. Heritage 2004: 224). Throughout the interaction, the participants jointly orient themselves towards different tasks (cf. Heritage 2004: 225), which closely follow the different information items in the CSG document. The document thus serves as a sort of 'agenda' for the interaction (cf. Svennevig 2012). Transfers between tasks are jointly agreed upon in the sense that neither of the participants attempts to impede the progression but instead confirms actions that initiate a transfer from one task to the next (cf. Heritage 2004: 228). Throughout the interaction, different resources are mobilised or invoked by the participants to support decision making and to prevent actions that could lead to the loss of potentially useful information.

Four excerpts from the empirical data have been selected for a close analysis of how decisions relating to the content of the CSG document are collectively made. Specifically, the analysis focuses on how different resources are jointly mobilised and assessed by the participants in the process.

The interaction displayed in Excerpt 1 (2.05–2.15) concerns the first part of the information given in the fourth bullet point displayed in the summary section of the CSG (highlighted by the red box in Figure 2). The text, in translation, reads "Our own 100% matches must be confirmed in Studio in the proof". In other words, this information specifies how a specific kind of TM matches should be handled. As is shown in the excerpt, the participants orient towards, and jointly assess, this specific piece of information. The analysis shows how the participants

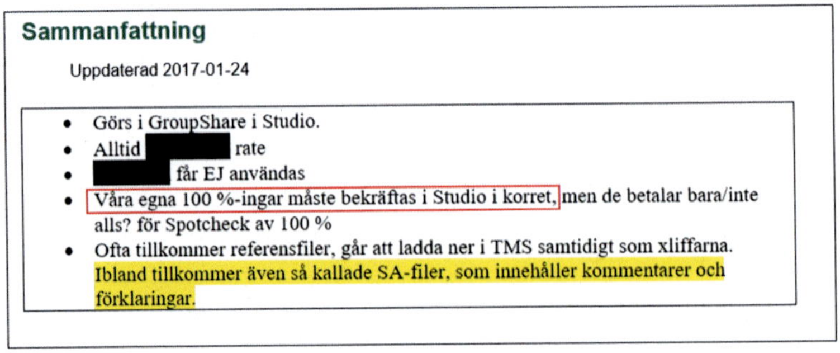

Figure 2.

Sammanfattning

Uppdaterad 2017-01-24

- Görs i GroupShare i Studio.
- Alltid ▮▮▮▮ rate
- ▮▮▮▮ får EJ användas
- Våra egna 100 %-ingar måste bekräftas i Studio i korret, men de betalar bara/inte alls? för Spotcheck av 100 %
- Ofta tillkommer referensfiler, går att ladda ner i TMS samtidigt som xliffarna. Ibland tillkommer även så kallade SA-filer, som innehåller kommentarer och förklaringar.

Figure 2. TM match management specification

interactively proceed from a state of uncertainty about the accuracy of the information to intersubjective agreement.

Excerpt 1. (2.05–2.15): Specifying conditions for TM match management

```
1 Maud: våra egna hundringar som sagt ehm ((CLIENT)) (0.5) har ju sina egna

2       hundringar och våra har jag för mej ä:r obekräftade i mallen (paus)
        our own hundreds again CLIENT has their own hundreds and ours I seem to recall are
        unconfirmed in the template

3 Linn: säîkert
        surely

4 Maud: m: jag tror att de är det
        m: I believe they are

5 Linn: jo de ja (0.3) [de] e dom
        yes they yes they are

6 Maud:              [m:]
```

Maud points to the item in the document to which they will jointly attend by echoing the initial formulation in the CSG: "our own hundreds again" (*"våra egna hundringar som sagt"*) (line 1). She then elaborates on the written text, adding that the client has their own 100% matches (lines 1–2), but hedges, "I seem to recall" (*"har jag för mig"*) (line 2), as she states that the LSP's matches are unconfirmed in the TMS template (line 2).[2] Maud's action of hedging makes a confirmation a conceivable relevant next action, and Linn does indeed confirm Maud's assumption (line 3). However, her response appears to be interpreted by Maud as an indication of sustained uncertainty (line 4), possibly because of the rising intonation. Linn, in turn, now reiterates her confirmation in a more assertive way: "yes they yes they are" (*"jo de ja de e dom"*) (line 5).

Maud's initial utterance, where she actually repeats the information in the CSG, could at first be interpreted as the manifestation of a certain epistemic status

---

2. The "template" mentioned here refers to a feature in Studio which allows for the compilation of resources such as term bases, TM, reference files, settings, etc.

on her part, simultaneously ascribing a less knowing status to Linn: had she expected Linn's level of knowledge to be identical to hers, an assertion of this kind would have been surprising (cf. Heritage 2012: 30). However, her addition *"har jag för mej"* ("I seem to recall") (line 2) signals a less certain epistemic stance with regard to the accuracy of the CSG information, which in fact states that the LSP's 100% matches "must be confirmed". Linn's response ("sä↑kert"), in turn, appears to indicate uncertainty on her part as well, given Maud's response *"m: jag tror att de är det"* ("m: I believe they are") (line 4), stressing the verb *"är"* ("are"). The sequence is brought to an end by Linn's response, now more assertive, and Maud's confirmation (lines 5–6). Two observations can be made here. First, indications of sustained uncertainty on part of the participants propels the interaction forward. Second, and more importantly, reaching a degree of certainty with regard to the CSG information is a joint accomplishment, as is also the (implicit) decision to keep the information about confirming 100% matches as it is. The participants then continue to the next item after discussing the consequences of not confirming TM matches (left out here), which further indicates that intersubjective agreement has been reached.

Whereas Excerpt 1 serves to illustrate how decisions about the CSG content emerge interactively, Excerpt 2 shows how Maud and Linn mobilise additional resources to support the assessment of the information, upon which decisions about its retainment, modification, or deletion rely. The action of particular interest to the analysis here is thus the collective mobilisation of an additional digital resource, an online invoicing system. The sequence follows after the one analysed in Excerpt 1 and concerns the second part of the fourth bullet point, which informs about payment for reviews of 100% matches (Figure 3; see text in red boxes), which originally reads, in translation, "they only pay for spot-checking of 100%".

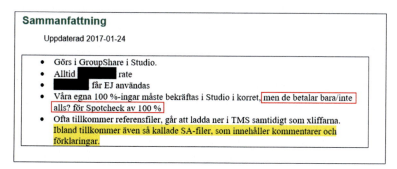

Figure 3. TM review payment specification

Excerpt 2. (2.39–2.53): Mobilising support for assessing TM match review payment

```
1 Maud: ehm och eh de betalar bara för spot check (.) av hundringarna jag vet

2      inte ens om dom gör de men vi kan ju hiva upp peon och titta efter

3      faktiskt (.) de är ju värt
       ehm and eh they only pay for spot-checking of hundred percent matches I
       don't even know whether they do that but let's find the purchase order
       and check actually it's worth it

4 Linn: bonjour le peo:: where are you internet explorer (1.0) tramsig jag e

5      idag
       bonjour le peo where are you internet explorer how silly I am today
```

As in Excerpt 1, the transition to the information to be attended to in Excerpt 2 is made by reiterating the CSG information: *"de betalar bara för spot check"* ("they only pay for spot-checking") (line 1). However, immediately thereafter, Maud expresses uncertainty about the accuracy of the information: *"jag vet inte ens om dom gör det"* ("I don't even know whether they do that") (lines 1–2). As in Excerpt 1, she thus immediately positions herself as less certain with regard to the information. She then proposes that they consult a purchase order, where the services that the client pays for are specified: *"vi kan ju hiva upp peon och titta efter"* ("let's find the purchase order and check") (line 2). Linn's response of locating a web browser, accompanied by her utterance (line 4) shows her acceptance of Maud's proposal. The prompt response also suggests the existence of common ground with regard to the potential value of the information stored in the invoicing system. That is, as no motivation is requested for the proposed action of finding the purchase order, one can assume that Linn has already acquired relevant knowledge of the contents and functionality of the invoicing system, as part of her general accumulated experience of tools and procedures in the workplace. Furthermore, Maud's proposal is indicative of her deontic authority, i.e., her right in the current situation to determine the future actions of another party (Stevanovic and Peräkylä 2012), and Linn's response also shows a reciprocity in their positioning towards the distribution of the mandate to propose courses of action.

As shown in Excerpt 2, mobilising additional material resources for support in the decision-making process is a collective accomplishment, which is conceivably suggestive of common ground. However, as is shown in Excerpt 3, the content of such additional resources is not necessarily self-explanatory. Having located the purchase order in the web-based invoicing system, the participants orient towards the information about payment for spot-checking of 100% matches (relating to the second part of the fourth bullet point shown in Figure 3). The analysis shows how the participants reach a shared interpretation of the information displayed.

Chapter 9. Co-constructing cognitive artifacts **215**

Excerpt 3. (4.22–4.50): Assessing information about TM match review payment

1 Maud: translation and reↆview technical noll näe   [( )]
    translation and review technical zero nope

2 Linn: [no̲l̲l̲] (isar)
    zeros

3 Maud: de står i (1.1) vahettere (1.1) för eftersom vi inte får för

4   hu̲ndringarna
    it says in what's it called because as we don't get paid for hundred
    percent matches

5 Linn: m: ↑m

6 Maud: å de inte står spot check: i (.) ta̲s̲kförklaringen
    and it doesn't say spot-checking in the task description

7 Linn: m:: ↑m eh vare va menar du i taskförklaringen [vart] vart tittar du då
    mm where is what do you mean in the task description where do you find
    that

8 Maud: [ehm:]

9 Maud: de e den här grejen=
    it's this thing

10 Linn: =a okej [mm]
    yes okay

11 Maud: [mm] de e liksom den som säger vad de är dom beställer så att

12   säga
    this specifies what they order so to speak

13 Linn: mm så då får vi inte betalt för dom heller
    mm so then we don't get paid for them either

14 Maud: ja ↑tror inte deↆ
    I don't believe so

Again, the participants orient towards information displayed on the screen. Maud reads from the purchase order ("translation and review technical"), adding "*noll nä*" ("zero nope") (line 1), indicating that no ("zero") payment is specified. As the more knowledgeable participant, Maud then starts explicating the significance of the information presented in the system (lines 3–4). As she mentions that "spot-checking" is not specified in the "task description" (line 6), Linn asks where the "task description" is displayed (line 7). Maud's reply "*de e den här grejen*" ("it's this thing") (line 9) is probably accompanied by a gesture towards the screen (even though the current data obviously do not provide clear evidence of gesturing). In any case, it is clear from Linn's response ("*a okej*") (line 10) that the participants' joint attention is aligned anew. Following Maud's explication of the function of the "task description" (line 11), Linn concludes that they do not get paid (line 13), which Maud possibly interprets as an indirect question as she replies that she does not believe so (line 14).

Although the participants reach a shared understanding regarding how to interpret the information in the invoicing system, the epistemic uncertainty about whether the client pays for reviews of 100% matches persists. This is crucial for

216 Raphael Sannholm

the action of particular interest in Excerpt 4, namely the joint mobilisation of social support for decision making. Immediately before the interaction displayed in Excerpt 4, Maud and Linn discuss the difficulty of interpreting information in the system (10.5 seconds, left out here). They then return to the information as Linn concludes anew that no payment is specified.

Excerpt 4 (5.01–5.43): Mobilising social support for assessing TM match review payment

```
1  Linn: precis men de står ju noll där å då=
          exactly but it says zero there and then

2  Maud: =a: =

3  Linn: =de brukar ju betyda att man inte får betalt för dom
          that usually means that you don't get paid for them

4  Maud: precis. (0.7) betalar dom för spot check då spelar de ingen roll hur

5        (.) många man lägger där utan då står de här att de ingår en spot check

6        ja har fått nån gång en:e vahettere faktura (0.6) innan du tar bort den

7        (1.0) mejla (.) ((PM))
          exactly. if they pay for spot-checking it doesn't matter how many you
          put there but then it says here that spotchecking is included I've
          received at some point a what's it called an invoice before you remove
          that send an email to (PM)

8  Linn: ((typing sounds 2.8 seconds))

9  Maud: precis (.) mejla ((PM)) eh vid tillfälle och fråga henne (0.8) att i i

10       gamla ins- att du håller på å går igenom admin [i] gamla
          exactly send an email to PM at some point and ask her that in old
          guide- that you are revising admin in old

11 Linn:                                                [m:]

12 Maud: instruktioner så står de att vi får betalt för spot check men när du

13       kollar på peon så så (0.5) förstår du inte riktigt vad det är som

14       faktiskt står
          guidelines it says that we get paid for spot-checking but when you
          check the purchase order you don't quite get what it actually says

15 Linn: ((typing sounds 3 seconds))

16 Maud: därmed så liksom (0.6) be henne förklara helt enkelt hur de

17       li[gger till vad] får vi
          therefore kind of ask her to explain what the deal is what we

18 Linn:  [yes:         ]

19 Maud: faktiskt betalt för
          actually get paid for

20 Linn: ja=
          yes

21 Maud: =m:
```

It is clear that the action of mobilising social support for deciding what to keep in the CSG is a joint accomplishment, where one party proposes a course of action and the other complies. Having reached agreement on the fact that the

Chapter 9. Co-constructing cognitive artifacts **217**

digit zero in the invoicing system specifies that the client does not pay for review (lines 2–4), Maud positions herself with more certainty towards the details about "spot-checking" (lines 4–5). Her next action points in a similar direction. Apparently anticipating that Linn might remove the information in the CSG, Maud prompts her to contact another actor, the project manager (PM): "*innan du tar bort den* (1.0) *mejla* (.) *((PM))*" ("before you remove that send an email to the PM") (lines 6–7), using an imperative. This action thus prevents the potential loss of information that would follow from its deletion. Again, this action and its response show how the participants collectively and interactively construct deontic authority when it comes to determining what course of action to take. Indeed, Linn responds to Maud's proposal (lines 6–7) by starting to type (line 8) what is presumably a draft email message. Maud, who shares Linn's visual space and therefore can monitor her actions, then confirms Linn's action (line 9), and reiterates the prompt to contact the project manager, now in a way that does not suggest this is to be done immediately (line 9). She then goes on to dictate the content of the email (lines 10, 12–14), which, again, is followed by Linn typing (line 15).

Maud's action of dictating the content of the email deserves particular attention, as it shows how the action of seeking social support to determine the contents of the CSG is a collective one. Here, Maud proposes a framing of the problem at hand, first providing background: "*du håller på å går igenom admin*" ("you are revising admin") (line 10), then pointing to the discrepancy between the CSG information and the details in the invoicing system ("*i gamla instruktioner står de at vi får betalt för spot check men när du kollar på peon så så* (0.5) *förstår du inte riktigt vad det är som faktiskt står*") ("in old guidelines it says that we get paid for spot-checking but when you check the purchase order you don't quite get what it actually says") (lines 12–14). Finally, Maud concludes: "*därmed så liksom* (0.6) *be henne förklara helt enkelt hur de ligger till vad får vi faktiskt betalt för*" ("therefore kind of ask her to explain what the deal is what we actually get paid for") (lines 16, 17, 19). At every turn, Linn's responses, both verbal and by means of typing, show that she does not reject Maud's proposal (lines 11, 15, 18, 20). This sequence also further evidences their joint construction of deontic authority: the right to determine future action, both in the immediate (what to put in the email) and in the long-term perspective (to eventually contact another social actor) is ascribed to Maud (cf. Stevanovic and Peräkylä 2012). Apparently, these rights even extend to depicting Linn as the less knowledgeable in the dictated message ("*så* (0.5) *förstår du inte riktigt*") ("you don't quite get") (line 13), even though the analysis has demonstrated that the uncertainty is not Linn's alone.

Finally, the dictation of the email content is also suggestive of an interplay between past experience and present situations. When faced with the problem of determining the accuracy of the information in a specific CSG document, the translators draw on their experience of general workplace procedures, including how to frame issues when communicating with actors in the workplace network. Such general workplace procedures can be seen as cultural practices which evolve over time. They provide partial and potential templates for addressing problems that arise at a later point in time (cf. Hutchins 2006: 379). I return to this point in the discussion.

As a coda, by contacting the PM, the final decision about which information to include in the CSG regarding the payment of 100% matches is postponed, which is reflected in the different options left in the text, as well as the question mark: "but they only pay/don't pay? for spot-checking of 100% matches" (see Figure 3 above). However, it is interesting to note that the information eventually found its final form. Figure 4 displays a later version of the same CSG, updated about 8 months after the interaction analysed in this chapter took place.

Sammanfattning

Uppdaterad 2017-11-02

- Görs i GroupShare i Studio.
- Alltid ▉▉▉▉ rate
- ▉▉▉▉ får **EJ** användas
- Vi har betalt för att korra 100 %-ingar sedan oktober 2017
- Ofta tillkommer referensfiler, går att ladda ner i TMS samtidigt som xliffarna. Ibland tillkommer även så kallade SA-filer, som innehåller kommentarer och förklaringar, men det har inte hänt sedan 2016.

Figure 4. Updated TM specifications

The information has now been changed to a statement, and the alternative formulations and the question mark removed. The text in point 4 now reads, in translation, "We get paid to proofread 100% matches since October 2017". In the next section, the results are discussed in light of the tenets of distributed cognition.

6. Discussion

6.1 Joint decision making as a distributed cognitive process

The analysis shows that decisions with regard to the contents of the CSG are jointly made by Maud and Linn through their interaction, including decisions to mobilise additional material resources necessary for assessing the accuracy of the information, and to contact other social actors. The analysis also shows how the document plays a part in the very decision-making process itself; based on the information in the CSG, the participants construct interpretations and propose courses of action. As Hutchins (2006:377) explains, "cognitive labor can … be distributed among persons". Similarly, Linell (2011:62) proposes that from the perspective of distributed cognition, conversations can be seen as a way in which different participants "contribute different parts of the thought process and (sometimes) function as a team that thinks and talks thoughts into being that the individuals themselves would not have been able to achieve as easily" (my translation).[3] These perspectives allow us to consider the cognitive task of decision making as distributed among the participants, assembled into a cognitive system together with various cognitive artifacts (the computer, the CSG itself, the invoicing system) (cf. Hutchins 2006: 378–379). As to the inclusion of cognitive artifacts, the most obvious case in the current analysis is the consultation of an invoicing system and a purchase order in order to ascertain whether spot-checking of 100% matches is paid for (Excerpts 2 and 3). This action shows how resources available in the cultural cognitive ecosystem may be mobilised to reach epistemic certainty and support decision making.

Moreover, the professional and interactional roles of participants have implications for how the cognitive system works. As previously explained, the joint assessment of the document forms part of a more general activity in which Maud is assigning certain clients to Linn. Therefore, being the more knowledgeable of the participants with regard to the client in question, Maud clearly has a mandate not only to propose future actions but also to close down anticipated future actions on the part of Linn. Nevertheless, Linn's responses are co-constitutive of the decisions about how to proceed at each moment. Here, I have used the concept of "deontic authority" (Stevanovic and Peräkylä 2012:297) to examine how the participants' respective mandate to propose actions is, in itself, constructed interactively.

6.2   Co-constructing the cognitive ecosystem

In this chapter, I have proposed that the CSG document jointly constructed by the participants can be thought of as a potential cognitive artifact, conceivably mobilised, e.g., for remembering workplace procedures. In the translation workplace, this cognitive artifact forms part of the continuously evolving infrastructure of resources that allow for collective cognition. As in the case at hand, the CSG can be seen as a scaffolding device for learning processes which is used when new

---

3. "bidrar med olika delar av tänkandet och där de (ibland) fungerar som ett team som tänker och pratar fram tankar som individerna inte själva så lätt hade kunnat åstadkomma" (Linell 2011:62)

co-workers are introduced to workplace procedures. In addition, learning encompasses not only mastering the physical execution of the procedures outlined in the document but also how to use and make sense of the contents of the document itself. This is not self-explanatory, as evidenced by the interaction analysed in this study, but involves acquiring knowledge about locally sanctioned ways of acting in the setting at hand. This serves to illustrate how learning the use of cognitive artifacts is integrated with learning cognitive practices (Menary and Gillet 2022: 366).

Through the careful dating of changes to the CSG, it also serves as a continuously updated means for remembering in the workplace, which should not necessarily be understood in the sense of an augmented memory of any individual co-worker in the workplace. Instead, it serves as a relatively stable meaning-making resource the existence of which, as well as the cognitive practice of its usage, is communicated to new co-workers. This resonates with Risku's (2010: 106) observation that "[t]ranslation work ... has a historical context of comparable previous work and documents, applicable professional standards, established working relationships". Moreover, the development of the cognitive artifact leads to the accumulation of more accurate "partial solutions to frequently encountered problems" (Hutchins 2006: 379) and, consequently, to the "development of cultural cognitive ecology" of the translation workplace. As Hutchins (2006: 379) points out, this can, in itself, be seen as a cognitive process of cultural learning.

7. Conclusions

This study investigates the joint construction of a cognitive artifact in a translation workplace. Using CA, the moment-to-moment interaction between two translators engaged in the activity of assessing the contents of a workplace document is analysed. In other words, the analysis concerns workplace discourse about workplace discourse, as it were. The analysis shows that the assessment of, and decisions about, the contents of the CSG are made collectively and interactively. This refers both to decisions regarding the contents of the CSG itself and decisions to mobilise additional support, for example, by consulting material resources, and contacting other social actors. When considered from the perspective of distributed cognition, the decision making can be seen to be distributed between the participants through their interaction with each other and with cognitive artifacts. Actions performed by the participants also reflect more general cultural practices, i.e., recurring ways of acting in the workplace. Activities in the past interact with activities in the present, and the translators' actions result in a further accumulation of knowledge and refinement of cognitive artifacts. In this process, there is also an interplay between the participants' positioning with regard to their knowledge of different domains (e.g., general workplace practices vs. particular practices connected to certain clients).

The study presented here hopefully serves to demonstrate that empirical investigations and the development of conceptualisations of activities within culturally situated cognitive systems constitute promising and productive foci for research within CTS, particularly with a focus on developing our understanding of the situated construction and use of cognitive artifacts. On a methodological note, this study also further demonstrates the potential of close analyses of interaction for advancing our knowledge about the nature of cognition in cultural ecosystems such as translation workplaces (cf. Hirvonen and Tiittula 2018). Indeed, using interaction analysis, the collective accomplishment of decision making, knowledge construction, and learning may be carefully examined and convincingly demonstrated. However, a limitation of the present study is that it is based primarily on audio data, which means that the potentially rich array of additional communicative resources in play in the interaction could not be properly included in the analysis. Investigating translators' use of embodied resources for meaning making necessitates video recordings of bodily postures, gaze, and gestures (cf. Hirvonen and Tiittula 2018).

Moreover, recordings of what happens in face-to-face interaction could be fruitfully combined with recordings of what happens on the screen, as they would allow for even more detailed investigations of joint meaning construction, problem solving, and decision making in extended translation processes.

Acknowledgements

First of all, I would like to thank the translators participating in the study. I would also like to thank my colleagues at Stockholm University for their valuable insights given at a data session where the data used in this chapter were discussed. A special thanks to Stefan Norrthon for reading and commenting on an earlier draft of this paper.

References

Alves, Fabio, and Arnt Lykke Jakobsen. 2021. "Grounding Cognitive Translation Studies: Goals, Commitments and Challenges." In *The Routledge Handbook of Translation and Cognition*, ed. by Fabio Alves, and Arnt Lykke Jakobsen, 545–554. London & New York: Routledge.

Angelelli, Claudia. 2004. *Medical Interpreting and Cross-Cultural Communication*. Cambridge: Cambridge University Press.

Arvola, Mattias. 2020. "Ett multimodalt perspektiv på kognition" [A Multimodal Perspective on Cognition]. In *Multimodal interaktionsanalys [Multimodal Interaction Analysis]*, ed. by Mathias Broth, and Leelo Keevallik, 235–250. Lund: Studentlitteratur.

Bowker, Lynne. 2022. "Computer-Assisted Translation and Interpreting Tools." In *The Routledge Handbook of Translation and Methodology*, ed. by Federico Zanettin, and Christopher Rundle, 382–409. London: Routledge.

Broth, Mathias, and Leelo Keevallik. 2020. "Multimodal interaktionsanalys — att studera mänskligt samspel" [Multimodal Interaction Analysis — Studying Human Interaction]. In *Multimodal interaktionsanalys [Multimodal Interaction Analysis]*, ed. by Mathias Broth, and Leelo Keevallik, 19–40. Lund: Studentlitteratur.

Broth, Mathias, Nigel Musk, and Rasmus Persson. 2020. "Inspelning och analys av interaktionsdata" [Recording and Analyzing Interaction Data]. In *Multimodal interaktionsanalys [Multimodal Interaction Analysis]*, ed. by Mathias Broth, and Leelo Keevallik, 41–74. Lund: Studentlitteratur.

Bundgaard, Kristine. 2017. "(Post-)Editing — A Workplace Study of Translator-Computer Interaction at Textminded Danmark A/S." Doctoral dissertation, Aarhus University.

Bundgaard, Kristine, and Tina Paulsen Christensen. 2019. "Is the Concordance Feature the New Black? A Workplace Study of Translators' Interaction with Translation Resources While Post-Editing TM and MT Matches." *The Journal of Specialised Translation* 31: 14–37.

Christensen, Tina Paulsen, Marian Flanagan, and Anne Schjoldager. 2017. "Mapping Translation Technology Research in Translation Studies. An Introduction to the Thematic Section." *Hermes* 56: 7–20.

Dragsted, Barbara. 2008. "Computer-Aided Translation as a Distributed Cognitive Task." In *Cognition Distributed: How Cognitive Technology Extends Our Minds*, ed. by Itiel E. Dror, and Stevan Harnad, 238–256. Amsterdam & Philadelphia: John Benjamins.

Ehrensberger-Dow, Maureen. 2021. "Translation, Ergonomics, and Cognition." In *The Routledge Handbook of Translation and Cognition*, ed. by Fabio Alves, and Arnt Lykke Jakobsen, 147–160. London & New York: Routledge.

Garbis, Christer. 2002. "The Cognitive Use of Artifacts in Cooperative Process Management." Doctoral dissertation, Linköping University.

Gavioli, Laura. 2015. "Conversation Analysis." In *Researching Translation and Interpreting*, ed. by Claudia V. Angelelli, and Brian J. Baer, 189–194. London Routledge.

Halverson, Sandra L. 2010. "Cognitive Translation Studies. Developments in Theory and Method." In *Translation and Cognition*, ed. by Gregory Shreve, and Erik Angelone, 349–369. Amsterdam & Philadelphia: John Benjamins.

ten Have, Paul. 2007. *Doing Conversation Analysis*. 2nd edition. London: Sage.

Heritage, John. 2004. "Conversation Analysis and Institutional Talk. Analyzing Data." In *Qualitative Research. Theory, Method and Practice*, 2nd edition, ed. by David Silverman, 222–245. London: Sage.

Heritage, John. 2012. "The Epistemic Engine: Sequence Organization and Territories of Knowledge." *Research on Language and Social Interaction* 45 (1): 30–52.

Heritage, John. 2013. "Epistemics in Conversation." In *The Handbook of Conversation Analysis*, ed. by Jack Sidnell, and Tanya Stivers, 370–394. Malden: Wiley Blackwell.

Chapter 9. Co-constructing cognitive artifacts **223**

Hirvonen, Maija. 2025. "Shared Cognition in the Translation Process: Information Processing and Meaning Production as Interactive Accomplishments." *Translation Studies* 18 (1): 61–82.

Hirvonen, Maija, and Liisa Tiittula. 2018. "How Are Translations Created? Using Multimodal Conversation Analysis to Study a Team Translation Process." *Linguistica Antverpiensia* 17: 157–173.

doi Hollan, James, Edwin Hutchins, and David Kirsh. 2000. "Distributed Cognition: Towards a New Foundation for Human-Computer Interaction Research." *ACM Transactions on Computer-Human Interaction* 7 (2): 174–196.

doi Hutchins, Edwin. 1995a. *Cognition in the Wild*. Cambridge & London: MIT Press.

doi Hutchins, Edwin. 1995b. "How a Cockpit Remembers Its Speed." *Cognitive Science* 19 (3): 265–288.

Hutchins, Edwin. 1999. "Cognitive Artifacts." In *The MIT Encyclopedia of the Cognitive Sciences*, ed. by Robert A. Wilson, and Frank C. Kiel, 126–127. Cambridge & London: MIT Press.

doi Hutchins, Edwin. 2001. "Cognition, Distributed." In *International Encyclopedia of the Social & Behavioral Sciences*, ed. by Neil J. Smelser, and Paul B. Baltes, 2068–2072. Amsterdam: Elsevier.

Hutchins, Edwin. 2006. "The Distributed Cognition Perspective on Human Interaction." In *Roots of Human Sociality. Culture, Cognition and Interaction*, ed. by Nick J. Enfield, and Stephen C. Levinson, 375–398. London: Routledge.

doi Hutchins, Edwin. 2008. "The Role of Cultural Practices in the Emergence of Modern Human Intelligence." *Philosophical Transactions of the Royal Society* 363: 2011–2019.

doi Hutchins, Edwin. 2010. "Cognitive Ecology." *Topics in Cognitive Science* 2: 705–715.

doi Hutchins, Edwin. 2013. "The Cultural Ecosystem of Human Cognition." *Philosophical Psychology* 27 (1): 34–49.

Hvelplund, Kristian Tangsgaard. 2017. "Translators' Use of Digital Resources During Translation." *Hermes* 56: 71–87.

doi Karamanis, Nikiforos, Saturnino Luz, and Gavin Doherty. 2011. "Translation Practice in the Workplace: Contextual Analysis and Implications for Machine Translation." *Machine Translation* 25: 35–52.

doi Koester, Almut. 2006. *Investigating Workplace Discourse*. London: Routledge.

doi Korhonen, Annamari, and Maija Hirvonen. 2021. "Joint Creative Process in Translation: Socially Distributed Cognition in Two Production Contexts." *Cognitive Linguistic Studies* 8(2): 251–276.

Linell, Per. 2011. *Samtalskulturer. Kommunikativa verksamhetstyper i samhället [Discourse Cultures. Communicative Activity Types in Society]*. Vol. 1. Linköping: Institutionen för kultur och kommunikation, Linköpings universitet.

doi Menary, Richard, and Alexander Gillett. 2022. "The Tools of Enculturation." *Topics in Cognitive Science* 14: 363–387.

doi Muñoz Martín, Ricardo. 2010. "On Paradigms and Cognitive Translatology." In *Translation and Cognition*, ed. by Gregory Shreve, and Erik Angelone, 169–187. Amsterdam & Philadelphia: John Benjamins.

Muñoz Martín, Ricardo. 2016. "Reembedding Translation Process Research: An Introduction." In *Reembedding Translation Process Research*, ed. by Ricardo Muñoz Martín, 1–20. Amsterdam & Philadelphia: John Benjamins.

Muñoz Martín, Ricardo. 2017. "Looking Toward the Future of Cognitive Translation Studies." In *The Handbook of Translation and Cognition*, ed. by John W. Schwieter, and Aline Ferreira, 555–572. Hoboken: Wiley Blackwell.

Norman, Donald. 1993. *Things that Make Us Smart. Defending Human Attributes in the Age of the Machine*. Reading: Addison-Wesley.

Norrthon, Stefan. 2020. "Teaterrepetitionens interaktion. Professionella praktiker i ett repetitionsarbete från manus till föreställning [The Interaction of a Theatre Rehearsal. Professional Practices in a Rehearsal Process from Script to Performance]." Doctoral dissertation, Stockholm University.

O'Hagan, Minako (ed). 2019. *The Routledge Handbook of Translation and Technology*. London: Routledge.

Risku, Hanna. 2002. "Situatedness in Translation Studies." *Cognitive Systems Research* 3 (3): 523–533.

Risku, Hanna. 2010. "A Cognitive Scientific View on Technical Communication and Translation. Do Embodiment and Situatedness Really Make a Difference?" *Target* 22 (1): 94–111.

Risku, Hanna, and Regina Rogl. 2021. "Translation and Situated, Embodied, Distributed, Embedded, and Extended Cognition." In *The Routledge Handbook of Translation and Cognition*, ed. by Fabio Alves, and Arnt Lykke Jakobsen, 478–499. London & New York: Routledge.

Risku, Hanna, and Florian Windhager. 2015. "Extended Translation. A Socio-Cognitive Research Agenda." In *Interdisciplinarity in Translation and Interpreting Process Research*, ed. by Maureen Ehrensberger-Dow, Susanne Göpferich, and Sharon O'Brien, 35–47. Amsterdam & Philadelphia: John Benjamins.

Risku, Hanna, Florian Windhager, and Matthias Apfelthaler. 2013. "A Dynamic Network Model of Translatorial Cognition and Action." *Translation Spaces* 2: 151–182.

Robbins, Philip, and Murat Aydede. 2009. "A Short Primer on Situated Cognition." In *The Cambridge Handbook of Situated Cognition*, ed. by Philip Robbins, and Murat Aydede, 3–10. New York: Cambridge University Press.

Rogl, Regina, and Hanna Risku. 2024. "Cognitive Artefacts and Boundary Objects: On the Changing Role of Tools in Translation Project Management." In *Translation, Interpreting and Technological Change: Innovations in Research, Practice and Training*, ed. by Marion Winters, Sharon Deane-Cox, and Ursula Böser, 13–36. London: Bloomsbury Academic.

Rothwell, Andrew, Joss Moorkens, María Fernández Parra, and Frank Austermuehl. 2023. *Translation Tools and Technologies*. London & New York: Routledge.

Sannholm, Raphael. 2021. "Translation, Teamwork, and Technology. The Use of Social and Material Scaffolds in the Translation Process." Doctoral dissertation, Stockholm University.

Sannholm, Raphael, and Hanna Risku. 2024. "Situated Minds and Distributed Systems in Translation. Exploring the Conceptual and Empirical Implications." *Target* 36 (2): 159–163.

Schegloff, Emanuel A., and Harvey Sacks. 1973. "Opening Up Closings." In *The Discourse Reader*, ed. by Adam Jaworski, and Nikolas Coupland, 263–274. London & New York: Routledge.

Stevanovic, Melisa, and Anssi Peräkylä. 2012. "Deontic Authority in Interaction: The Right to Announce, Propose, and Decide." *Research on Language and Social Interaction* 45 (3): 297–321.

Svennevig, Jan. 2012. "The Agenda as Resource for Topic Introduction in Workplace Meetings." *Discourse Studies* 14 (1): 53–66.

Wadensjö, Cecilia. 1998. *Interpreting as Interaction*. London & New York: Longman.

Appendix 1. Transcription conventions

[ ]	Brackets: overlapping speech
(.)	Pause shorter than 0.3 seconds
(0.6)	Pause length
ins-	Dash: interrupted utterance
m:	Colon: Preceding speech sound is prolonged
(isar)	Words within parentheses or empty parentheses: uncertain transcription
((typing sounds))	Double parentheses: transcriber's comments
är	Underlining: emphasis
side?	Question mark: rising tone
sä ↑ kert	Upwards arrow: rising tone in following syllable
ja= =m:	Equal signs: latching, i.e., no discernible pause between two utterances

CHAPTER 10

Revision files as cognitive ethnographic data

Artefact analysis of file and software features combined with systemic functional discourse analysis

Annamari Korhonen
Tampere University

I apply artefact analysis and systemic functional discourse analysis as independent but complementary methods to examine revision files exported from Trados Studio translation software. The methods are intended to be used as part of cognitive ethnographic investigations of professional translation contexts and the distributed cognitive systems that exist in those contexts. The artefact analysis spotlights how the affordances of the files influence the cognitive work. Comments added to the revised texts inform us of how the translator and reviser as translation process participants position themselves in the cognitive system, and an analysis of shifts at the thematic, ideational and interpersonal levels of translational meaning-making show how they distribute the cognitive labour and direct their individual cognitive focus.

Keywords: cognitive translation studies, cognitive ethnography, distributed cognition, artefact analysis, systemic functional linguistics, translation revision, cognitive collaboration

1. Introduction

The aim of this chapter is to further develop cognitive ethnographic methodology (see Hutchins 1995a: 370–371) to be used for investigating the cognitive collaboration of translators and revisers (for an additional perspective on the translator-reviser relationship, see also Riondel, Chapter 8, this volume). The focus is on an underutilised data type, revision files, whose potential as cognitive ethnographic data will be explored by testing two analysis methods. The theoretical lens

https://doi.org/10.1075/btl.165.10kor
Available under the CC BY-NC 4.0 license. © 2025 John Benjamins Publishing Company

being employed in both is that of (socially) distributed cognition (Hutchins 1995a, 1995b; Perry 1999; Korhonen and Hirvonen 2021; Sannholm and Risku 2024; see also Sannholm, Chapter 9, this volume). The term revision refers to the part of the translation workflow that constitutes "bilingual examination of target language content … against source language content … for its suitability for the agreed purpose" as defined in the ISO 17100 translation industry standard (International Organization for Standardization 2015); by revisers, I mean the translation professionals who perform revision. Since this chapter does not aim to present a full ethnographic study, no data will be presented on the context of the work and the background or position of the process participants, with the exception of some knowledge of their native languages.

The first of the two methods is artefact analysis described by Lueger (2000: 140–186) and Risku (2009: 114–115). This method has already been used in cognitive translation ethnography to describe several different artefacts (Risku 2009; Sannholm 2021) but has not been applied to revision files or the software features relevant to the processing of these files. The second method is discourse analysis of the translation and revision solutions and comments contained in the revision files. The discourse analysis is carried out using systemic functional linguistics (SFL; see Martin and White 2005; Halliday and Matthiessen 2014; for quick reference, also see Banks 2019 or Matthiessen, Teruya, and Lam 2010). The aim of the discourse analysis is not to describe the texts as such. Rather, the linguistic properties of the translation as well as the revision changes and comments are analysed as indications of how the cognitive labour of linguistic meaning-making is being distributed: on which lines of meaning the translator and reviser focus. This definition of scope and focus naturally also means that many crucial systemic functional aspects of translated texts, such as cohesion, are here left uncharted. As the latter method is more novel for cognitive translation studies and required the development of a multi-stage analysis procedure, it also receives more space in this chapter. A full ethnographic research project, complete with observation, interviews and artefact data, could utilise one or both of these methods.

The revision files that will be used in these methodological explorations are bilingual Microsoft Word files that have been exported from the Trados Studio translation environment solely for revision purposes; for an overview of the file format, see Section 2. The use of revision files as data in cognitive translation studies is based on the fact that the distribution of a cognitive task always assumes some communication between the parties (Perry 1999), and the revision files constitute such communication. The overarching research question that I aim to answer is the following: What can we learn about the cognitive collaboration in translation contexts by using revision files as data? Since other communication between translators and revisers is often sporadic or even non-existent, the revision files may prove to be an invaluable source of information on this topic. An analysis of these files can tell us firstly, how they as artefacts steer, limit, or enable the cognitive work, and secondly, how the cognitive labour is distributed among the participants. The methods selected for this pilot study address both of these aspects. While I present some results achieved through these methods, the limited scope of the data prevents any firm conclusions. The analyses are intended as tests, and the results merely illustrate their potential. The primary contribution being made here is methodological.

Using different versions of translations as they proceed in the workflow as part of ethnographic data is not a new idea in translation studies; such data have been used for example by Koskinen (2008: Chapter 6) in her ethnographic research on the culture and institutional identities of translators in European Union's translation operations. Van de Geuchte and Van Vaarenbergh (2016) also use text versions in their investigation of how external processes influence the translation creation process. Research into cognitive processes in a translation context, however, usually relies on accounts of the translator's (or reviser's) behaviour, which is observed either by using, e.g., eye-tracking technology or field observation methods, and is considered to inform the researchers of cognitive processes. When using a written translation artefact as cognitive data, we are essentially looking for traces of the translation professionals' behaviour in that artefact instead of observing them directly. The revision file contains information of more than one stage of the work at the same time in the form of the original translation and the changes made by the reviser. It is therefore a promising data type for investigating how translation collaboration takes shape in shared files and digital systems at this stage of the workflow. While we can learn much by observation and by investigating the properties of tools and artefacts that are used as scaffolds in the cognitive ecosystem (see Sannholm 2021), a full analysis of (socially) distributed cognition also requires evidence of how cognitive input is conveyed between the participants. Ideally, such data needs to include all the different types of communication between the participants — not only conversations and messages, but also the communication that takes place in the translation and revision files sent between the process parties.

The translation context under study here is commercial specialised translation carried out by language service providers (LSPs). In the LSP workflow, the reviser may be another translator, a project manager, or a linguist who specialises exclusively on revision. Once the translator has produced their version of the translation, they send the text to the reviser in an editable format. The translator and reviser may both be employees of the company, or not; they may know each other, or not; and there may be an intermediary, typically a project manager, between them, or not. The exact workflow and file format depends on the translation tools that are being used and the production principles adopted in that specific company. Several different tools are available; most of them include similar main features, such as storage of translated segments into a translation memory database and some translation automation features. For the revision process, the tools include two main options: revising the text within the translation software, or exporting it so that it can be processed in a generic text processing software, and then imported back into the translation memory tool.

In the following sections, I will first describe the data and the two methods being tested. Next, I will present the analysis results that were achieved through both methods. In the discussion section, I evaluate the analysis methods with regard to their usefulness for cognitive ethnography and consider some future paths.

2. Description of data and the two methods

2.1 The data

The data under investigation here consists of seven .docx files (Figure 1), each of which contains a translated text exported from the Trados Studio translation software. The data was gathered in several stages; the first batch was received in 2020, with other files following in 2021 and 2022. The criteria for this dataset were that the files should display the source text, the translation and the changes made by a reviser. All the texts are non-confidential, and permissions for using them have been received from the LSPs, who were also requested to ask the clients in question for their permission. Gathering textual data from LSPs was found to be somewhat challenging due to the customer confidentiality deeply ingrained into the companies' operations. Typically, LSPs handle all customer texts as confidential, and are not eager to hand them over to anyone.

2	Translated (0%)	Energistä aamua.	I hope you'_are all having an energy-filled morning!
3	Translated (0%)	<8>M</8>aailma sähköistyy vauhdilla<14>.</14>	<8>T</8>he world is rapidly electrifying.
4	Translated (83%)	Tällä hetkellä vajaa neljännes energiankäytöstä Euroopassa on sähköä.	Electricity now accounts for around 24 percent of Europe's total energy consumption,
5	Translated (99%)	Tulevaisuudessa osuus voi ylittää 60 %.	but in the future this figureit maycould exceed 60 percent in the future.

Figure 1. An excerpt of an exported revision file

In the revision file, the text and some metadata have been organised into four columns. The first column contains the translation segment ID number. The second column indicates the translation status of the segment (e.g., Not Translated, Draft, or Translated) as well as the translation memory match percentage; in this example, no memory match has been found for segments 2 and 3, but 83% and 99% matches are available for segments 4 and 5, respectively. The colour coding reflects the match level. The third column contains the source text, and the fourth contains the target text. The reviser will only edit the text in the fourth column.

A summary of the data is presented in Table 1, including the language pairs (English, Finnish), source and target word counts, the number of translation segments, the number of comments, and the text genre. Comment data was not available for F1 and F2.

Table 1. The revision files included in the primary data

ID	Lang. pair	Source words	Target words	Segm.	Comm.	Genre
F1	EN-FI	629	464	63	N/A	Chemistry, Instruction
F2	EN-FI	583	422	70	N/A	Medical, User instr.
F3	EN-FI	699	464	39	0	Business, Strategy summary
F4	FI-EN	988	1611	85	2	Business, Web article
F5	FI-EN	292	462	26	2	Energy, Press release
F6	FI-EN	174	272	17	3	Energy, Speech
F7	FI-EN	526	904	52	0	Energy, Web article
Total		3891	4599	352	7	

Analyses of these files as digital artefacts and ethnographic data require knowledge of how the files are positioned in the LSP workflow and operations. In the absence of observational data, I have drawn this information from my experience as a translator working at an LSP, as well as from 20 interviews with translation professionals carried out at eight LSPs and with two independent professionals in 2020 and 2021, and three guided tour protocols (see Olohan 2021: 125) focusing on how revisers work and carried out in 2020 with two independent professionals and with one reviser employed by an LSP. No analysis of these supporting datasets will be presented here.

2.2 The artefact analysis method

When using theories of distributed or extended cognition (Hutchins 1995a, 1995b; Clark and Chalmers 1998) as the lens to investigate cognitive action, tools and artefacts are considered an integral part of the action: they give structure to the situation and the activities and thus form an essential part of the observed action (Risku 2009: 114–115). The artefacts always reflect certain assumptions about the work, and the researcher needs to identify these assumptions, how they become visible in the artefact, and how they support a specific way of working. The research questions that could be answered by this method include the following: How does the artefact steer, limit, or enable the (cognitive) action? What operations does it afford, and what impact does this have on the overall cognitive task?

The impact of artefacts on any action can be understood through their affordances, defined as "the opportunity of actions offered by the environment" by Borghi (2021:12485); different affordances of the same artefact may be utilised in different situations. The concept of affordances was first developed to account for the relationship of animals to their environment (Gibson 1979) but has later been extended to other fields, such as human-computer interaction. The affordances of sociocultural objects (see Cosentino 2021) such as translation tools afford actions that have significance in their context of usage. For example, the translation memory software affords the storage of translated segments. Through affordances, the artefacts have an impact on how they are used.

The overall aim of artefact analysis is to make a complex object easier to grasp and to discuss, and to understand the meanings assigned to artefacts in their context of use. A thorough description of the artefact will also help us understand the extensive system in which the individual cognitive work takes place. Risku (2009:114–115) describes a practical artefact analysis method that can be used to inform us about social and cognitive aspects of the situation as they materialise in translation artefacts. As the first step of the analysis, a written description of the artefact is produced. Ideally, the description includes an account of the artefact's external characteristics, elements, author (or possible another initiator), location, and explicitly stated purposes of use. The potential, activity- and situation-dependent affordances of the artefact are also described; according to Risku, this requires some knowledge of the context. In the second step of the analysis, the description is followed by a comparison of the explicitly stated uses of the artefact, the actual observed uses, and the internal logic of the artefact itself. The artefacts also change during the process, and these changes need to be accounted for (Risku 2009:115).

In a full ethnographic research project, knowledge of the actual affordances employed by the users is obtained through observation, together with other contextual information. In the absence of such a research project, the test analysis presented here focuses on describing the external characteristics and elements of the artefacts. The potential revision-related affordances of the artefacts are deciphered from the characteristics of the artefacts and the software used to process them, with usage information obtained from the artefacts themselves and through the author's first-hand experience of how this artefact type is used at LSPs. The artefact's steering, limiting or enabling impact on the reviser's share of the cognitive work is then discussed based on these descriptions.

2.3 Discourse analysis using systemic functional linguistics

2.3.1 *SFL as the tool of analysis*

In the second methodological test, systemic functional linguistics will be used to analyse how cognitive collaboration takes shape in the communication contained in the revision file. The suggestion that SFL might be applied in the way proposed here is based on its nature as a functional grammar that spotlights the meaning-making capacity of language; in this chapter, SFL is used as an analytical framework that allows us to get closer to the linguistic meaning-making activity of translators and revisers. The analytic categories available in SFL allow modelling the cognitive task of translators and revisers as the manipulation of the three lines of meaning that are present in all language. The manipulation becomes particularly observable in translation shifts (for a thorough discussion of using SFL for the analysis of translation shifts, see Hill-Madsen 2020).

Two different communication features can be identified in the files: comments, and the translated text itself (including the changes introduced by the reviser). The comments, typically displayed in the margin, constitute direct communication between the process participants. They are usually written by the reviser for the translator, although the opposite direction is also possible. The comments may reveal how the participants position themselves and others in the overall cognitive process: which role they adopt, and how much space they yield to the other participant.

The translated text contained in the revision file can be seen as communication on two different levels. Firstly, it constitutes communication that originates from an external party, the client, and is being translated into another language on their behalf; this level of communication will not be analysed here. Secondly, it is a vehicle for negotiating translation solutions between the translator and the reviser. The text contains the translation solutions chosen by the translator, and the revision changes made by the reviser. Each change that the reviser has made to the file using the Track Changes feature can be seen as an instance of communication that aims at proposing or requiring modifications to the wording. These changes are thus a visible indication of a distributed cognitive system in action, and they can be subjected to a linguistic analysis that informs us of the nature of this system. In other words, as the participants negotiate the solutions using the features of the text processing software, the division of linguistic labour becomes visible in the text. In the current test analysis, distribution of the linguistic labour of meaning-making in the text is investigated by an analysis of the three metafunctions (textual, ideational, and interpersonal) that form the three lines of meaning described in SFL (Table 2).

Table 2. The three metafunctions of systemic functional linguistics (Halliday and Matthiessen 2014:83)

Metafunction	Type of meaning	Structure or system
Textual	Message	Theme + Rheme
Ideational	Representation	Process + participants + circumstances
Interpersonal	Exchange	Mood, modality, appraisal

The textual metafunction is perhaps the easiest of these to apply in an analysis: "the Theme of a clause is the first group or phrase that has some function in the [ideational] structure of the clause" (Halliday and Matthiessen 2014:91). Theme and Rheme function in a very similar way in both English and Finnish, setting the information structure of the clause (Hakulinen et al. 2004:1308; Halliday and Matthiessen 2014:88).

The ideational metafunction bears some resemblance to a traditional grammatical analysis, but instead of grammatical subjects, objects and adverbials, etc., it deals with process types, the logical subject, and other participants defined by their semantic relationships. The process types, expressed by verbs, are material, behavioural, mental, verbal, relational and existential; the related logical subjects are Actor, Behaver, Senser, Sayer, Carrier and Token, and Existent (Halliday and Matthiessen 2014:214, 219). Together with possible other participants, the logical subjects are involved in the process expressed by the process verb. Circumstances, on the other hand, are phrases that add some temporal, spatial, causal or other similar aspect to the clause (Halliday and Matthiessen 2014:221). The ideational metafunction also includes the logical function, which deals with complex structures and is therefore not included in the current analysis.

The interpersonal metafunction deals with two kinds of relationships: those between the speaker/writer and the addressee, and those between the speaker/writer and the message content (Banks 2019:47). The interpersonal layer of meaning may be the most demanding of the three metafunctions to analyse, as it can be manifested in the clause using several different systems. The first of these is the system of Mood: whether the clause is a question, statement, or instruction (Halliday and Matthiessen 2014:134–166). All these clause types establish specific relationships between the speaker/writer and the addressee. The systems that are used to express relationships with the content are Modality and Appraisal; Modality includes expressions of probability as well as permission and obligation

(Banks 2019:50). Appraisal, which can be manifested as a wide variety of grammatical and lexical systems and features, concerns expressions of engagement, affect, judgement, appreciation or graduation (Martin and White 2005:35; Banks 2019:84–89).

As a linguistic and grammatical approach that emphasises meaning and the use of language in functional communication, SFL resonates strongly with translation studies, and can be used as a linguistic tool for comparative discourse analysis of translations (Munday 2021:84; see also Munday 2012). For accounts of how SFL has been previously used in translation studies research, see Kim and Matthiessen (2015), Hill-Madsen (2020:143–144), Kim et al. (2021) and Chen, Xuan, and Yu (2022). Ideally, a systemic functional analysis of more than one language version should be based on descriptions of each language (see, e.g., Halliday and Matthiessen 2014:55–56; Munday 2021:84). Unfortunately, there is no full description of Finnish that uses a purely systemic functional approach, although major steps towards such a description have been taken by Shore, whose dissertation (Shore 1992) gives a partial systemic functional account of Finnish, and whose subsequent grammar of Finnish (Shore 2020) combines functional and traditional approaches. The lack of a full description does not, however, pose major problems to the present analysis, which focuses on shifts in clause-level metafunctions. A more detailed analysis of how the metafunctions manifest in the texts, and whether the shifts are obligatory or optional, should be based on thorough descriptions of the languages; however, such analysis will not be presented here. At the level being applied here, the lexicogrammatical and semiotic resources of Finnish and English are adequately similar, so that the Finnish texts can be analysed using the English-based theoretical presentations of systemic functional grammar, primarily the one by Halliday and Matthiessen (2014).

2.3.2 Description of the discourse analysis procedure

Systemic functional analysis was carried out for both the comments found in text margins, and the translation solutions being proposed in the text itself. The focus of these two parts of the analysis was slightly different. The comments added to the text margins are a form of direct interaction that helps establish the relationship between the translator and the reviser. Therefore, the analysis of the comments focuses on the interpersonal line of meaning-making, particularly on how the authors of the comments utilise the systems of Mood and Modality to construct their own role, and that of the recipients — in other words, how they position themselves as part of the socio-cognitive system.

The analysis of the solutions being proposed within the text by the translator and the reviser was focused on shifts that could be identified with regard to any of the three metafunctions: textual, ideational, and interpersonal. The unit of analysis was the clause, as required by the SFL framework, although the figures being presented here are based on translation segments, which are typically comprised of one sentence. This presentation method is based on the typical procedure in retrospective translation analysis following Toury's (1995) coupled pairs method, also applied by Hill-Madsen (2020:147). In retrospect, presenting clause-based results would have resulted in improved precision and accuracy; this is recommended for future applications of the method.

When analysing the reviser's intervention, I went through all the segments that contained changes made by the reviser, and established whether the change was an edit that aimed at improving the text, or constituted correction of a language mechanics error (grammar, spelling, punctuation etc.) or accuracy error (mistranslation; see, e.g., Mossop 2020:136, 138–141). While it is often a matter of opinion whether some revision changes are necessary or not, errors are here defined as changes that I, based on my experience as a translation professional, deemed necessary without doubt, as they led, e.g., to ungrammatical or inaccurate translations. The error corrections were excluded from the analysis of the metafunctions. This allowed focusing on the creative undertaking of translation production instead of the more mundane effort of correcting errors.

For the segments that contained changes classified as edits, I examined whether they included a metafunctional shift, and which metafunctions were concerned; as Hill-Madsen (2020:147) states, "any TT wording may represent a shift in more than one metafunction at the same time". The shifts were quantified to find out how revisers divided their cognitive focus between the different metafunctions. Next, I took a step back and carried out the same analysis for the translations: which metafunctional shifts had taken place during translation? This allowed drawing conclusions about the translators' cognitive focus. Combining the analysis of metafunctional shifts found in the translators' and the revisers' interventions, I examined how they distribute the cognitive labour of meaning-making between them. This quantitative analysis revealed substantial differences between the individual files. To explain these differences, I looked at the genre of each text and how it may have impacted the roles that the translator and reviser had adopted.

While carrying out the analysis of metafunctional shifts, I excluded elliptical structures as well as the mechanisms of explicitation and implicitation, and did not engage in any analysis of whether the shifts were obligatory or optional. All of these topics could constitute interesting areas for study from a cognitive perspective, but require thoroughness that the scope of the present chapter does not allow. While an analysis of obligatory and optional shifts would naturally improve the precision of the analysis, conducting such analysis in terms of systemic functional grammar would require the availability of a full description of both languages, but as mentioned above, such a description of Finnish is currently not available.

3. Outcomes of the methodological tests

3.1 Artefact analysis

In this analysis of the exported Trados Studio revision files as digital artefacts, I describe the artefacts' external characteristics and elements, focusing on the revision-related affordance potential of the files and the Microsoft Word software that is used to process these files. The data also contains some evidence of the actual usage of the software's affordances. When describing the various characteristics, I also discuss how they steer the cognitive focus of revisers and may help or hinder them in their task.

The most important revision-related characteristics of the .docx revision file are found in its special formatting. The file contains the source text and the translated text in a table format (see Figure 1 for an example). The segment ID is in the first column, and information about the TM match in the second. The match level is repeated in the file as colour coding: in the current data, full matches are displayed on a green background, and partial matches on a yellow background. The colours can be changed in Trados Studio's settings. The third and fourth columns contain the source and target text segments, positioned side by side.

These formatting characteristics guide the reviser's attention towards comparing each translation segment to the source, and away from textual features such as cohesion and the organisation of the text. Paragraph breaks are not displayed at all, which makes it impossible to edit paragraph structures without external references such as the original source text or a formatted target text. Paragraph-level editing is further prevented by the segmentation of the text, which must not be changed as that would lead to incompatibility with the translation software. Tags often indicate some formatting features such as bolding, but headings and lists, for example, are often not indicated unless they have, e.g., numbering. The formatting tags may also be displayed in a condensed form, leaving their meaning unclear; this was the case in some of the files in the current data (see Figure 1). The files thus do not afford the reliable revision of many textual features.

The file affords detailed information on the TM match level. An obvious consequence is that the reviser may not read full matches at all, or only cursorily, as these are assumed to have been revised previously. This may further hinder the revision of the text as a coherent whole. The reviser's cognitive focus is thus steered towards economical checking of the translation segments which are most likely to contain errors. On the other hand, there is no indication of which part of a partial match segment is new and which is a legacy translation; such information could help the reviser work in an even more economical manner.

All the normal functionality of .docx files processed in MS Word is available for the revision files. These cannot, however, be used freely, as any changes might again result in incompatibility with the translation environment, and failure when importing the revised translation. The revisers are only expected to use MS Word's review functionality (Figure 2). The current data shows that revisers use the Track Changes function to make their edits visible in the text, and may also use the commenting functionality to add comments that are directly related to specific parts of the text. Other functions available to them include switching between the All Markup and Simple Markup views, which show or hide the edits, respectively, and allow a shift in focus from the changes to the final text version. The Simple Markup view helps revisers to ensure that they have not introduced new problems to the text. In addition, the Show Markup menu can be used to show or hide various markup types, such as formatting changes. Usage of these features largely depends on the individual preferences of the revisers.

Figure 2. The main review functionality of MS Word

Since the MS Word software has been developed for text processing and not for translation, the translation process must adapt to the functionality that is available. The formatting of the revision file has been designed by translation software developers to include information that is relevant for translation. Nevertheless, the result is a trade-off between an easy process (as the reviser does not need to buy a translation software license) and having available a full range of features, such as the translation memory database and original text formatting information, that would support translation and the cognitive effort of revisers in the best possible manner. Based on this analysis, the revision file's characteristics steer and limit the revisers' cognitive work considerably. The absence of text formatting information also seems to indicate that software developers have assumed that the purpose of revision is not to improve the translated texts, but mainly to check them for errors in accuracy and language mechanics.

3.2 The communication contained in the revision files

In this second part of the analysis of revision files, I turn the focus on what is being communicated in them. As was mentioned above, the files contain two types of communication between the participants: comments that are used as direct messages; and the translated text itself, which communicates the translation and revision solutions being proposed. I will first analyse the comments for evidence of how the revisers position themselves and the translators in the process. After this, I will turn my focus to the translated texts and examine how the participants distribute labour in the joint cognitive activity of creating a translation.

3.2.1 *The comments as interaction*

The commenting function of MS Word fosters direct communication between the translator and reviser and therefore has special importance for constructing their cognitive collaboration. While the translator may add comments directed to the reviser, the current data only contains comments added by revisers. Three of the seven files included a total of seven comments: two in both F4 and F5, and three (written by two different revisers, although only one had revised the text itself) in F6. In all of these instances, the language pair of the translation is FI–EN, and English is the revisers' L1.

The tone of voice in these comments is generally informative and polite, aiming to help the other participant in their cognitive task while giving them the freedom to carry out that task as they choose. The revisers use declarative sentences to offer background information and their own views of correct English usage. They show a willingness to yield decision-making power to the other parties and soften their statements with modal verbs and expressions of uncertainty: "I would capitalise because ..., but reject if you think it should be ..."; "I'm not sure of the difference ..., but I guess they know what they're talking about". The revisers also justify their views; four of the seven comments refer to an online source originating from the client, and two others include the reviser's own knowledge about culturally appropriate usage or rhetorical devices. Both of the references to the revisers' own knowledge are carefully hedged, presumably to avoid seeming too authoritative – although the assumption in LSP contexts usually is that the L1 reviser has authority on such issues. The only case of imperative mood is found in the clause quoted above, instructing the translator to reject the suggestion if they disagree with it. Since obligatory correction requests would be given using the Track Changes function, there is no need to use the imperative in the comments.

The majority of the comments in the data are unidirectional communication and have no responses, with one exception (in F6). It seems that in this case, the revised text has been sent to a second reviser for commenting or further improvement. The second reviser has, however, refrained from making any further changes, and has only added one fairly neutral comment. The scarcity of the other reviser's input may indicate unwillingness to correct a fellow reviser's work. The original reviser has responded to this comment, but it is unlikely that the author of the first comment would ever see it, as the working processes of LSPs are usually streamlined so that back-and-forth discussions rarely occur. As the responding reviser should be well aware of this, the intended reader of the comment is probably the translator.

3.2.2 Systemic functional analysis of metafunctional shifts as indications of distributed cognitive labour

In this section, I will first present a primarily quantitative analysis of the distribution of indications of cognitive labour of meaning-making in the revision files; this part of the analysis reveals some interesting trends related to text genre. After this, the cognitive focus of translators and revisers will be examined separately. In all these analyses, cognitive labour is operationalised through the three aspects of meaning that are manifested through the three metafunctions.

The revisers' task scope is usually understood as correcting errors, and unnecessary changes are advised against (see Martin 2007; Mossop 2020). In the current data, however, many reviser interventions did not constitute corrections of errors (language mechanics or accuracy). Looking at the data as a whole, it is thus clear that revisers do not restrict their cognitive work to locating and correcting errors. Instead, they seem to engage in a much more extensive translation and editing task, aiming at the overall improvement of the target text both as a reproduction of the source and as an independent text.

Table 3. Indications of distributed cognitive labour between translator and reviser

	Total segm.	Genre	Shifts by translator	Reviser interv.	Shifts by reviser
F1 (EN-FI)	63	Chemistry, Instruction	13 (21%)	11 (17%)	2 (3%)
F2 (EN-FI)	70	Medical, User instr.	11 (16%)	5 (7%)	1 (1%)
F3 (EN-FI)	39	Business, Strategy summary	31 (79%)	15 (38%)	5 (13%)
F4 (FI-EN)	85	Business, Web article	52 (61%)	19 (22%)	2 (2%)
F5 (FI-EN)	26	Energy, Press release	12 (46%)	4 (15%)	0
F6 (FI-EN)	17	Energy, Speech	5 (29%)	11 (65%)	4 (24%)
F7 (FI-EN)	52	Energy, Web article	21 (40%)	28 (54%)	7 (13%)

The file-specific characteristics of cognitive labour distribution are given in Table 3 and Figure 3. In addition to the number of segments and the genre, the table presents information on the metafunctional shifts introduced by the translator, the reviser's total intervention (error correction and other edits combined; note that not all of the edits contain a metafunctional shift), and the metafunctional shifts introduced by the reviser. The figure only shows the percentages of segments in which an intervention or shift occurred. The total intervention rate of the translator is not displayed here, since it must naturally always be 100 per cent (or very near it, taking into account that some segments may not require a translation).

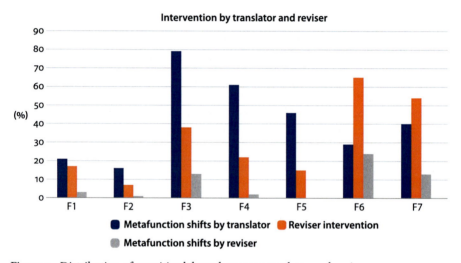

Figure 3. Distribution of cognitive labour between translator and reviser

It seems that the values and ratios presented above can be connected to specific cognitive configurations in which the apparent quality level produced by the translator, the role adopted by the reviser (reflected in the overall number of changes, the number of errors corrected and the number of metafunctional shifts introduced), and the requirements set by the text genre come together. These cognitive configurations are discussed below. I will discuss genre here as a translation-relevant phenomenon that is related to the need to use the style and register that are appropriate for each text in the target culture. Due to the small number of files being examined, I will conceptualise genre using a simple stylistic dichotomy of *fluent translations* which emphasise smoothness of style (typically marketing texts, articles etc.), and *precise translations* that prioritise accuracy (e.g., legal texts, user manuals and administrative texts). This dichotomy has been presented based on my interview data in Korhonen (2022: 175); as to what consti-

Chapter 10. Revision files as cognitive ethnographic data **241**

tutes smoothness, see Mossop (2020: 53–58). In the current data, the first of these genre types (files F3–F7) encourages linguistic creativity that manifests as a high number of metafunctional shifts introduced by both the translator and reviser, while the latter type (F1 and F2) contain considerably fewer shifts.

F1 and F2 are technical texts, and stylistically very straight-forward. However, F1 contains some demanding technical terminology, and some sections of the English source text are difficult to decipher (as demonstrated in Example 1). This implies high requirements not only for the translator's terminological knowledge, but also for their subject matter expertise. In order to be able to translate the text well, the translator would need to fill in information that is missing or misleadingly expressed in the source text. Example 1 shows a case in which the translator clearly did not possess this expertise, but the reviser did and added information that was not expressed directly in the source text. The role of the reviser thus approaches that of content editor.

Example 1. A translation segment from file F1

(1) **Source text:**   **This XXXX Styrene monomer product does contain inhibitor (TBC) as 14–18 ppm once leave from the XXXX storage tanks.**

  Raw translation: *Tämä XXXX-styreenimonomeerivalmiste ei sisällä inhibiittoria (TBC), kun 14–18 ppm on poistunut XXXX-säiliöistä.*

  'This XXXX Styrene monomer product does **not** contain inhibitor (TBC) when 14–18 ppm has left from the XXXX storage tanks.'

  Revised *Tämä XXXX-styreenimonomeerivalmiste ei sisällä inhibiittoria (TBC)*
  translation: *pitoisuudessa 14–18 ppm sen jälkeen, kun valmiste on siirretty XXXXin varastosäiliöistä.*

  'This XXXX Styrene monomer product does **not** contain inhibitor (TBC) **at the concentration of** 14–18 ppm **after the product has been moved** from the XXXX storage tanks.'

F2 is a user instruction text, again stylistically uncomplicated and with few metafunctional shifts by either the translator or reviser. The translation contains a very high number of full and partial translation memory (TM) matches, which may explain the infrequency of reviser intervention. The segments that are full TM matches contain no reviser interventions, which might mean that the reviser has been instructed not to change them, or even not to read them at all to save time and costs. The TM match level also complicates the analysis of translator intervention, since the file does not reveal whether any shifts were introduced by the person who translated this text or by those who wrote the legacy translations now being drawn from the TM.

The low number of metafunctional shifts found in F1 and F2 seems to point at a connection between the number of metafunctional shifts and the genre:

in stylistically simple texts, producing an adequate translation does not seem to require linguistic creativity that would necessitate many metafunctional shifts. These files can be translated between English and Finnish with relatively little creativity, following the source text closely and focusing on accuracy. However, to confirm this relationship, a stylistic analysis would be necessary. As such an analysis is not part of the current test setup, no definite conclusions can be drawn regarding this matter.

The other five files are of genres that prioritise fluency over detailed accuracy. All of them are directed at fairly large audiences, in most cases through online publication. In F3, F4 and F5, it seems that the translator has aimed for a smooth target text, introducing a fairly large number of metafunctional shifts and thus taking on nearly all of the cognitive work of producing the translation. There are, however, differences in how the revisers have worked: in F3, the reviser has introduced a considerably larger number of metafunctional shifts than the revisers of the other two files — regardless of the fact that the translator had already introduced a very high number of shifts. It seems that the reviser has made changes that are not strictly necessary (see Example 2).

Example 2. A translation segment from file F3

(2) **Source text:** **We invest in R&D, with a particular focus on sustainability.**

Raw translation: *Investoimme tuotekehitykseen **kiinnittäen** erityistä huomiota vastuullisuuteen.*

'We invest in R&D **attaching** particular attention on sustainability.'

Revised translation: *Investoimme tuotekehitykseen **ja kiinnitämme** huomiota erityisesti vastuullisuuteen.*

'We invest in R&D **and attach** particular attention on sustainability.'

In F4, the reviser has focused on correcting (minor) errors and has made few other edits. In F5, this tendency is even more pronounced. All three revisers have received a translation with little to correct but have made different choices in how to approach it: the reviser of F3 (EN-FI) has decided to make further stylistic improvements, while the revisers of F4 and F5 (both FI-EN) have restricted their cognitive effort mostly to correcting minor errors such as punctuation and prepositions.

Files F6 and F7 differ from the others in that the proportion of segments with reviser intervention is much higher than in the other files, and also high when compared to the number of metafunctional shifts introduced by the translator. It seems that the revisers have assumed a large share of the cognitive work in these two instances. The reasons for this differ greatly between these two texts. F6 is a short speech, which makes it difficult to draw conclusions based on the number of metafunctional shifts; however, some general observations can be made. While there are not many actual errors in the raw translation, the reviser has edited it to make it more idiomatic and natural. The result is a well-written speech that runs smoothly. The translator is clearly not a native speaker of the target language, but the reviser is. This is a good example of the division of cognitive work between non-native and native translation professionals.

F7, on the other hand, is characterised by an unpolished source text that contains many language errors, a translator who has not been able to cope with this, and a reviser who seems to have lost their motivation facing a task that may have been impossible to perform in the allotted time. While the proportion of segments with reviser interventions was higher in F6, F7 is a much longer text and often contains several corrections within the same segment. The level of reviser's intervention thus actually seems to be higher. The reviser takes on a relatively high proportion of the cognitive labour and seems to have invested much effort in correcting terms and grammar as well as the style of the text (reflected in metafunctional shifts), trying to compensate for the shortcomings of the earlier versions. The final translation still contains numerous errors.

Next, let us look at what metafunctional shifts can tell us about which aspects of meaning-making the translator and the reviser take on as part of their cognitive work. The translators' cognitive focus is presented in Table 4 and Figure 4. They show, for each file, the proportion of segments that contain one or more metafunctional shifts, and the proportions of segments that contain a thematic, ideational, or interpersonal shift. Note that shifts in more than one metafunction may occur at the same time, which is why the numbers add up to more than the total number and percentage of shifts for each text.

Table 4. Distribution of the translators' cognitive focus between different aspects of meaning-making

	Shifts by translator	Thematic shifts	Ideational shifts	Interpersonal shifts
F1 (EN-FI)	13 (21%)	4 (6%)	8 (13%)	4 (6%)
F2 (EN-FI)	11 (16%)	6 (9%)	4 (6%)	2 (3%)
F3 (EN-FI)	31 (79%)	16 (41%)	30 (77%)	4 (10%)
F4 (FI-EN)	52 (61%)	26 (31%)	37 (44%)	13 (15%)
F5 (FI-EN)	12 (46%)	3 (12%)	10 (38%)	1 (4%)
F6 (FI-EN)	5 (29%)	3 (18%)	4 (24%)	1 (6%)
F7 (FI-EN)	21 (40%)	8 (15%)	13 (25%)	2 (4%)
Total	**145**	**66**	**106**	**27**

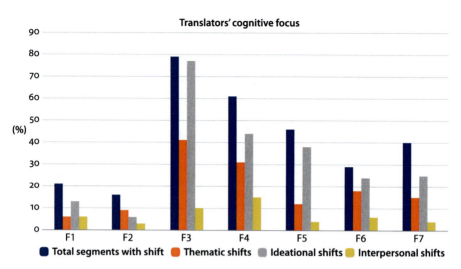

Figure 4. Distribution of the translators' cognitive focus between different aspects of meaning-making

The main trend of more frequent metafunctional shifts being found in texts which require a smooth and fluent style was discussed above. Now we turn to the individual metafunctions: which of them do translators spend the most cognitive energy on? The answer is clear: the cognitive work of translators is predominantly directed at managing the ideational metafunction, that is, presenting the flow of events consisting of processes, participants and circumstances. When looking at all seven files combined (see Table 4), a total of 73% of segments that contain a metafunctional shift (145 segments) have an ideational shift (106 segments), which may also coincide with either a thematic or interpersonal shift. Thematic shifts are the second most frequent area of translators' cognitive focus.

The interpersonal metafunction receives the least attention from the translator. The relationships and attitudes expressed in the texts seem to change very little even though the texts are being translated for new audiences. There are only two noteworthy exceptions to this in the data, found in F1 and F4. F1, which is a technical instruction text, contains as many interpersonal as thematic shifts introduced by the translator. Several of the interpersonal shifts in this file are changes in how compelling an instruction is (see Example 3). The shifts have probably been considered necessary due to cultural differences: Finnish readers might well consider less compelling instructions optional.

Example 3. A translation segment from file F1
(3) Source text: ... an inhibitor ... should be maintained at ...
    Raw translation: *Inhibiittorin ... pitoisuutena on pidettävä ...*
                     'Inhibitor's ... concentration **must be** maintained at ...'

F4 is another file with relatively many interpersonal shifts. The text recounts the career of one person, and most of these shifts are related to how he is being referred to. In the original Finnish, first name is used throughout the text, creating a comfortable informal tone; the translator has replaced these with the surname, catering for an international audience which might not be comfortable using first names. This could be analysed as an example of a cultural filter at work (see, e.g., House 2006: 347–353), although there is no single target culture at play.

Moving on to the metafunctional shifts introduced by the revisers (Table 5 and Figure 5), it becomes evident that the current data is too limited and does not contain enough shifts to draw any firm quantitatively based conclusions. However, the revisers seem to focus on the ideational and thematic areas of meaning-making, accepting the interpersonal aspects of the texts as they were. In this respect, the results do not differ greatly from those presented on translators above. It seems that the translators and revisers distribute their focus between different areas of meaning-making in very similar ways.

Table 5. Distribution of the revisers' cognitive focus between different aspects of meaning-making

	Shifts by reviser	Thematic shifts	Ideational shifts	Interpersonal shifts
F1 (EN-FI)	2 (3%)	0	2 (3%)	1 (2%)
F2 (EN-FI)	1 (1%)	0	1 (1%)	0
F3 (EN-FI)	5 (13%)	4 (10%)	4 (10%)	0
F4 (FI-EN)	2 (2%)	1 (1%)	0	1 (1%)
F5 (FI-EN)	0	0	0	0
F6 (FI-EN)	4 (24%)	3 (18%)	3 (18%)	0
F7 (FI-EN)	7 (13%)	3 (6%)	5 (10%)	0
Total	**21**	**11**	**15**	**2**

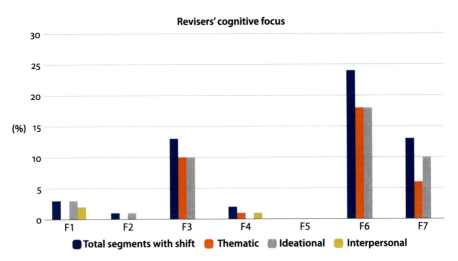

Figure 5. Distribution of the revisers' cognitive focus between different aspects of meaning-making

4. Discussion

The methodological tests presented here yielded some interesting results and illustrated ways in which these methods could be used for investigating the cognitive tasks and distribution of labour of translators and revisers. The artefact analysis of the files as digital artefacts spotlighted the ways in which the file format and the affordances steer the reviser's work, and the account of how revisers position themselves in their comments revealed that they yield plenty of space for the translators to make final translation decisions. The artefact analysis and the analysis of the comments as interaction appear to be useful methods that could be adopted in many types of cognitive or socio-cognitive studies of translation. The exact way of using or combining them would depend on the goals of each study.

The analysis of the distribution of labour manifested through the numbers of metafunctional shifts and their ratio to the total intervention proved to yield the most fruitful results when connected to text genre; the cognitive input of translators and revisers was relatively easy to trace in the files. Based on this part of the study, we can hypothesise that when the text genre requires what can be called a fluent translation (instead of a very precise one), and the language pair is English to Finnish, a high number of metafunctional shifts often takes place. The shifts typically concern the ideational metafunction and, perhaps to a slightly smaller extent, the thematic metafunction. It would be interesting to see whether similar trends exist in other language pairs.

The interpersonal metafunction, which concerns attitudes, emotions, and social relationships between writer and audience, constitutes a very interesting area of meaning-making and of the cognitive effort of translation production. It seems that translators and revisers do not often make changes to the interpersonal aspects of the texts. With a few exceptions, the interpersonal relationships mostly remain the same despite changing audiences. This may be an indication of the translators' desire to remain invisible. If they adopted a more active interpersonal role and position between author and audience or inserted any value-related discourse that could be interpreted as their own, they might lose that invisibility. They may also be saving their cognitive resources by focusing on transfer instead of developing a stance towards the subject matter.

The last part of the analysis focused on the individual tasks of the translator and reviser, and how they direct their cognitive focus. Both seem to give the most attention to the ideational content of the texts, and the least to interpersonal. Quantitative comparison between the two was, however, prevented by the small total number of metafunctional shifts made by the revisers in this limited dataset. If such comparisons are to be made, more extensive datasets or different analysis methods are needed.

It is important to note that if the type of discourse analysis presented here is applied, its role in the overall study must be considered carefully. As a grammatical framework, SFL has been developed for analysing language. Here, it has been used to explore what the language used in the texts can tell us about the process participants' cognition. While the results seem to indicate that useful results can be thus obtained, the method should not be applied blindly and is likely to require further development to meet each research project's needs. It may even be necessary to replace SFL with another linguistic framework. Choosing SFL for this pilot analysis is not meant to imply that it is the only possible option for cognitive ethnographic analysis.

An analysis of real-world translations between languages such as English and Finnish, which belong to different language families and therefore have not only different grammatical constructions but different ways of building discourse, is never easy. While SFL may offer a better tool for this than other grammatical theories, the analysis can still be tricky. Other kinds of difficulties resulted, as could be expected, from missing contextual information. It is difficult to know based on textual data alone whether some inconsistencies between the source and raw target texts are due to purposeful edits done by the translator, or just translation errors. The problem extends to the reviser — if they have not corrected the inconsistency, does that mean that they agree on the edit, or that they just have not noticed the error?

An analysis of seven files and 352 translation segments was, while time-consuming, still possible without any particular digital analysis tools. A more extensive analysis of the linguistic manifestations of the distribution of cognitive labour would require the adoption of, e.g., corpus tools. Similarly, adding detail to the systemic functional analysis would increase the analysis effort exponentially. When working without any automation, the analysis should always be limited to some carefully selected linguistic features instead of attempting to include all aspects of meaning-making in one analysis.

As stated in the introduction, the methods presented here are not intended to be used independently, but as part of ethnographic studies. In such research projects, the situational context in which the translations are being created would be described, together with the background and position of the translators and revisers. The text would also need to be followed all the way as proposed by Koskinen (2008, 2020) to fully describe the different phases of collaboration between the translator and the reviser. Most importantly, the final version produced by the translator based on the reviser's suggestions would need to be obtained in order to examine the translator's interventions at this stage. Furthermore, if the client joins the cognitive work by making or requesting changes to the translation after delivery, these would need to be recorded and analysed. Observation and interviews could also reveal the participants' competence profiles, attitudes, and their goals when working on the translations. A specific interview method described by Olohan (2021: 12, 125), called the 'guided tour' or 'contextual inquiry', takes place while the interviewee is working and could be very useful for this purpose. Observational data could also allow taking the artefact analysis further with a comparison of the artefact's explicitly stated purposes and functions with its observed, actual uses. This could reveal differences between how the organisation wants to use the artefacts, the usage intended by the artefact's designers, and the context-bound actual use (Risku 2009: 115).

The exploratory analyses presented here lead to many new questions that could be answered in future studies, helping to improve the methods further. For example, a larger dataset could allow a more extensive examination of the interaction that translators and revisers engage in using the commenting function. Methods and theories not adopted here, such as an analysis of the comments as written discourse (see Cameron and Panović 2014), could prove useful. Within the translated texts, phenomena such as explicitation and implicitation, with the related grammatical concept of ellipsis, could also be investigated to find out more about how translators and revisers share the task of meaning-making.

An understanding of how artefacts and their affordances connect to human cognition is key to all successful human-computer interaction. It is therefore vital that translation studies researchers stay up to date on which artefacts are being used by professionals, and how. As Hutchins (1995a: 371) says, "[s]tudying cognition in the wild is difficult, and the outcomes are uncertain"; to ensure the best possible results, we need to continue testing and developing new methods for investigating situated cognitive functions in translation contexts.

References

Banks, David. 2019. *A Systemic Functional Grammar of English. A Simple Introduction.* New York: Routledge.

Borghi, Anna M. (2018) 2021. "Affordances, Context and Sociality." *Synthese* 199: 12485–12515.

Cameron, Deborah, and Ivan Panović. 2014. *Working with Written Discourse.* London: Sage.

Chen, Shukun, Winfred Wenhui Xuan, and Hailing Yu. 2022. "Applying Systemic Functional Linguistics in Translation Studies. A Research Synthesis." *Babel* 68 (4): 517–545.

Clark, Andy, and David Chalmers. 1998. "The Extended Mind." *Analysis* 58 (1): 7–19.

Cosentino, Erica. (2019) 2021. "Artifacts and Affordances." *Synthese* 198 (Suppl. 17): 4007–4026.

Gibson, James J. 1979. *The Ecological Approach to Visual Perception.* Boston: Houghton-Mifflin.

Hakulinen, Auli, Maria Vilkuna, Riitta Korhonen, Vesa Koivisto, Tarja Riitta Heinonen, and Irja Alho. 2004. *Iso suomen kielioppi* [*The Big Grammar of Finnish*]. Helsinki: Suomalaisen Kirjallisuuden Seura.

Halliday, Micheal A. K., and Christian M. I. M. Matthiessen. 2014. *Halliday's Introduction to Systemic Functional Grammar.* Abingdon: Routledge.

Hill-Madsen, Aage. 2020. "SFL and Descriptive Translation Studies: Systemic-Functional Grammar as a Framework for the Analysis of Shifts in Translation." *Globe: A Journal of Language, Culture and Communication* 10: 143–169.

House, Juliane. 2006. "Text and Context in Translation." *Journal of Pragmatics* 38: 338–358.

Hutchins, Edwin. 1995a. *Cognition in the Wild.* Cambridge, MA: MIT Press.

Hutchins, Edwin. 1995b. "How a Cockpit Remembers Its Speeds." *Cognitive Science* 19: 265–288.

International Organization for Standardization. 2015. ISO 17100 Translation Services — Requirements for Translation Services.

Kim, Mira, and Christian M. I. M. Matthiessen. 2015. "Introduction." *Target* 27 (3): 335–350.

Kim, Mira, Jeremy Munday, Zhenhua Wang, and Pin Wang (eds). 2021. *Systemic Functional Linguistics and Translation Studies.* London: Bloomsbury.

Korhonen, Annamari. 2022. "When and How to Revise? Building a Cognitive Dyad of Translator and Reviser through Workflow Adjustment." *Translation, Cognition & Behavior* 5 (2): 165–186.

Korhonen, Annamari, and Maija Hirvonen. 2021. "Joint Creative Process in Translation: Socially Distributed Cognition in Two Production Contexts." *Cognitive Linguistic Studies* 8 (2): 251–276.

Koskinen, Kaisa. 2008. *Translating Institutions: An Ethnographic Study of EU Translation*. Manchester: St. Jerome.

Koskinen, Kaisa. 2020. "Translatorial Linguistic Ethnography in Organizations." In *Understanding Multilingual Workplaces: Methodological, Empirical and Pedagogic Perspectives*, ed. by Sierk Horn, Philippe Lecomte, and Susanne Tietze, 60–77. New York: Routledge.

Lueger, Manfred. 2000. *Grundlagen qualitativer Feldforschung: Methodologie – Organisierung – Materialanalyse* [*Foundations of Qualitative Field Research: Methodology – Organisation – Materials Analysis*]. Wien: WUV.

Martin, James R., and Peter R. R. White. 2005. *The Language of Evaluation: Appraisal in English*. Basingstoke: Palgrave Macmillan.

Martin, Timothy. 2007. "Managing Risks and Resources: A Down-to-Earth View of Revision." *JoSTrans* 8: 57–63.

Matthiessen, Christian M. I. M., Kazuhiro Teruya, and Marvin Lam. 2010. *Key Terms in Systemic Functional Linguistics*. London & New York: Continuum.

Mossop, Brian. 2020. *Revising and Editing for Translators*. 4th edition. Abingdon: Routledge.

Munday, Jeremy. 2012. *Evaluation in Translation. Critical Points of Translator Decision-Making*. Abingdon: Routledge.

Munday, Jeremy. 2021. "Systemic Functional Linguistics as a Framework for the Analysis of Translator/Interpreter Intervention." In *Systemic Functional Linguistics and Translation Studies*, ed. by Mira Kim, Jeremy Munday, Zhenhua Wang, and Pin Wang, 83–98. London: Bloomsbury.

Olohan, Maeve. 2021. *Translation and Practice Theory*. London: Routledge.

Perry, Mark. 1999. "The Application of Individually and Socially Distributed Cognition in Workplace Studies: Two Peas in a Pod?" In *Proceedings of the 3rd European Conference on Cognitive Science*, ed. by Sebastiano Bagnara, 87–92. Siena, Italy.

Risku, Hanna. 2009. *Translationsmanagement: Interkulturelle Fachkommunikation im Informationszeitalter* [*Translation Management: Intercultural Specialized Communication in the Information Age*]. Tübingen: Narr.

Sannholm, Raphael. 2021. "Translation, Teamwork, and Technology: The Use of Social and Material Scaffolds in the Translation Process." Dissertation, Stockholm University. http://urn.kb.se/resolve?urn=urn:nbn:se:su:diva-197921

Sannholm, Raphael, and Hanna Risku. 2024. "Situated Minds and Distributed Systems in Translation. Exploring the Conceptual and Empirical Implications." *Target* 36 (2): 159–183.

Shore, Susanna. 1992. "Aspects of a Systemic-Functional Grammar of Finnish." Dissertation, Macquarie University.

Shore, Susanna. 2020. *Lauseita ja vesinokkaeläimiä. Perinteisestä funktionaaliseen lauseoppiin* [*Clauses and Platypuses. From Traditional to Functional Syntax*]. Helsinki: SKS.

Toury, Gideon. 1995. *Descriptive Translation Studies and Beyond*. Amsterdam & Philadelphia: John Benjamins.

Van de Geuchte, Sofie, and Leona Van Vaerenbergh. 2016. "Text Creation in a Multilingual Institutional Setting." *Translation Spaces* 5 (1): 59–77.

CHAPTER 11

Thinking with actor-network theory to unearth the (in)visibility of translation in a journalistic setting

Marlie van Rooyen
University of the Free State

Translation in a journalistic setting often disappears in the news production process. On the one hand, news organisations rarely appoint translators, and on the other hand, the task of translation is typically embedded into the news workers' daily activities. Journalists' perception of translation as an interlingual activity also reinforces the seeming invisibility of translation. This chapter illustrates that it is possible to shed light on less obvious instances of translation in radio station newsrooms when thinking with Bruno Latour's actor-network theory. Latour's 'travel guide' provides a framework to trace and showcase the human and nonhuman actors involved in translation activities, the translated products, and the multiple sources incorporated in the news production process.

Keywords: actor-network theory (ANT), fieldwork, news translation, visibility, community radio news

1. Introduction

Venuti (1995) was one of the first scholars who studied the visibility and/or invisibility of translation, albeit within literary translation. According to Venuti, a translated product could be visible or invisible as such depending on the translation strategy followed, e.g., domestication or foreignisation. The argument is that a translation product would usually only become visible as such if a researcher or a reader could identify the translator(s) or gain access to translation notes, or any other documentation related to the publication of the work. However, in the case of informative texts (such as news items), it is generally more challenging to identify translation.

After more than two decades of journalistic translation research (JTR), translation as practice and product is still argued to be invisible in the news production process. On the one hand, journalists view translation as a separate process from

https://doi.org/10.1075/btl.165.11van
Available under the CC BY-NC 4.0 license. © 2025 John Benjamins Publishing Company

the writing and editing of news texts (Bielsa 2007:143), and reporters would rather refer to a translation-related task "as an auxiliary activity" than as part of their regular job responsibilities (Davier 2014:61; see also Koskinen, Chapter 1, and Steinkogler, Chapter 6, on paraprofessional translation, this volume). On the other hand, researchers investigating the textual transfer from one language into another in newsrooms could miss translation in the news production process if they are not physically present in these newsrooms.

One of the greatest challenges for the translation studies (TS) scholar is that journalists themselves often have a very narrow perception of translation. It would thus be difficult for the researcher to identify news translation practices only based on experiences shared by a journalist during an interview. This is why Bani refers to the tendency that translation and those responsible for news translation become "completely invisible" (2006:35) in a newsroom. The research endeavour becomes even more tricky as journalists are often uneasy to include translation as part of their daily activities, specifically because they mostly view translation as a literal interlingual translation practice (Bielsa and Bassnett 2009:15). These journalists would rather refer to themselves as reporters with knowledge of other languages (Bielsa and Bassnett 2009:15). Nonetheless, in the case where news needs to be produced in more than one language and the journalists are either bilingual or multilingual individuals, they would be able to translate "foreign sources" into the expected target language (Tyulenev 2014:75). Furthermore, the integrated nature of journalistic and translation activities, within a single actor, further contributes to the invisibility of translation (Kang 2022:108–109). In this instance, the journalists are so-called "paratranslators" and their professional tasks would include "translation- or interpreting-related" elements (Tyulenev 2014:75).

In terms of research, Van Doorslaer (2010:181) has shown that translation forms part of the newsgathering stage and is also part of the writing and editing of news stories. Numerous scholars have also presented evidence that a journalist's job could include multiple elements of translation, for example, borrowing (Osaji 1991), cutting (Bani 2006), deletion (Van Rooyen and Naudé 2009), domestication (Bielsa 2007), reframing (Federici 2010), synthesising multiple sources (Bielsa and Bassnett 2009), and transediting (Stetting 1989). Nonetheless, translation in journalistic settings is often (if not mostly) either forgotten or "simply erased or glossed over" by both journalists and researchers alike (Scammell and Bielsa 2022:1434).

Conway (2010:981) adds that if the translation process is not signalled in some way, it would not be possible to identify the product as a translation. Schäffner and Bassnett (2010:10) argue that in some cases the fact that a (news) text is a translation would only become visible as such through mistranslation or translation errors. Other constraints in identifying the news translation product could be related to the absence of physical records or electronic archives of journalistic texts. Conway describes how he was unable to find any evidence in a historical study of news translation at the Canadian Broadcasting Corporation, as "there are no texts to examine because they were never produced" (2014: 624). He found that the CBC and Radio Canada have a sizeable archive of video recordings of the news programmes, but the documentation and records of written news texts are mostly ad hoc, "made up of items different people at different times thought were important, but without a clear guiding principle" (Conway 2014: 625). I found a similar situation when I investigated radio news translation at community radio stations in South Africa. In some instances, the texts (written by hand) were merely dumped into a steel cabinet (Figure 1) without any filing system (Van Rooyen 2019a: 182).

Figure 1. A steel cabinet and archived news bulletins

In terms of source texts, Gambier argues that a journalistic setting is often characterised by "complex multi-source situations" (2016: 900), which, in the words of Davier, is "a patchwork of many different sources, many of which were originally in a different language" (2014: 58). More recently, Gambier emphasised the challenge of tracking the source text(s) and that this process would be "time consuming and make collection of a corpus difficult" (2022: 96). Davier (2014: 64) relays the experience of an editor at the European-based news agency, Agence télégraphique suisse (ATS), who views translation as "posing a general risk for the transmission of news" (Davier 2014: 64) as "there's not much left of the original message anymore" (Davier 2014: 64). Davier deduces that some of the journalists might "not really trust translation" (2014: 65), because it produces "double abstraction" when journalists themselves "rarely go into the field" (Davier 2014: 65). Thus, the journalists are removed from a news story on two levels: first, because the journalists who are stuck in the newsroom did not attend the news event themselves; and, second, because the journalists in the newsroom have to translate news stories from one language into another. This is similar to what one would find in community radio newsrooms where the news writers responsible for translation very rarely, if ever, leave the office to attend a news event.

In this contribution, I present and describe data collected from community radio stations in South Africa. In line with the work of Farías, Blok, and Roberts, I try to 'think and speak near ANT', which means "not simply deploying the existing ANT canon of concepts, research strategies and writing experiments, but keeping them near as a source of questions, problems and inspiration" (2019: xxii). ANT is thus not a prescriptive method, but rather a thinking tool to unearth translation activities, the actors (e.g., journalists performing translation tasks), the translated product (e.g., newspaper stories or radio news bulletins) and/or the source text(s) consulted in the news production process.

2. Actor-network theory as *slow*ciological approach

A sociological approach to investigating translation includes an examination or interest in the sociology of the translated product, the sociology of the translator (or agent), and the sociology of translation work or translation activities. In the sociological turn in TS, it is particularly Bourdieu's concepts of habitus, capital and his field theory that has been taken up by scholars in TS, e.g., by Simeoni (1998), Inghilleri (2003), and Heilbron and Sapiro (2007). Tyulenev (2012) incorporates Luhmann's social systems theory in TS, while Bielsa and Bassnett (2009) and Van Rooyen (2013) apply Giddens's structuration theory in the investigation of news translation. The number of scholars working with ANT has significantly grown over the past few years, including, among others, Buzelin (2005, 2007), Kung (2009), Bogic (2010), Abdallah (2012), Risku and Windhager (2013), Luo and Zheng (2017), Van Rooyen (2019a, 2019b), and Cherchari (2021). According to Luo, these and other TS scholars have recognised that translation is not only linguistic but is also "an outcome of practical activities made by various translation actors or agents" (2020: 202).

Latour moves from the traditional "sociology of the social" to a "sociology of associations" (2005: 9). The "sociology of the social" could be applied when investigating an already stabilised society, but it would not be successful when investigating that which is not yet "*assembled*" (Latour 2005: 12, italics in the original). In contrast, the "sociology of associations" (Latour 2005: 9) is an investigative process, according to which the ANT researcher becomes a little ant — "a blind, myopic, workaholic, trail-sniffing, and collective traveller" (Latour 2005: 9) who traces the effects of how the social is formed (Mol 2010: 261). The social (or society) would thus only assemble as a "consequence of associations and not their cause" (Latour 2005: 238). For Latour, "everything is data" (2005: 133) and therefore researchers should take meticulous care when tracing the effects of the interactions between different actors (whether human or nonhuman) to ensure that they do not miss out on the valuable processes and connections between the different actors (Latour 2005: 133). As a result, Latour proposes a slower ontology, or slowciological approach (2005: 25), which also aligns with ethnographic methods to shed light on the often invisible "heterogeneous and multi-layer[ed]" everyday practices (Nimmo 2011: 113). In TS, for example, Abdallah reports that ethnographic methods could also assist an ANT researcher to "follow the actors by observing, from the inside, how the network is built" (2012: 25). Thus, the Latourian observer is *in* the moment when doing ethnographic research.

Thinking with ANT implies an understanding of all the tools available to the investigator. Law (2009: 142) relates ANT to "a toolkit", which can be adapted and applied for the sake of doing research (Mol 2010: 265). ANT is thus not a theory "for causal explanations of social phenomena, but a tool for discovering hidden factors" (Kim 2019: 361). Law (2009: 141) argues more explicitly that ANT is more practical and descriptive, rather than theoretical. Furthermore, Janicka infers that ANT is "a rigorous approach" to highlight the "agents of change that have been heretofore invisible" (2022: 4). The framework becomes the ANT observer's "travelling companion", or, as proposed by Farías, Blok, and Roberts, a way to think "near ANT" (2019: xx). Latour's infralanguage (or vocabulary) provides a toolkit to investigate the associations between actors rather than only relying on "the observer's notions, to trace the empirical construction of the phenomenon itself" (Kim 2019: 361).

Latour's infralanguage includes, among others, terms and concepts such as 'actor', 'actant' (human or nonhuman), 'actor-network', 'mediator', 'intermediary', 'black box', 'TRANSLATION',[1] 'spokesperson', 'obligatory passage point' (OPP), 'agency' and 'power', which are all necessary to "allow an account, an empirical description, to be assembled" (Sayes 2013: 142). Some terms overlap and as a result, the ANT researcher needs to clarify the terminology chosen in a given study to avoid any possible confusion.

One of the most distinctive aspects of ANT is the expansion of the term 'actor' to include both human and nonhuman entities when studying the social (Latour 1996: 2). In line with ANT, the actors are 'actants'[2] (a term borrowed from semi-

---

1. I have taken the decision to use TRANSLATION in small caps when the concept is used in Latourian terms.

2. As in a previous publication (Van Rooyen 2019a), I take a pragmatic decision to use the term 'actor' throughout, adding, where applicable, the denominators of either human or nonhuman to remind the reader that both could be significant agents of change.

otics) that "can literally be anything provided it is granted to be the source of an action" (Latour 1996: 7). Latour includes various nonhumans in his own research, for example "mosquitoes, parasites, rats, fleas" (1987: 111) and "microbes, scallops, rocks, and ships" (Latour 2005: 10). In a newsroom, for example, possible nonhuman actors would include a desk, a mobile phone, computers, internet connection and printers (Van Rooyen 2019a: 108). As stated by Latour, the ANT researcher would only consider those actors that are relevant and would leave a "visible effect on other agents" (2005: 79). In other words, actors would only be valuable (thus, have an effect) if they "make a difference" (Archetti 2014: 587).

In Latourian terms, such actors that "make a difference" are 'mediators' (2005: 217). The brief moment when mediators come together and interact with one another is what Latour (1996: 379) defines as TRANSLATION. The effect of Latourian TRANSLATION is different forms of transformation, modification, distortion or change that would then allow for some form of meaning making (Latour 1996: 379). This implies that the mediator has the potential to exert power and display agency when interacting with other actors.

In contrast to 'mediators', 'intermediaries' are human or nonhuman actors that do not make a difference or have any effect in their interactions with any other human or nonhuman actors. The intermediary merely "transports meaning ... *without* transformation" (Latour 2005: 39, emphasis added) and is in effect a black box, which counts for one, "even if it is internally made of many parts" (2005: 39). The observer would not be able to identify any of the processes involved to create the intermediary (or black box), because all these processes and interactions are hidden. The black box is when "many elements are made to act as one" (Latour 1987: 131), for example some form of infrastructure or technology that has been stabilised in a given network and is often taken for granted, such as computers, mobile phones or a messaging tool such as *WhatsApp* (Van Rooyen 2019a: 61). In other words, a black box is a "closed-off product" (Van Rooyen 2019a: 61), and one would mostly only see the different parts of the black box when something goes wrong, for example if a computer breaks down. I have argued elsewhere that, in a journalistic setting, the final news product (whether it is a newspaper article or broadcast news bulletin), is "a closed-off product and, in translation terms, a final target text" (Van Rooyen 2019a: 61). One would probably only become aware of the multiple (possibly invisible) activities and practices involved in the news translation process if there is a mistranslation. ANT therefore provides a framework to understand "the sociological processes, activities and associations involved in creating the news translation product" (Van Rooyen 2019a: 61).

To reveal some of the hidden actors (i.e., intermediaries or black boxes), Latour puts forward the notion of 'spokesperson' that would speak on behalf of those who "do not speak" (Latour 1987:71). The spokesperson could be a scientist (or TS researcher as is the case in this chapter) who is "simply commenting, underlining, pointing out, dotting the i's and crossing the t's, not adding anything" (Latour 1987:71). Teurlings (2013:104) equates the "TRANSLATOR-spokesperson" to someone who would be TRANSLATING other actors and who would try "to mobilize them in an actor-network". In effect, "each TRANSLATION reshuffles the connections between elements" (Latour 1987:238, emphasis added) to form 'networks'. These types of networks are strongly linked to the process of working that Latour rather relates to a "*worknet*" or "*action net*" (2005:132, italics in original). Latour's network is a way in which a researcher could "describe something" and is not "what is being described" (2005:134). Teurlings provides an example of an actor-network in the form of a "driving car" (2013:104). The actor-network would not be able to function without nonhuman actors such as fuel and wheels (Teurlings 2013:104). Without these crucial nonhuman elements, the car would break down and would no longer function. In the same way "writing or translating or editing or reading news, could also be actor-networks" (Van Rooyen 2019a:63). I argue that ANT researchers could gain access to several 'invisible' actors in the news translation production process that are hidden in the form of black boxes and intermediaries if they follow an ANT methodology. Tracing the nonhuman actors (especially if they are hidden as intermediaries) could reveal translation processes (whether interlingual or intralingual) in the newsroom under investigation.

In this study, I propose that Latour's slowciological approach can serve as a conceptual and analytical tool to analyse the social (whether it is the actor, process or product). For this purpose, I refer to the work of Callon (1984) who identified four moments (or phases) of TRANSLATION. He argues that these moments can be used as a tool to determine "the identity of actors, the possibility of interaction and the margins of manoeuvre" (1984:203). These four moments, which can overlap, are *problematisation, interessement, enrolment* and *mobilisation* (Callon 1984:203).

In the first TRANSLATION moment, *problematisation*, the ANT researcher produces a written account of what she has observed in a real-life setting (Callon 1984:204). As such, *interessement* is a dynamic process in which the researcher identifies the key role-players and also the "associations between entities" (Callon 1984:203). An ANT researcher thus describes and identifies actors in such a manner that it is possible to uncover obligatory passage points (OPPs) (Callon 1984:204). In terms of news production, Kumar and Haneef (2016:107) posit that OPPs are human or nonhuman actors who have become indispensable in the process of creating news content. Furthermore, an actor will only qualify as an OPP if all other actors touch (or associate with) the OPP (Kumar and Haneef

2016:119). The visual representations (see Figures 2, 3, 5, 6 and 7 in the present paper) represent the actors, mediators, intermediaries, OPPs and the "associations between entities" (Callon 1984:206) in the radio news production process.

During the second TRANSLATION moment (*interessement*), the ANT researcher recruits the actors that she defined during the moment of *problematisation* (Callon 1984:207–208). The ANT researcher thus aims to be interested in, and showcase, the actors and the entities with whom these actors are associated (Callon 1984:210). Ultimately, the researcher's interest would allow her to capture the OPPs involved in the process (Callon 1984:203).

The third moment, *enrolment*, includes detailed descriptions of the interactions between all the actors concerned (Callon 1984:206). Kumar and Haneef (2016:109, emphasis added) define *enrolment* in a newsroom study as "[t]he process by which actor(s) interact with other actors and an actor's space gets expanded through the *enrolment* of more actors into its alliance". *Enrolment* is furthermore an ongoing process that involves the creation of multiple actor-networks (Kumar and Haneef 2016:109).

Callon's (1984:209) final moment is *mobilisation* in which some actors might be displaced (or TRANSLATED) by others. The researcher's written accounts should display how human and nonhuman actors are displaced from "one frame of reference to the next" (Latour 2005:30). In addition, Callon (1984:214) raises 'Who'-questions, namely: "Who speaks in the name of whom? Who represents whom?". In the *mobilisation* moment, "[a] series of intermediaries ... are put into place which lead to the designation of the spokesman" (Callon 1984:216). The spokesperson(s) will come to the fore, even if the chains of intermediaries, interactions and associations are quite long (Callon 1984:216). Furthermore, the spokesperson(s) will communicate on behalf of other actors and convey "what others say and want, why they act in the way they do and how they associate with each other" (Callon 1984:213–214).

Essentially, Latourian TRANSLATION entails the movement and the processes when different human and nonhuman actors work together (Latour 1996:378). As a result, ANT takes us beyond translation linked to language, because the ANT definition of TRANSLATION includes "a geometric meaning (moving from one place to another)" (Latour 1987:11).

In the following section, I present how and where I travelled to collect data to determine what is worth seeing (Latour 2005:17) with the aim to unearth interlingual and/or intralingual translation in the news production process in a specific journalistic setting.

3. Thinking with ANT to collect and analyse data

The Latourian observer should be open to change and uncertainties, especially when she is searching for answers in a setting where "things are changing fast" (Latour 2005:142), such as a radio newsroom. Latour presents his thinking tool in the form of a travel guide or travel companion, but, to complicate matters even further (at least initially), this guide is not clearly defined as either a theory or a method.

In the late 1990s, Callon wrote that ANT scholars "never claimed to create a theory" (1999:194), with Law agreeing that ANT "is not a theory" (2009:141). At times even Latour himself made it difficult for the academic audience to follow his arguments. In *Reassembling the Social*, Latour states that ANT is a "strong theory", because it shows "*how* to study things, or rather how *not* to study them ... [and] how to let the actors have room to express themselves" (2005:142). A few chapters further, Latour indicates that ANT is an "empty, relativistic grid" (2005:221), which also aligns with Mol's conceptualisation of ANT as a "kaleidoscope" or a "repertoire" (2010:261). Furthermore, ANT is not a frame or a box, but a way of working, doing research and thinking. In fact, ANT is a tool (i.e., a method), which Latour equates to "the name of a pencil or a brush [rather] than the name of a specific shape to be drawn or painted" (2005:142). The aim is therefore to work *near ANT* or *with ANT*.

The data presented in this chapter link to a project which unfolded over a period of six years. The design evolved into an emergent qualitative actor-network approach consisting of two phases: a concurrent mixed-method design, followed by a multiple case study design (Van Rooyen 2019a). In the first phase, I visited twelve community radio stations in the Free State province of South Africa. I followed in the footsteps of Latour as I travelled "from one spot to the next, from one field site to the next" (1999:20), in some instances not knowing the physical address, nor the name and number of a contact person at the radio stations that should be my next research site. As far as possible, I was doing research *with* ANT as "we go, we listen, we learn, we practice, we become competent, we change our views" (Latour 2005:146). During the period of fieldwork, it was often necessary to negotiate entrance to the research sites by listening carefully to learn from the participants and to collect data with the anticipation to uncover the intricacies of news translation in community radio.

The qualitative data collection methods used in this study mostly align with what one would expect in an ethnographic study. I entered each research setting as a former insider to radio journalism in South Africa with experience in the production (and translation) of commercial, community and student radio news. I could identify with the work of Tsai (2005) who emphasised the value of her prior knowledge as a journalist because it provided her some perspective to exclude redundant "noise" (i.e., distractions) when observing and interacting with participants. Hemmingway (2008:35), another former journalist, postulates that her insider view gave her the necessary insight to illuminate the intricate news production processes (see also Hokkanen, Chapter 4, and Staudinger, Chapter 5, this volume, for their insights on insider roles in different settings).

The qualitative data collection methods employed included observations, fieldnotes, conducting interviews, and the collection of documents, audio, and visual material. As a former insider I was fully aware of the time constraints in a broadcast newsroom, and therefore always attempted to be a distant observer, only interacting with members of the news team when it was necessary. Field conversations were particularly valuable in building rapport with participants, especially in a setting where I had "little or no previous contact with the person being interviewed" (Hammersley and Atkinson 2007:109) and specifically also because it was important to gain the trust of participants (Babbie and Mouton 2014:273). It soon became clear that building rapport and establishing trust would differ from one radio station (context) to the next (Van Rooyen 2019a:92). In some cases, I often relied on my former insider perspective as a radio news journalist in different tiers of radio, namely student, community and commercial (Van Rooyen 2019a:92). In other instances, I would reflect on shared experiences with participants in the radio newsrooms, for example, if the participant and I had studied at the same university or if we had worked with the same colleagues in other settings (Van Rooyen 2019a:92). During these periods of observation, I captured as much as possible of these experiences in the form of fieldnotes that would eventually be used to produce Latourian written accounts. As claimed by Abdallah (2012:24), the written accounts stabilise events in the research setting that would make it possible for the researcher to investigate and understand all the processes and activities relevant to translation in the community radio newsroom and to identify all the OPPs in these processes. This is an example of the TRANS-LATION moment of *interessement* where the written accounts capture what lies in "between the meshes" (Latour 2005:242).

All the documents collected during the study were publicly available and included, among others, radio news reports, newspapers, news timetables, and policy documents. With permission, I photographed as much as possible during the visits to the radio stations. Video-recordings (with a mobile phone) were invaluable to capture movement, changes, and interactions between different actors. This aligns with an ANT account which aims "to represent, or more exactly to re-represent — that is — to present *again* — the social to all its participants, to *perform* it, to give it a form" (Latour 2005:139, emphasis in original).

In terms of data analysis, the Latourian written account is a "description ... where all the actors *do something* and don't just sit there" (2005:128). Actors become mediators when they make a difference through their actions, interactions, and connections with other actors, and will therefore be included in the observer's written account (Latour 2005:14). In contrast, there is no value in adding actors to a written account if they make no difference and have no effect related to the aim of the study (i.e., the intermediaries). In essence, the written account provides "an arena, a forum, a space, a representation" for the social or the collective (Latour 2005:256). Once the researcher has analysed the data, the conclusions should highlight the mediators and reveal their "real names" (i.e., who or what they are) (Latour 2005:240). In this way it should be possible to uncover what lies "between the meshes" (and thus might have been invisible), because the data that are not actually part of the net, will be "unconnected" and would in effect be unblackboxed (Latour 2005:242). In the next section, I present and describe data I collected from community radio stations in South Africa.

4. Tracing the actors, associations and connections

4.1 Community radio in South Africa

In South Africa, radio broadcasting consists of three types of radio licences, namely the public broadcaster (South African Broadcasting Corporation); commercial (or private) radio stations; and community radio stations, which emerged in the 1990s as an alternative to the government-owned media. The Independent Communications Authority of South Africa (ICASA) started issuing the first radio licences to community radio stations shortly after South Africa's first democratic elections in 1994 (Olorunnisola 2002:31). Community radio stations are defined according to the community they serve, whether cultural, geographic, or related to any other interest (Bosch 2005: 4).

In South Africa, community radio stations are tasked to tell the stories of particular communities in the relevant language(s) of the respective audiences (Govender 2010:184). Furthermore, community radio stations are not run for profit, but owned by the community they serve (Govender 2010:184). It is especially "participation and communication" that played a cardinal role "in contexts with histories of exclusion and discrimination", such as Africa, Asia and Latin America (Olorunnisola 2002:132).[3]

---

3. See Van Rooyen (2019a:11–25) for a detailed overview of the South African media landscape.

In Van Rooyen (2019a, 2019b), I highlighted the undeniable prominence of translation in community radio stations. Bielsa attests that researching news translation in these settings is "interesting in its own right" where the focus is on the "highly heterogenous contexts and forms of translation ... in contrast with the mainstream where more uniform practices tend to prevail" (2022:7). Next, I present the data collected and analysed in the form of an ANT-inspired written account.

4.2 The written account: Data analysis and presentation

As mentioned above, I collected descriptive and demographic data from radio station managers and news participants at twelve radio stations in the Free State. Further to this, I returned to three of these radio stations for a longer period of time. As an illustration of what we could learn from thinking with ANT, I present an account from Radio Station L,[4] a radio station situated in the largest informal settlement in the Free State. At the time of data collection, the radio station had 102,000 listeners and broadcasted in four languages, namely Sesotho, English, Setswana and isiXhosa (South African Advertising Research Foundation 2016:3).

I visited the radio station for two weeks in November 2016. The radio station was housed in the building of a non-governmental organisation with only two rooms — one being the broadcast studio, and the other, a multipurpose office. During my stay, I observed and captured numerous human and nonhuman actors, mediators, intermediaries, actor-networks, and obligatory passage points (OPPs). In this example, I aim to describe the multiple intricacies during one of the afternoon news shifts in the news office.

The Latourian written account would ideally only represent and include mediators but exclude intermediaries because they are not making a difference. However, I wanted to include as many as possible of all these actors in the written accounts to showcase how I had wrestled to uncover the relevant actors and actions while investigating the role or position of translation in community radio newsrooms that deliver news to audiences in multiple languages (Van Rooyen 2019b:45).

Scene 1
The small office is abuzz with visitors and staff members. The room functions as a reception area, news office, marketing office. There are a few chairs, a table, a bookcase with files, a steel cabinet, a broken air-conditioning unit, old desktop computers. The afternoon news writer arrives a few minutes past 10:00. We greet

---

4. The name of the radio station has been anonymised.

Chapter 11. Thinking with actor-network theory 263

briefly because we have met before. There are too many people and too few chairs. Lesedi[5] takes a seat on a computer box in front of a desk at the back of the office. He picks up a pen and starts writing on a piece of paper in Sesotho. Lesedi turns around, opens a drawer in the filing cabinet (see Figure 1), and flips through old news bulletins.

Figure 2 is a visual representation of how I worked with ANT as a method (or a paintbrush) to uncover the human and nonhuman actors in Scene 1. The figure is not meant to represent a static network, but rather to show (and make visible) all the actors as they became enrolled in the news production process. These processes are examples of the TRANSLATION moments of *problematisation* and *enrolment*. If an actor does not make a difference, it is an intermediary and can be excluded (or at least be moved to the background) in the ANT account. Even though it might be challenging to make it clear who or what makes a difference, the researcher should always keep the aim of the study in mind to make

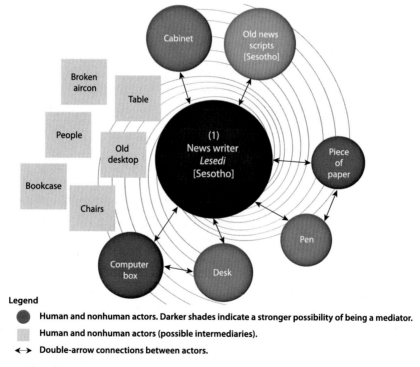

Figure 2. The afternoon news writer in action (Scene 1)

---

5. Pseudonym for the Sesotho news writer.

these distinctions. Therefore, if the actor (human or nonhuman) was not specifically involved in the news production process, the actor would be identified as an intermediary, and thus be moved to the background (see the light grey areas in Figure 2).

The afternoon news writer enrolled a pen and a piece of paper (as mediators) to write a text (a news story) in Sesotho (the TRANSLATION moment of *enrolment*). These nonhuman actors were mediators because the writer would not be able to capture the news story without these utensils. Other mediators include old news scripts, a desk, computer box, a steel cabinet, and the news writer himself (see the darker grey circles in Figure 2). The visualisation in Figure 2 reveals many interactions (the double-arrowed lines) that show the connections between the different human and nonhuman actors. I found that one of the mediators, the news writer, is an OPP, because he was indispensable at this stage of the unfolding events.

Scene 2

The morning news writer, Mpho, enters the office and finds her way to the corner where Lesedi and I are sitting. I know Mpho very well. I've been observing her newswriting for quite a few days already. She has just returned from the nearby supermarket. She hands Lesedi a pile of English newspapers, as well as her handwritten Sesotho news bulletins from the morning shift. Mpho shares the latest information about a developing news story. The story is local. It's a brutal crime. It shocks. A 14-year-old boy was killed after stealing R500 [± 25 Euro]. Two men had beaten up the boy and left him for dead ... After a short discussion Mpho greets and leaves the office. Lesedi flips through the morning news bulletins, checks something in an English newspaper, and continues writing stories for the 11:00 news bulletin in Sesotho. He finishes one story after the other. Just before 11:00 he leaves for the studio.

The account in Scene 2 (see Figure 3) enrolled several new actors as part of the TRANSLATION moment of *enrolment* and displaced some of the intermediaries presented in Scene 1. The displacement (or in Latourian terms, TRANSLATION) forms part of Callon's (1984: 209) final moment of TRANSLATION, *mobilisation*. Furthermore, the spokesperson(s) become visible during the process of *mobilisation*, even if the chains of intermediaries, interactions and associations are quite long (Callon 1984: 209). In this context, "to mobilise" means that all of the actors involved are displaced and thereafter "reassembled at a certain place at a particular time" (Callon 1984: 217). The spokesperson(s) will then communicate on behalf of other actors.

As a result of the TRANSLATION moment of *enrolment*, it is possible to identify the intermediaries that had no specific effect on the news production process, such as a broken air conditioner, the table, other people, chairs, an old desktop,

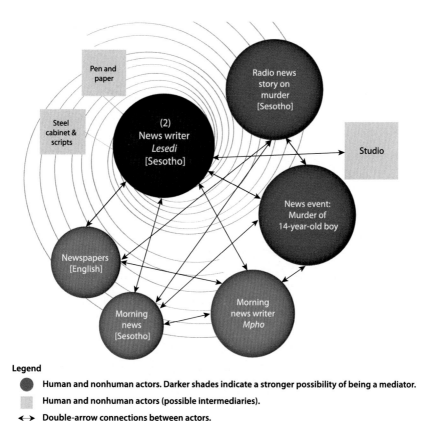

Figure 3. Local developing news story (Scene 2)

and the bookcase. I could move some actors that might have been relevant in Scene 1 (see Figure 2) into the shadows, because, for example, the cabinet and the old news scripts in the steel cabinet no longer played a direct role in the news production process (see Figure 3 for the intermediaries presented in the form of squares in a lighter shade of grey). This was also relevant to the two nonhuman mediators, pen and paper. They had been enrolled (TRANSLATION moment of *enrolment*) and stabilised in Scene 1 (TRANSLATION moment of *interessement*). In Scene 2, they have been grouped together to form an intermediary, which merely "transports meaning ... without transformation" (Latour 2005: 39).

The early morning news writer, Mpho, became part of the afternoon news interactions when she returned to the office. She was a mediator that brought about change when she handed over newspapers and the early morning news scripts to the afternoon news writer. In turn, the newspapers and news scripts influenced Lesedi when he continued writing the news. The nonhuman actors were responsible for Lesedi *doing* (i.e., writing) the news. The developing news story (about the murder of a 14-year-old boy) moved into a more central position in the news production process. Therefore, the TRANSLATION moment of *problematisation* provides me the opportunity to identify the strongest OPPs, which include the news event (the murder), the news writer and the radio news story about the news event (written in Sesotho) (in Figure 3 the strongest OPPs are circles and in a darker shade of grey). The other mediators enrolled in Scene 2 (Figure 3) are the English newspapers, the morning news scripts in Sesotho, and the morning news writer (TRANSLATION moment of *enrolment*).

Scene 3
Lesedi returns to the office after quite some time. Smoke break. He must have spoken to someone about something, because there is some form of urgency in his demeanour. Lesedi is busy with his phone. He looks up and explains to me that he is trying to buy mobile top-up to recharge the SIM card with airtime.[6] *The radio station has no internet connection, whether wireless, cable or broadband. A few moments later, his phone beeps. WhatsApp. It is an English media statement from the police. Lesedi phones the police spokesperson and conducts a quick interview in Sesotho about a memorial service for the 14-year-old boy. Lesedi records the interview using a second mobile phone (Figure 4).*

Figure 4. Mobile phones in action

---

6. The newswriter is uploading airtime to his pre-paid mobile phone in order to make voice calls, text messages and access the internet. In a developmental context such as South Africa, prepaid airtime is less expensive (Vincent and Cull 2010: 167) in comparison to far less affordable mobile data (Moyo and Munoriyarwa 2021: 367). Further to this, people often rather top-up with airtime rather than mobile data as "older and entry-level handsets are not data-enabled" (Donovan and Donner 2010: 264). For the sake of clarity, the non-human actor will be referred to as 'prepaid phone credit'.

Scene 3 in Figure 5 represents a shift in the movement between the different actors involved. During the Latourian TRANSLATION process, the researcher enrols more actors into the actor-network (TRANSLATION moment of *enrolment*), but consequently a number of actors are also displaced (TRANSLATION moment of *mobilisation*). I have been able to move some of the intermediaries into the shadows, namely the morning news scripts and newspapers, as well as the morning news writer. The information Lesedi selected from the news scripts and the newspapers have now become part of the Sesotho news story about the murder of a 14-year-old boy. All these mediators have been displaced and formed a single black box. It is extremely important to highlight that I would not have been aware of these source texts and the inter- and intralingual translation processes if I had not been present in the moment, following the actors as the events unfolded.

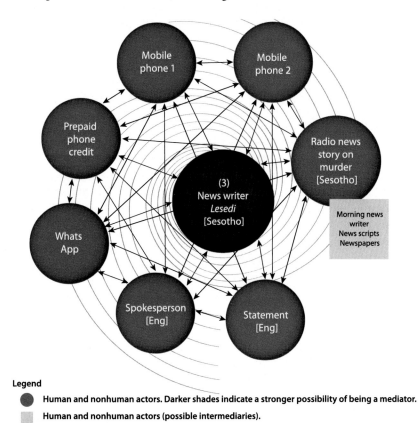

Legend
- ● Human and nonhuman actors. Darker shades indicate a stronger possibility of being a mediator.
- ▪ Human and nonhuman actors (possible intermediaries).
- ←→ Double-arrow connections between actors.

Figure 5. A spiral of mediators (Scene 3)

The ANT paintbrush also gave me access to a myriad of new mediators, for example the nonhuman actor 'prepaid phone credit' that has gained significant power and agency, because the news writer would not be able to access the latest information about the developing news story without any prepaid phone credit (TRANSLATION moment of *problematisation*). Furthermore, the phone needed prepaid phone credit to receive the police statement via the message application, *WhatsApp*. The news writer also enrolled the police spokesperson using prepaid phone credit when conducting the interview (TRANSLATION moment of *enrolment*) (Figure 5). Other actors included two mobile phones, a police statement, and an interview with the police spokesperson (in Figure 5 all the circles are indicated in a darker shade of grey).

All these actors were mediators because they had some kind of effect on one another. It became quite complicated to differentiate between the various mediators in this scene as they are fairly equally linked to one another. It is as if the actor-network presented in Figure 5 is held together with such tension that if any of these mediators should fail, the whole process might collapse (visually represented by the darker background and the darker shaded circles in Figure 5).

Scene 4

Lesedi listens to the recording of the interview in Sesotho he had with the police spokesperson. He writes in Sesotho with his pen on a piece of paper. He stops. He seems concerned, turns to me, and explains that he recorded the clip on the wrong phone, because this phone cannot play and pause. Lesedi needs this function to play (and then pause) the soundbite while reading and presenting the news story in the broadcast studio. He will not be able to cut the soundbite at the right time if the phone cannot pause. It is now 11:53. The next bulletin is at 12:00. Lesedi's hands tremble slightly. The soundbite is 49 seconds long. Lesedi re-records the soundbite on the other mobile phone. He grabs the rest of the news bulletin and rushes off to the broadcast studio. I grab my phone and follow him into the room next door. Lesedi moves in behind the microphone. The presenter sits opposite from him. She controls the mixing desk. The news jingle plays and Lesedi starts reading the news. The story about the boy's memorial service leads the bulletin. Lesedi reads the introduction to the story. He holds the phone's speaker close to the microphone right in front of him. The soundbite plays. He pauses the phone at exactly 49 seconds. Lesedi waits a second or two and continues with the rest of the news bulletin.

In Scene 4 (Figure 6), the news writer was still an OPP, together with the two mobile phones, the soundbite, the news story, the news bulletin, and the studio (TRANSLATION moment of *problematisation*). The studio included the mixing desk, microphone, news jingle and presenter. The news writer made one small mistake by recording the interview on the wrong phone. At that moment, the tightly knitted actor-network, described in Scene 3 (see Figure 5), started showing cracks. The TRANSLATION moment of *interessement* highlights the stabilised and strong OPP (i.e., the news writer) who began trembling when the mediator, 'time constraints', was also enrolled into the news production process (TRANSLATION moment of *enrolment*). The news writer was quick to re-record the soundbite on another phone. The actor-network slightly rocked to and fro, but it swiftly stabilised and the news production process could continue (TRANSLATION moment of *mobilisation*).

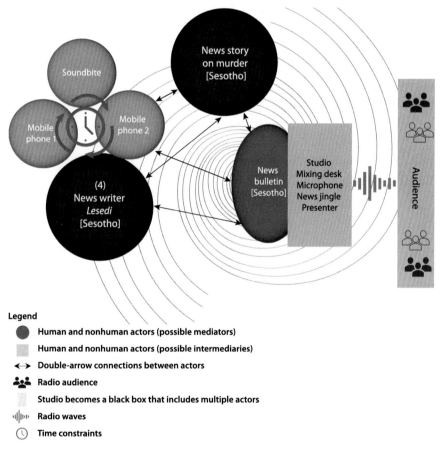

Figure 6. Time constraints in the newsroom (Scene 4)

As the reader presented the news, some of the actors that previously served as mediators started moving into the background, including the prepaid phone credit and *WhatsApp*. These two actors were no longer visible in the actor-network (see Figure 6). In addition, the news writer previously incorporated (i.e., either interlingually or intralingually translated) information from the police statement into the news story about the 14-year-old boy. The audience would not be aware of the police statement, nor the issues with prepaid phone credit, *Whats-App*, and a broken mobile phone. The listener would only hear the news writer presenting the bulletin, as well as the voice of the police spokesperson when the soundbite was played during the news broadcast. As a TS scholar, I would have missed all the translational activities, as well as the source texts (in the form of the police statement, *WhatsApp* and interview) if I had not been following the actors as the process unfolded.

5. Conclusion

The aim of this chapter was to illustrate the value of thinking with and near ANT when investigating the (in)visibility of translation in community radio news. An ANT researcher becomes a spokesperson for both the human (e.g., the news writers and all other participants) and the nonhuman (in the form of materiality or processes and practices) by TRANSLATING the findings for the audience (Clark 2019:163). The ANT-inspired observer became a little ant who painstakingly followed the actors to shed light on the traces of translation in community radio news.

I have demonstrated the value of Callon's (1984) four moments of TRANSLATION, namely *problematisation, interessement, enrolment* and the *mobilisation* to uncover the actors, translation processes and activities in a community radio newsroom. The moment of *problematisation* assisted the researcher to identify human and nonhuman actors. Numerous actors were identified, for example human actors such as a police spokesperson, morning news writer, afternoon news writer, and a presenter. Nonhuman actors included prepaid phone credit, the messaging tool *WhatsApp*, a police statement, mobile phones, the news story itself, pens and paper, the studio, mixing desk, microphone and news jingle. It is through the near-simultaneous translation moment of *interessement* that the researcher can recruit all these actors "into the project using a variety of techniques of getting the actants interested" (Tyulenev 2014:166).

Through the moments of, first, *problematisation*, and of *interessement*, it becomes possible to identify those actors that served as mediators and intermediaries. It also happens that actors that might have had a more prominent position earlier in the unfolding of the events (presented in the written accounts from Scene 1 to Scene 4) disappear into the background. Examples include a pen and a piece of paper as a mediator in Scene 1 (see Figure 2) that moved to the background as an intermediary in Scene 2 (see Figure 3), because it was enveloped by stronger actors (thus mediators and OPPs) such as the news writer and the radio news story itself, with both becoming the strongest OPPs (see Figure 7). These two OPPs and the broadcast facilities (including the studio, mixing desk, microphone and presenter) are indispensable in the translation of community radio news (see Figure 7). The different actor-networks (in which the different moments of TRANSLATION are encapsulated) are represented by the double-arrowed connections between the different actors, and it became clear that those mediators connected to most of the other actors eventually surface as the OPPs (see the highly strung associations between actors in Figure 5).

The third TRANSLATION moment, *enrolment*, is closely linked to the moment of *interessement* as it describes the associations, relationships and interactions between the different actors. *Enrolment* implies that the actors should accept the roles of being included in the social. An intralingual or interlingual translation process would only be successful if the newswriter accepted the role of participating in the translation process. The final moment, *mobilisation*, clarifies the role of the spokesperson. In this study, the news writer, via the news story and the broadcasting facilities, becomes the spokesperson for multiple actors, from the news event (the murder) to mobile phones to prepaid phone credit. Another spokesperson, not represented in the visualisations, is the researcher herself (thus me). On the level of research, I have become the spokesperson to share the results of an ANT-inspired study with scholars in (and possibly even beyond) the discipline.

The final visual representation (see Figure 7) displays all the actors that served as mediators at some point in the news production process, even though some of them would not have been visible (or audible) by the end of Scene 4. For the sake of the argument, the intermediaries are once again slightly visible in Figure 7 to illustrate that these actors were part of the news production process. These actors were visible, and they did leave traces.

If an ANT observer follows the actors as events unfold, it is possible to trace the translation activities, the translators, the translated product(s) and the source texts. However, if the observer entered the room an hour later, the moment would have been lost. The only remaining mediators were the news writer, the news story, and the broadcast studio — all three obligatory passage points without which the news production (and translation) process would not have been completed. The intermediaries had been displaced as part of the TRANSLATION moment of *mobilisation* and were no longer accessible. This is one of the reasons why a TS scholar would not be able to access the source texts that formed part of the translation process if she did not follow and observe the actors and the activities for an extended period of time. The news story about the murder of a 14-year-old boy is not a single, homogeneous thing with a single source text. In fact, the

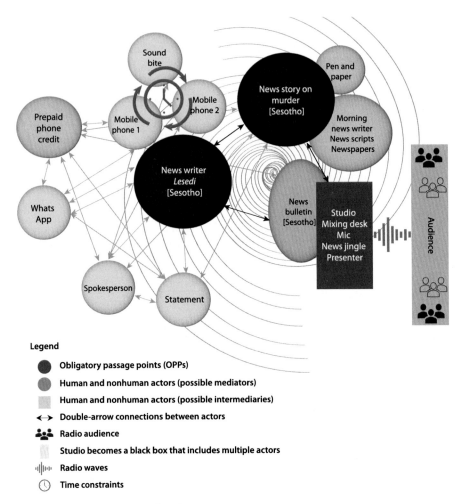

Figure 7. A concatenation of mediators

news story is a "concatenation of mediators", which includes a series of interconnected actors (Latour 2005: 137).

Thus, I argue, thinking with ANT makes it possible to deploy (and thus unravel) all the actors and actions involved in the news translation process. Ultimately, if the ANT observer had not been present as the news production process progressed and evolved, she would have missed every*thing*, and every*one* involved in the process.

References

Abdallah, Kristiina. 2012. Translators in Production Networks: Reflections on Agency, Quality and Ethics. Doctoral dissertation. University of Eastern Finland: Joensuu.

Archetti, Christina. 2014. "Journalism and the City: Redefining the Spaces of Foreign Correspondence." *Journalism Studies* 15 (5): 586–595.

Babbie, Earl J., and Johann Mouton. 2014. *The Practice of Social Research.* 15th edition. Cape Town: Oxford University Press Southern Africa.

Bani, Sara. 2006. "An Analysis of Press Translation Process." In *Translation in Global News: Proceedings of the Conference Held at the University of Warwick*, ed. by Kyle Conway, and Susan Bassnett, 35–46. Coventry: Centre for Translation and Comparative Cultural Studies, University of Warwick.

Bielsa, Esperança. 2007. "Translation in Global News Agencies." *Target* 19 (1): 135–155.

Bielsa, Esperança. 2022. "Introduction: Translation and/in/of Media." In *The Routledge Handbook of Translation and Media*, ed. by Esperança Bielsa, 1–10. London: Routledge.

Bielsa, Esperança, and Susan Bassnett. 2009. *Translation in Global News.* London: Routledge.

Bogic, Anna. 2010. "Uncovering the Hidden Actors with the Help of Latour: The 'Making' of the Second Sex." *MonTI* 2: 173–192.

Bosch, Tanja. 2005. "Community Radio in Post-Apartheid South Africa: The Case of Bush Radio in Cape Town." *Transformation* 10: 1–10. http://hdl.handle.net/10019.1/41380

Buzelin, Hélène. 2005. "Unexpected Allies: How Latour's Network Theory Could Complement Bourdieusian Analyses in Translation Studies." *The Translator* 11 (2): 193–218.

Buzelin, Hélène. 2007. "Translations 'in the Making'". In *Constructing a Sociology of Translation*, ed. by Michaela Wolf, and Alexandra Fukari, 135–170. Amsterdam & Philadelphia: John Benjamins.

Callon, Michel. 1984. "Some Elements of a Sociology of Translation: Domestication of the Scallops and the Fishermen of St Brieuc Bay." *The Sociological Review* 32: 196–233.

Callon, Michel. 1999. "Actor-Network Theory: The Market Test." *Sociological Review* 46: 181–195.

Cherchari, Elena. 2021. Sociological Translations at Inter Press Service (IPS). Unpublished doctoral dissertation. School of Translation and Interpreting, University of Ottawa, Canada.

Clark, Nigel. 2019. "What Can Go Wrong When People Become Interested in the Non-Human?" In *The Routledge Companion to Actor-Network Theory*, ed. by Anders Blok, Ignacio Farías, and Celia Roberts, 158–167. London: Routledge.

Conway, Kyle. 2010. "Paradoxes of Translation in Television News." *Media, Culture & Society* 32 (6): 979–996.

Conway, Kyle. 2014. "Vagaries of News Translation on Canadian Broadcasting Corporation Television: Traces of History." *Meta* 59 (3): 620–635.

Davier, Lucile. 2014. "The Paradoxical Invisibility of Translation in the Highly Multilingual Context of News Agencies." *Global Media and Communication* 10 (1): 53–72.

Donovan, Kevin, and Jonathan Donner. 2010. "A Note on the Availability (and Importance) of Pre-paid Mobile Data in Africa." In *Proceedings of the 2nd International Conference on M4D Mobile Communication Technology for Development (M4D2010)*, 10–11 November 2010, Kampala, Uganda, ed. by Jakob Svensson, and Gudrun Wicander, 263–267. Sweden: Karlstad University.

Farías, Ignacio, Anders Blok, and Celia Roberts. 2019. "Actor-Network Theory as a Companion: An Inquiry into Intellectual Practices." In *The Routledge Companion to Actor-Network Theory*, ed. by Anders Blok, Ignacio Farías, and Celia Roberts, xx–xxxv. London: Routledge.

Federici, Federico M. 2010. "Translations in Italian Media: The Calipari Case and Legitimised Texts." In *Political Discourse, Media and Translation*, ed. by Christina Schäffner, and Susan Bassnett, 116–141. Newcastle: Cambridge Scholars.

Gambier, Yves. 2016. "Rapid and Radical Changes in Translation and Translation Studies." *International Journal of Communication* 10: 887–906.

Gambier, Yves. 2022. "Revisiting Certain Concepts of Translation Studies Through the Study of Media Practices." In *The Routledge Handbook of Translation and Media*, ed. by Esperança Bielsa, 91–107. London: Routledge.

Govender, Anusharani. 2010. "Community Radio in KwaZulu-Natal: An Idealised Public Sphere." In *The Citizen in Communication: Re-Visiting Traditional, New and Community Media Practices in South Africa*, ed. by Nathalie Hyde-Clarke, 179–200. Claremont: Juta.

Hammersley, Martyn, and Paul Atkinson. 2007. *Ethnography: Principles in Practice*. 3rd edition. London: Routledge.

Heilbron, Johan, and Gisèle Sapiro. 2007. "Outline for a Sociology of Translation. Current Issues and Future Prospects." In *Constructing a Sociology of Translation*, ed. by Michaela Wolf, and Alexandra Fukari, 93–107. Amsterdam & Philadelphia: John Benjamins.

Hemmingway, Emma. 2008. *Into the Newsroom: Exploring the Digital Production of Regional Television News*. London: Routledge.

Inghilleri, Moira. 2003. "Habitus, Field and Discourse: Interpreting as a Socially-Situated Activity." *Target* 15 (2): 243–268.

Janicka, Iwona. 2022. "Processes of Translation: Bruno Latour's Heterodox Semiotics." *Textual Practice* 37 (6): 847–866.

Kang, Ji-Hae. 2022. "The Translating Agent in the Media: One or Many?" In *The Routledge Handbook of Translation and Media*, ed. by Esperança Bielsa, 108–121. London: Routledge.

Kim, Shinhaeng. 2019. "On 'Infra-Theory' or 'Infra-Language.'" *Journal of Asian Sociology* 48 (3): 359–376.

Kumar, Anoop, and M. Shuaib Mohammed Haneef. 2016. "Convergence of Technologies and Journalists: Translation of Journalistic Practices through ANT Perspective." *Estudos em Comunicação* 22: 105–122.

Kung, Szu-Wen Cindy. 2009. "Translation Agents and Networks, with Reference to the Translation of Taiwanese Novels." In *Translation Research Projects 2*, ed. by Anthony Pym, and Alexander Perekrestenko, 123–138. Tarragona: Intercultural Studies Group, URV.

Latour, Bruno. 1987. *Science in Action: How to Follow Scientists and Engineers Through Society*. Cambridge, MA: Harvard University Press.

Latour, Bruno. 1996. "On Actor-Network Theory: A Few Clarifications Plus More than a Few Complications." *Soziale Welt* 25 (3): 369–381.

Latour, Bruno. 1999. "On Recalling ANT." *The Sociological Review* 46: 15–25.

Latour, Bruno. 2005. *Reassembling the Social: An Introduction to Actor-Network Theory*. Oxford: Oxford University Press.

Law, John. 2009. "Actor Network Theory and Material Semiotics." In *The New Blackwell Companion to Social Theory*, ed. by Bryan S. Turner, 141–158. West Sussex: Wiley-Blackwell.

Luo, Wenyan. 2020. *Translation as Actor-Networking: Actors, Agencies, and Networks in the Making of Arthur Waley's English Translation from the Chinese 'Journey to the West'*. London: Routledge.

Luo, Wenyan, and Binghan Zheng. 2017. "Visiting Elements Thought to Be 'Inactive': Nonhuman Actors in Arthur Waley's Translation of 'Journey to the West'." *Asia Pacific Translation and Intercultural Studies* 4 (3): 253–265.

Mol, Annemarie. 2010. "Actor-Network Theory: Sensitive Terms and Enduring Tensions." *Kölner Zeitschrift für Soziologie und Sozialpsychologie* 50 (1): 253–269. https://hdl.handle.net/11245/1.330874

Moyo, Dumisani, and Allen Munoriyarwa. 2021. "'Data must Fall': Mobile Data Pricing, Regulatory Paralysis and Citizen Action in South Africa." *Information, Communication & Society* 24 (3): 365–380.

Nimmo, Richie. 2011. "Actor-Network Theory and Methodology: Social Research in a More-Than-Human World." *Methodological Innovations Online* 6 (3): 108–119.

Olorunnisola, Anthony. 2002. "Community Radio: Participatory Communication in Postapartheid South Africa." *Journal of Radio Studies* 9 (1): 126–145.

Osaji, Debe. 1991. "The Place of Broadcasting Translation in Multilingual Nigeria." *Babel* 37 (1): 54–62.

Risku, Hanna, and Florian Windhager. 2013. "Extended Translation: A Sociocognitive Research Agenda." *Target* 25 (1): 33–45.

Sayes, Edwin. 2013. "Actor-Network Theory and Methodology: Just What Does It Mean to Say that Nonhumans Have Agency?" *Social Studies of Science* 44 (1): 134–149.

Scammell, Claire, and Esperança Bielsa. 2022. "Cross-Cultural Engagement Through Translated News: A Reception Analysis." *Journalism* 23 (7): 1430–1448.

Schäffner, Christina, and Susan Bassnett. 2010. *Political Discourse, Media and Translation*. Newcastle upon Tyne: Cambridge Scholars Publishing.

Simeoni, Daniel. 1998. "The Pivotal Status of the Translator's Habitus." *Target* 1: 1–39.

South African Advertising Research Foundation. 2016. Community Station Summary: Station Audience — Past 7 Days. *Radio Audience Measurement Survey*, March 2016. http://www.saarf.co.za/rams-community/2016/RAMSMAR2016-AudienceCommunity.pdf

Stetting, Karen. 1989. "Transediting. A New Term for Coping with a Grey Area Between Editing and Translating." In *Proceedings from the Fourth Nordic Conference for English Studies*, ed. by Jørgen E. Nielsen, Arnt L. Jakobsen, Kirsten Haastrup, Graham Caie, Jorgen Sevaldsen, Henrik Specht, and Arne Zettersten. 371–382. Copenhagen: University of Copenhagen.

Teurlings, Jan. 2013. "Unblackboxing Production: What Media Studies Can Learn from Actor-Network Theory." In *After the Break: Television Theory Today*, ed. by Marijke de Valck, and Jan Teurlings, 101–116. Amsterdam: Amsterdam University Press.

Tsai, Claire. 2005. "Inside the Television Newsroom: An Insider's View of International News Translation in Taiwan." *Language and Intercultural Communication* 5 (2): 145–153.

Tyulenev, Sergey. 2012. *Applying Luhmann to Translation Studies: Translation in Society*. London: Routledge.

Tyulenev, Sergey. 2014. *Translation and Society: An Introduction*. London: Routledge.

van Doorslaer, Luc. 2010. "Journalism and Translation." In *Handbook of Translation Studies, Volume 1*, ed. by Yves Gambier, and Luc van Doorslaer, 180–184. Amsterdam & Philadelphia: John Benjamins.

van Rooyen, Marlie. 2013. "Structure and Agency in News Translation: An Application of Anthony Giddens' Structuration Theory." *Southern African Linguistics and Applied Language Studies* 31 (4): 495–506.

van Rooyen, Marlie. 2019a. "Tracing the Translation of Community Radio News in South Africa." Unpublished doctoral dissertation. KU Leuven.

van Rooyen, Marlie. 2019b. "Tracing Convergence in the Translation of Community Radio News." In *Journalism and Translation in the Era of Convergence*, ed. by Lucile Davier, and Kyle Conway, 155–176. Amsterdam & Philadelphia: John Benjamins.

van Rooyen, Marlie, and Jacobus A. Naudé. 2009. "A Model for the Translation of News Agency Texts (Sapa) for Radio (OFM) News." *Communicatio: South African Journal for Communication Theory and Research* 35 (2): 251–275.

Venuti, Lawrence. 1995. *The Translator's Invisibility: A History of Translation*. London: Routledge.

Vincent, Katharine, and Tracy Cull. 2010. "'Ten Seeds': How mobiles have contributed to growth and development of women-led farming cooperatives in Lesotho." In *Proceedings of the 2nd International Conference on M4D Mobile Communication Technology for Development (M4D2010)*, 10–11 November 2010, Kampala, Uganda, ed. by Jakob Svensson, and Gudrun Wicander, 160–168. Sweden: Karlstad University.

PART IV

Integrating marginalised groups and phenomena

CHAPTER 12

Field research on reading translated fiction
Methodological considerations and challenges

Duygu Tekgül-Akın
Bahçeşehir University

Fieldwork has been used by translation and interpreting studies (TIS) scholars in a variety of settings. Studies employing this methodology have focused on the agents, processes and contexts of production, paying relatively less attention to the users of translation. This chapter highlights the relevance of fieldwork to study the reading of translated literature. It discusses the benefits of this methodology for rigorous and reflexive research as well as the challenges, ethical considerations, and limitations involved. The chapter addresses ethical issues and considerations related to the visibility and positionality of the researcher, followed by logistical and pragmatic difficulties of reader research. It also covers a discussion of online research with readers. Potential pitfalls are identified and future directions are outlined.

Keywords: readers, reading, book clubs, fiction in translation, researcher positionality

1. Introduction

In a 2018 paper, anthropologist Adam Reed wrote that fiction reading is thought to be an activity "whose best days are behind it" (Reed 2018:36). During the COVID-19 pandemic, the disruption of the global circulation of people and goods, and the greater need for human connectivity catapulted solitary fiction reading to a new prominence. "Pestilential" classics, in Towheed's (2020) words, like Albert Camus' *The Plague* ([1947] 2002) became virtual reading group favorites in the UK during lockdown as people sought 'immersive' reading experiences.[1] Penguin Classics reportedly struggled to keep up with demand, and sales

---

1. In modern times, with widespread literacy and availability of reading material, reading as a cognitive activity is usually undertaken as a solitary experience, in contrast to the collective

https://doi.org/10.1075/btl.165.12tek
Available under the CC BY-NC 4.0 license. © 2025 John Benjamins Publishing Company

Chapter 12. Field research on reading translated fiction **279**

shot up in Italy and France as well (Flood 2020). Books will probably be around for a little longer to help us make sense of the world, and the enduring appeal of book groups as spaces for collective deliberation attests to their relevance in contemporary participatory culture.

This chapter addresses the methodological considerations and challenges related to fieldwork with readers of fiction in translation. Fieldwork has been used by TIS scholars in a variety of settings. To date, studies based on this methodology have focused on the agents, processes and contexts of production (see Flynn 2010; Buzelin 2022; Marin-Lacarta and Yu 2023), paying relatively less attention to the users of translation and interpreting services. There are few studies exploring reading in naturally occurring situations (cf. Tekgül 2017, 2019, Tekgül-Akın 2022). On the other hand, there is no doubt that reading and discussing translated fiction falls under the remit of translation and interpreting practices: not only because the object at hand is a text that has been translated from another language but also because those discussions are 'translations' of readers' life experiences and their projections onto life, hence, cultural self-translations. The chapter highlights the necessity and relevance of fieldwork to analyze the reading of translated literature. It aims to discuss the benefits of this methodology for rigorous and reflexive, *in situ* research as well as the challenges, ethical considerations, and limitations involved.

In the context of print culture, fieldwork as a research methodology would encompass observations and interviews conducted in venues such as bookshops (Smith 2022), classrooms (Moser 2022), literary events (Rehberg Sedo 2010), and festivals (Dane 2020). However, these methods do not yield data directly related to the act of textual interpretation and meaning-making. The cognitive aspect of reading cannot be captured through external — i.e. participant or non-participant — observation; on the other hand, the new, computational method of eye-tracking has proven useful in gauging this dimension of reading (see Kruger 2013). However, for the purposes of this chapter, fieldwork is understood to involve ethnography (cf. Marin-Lacarta and Yu 2023: 2), mostly because the vast majority of studies on reading based on fieldwork have utilized this methodology. The most feasible way to analyze reading patterns through the ethnographic methods of participant and non-participant observation is to engage with readers as they talk about their reading, which, considering the challenges stemming from logistics and the involvement of the researcher with their various subjectivities, entails perhaps the greatest methodological complexity compared to other methods of data

---

reading of the 19th century, for example, when books and newspapers were read aloud for friends and family. The discussion of the reading material, however, where the meaning-process continues to take shape, still requires a group setting, in person or online.

collection from readers. The principal setting for participant observation with readers has so far been book groups, which constitutes the thrust of this intervention. Throughout the chapter, the umbrella terms 'fieldwork' and 'ethnography' are used interchangeably, with occasional references to focus groups, interviews, questionnaires/surveys and 'netnography' as well, which might be used in combination with immersive, face-to-face ethnography.

2. Methodology

The study aims to answer the following research questions: (1) What does fieldwork contribute to the study of reading translations? (2) What are the methodological challenges involved in doing fieldwork with readers? (3) What are the implications of the researcher's positionality, as an academic, as an outsider to the intimate community of reading, and sometimes, as a cultural Other? (4) Which ethical considerations arise from doing ethnography with readers?

This contribution builds on my research interest in reading translations: I draw on my experience of researching reader responses to translated fiction using empirical data from book groups. For my PhD, I conducted fieldwork with reading group members in London, Devon, Shropshire, Dorset and Staffordshire in Britain, joining 32 discussions across 12 different groups between 2009 and 2011. I used the method of participant observation, which means that I read the book of the month and contributed to the discussion with my personal comments. 23 of the group meetings I joined convened in public libraries, six in bookshops and three were private book groups that convened in homes. 19 book group meetings discussed novels translated from a variety of languages whereas the remaining 14 were dedicated to novels originally written in English. I complemented my fieldwork with book groups with three semi-structured focus groups and 18 interviews with individual readers. Many of the interview respondents were people I met in the book groups and some contacted me in response to posters I left on the university campus and at a café in the city centre. The book group meetings lasted about an hour to an hour and a half whereas the interviews lasted between half an hour and an hour. I used a voice recorder in all book group meetings and interviews except for one library meeting and one bookshop meeting. The book groups were moderated by either a librarian or a bookseller and in the interviews I used guidelines that I had prepared based on the book in question. I transcribed the book group and interview recordings myself and analyzed them thematically using selective sampling. Earlier publications based on this fieldwork have addressed the aesthetic dimension (Tekgül 2017, Tekgül-Akın 2022) and the intercultural communication aspect (Tekgül 2019) of reading translated fiction whereas this particular chapter elaborates on methodological considerations. In addition to the methodological concerns entailed in participant observation, this chapter also covers a brief discussion of online research, or "netnography" (Kozinets 2010) with readers: potential pitfalls will be identified and future directions will be outlined.

In what follows, I first outline a rationale for ethnographic studies of reading translations within a theoretical framework. The second issue to be addressed is ethics and the existence and visibility of the researcher with her or his positionality. The next section elaborates on pragmatic challenges involved in reader research, including how to access real readers in naturally occurring situations and how to gain their trust. I conclude by discussing the methodological aspects of online ethnographies of reading.

3. Theoretical framework

Ethnographic approaches to reading translated fiction are necessary and relevant not only because they constitute a veritable strand of translation criticism but also because these studies reveal a great deal about the readers themselves and the process of meaning-making. Anthropologists have shied away from conducting ethnographic studies of reading because the activity is not tangibly observable from the outside (Reed 2011: 18). Although much of contemporary reading takes place as an internal experience, discussing textual material is one way of externalizing it. In her manifesto for a cultural sociology of reading, Thumala Olave (2018: 418) argues that

> [s]ocial actors, irrespective of their social position, can and do leave their situations when they read and because they read. Through the pleasures offered by fiction readers can both orient and care for themselves as well as relate to others.

Translated fiction, which usually involves a degree of cultural difference, is in a unique position to accentuate the externalization of the Self. Contact with cultural Others, albeit imaginative, reinforces aspects of the Self (Hall 1991; Smith 2022) and decentres assumptions previously taken for granted. Characters, settings or events considerably different from one's own help relate the inner Self to social reality. There exists a robust tradition of research that regards reading as social practice (Griswold, McDonell, and Wright 2005; Wright 2006; Fuller 2008; Benwell 2009; Fuller and Procter 2009; Swann and Allington 2009; Rehberg Sedo 2011a). Books provide fodder for conversations with others, but the idea of reading as a social practice is based on the premise that the fictional characters in the text as well as the physically absent other readers of the same material form an "imagined community" (cf. Anderson 1983). Readers use their agency to construct not only their own identity but also the characters they read about through their discussions with fellow readers (Hall 2009; Swann and Allington 2009). Philosopher Gregory Currie's (1998) suggestion that literature can be utilized for life-planning and moral change is a telling logical extension of this idea. However, the potential of fiction in translation in this regard has not been explored in full.

Studies on reading translations undertaken by TIS scholars seem to relate patterns of reading to the various features of target texts, which are, after all, shaped by the strategies of the translator and/or the author. This might be attributed to the influence of a Literary Studies methodology, which favors the close reading of texts. Textual properties such as style, register, domestication and foreignization gain primacy over the readers' agency in explaining patterns of reception (see e.g. Ruokonen 2011; Kruger 2013; Walker 2021). In reference to Radway ([1984] 1991) and Long (2003), the pioneers of the cultural studies methodology in exploring reading in book group contexts, Travis (2003:137) writes that these two researchers "renounce[d] their own status as 'experts' privy to the 'true' meanings of discrete 'texts'". This perspective has much to offer our discipline, where translation scholars should perhaps also relinquish their own power to the readers to discuss aspects of translated texts.

Ethnographic studies are often based on a constructivist ontology, underpinned by the idea that reality is constructed by people who address it. Constructing reality means "making accounts of the world around us and gaining impressions on culturally defined and historically situated interpretations and personal experiences" (Sarantakos 2004:37). Through the process of interpretation, readers reflectively assess the impressions they glean from the reading material, weaving them together with the help of fellow readers. These interpretations are then co-constructed by the researcher who studies the agents and context of reading (see Marin-Lacarta and Yu 2023:3).

Ethnography therefore provides a fuller picture of reading, compared to, for example, surveys, interviews and focus groups, taking stock of the agency of the reader and the multiple interests to be gained in textual consumption: entertainment, information, pleasure and status. In other words, the reader is free to foreground whichever function of reading they see fit under the given circumstances: for some, appreciating the finer qualities of a translated text by a 'lesser-known' author is a source of prestige while reading about other cultures offers others an experience that may be described as "virtual travelling" (see Tekgül 2019, Tekgül-Akın 2022). Childress' research (2017:197–201) has shown that readers' interpretations of literary texts can change after group discussions, which means that the interactive reading group setting is a significant factor in the meaning-making process. Arguably, ethnographic studies offer the most rigorous methodology to unravel the multifaceted process of interpretation.

I have argued earlier (Tekgül-Akın 2022) that such a methodology calls for an analysis of "consumption", rather than the conventional idea of reception: the former attributes greater agency to the reader than the latter, which relegates the reader to a more passive role of the "recipient". This understanding goes above and beyond "giving voice" to fieldwork participants and informants, placing their perspective at the forefront. In turn, a focus on consumption implies a methodological shift towards ethnography as opposed to reception, in line with Reed, who champions ethnography "as a means of recovering the role of the hitherto marginalised reader" (Reed 2011:24).

According to Flynn (2010), one of the three assumptions of ethnographic research is thick description (Geertz 1973:6). In a similar vein, the kind of thick description that brings out the web of meanings in an ethnographic setting is paralleled by the "thick self-translation" (after Appiah 1993), from a cultural perspective, of readers' engagement with the text. The other two assumptions are the inseparability of language from its users and context, and the grounded nature of research. These are further compounded by the need, on the part of the researcher, to establish rapport with respondents and to exercise reflexivity during the writing up stage. These considerations can best be addressed by engaging with readers in pre-existing social networks and in natural settings: in this sense, participant observation with book clubs yields richer and more authentic data than focus groups.

4. Methodological and ethical considerations

Fieldwork with readers is subject to the usual protocols of research with human respondents: ethics clearance applications must anticipate potential pitfalls, including trauma triggers to be found in the reading material. In cases where the researcher sets the reading material, it would be wise to avoid texts exploring themes likely to cause upset. On the other hand, unless the researcher personally knows the respondents — not an ideal research design, for reasons of validity — it is almost impossible to know which passages in a text would be triggering for which readers. Book group talk proceeds in all kinds of directions and the researcher could at best try and deflect tension with their personal comments as a participant observer. References to traumatic life experiences may actually enhance empathy between the researcher and the respondents (see Ellingson 1998), however, from an ethical point of view, the first and foremost benchmark is the intent, although of course the researcher should ideally try and pre-empt unintended consequences as well. Huang, Cadwell, and Sasamoto (2023) remind us that the three principles of ethical engagement with respondents applies to TIS research as well: avoiding harm, making sure the relationship is of benefit to the respondent as well, and respecting respondents' rights (see Murphy and Dingwall 2007).

In ethnographic settings, the outsider status of the researcher sharpens the analytical lens (see Merriam et al. 2001). Cultural difference certainly provides an advantage in that it helps put things in perspective but doing ethnography as an international researcher in TIS generates a particular set of methodological questions. In my case, I set out to investigate how readers respond to cultural difference, but me referring to my own life experiences as a participant observer meant that I was the embodiment of cultural difference in the book group setting: I was usually the only non-British, and often the only non-white person in the group, and the only one to come from a Middle Eastern/Muslim background. In a comparable fieldwork setting where Long (2003) was the only white participant in an African American book club, she implies that her presence was more visible, perhaps with more "distorting effects on the 'natural' interaction" (2003: xv). Cognizant of such inevitable visibility, I did my best to avoid dominating the group discussion with "my own agenda" (cf. Berger 2015: 225), a self-conscious reflex that needed to be balanced out with my desire to contribute to the conversation as a *bona fide* group member.

On the other hand, my background in a non-Western culture, my accent in English and concomitantly, my apparent immigrant status likely resulted in a power differential with my mostly white, British respondents. Beals, Kidman, and Funaki (2020) contend that researchers occupying a minority or minoritized status struggle with perspective taking. The authors problematize the dichotomy between "insider" and "outsider" statuses and recommend instead embracing the "edge" (after Krebs 1999) to self-consciously navigate the boundaries (see also Steinkogler, Chapter 6, this volume, who echoes this discussion using the concept of 'boundary work'). Researchers have for some time grappled with issues of insider/outsider status in terms of race, ethnicity, gender, class and profession (e.g. Merton 1972; Kusow 2003; Shankar 2006; Ademolu 2023), concluding that sameness and difference may be more than meets the eye. In my case, notwithstanding the differences, the readers and I presumably shared a passion for fiction. On the other hand, coupled with my academic identity, our shared passion could potentially flip the above-mentioned power differential by conferring cultural authority to me: it is important to remember that readers might be tempted to engineer responses to cater to the researcher's status as a person with high literary capital (cf. Earl 2008: 402). A critical reflexive methodology should accommodate the

Chapter 12. Field research on reading translated fiction 285

ambiguous boundaries between the researcher and the respondents that are in constant flux (Sherif 2001: 435).

According to Benwell (2009: 305),

> rather than attempting to simply limit the researcher's imprint on the data and then assume its effects are negligible, an ethnomethodological, participant-oriented approach examines the data on its own terms, accounting for effects of local context as they are revealed in the data itself.

In a similar vein, my analysis was sensitive to how my existence was instrumental in bringing out some of the reader responses. In the face of cosmopolitanism as a positive norm in cultural consumption (see Tekgül 2017), my existence as the cultural Other sometimes created tension; I, nevertheless, tried to channel this into a productive one. In a Devon book club that I attended regularly between 2009 and 2011, we were discussing Irène Némirovsky's (2008) *All Our Worldly Goods* in English translation when I offered my personal take, which revealed my Muslim background. Although I subsequently identified myself as "not a religious person", one member responded to my comment in an exuberantly affirmative way. In an effort to make me feel welcome in that cultural space, he reiterated a few times how he found my comment "very interesting". Rumsby and Eggert (2023) point out how a researcher's religious background may both be a source of challenge and insight; concluding that religious positionalities must be neither essentialized nor ignored. In line with a reflexive methodology, I chose to interpret this gesture as an act of "cultural hospitality", foregrounded by the element of cultural difference supplied by the translated reading material (Tekgül 2019: 385–386).

On another occasion, my existence as a cultural Other might have enhanced readers' self-reflexivity regarding national and cultural images. In another Devon reading group, we had convened to discuss the English translation of Alaa al Aswany's (2007) *Yacoubian Building*. The consensus was that some of the descriptions of Egyptian society in this book are at best questionable, potentially prompting sweeping generalizations on the part of the reader. Engagement with narratives brings about belief formation or re-formation (Currie 1998: 177). Recognizing this potential, one reader asked me how I feel about the possibility of 'Westerners' reading the book and thinking "[t]hat's what Islamic countries are like, they're corrupt, they're sexist, they're this and that" (Tekgül 2019: 388). These examples demonstrate how reception is not a set of stable and fixed instances of meaning-making but co-constructed by the researcher.

Research has established that articulations of taste in book clubs are inflected by readers' perceived cultural authority (González 1997; Howie 2011; Rehberg Sedo 2011b; Leypoldt 2021). Although digital technologies have democratized conventional understandings of cultural authority, especially for online book clubs (Murray 2018: 383–384), no book group is an egalitarian heaven, as there will always be some readers who assert more cultural authority than others — discussion leaders, at the very least (see Travis 2003) (whether appointed/elected permanently or on a rotating basis), and those readers with more literary capital, which parallels education/social class and age. The issue of cultural authority constitutes a legitimate research question in relation to discussing fiction in translation: the authority might be shaken by unfamiliarity with the source language and the literary canon, which could allow the researcher to pose productive questions about taste and status. In my own fieldwork, for example, a certain authority was conferred to those book club members who had lived in the country where the translated book was set, or even those who have been there on touristic visits. In cases when we discussed a novel translated from Turkish, readers certainly treated me as an expert, because I was from the country and I spoke the source language. In a Devon book club, for example, we were tackling Latife Tekin's (2007) novel *Swords of Ice*, which is peppered with recurrent French borrowings, like *perspektif, sistematik* and *organizasyon*. Translators Saliha Paker and Mel Kenne have decided to foreignize these elements in order to convey the sociolinguistic associations of dropping French words into daily language. One reader commented on this strategy but needed confirmation from me as a Turkish speaker. This overlaps with my perceived authority as a researcher, as mentioned above, but since Turkish is not a widely spoken language in the UK, anyone who speaks Turkish would presumably be treated with the same deference.

5. Methodological challenges and practical issues

One major challenge concerns logistics: locating and contacting, and then visiting groups. A sensible starting point would be to search for book club listings by public libraries and bookshops on social media and on the Internet in general. Private book groups that are not publicly advertised are naturally more difficult to access, but with the snowballing technique the researcher may enlist the help of readers who are members of multiple groups simultaneously. Joining private book groups meeting at homes and other venues may raise safety concerns, which must be assessed by the researcher.

Depending on how homogeneous or heterogeneous the 'field' is envisioned to be, the fieldworker will need to cast a wide enough net in order to achieve a level of representativeness in the sample. For example, Reed's (2011) study is based on a single literary society in Britain, with a well-defined membership and focus. My fieldwork, in contrast, covered engaged readers resident in Britain, which entails far more breadth and complexity, also incurring additional travel expenses.

In their multi-sited ethnography spanning five continents, Procter and Benwell (2015) have resorted to video recordings arranged by local research associates. Although this strategy reduces researcher intrusion (see Procter and Benwell 2015: 216), it also undermines thick description, which is maximized in cases of participant observation. The same concern is valid for participation in online book clubs (see discussion below).

Returning to representation, one seemingly valid question in Davies, Lupton, and Gormsen Schmidt's (2022: 6) study on fiction reading in Denmark and the UK arose from the overwhelming majority of 'white women' among their respondents: the researchers pondered whether it would be necessary or legitimate to try and recruit more respondents from diverse ethnic backgrounds and more male readers. The authors finally decided not to intervene in this way; however, their research acknowledges the fact that their sources of data are skewed. In other words, their random sampling produced a dataset that representatively reflects the asymmetries of their field(s).

One limitation of ethnography, as pointed out by Kotze et al. (2021: 153), is the small size of the dataset that does not allow generalization. Although generalizability has a certain methodological appeal, the trade-off with particularity makes it problematic. A large dataset is not a prerequisite in qualitative research; on the other hand, with the right funding, large-scale studies can be undertaken (see Procter and Benwell 2015).

Once initial contact is established, the next step is obtaining advance informed consent, which is also subject to institutional protocols. In the context of reading groups, establishing trust includes anticipating or, when necessary, addressing respondents' concerns about potential commercial interest: given that the publishing industries in industrialized societies are very market-driven (see Squires 2009), readers have reason to suspect the data collected may end up being used for market research purposes.

When it comes to the actual data collection in the book club setting, the interactive nature of the conversation presents both opportunities and challenges. In relation to the situated nature of research (see Flynn 2010: 118) the researcher's engagement with readers in casual, unstructured conversation makes it possible to ask questions and gauge relevant data, but there is the risk of being disruptive, which would not only compromise validity but also raise ethical questions. Readers' utterances are rarely unmediated fragments of research data and must always be contextualized. Benwell states that data collected in artificially generated contexts such as interviews and focus groups is not "a direct reflection of reality" (2009: 301). Such is the case with data collected through participant observation as well, which is inevitably co-constructed by the researcher. In settings where aesthetic judgements are made, for example, individuals might be especially motivated to articulate aesthetic positions by instrumentalizing the cultural object. Among individuals who have been convening for the aesthetic exercise of discussing books, it is possible to identify a degree of interest in generating symbolic profit through negative judgements, which are believed to signal a heightened sensibility (see Tekgül-Akın 2022). For a reflexive analysis, therefore, the researcher must take into consideration the situated origin of the ethnographic data.

One practical issue regarding data management is the tracking of individual speakers in a group setting: it might be difficult to distinguish between voices in the recordings, especially in the case of overlapping speech, which is common in focus groups and semi-structured interviews. Moreover, with a larger number of speakers, it might also be easy to confuse pseudonyms when anonymizing the transcript. In cases of multilingual data collection, which might be the outcome of multi-sited ethnography, transcribed recordings would also need to be translated, which actually brings methodological considerations regarding ethnography and translation full circle (see Sturge 2014).

6. A 'netnography' of reading

The word "netnography" was coined by Robert Kozinets, who defines it as "a specialized form of ethnography adapted to the unique computer-mediated contingencies of today's social worlds" (2010:1) and a "participant-observational research based in online fieldwork" (Kozinets 2010:60). This methodology gained a new relevance during the COVID-19 pandemic, when lockdowns forced individuals to find ways of virtual socialization and online shopping became the new normal (see Davier, Chapter 7, for another discussion of remote fieldwork in this volume). Online can no longer be dismissed as 'unnatural' as patterns of analogue and digital engagement with texts — including book browsing, reading, discussing and commenting — are increasingly fused. However, complexities arising from the "public vs. private fallacy" regarding computer-mediated communication are still pertinent (see Kozinets 2010:140–142), which raises ethical dilemmas: once the researcher has gained access to a private circle on the Internet, it is too easy to forget that data collected here may not have been intended for the public domain. Moreover, although social media platforms have been lauded for offering data that is "unsolicited and unprompted by the researcher" (McCormick et al. 2017:392) they have increasingly blurred the boundaries between "public" and "private" on the Internet.

Field research on reading translations may draw solely on virtual, synchronous book club discussions that take place on videoconferencing platforms whereas blended, mixed-methods research designs may employ data from online interviews, discussion forums, listservs, blogs, social media posts, surveys and customer reviews on online booksellers in concert with data collected through conventional, face-to-face ethnographic fieldwork. These methods of data collection occupy varying positions on the spectrum of immersive vs. unobtrusive research: a careful balance must be struck based on an evaluation of available resources.

Online studies of reading partially circumvent the logistical challenges of face-to-face research outlined above: it might be easier to recruit respondents through social networks and forums (see Davies, Lupton, and Gormsen Schmidt 2022: 6), and the researcher could also join meetings in the comfort of their living room, the automatic transcription offered by the videoconferencing platforms facilitating identifying and tracking themes when asking follow-up questions.[2] Furthermore, online meetings could provide easier access when it comes to certain reader groups: young adults, readers with disabilities, individuals with reduced mobility, including inmates and care home residents. Fieldwork with these demographic groups of course brings to mind questions about the vulnerability of research participants (see Kozinets 2010: 140; Huang, Cadwell, and Sasamoto 2023: 9–10). Virtual book clubs are more convenient for like-minded readers scattered over geographical distances to come together — virtually — over a shared interest (Long 2003: 213–214).[3] This is a relevant advantage for translation research, which often concentrates on texts representing a common source language or literature. The Portuguese in Translation Book Club,[4] for example, has been convening every other month on Zoom since the pandemic, with 2804 followers on X as of November 2023. Rehberg Sedo (2011b: 106) seems to suggest that online book groups are generally more democratic and open-minded than face-to-face ones, which means that members might be more willing to read and discuss fiction in translation, from languages of low diffusion, for example.

On the other hand, a particular set of pitfalls present themselves in the case of online ethnographies. The most pressing problem involves establishing rapport with readers. Not only might online groups have a transient membership, but

---

2. That said, it is important to consider potential confidentiality risks when using such software. Questions remain about how automatic transcriptions and recordings are managed and stored online, raising ethical concerns about the privacy and security of sensitive information.

3. Long (2003) worked with discussion forums at a time when videoconferencing technology was not available. Due to the fast pace of technological advancement, a considerable portion of literature on the methodological aspects of online research predates possibilities afforded by the latest developments.

4. https://www.pintbookclub.com/

the range of topics addressed might be less diverse. In her own research, Rehberg Sedo (2011b) has noticed that participants in online groups tend to digress less from the book, with fewer references to personal or political issues. In her earlier research (Rehberg Sedo 2003) she suggests that readers may feel more at ease expressing themselves online, but this is largely limited to listservs and forums, which actually give members the opportunity to comment anonymously. Virtual, synchronous book club meetings mimic face-to-face gatherings, where it takes time and effort for discursive norms to coalesce.

The discursive norms might have changed since the pandemic, due to the conflation of public and private spheres on virtual meetings. Readers might now feel more comfortable divulging personal details thanks to the normalizing effect of social isolation for online encounters. Advances in technology and a shift in people's attitudes notwithstanding, it is worth remembering that non-verbal cues and body language are difficult to register in an online meeting, with implications for thick description.

If user comments from online social media platforms and forums are to be quoted, caution must be exercised in terms of privacy: even if names are anonymized, it might still be possible to track down commenters by entering verbatim quotes into search engines. This was the case, for example, in Allington's study on Amazon.co.uk reviews at the time of writing this chapter (see 2021: 256–262). Regarding nicknames, Kozinets (2010: 144–145) warns that they function like names and should be treated as such: it is possible to accumulate a reputation with a nickname, as many examples from social media attest. Listservs allow more privacy (see Rehberg Sedo 2011b), and so does interlingual translation, if readers' comments were originally written in a language other than the language of research/publication. There are two sides to the ethical impasse here: not crediting the commenters would go against the grain of reflexive research, especially in the face of the "participants as co-researchers" approach (see Boylorn 2008); on the other hand, the lack of informed consent would also be problematic from a methodological perspective. Another methodological issue inherent in online reviews research concerns data management: commercial platforms may deny or restrict access to data at any point of the research process (Murray 2018: 378). For these reasons, social media platforms and forums are perhaps best used to recruit respondents for one-on-one interviews (either online or face-to-face) to complement in-person participant observation.

7. Conclusion

The chapter provides an outline of the ethical considerations and methodological challenges pertaining to fieldwork with readers of translations. The topics addressed above demonstrate the complexity of ethnography as a methodology, which nevertheless provides a rewarding fieldwork experience for the researcher. Even if the benefits of computational and online data collection methods seem to outweigh those of face-to-face ethnography, the methodology is likely to have enduring relevance. As Price (2019:50) reminds us, "[n]o matter how many keystrokes you track and blinks you time, others' reading remains as hard to peer into as others' hearts". With due respect to the said methods, ethnography remains the most attuned methodology to tap into affective responses to texts. Furthermore, while fieldwork accounts in TIS have so far focused on professional, paraprofessional or non-professional contexts of translation production, this chapter contributes to the literature by focusing on a context of translation consumption.

The ethnographic study of contemporary reading has mostly been confined to the novel and to Western contexts (exceptions are Benwell 2009; Procter and Benwell 2015; Rosen 2015; Raia 2022). This ties in with the European historical and cultural origins of the genre (see Reed 2018:34). More research is needed in order to investigate the reading of creative texts — including in translation — other than novels, in non-European languages, and in non-Western contexts. Other genres include poetry and non-fictional literary narratives like memoirs, and multimedia productions like comic novels and subtitled/dubbed films or remakes. Moreover, further research could consider different age groups (cf. Rehberg Sedo 2011b; Kruger 2013; Norrick-Rühl 2022).

One glaring gap is the study of textual engagement with holy texts, which are often translations but couched within a non-fiction frame of reference. Luhrmann (2012) has explored one context in which readers experimented with the fictional potentialities of the Bible. Other studies in other contexts could bring together considerations related to orality and the consumption of written texts, with insights from Religious Studies integrated.

Ethnographic studies of fiction reading have examined the implications of gender (Flynn and Schweickart 1986; Radway [1984] 1991; Long 2003; Shankar 2006; Howie 2011; Thumala Olave 2018) and genre (Radway [1984] 1991; Michelson 2021). Similarly, translation scholars may choose to focus on any given parameter related to the text or its readers (cf. Huang, Cadwell, and Sasamoto 2023). For example, Procter and Benwell (2015) distinguish between literal and metaphorical reading. How do these strategies play out in the case of translated fiction?

One way of approaching the reading of fiction in translation is to compare and contrast it with the reading of non-translated fiction (see Tekgül 2017). It has been suggested (see Howie 2011:142) that women tend to engage in more "social talk" than men in book groups. It would be interesting to see what happens when translated texts enter the equation. Are readers more inclined to digress when the plot is set in a different society? Childress (2017) has "connected the circuit" by tracing the creation, production, promotion and reception of a single novel (see also Özçelik 2010). Similarly, translation research could also link production and consumption with each other. Finally, in blended methodologies, eye-tracking studies (Kruger 2013; Walker 2021) could be integrated into ethnographic work to focus on specific aspects of texts. Data visualization tools such as network diagrams, word clouds, and user traffic and sentiment-analysis graphs could also complement data collected through ethnographic methods (see Murray 2018:378).

References

Ademolu, Edward. 2023. "Birds of a Feather (Don't Always) Flock Together: Critical Reflexivity of 'Outsiderness' as an 'Insider' Doing Qualitative Research with One's 'Own People'." *Qualitative Research* 4 (2): 344–366.

Allington, Daniel. 2021. "Customer Reviews of 'Highbrow' Literature: A Comparative Reception Study of *The Inheritance of Loss* and *The White Tiger*." *American Journal of Cultural Sociology* 9: 242–268.

Anderson, Benedict. 1983. *Imagined Communities: Reflections on the Origins and Spread of Nationalism*. London: Verso.

Appiah, Kwame Anthony. 1993. "Thick Translation." *Callaloo* 16 (4): 808–819.

Aswany, Alaa al. 2007. *Yacoubian Building*. Translated by Humphrey Davies. London & New York: Harper Perennial.

Beals, Fiona, Joanna Kidman, and Hine Funaki. 2020. "Insider and Outsider Research: Negotiating Self at the Edge of the Emic/Etic Divide." *Qualitative Inquiry* 26 (6): 593–601.

Benwell, Bethany. 2009. "'A Pathetic and Racist and Awful Character': Ethnomethodological Approaches to the Reception of Diasporic Fiction." *Language and Literature* 18 (3): 300–315.

Berger, Roni. 2015. "Now I See it, Now I Don't: Researcher's Position and Reflexivity in Qualitative Research." *Qualitative Research* 15 (2): 219–234.

Boylorn, Robin M. 2008. "Participants as Co-Researchers." In *The SAGE Encyclopedia of Qualitative Research Methods*, ed. by Lisa M. Given, 600–601. Thousand Oaks, CA: Sage.

Buzelin, Hélène. 2022. "Ethnography in Translation Studies: An Object and a Research Methodology." *Slovo Ru: Baltic Accent* 13 (1): 32–47.

Camus, Albert. (1947) 2002. *The Plague*. Translated by Robin Buss. London: Penguin.

Childress, Clayton. 2017. *Under the Cover: The Creation, Production, and Reception of a Novel.* Princeton: Princeton University Press.

Currie, Gregory. 1998. "Realism of Character and the Value of Fiction." In *Aesthetics and Ethics: Essays at the Intersection*, ed. by Jerrold Levinson, 161–181. Cambridge: Cambridge University Press.

Dane, Alexandra. 2020. "Cultural Capital as Performance: Tote Bags and Contemporary Literary Festivals." *Mémoires du livre / Studies in Book Culture* 11 (2): 1–29.

Davies, Ben, Christina Lupton, and Johanne Gormsen Schmidt. 2022. *Reading Novels During the COVID-19 Pandemic.* Oxford: OUP.

Earl, Benjamin. 2008. "Literary Tourism: Constructions of Value, Celebrity and Distinction." *International Journal of Cultural Studies* 11 (4): 401–417.

Ellingson, Laura L. 1998. "'Then You know How I Feel': Empathy, Identification, and Reflexivity in Fieldwork." *Qualitative Inquiry* 4 (4): 492–514.

Flood, Alison. 2020. "Publishers Report Sales Boom in Novels about Fictional Epidemics" *The Guardian*, 5 March, https://www.theguardian.com/books/2020/mar/05/publishers-report-sales-boom-in-novels-about-fictional-epidemics-camus-the-plague-dean-koontz

Flynn, Peter. 2010. "Ethnographic Approaches." In *The Handbook of Translation Studies, Volume 2*, ed. by Yves Gambier, and Luc van Doorslaer, 116–119. Amsterdam & Philadelphia: John Benjamins.

Flynn, Elizabeth, and Patrocinio Schweickart (eds). 1986. *Gender and Reading: Essays on Readers, Texts, and Contexts.* Baltimore: Johns Hopkins University Press.

Fuller, Danielle. 2008. "Reading as Social Practice: The Beyond the Book Project." *Popular Narrative Media* 1 (2): 211–216.

Fuller, Danielle, and James Procter. 2009. "Reading as 'Social Glue'? Book Groups, Multiculture, and Small Island Read 2007." *Moving Worlds* 9 (2): 26–40.

Geertz, Clifford. 1973. *The Interpretation of Cultures.* New York: Basic Books.

González, Norma Linda. 1997. "Nancy Drew: Girls' Literature, Women's Reading Groups, and the Transmission of Literacy." *Journal of Literacy Research* 29 (2): 221–251.

Griswold, Wenny; Terry McDonell, and Nathan Wright. 2005. "Reading and the Reading Class in the Twenty-First Century." *Annual Review of Sociology* 31: 127–141.

Hall, Stuart. 1991. "The Local and The Global: Globalization and Ethnicity." In *Culture, Globalization and the World System*, ed. by Anthony D. King, 19–40. Basingstoke: MacMillan.

Hall, Geoff. 2009. "Texts, Readers — and Real Readers." *Language and Literature* 18 (3): 331–337.

Howie, Linsey. 2011. "Speaking Subjects: Developing Identities in Women's Reading Communities." In *Reading Communities from Salons to Cyberspace*, ed. by DeNel Rehberg Sedo, 140–158. Basingstoke: Palgrave.

Huang, Boyi, Patrick Cadwell, and Ryoko Sasamoto. 2023. "Challenging Ethical Issues of Online Ethnography: Reflections from Researching in an Online Translator Community." *The Translator* 29 (2): 157–174.

Kotze, Haidee, Berit Janssen, Corina Koolen, Luka van der Plas, and Gys-Walt van Egdom. 2021. "Norms, Affect and Evaluation in the Reception of Literary Translations in Multilingual Online Reading Communities: Deriving Cognitive-Evaluative Templates from Big Data." *Translation, Cognition & Behavior* 4 (2): 147–186.

Kozinets, Robert V. 2010. *Netnography: Doing Ethnographic Research Online*. London: Sage.

Krebs, Nina B. 1999. *Edgewalkers: Defusing Cultural Boundaries on the New Global Frontier*. New York: New Horizon Press.

Kruger, Haidee. 2013. "Child and Adult Readers' Processing of Foreignised Elements in Translated South African Picturebooks: An Eye-Tracking Study." *Target* 25 (2): 180–227.

Kusow, Abdi. 2003. "Beyond Indigenous Authenticity: Reflections on the Insider/Outsider Debate in Immigration Research." *Symbolic Interaction* 26 (4): 591–599.

Leypoldt, Günter. 2021. "Spatial Reading: Evaluative Frameworks and the Making of Literary Authority." *American Journal of Cultural Sociology* 9: 150–176.

Long, Elizabeth. 2003. *Book Clubs: Women and the Uses of Reading in Everyday Life*. Chicago & London: University of Chicago Press.

Luhrmann, Tanya M. 2012. *When God Talks Back: Understanding the American Evangelical Relationship with God*. New York: Knopf.

Marin-Lacarta, Maialen, and Chuan Yu. 2023. "Ethnographic Research in Translation and Interpreting Studies." *The Translator* 29 (2): 147–156.

McCormick, Tyler H., Hedwig Lee, Nina Cesare, Ali Shojaie, and Emma S. Spiro. 2017. "Using Twitter for Demographic and Social Science Research: Tools for Data Collection and Processing." *Sociological Methods & Research* 46 (3): 390–421.

Merriam, Sharan B., Juanita Johnson-Bailey, Ming-Yeh Lee, Youngwha Kee, Gabo Ntseane, and Mazanah Muhamad. 2001. "Power and Positionality: Negotiating Insider/Outsider Status within and across Cultures." *International Journal of Lifelong Education* 20 (5): 405–416.

Merton, Robert K. 1972. "Insiders and Outsiders: A Chapter in the Sociology of Knowledge." *American Journal of Sociology* 78 (1): 9–47.

Michelson, Anna. 2021. "The Politics of Happily-Ever-After: Romance Genre Fiction as Aesthetic Public Sphere." *American Journal of Cultural Sociology* 9: 177–210.

Moser, Nelleke. 2022. "A Bookshelf of the World: Bringing Students' Books Inside the Classroom — A Means for Epistemic Equality?" In *Bookshelves in the Age of the COVID-19 Pandemic*, ed. by Corinna Norrick-Rühl, and Safquat Towheed, 215–236. Cham: Palgrave.

Murphy, Elizabeth, and Robert Dingwall. 2007. "The Ethics of Ethnography." In *Handbook of Ethnography*, ed. by Paul Atkinson, Amanda Coffey, Sara Delamont, John Lofland, and Lyn Lofland, 339–351. Los Angeles: Sage.

Murray, Simone. 2018. "Reading Online: Updating the State of the Discipline." *Book History* 21: 370–396.

Némirovsky, Irène. 2008. *All Our Worldly Goods*. Translated by Sandra Smith. London: Chatto & Windus.

Norrick-Rühl, Corinna. 2022. "*Elmer the Elephant* in the Zoom Room? Reflections on Parenting, Book Accessibility, and Screen Time in a Pandemic." In *Bookshelves in the Age of the COVID-19 Pandemic*, ed. by Corinna Norrick-Rühl, and Safquat Towheed, 195–214. Cham: Palgrave.

Özçelik, Nil. 2010. *Translation and Reception of Feminist Speculative Fiction in Turkey: A Multiple-Foregrounding Analysis*. Saarbrücken: LAP Lambert Academic Publishing.

Price, Leah. 2019. *What We Talk about When We Talk about Books: The History and Future of Reading*. New York: Basic Books.

Procter, James, and Bethany Benwell. 2015. *Reading Across Worlds: Transnational Book Groups and the Reception of Difference*. Basingstoke: Palgrave Macmillan.

Radway, Janice. (1984) 1991. *Reading the Romance: Women, Patriarchy, and Popular Literature*. Chapel Hill & London: University of North Carolina Press.

Raia, Annachiara. 2022. "Easy to Handle and Travel with: Swahili Booklets and Transoceanic Reading Experiences in the Indian Ocean Littoral." In *The Cultural Sociology of Reading: The Meanings of Reading and Books Across the World*, ed. by María Angélica Thumala Olave, 169–208. Cham: Palgrave.

Reed, Adam. 2011. *Literature and Agency in English Fiction Reading: A Study of the Henry Williamson Society*. Manchester: Manchester University Press.

Reed, Adam. 2018. "Literature and Reading." *Annual Review of Anthropology* 47: 33–45.

Rehberg Sedo, DeNel. 2003. "Readers in Reading Groups: An On-Line Survey of Face-to-Face and Virtual Book Clubs." *Convergence: The Journal of Research into New Media Technologies* 9 (1): 66–90.

Rehberg Sedo, DeNel. 2010. "Cultural Capital and Community in Contemporary City-wide Reading Programs." *Mémoires du livre / Studies in Book Culture* 2 (1): 1–23.

Rehberg Sedo, DeNel. 2011a. "An Introduction to Reading Communities: Processes and Formations." In *Reading Communities from Salons to Cyberspace*, ed. by DeNel Rehberg Sedo, 1–24. Basingstoke: Palgrave.

Rehberg Sedo, DeNel. 2011b. "'I Used to Read Anything That Caught My Eye, But…': Cultural Authority and Intermediaries in a Virtual Young Adult Book Club." In *Reading Communities from Salons to Cyberspace*, ed. by DeNel Rehberg Sedo, 101–122. Basingstoke: Palgrave.

Rosen, Matthew. 2015. "Ethnographies of Reading: Beyond Literacy and Books." *Anthropological Quarterly* 88 (4): 1059–1083. https://www.jstor.org/stable/43955502.

Rumsby, Seb, and Jennifer P. Eggert. 2023. "Religious Positionalities and Political Science Research in 'the Field' and Beyond: Insights from Vietnam, Lebanon and the UK." *Qualitative Research* 24 (3): 525–547.

Ruokonen, Minna. 2011. "Target Readers' Expectations and Reality: Conformity or Conflict?" In *Beyond Borders — Translations Moving Languages, Literatures and Cultures*, ed. by Pekka Kujamäki, Hannu Kemppanen, Leena Kolehmainen, and Esa Penttilä, 73–100. Berlin: Frank & Timme.

Sarantakos, Sotirios. 2004. *Social Research*. Basingstoke: Palgrave MacMillan.

Shankar, Avi. 2006. "Book-Reading Groups: A 'Male Outsider' Perspective." In *Consuming Books: The Marketing and Consumption of Literature*, ed. by Stephen Brown, 114–125. London & New York: Routledge.

Sherif, Bahira. 2001. "The Ambiguity of Boundaries in the Fieldwork Experience: Establishing Rapport and Negotiating Insider/Outsider Status." *Qualitative Inquiry* 7 (4): 436–447.

Smith, Daniel R. 2022. "Reading, Novels and the Ethics of Sociability: Taking Simmel to an Independent English Bookshop." In *The Cultural Sociology of Reading: The Meanings of Reading and Books Across the World*, ed. by María Angélica Thumala Olave, 361–384. Cham: Palgrave.

Squires, Claire. 2009. *Marketing Literature: The Making of Contemporary Writing in Britain.* Basingstoke: Palgrave Macmillan.

Sturge, Kate. 2014. "Translation Strategies in Ethnography." *The Translator* 3 (1): 21–38.

Swann, Joan, and Daniel Allington. 2009. "Reading Groups and the Language of Literary Texts: A Case Study in Social Reading." *Language and Literature* 18 (3): 247–264.

Tekgül-Akın, Duygu. 2022. "Towards a Sociology of Consuming Translated Fiction: Pleasure, Status, and Textual-Linguistic Intolerance." *Translation in Society* 1 (2): 157–176.

Tekgül, Duygu. 2017. "The Destabilization of Symbolic Boundaries in the Consumption of Translated Fiction." *Mémoires du livre / Studies in Book Culture* 9 (1): 1–22.

Tekgül, Duygu. 2019. "Book Club Meetings as Micro Public Spheres: Translated Literature and Cosmopolitanism." *Language and Intercultural Communication* 19 (5): 380–392.

Tekin, Latife. 2007. *Swords of Ice.* Translated by Saliha Paker and Mel Kenne. London: Marion Boyars.

Thumala Olave, María Angélica. 2018. "Reading Matters: Towards a Cultural Sociology of Reading." *American Journal of Cultural Sociology* 6: 417–454.

Towheed, Safquat. 2020. "New Worlds or Old Habits? Reading During the Pandemic" *Reading the Pandemic*, 18 November 2020. https://www.youtube.com/watch?v=Awc_i76hqGw

Travis, Trysh. 2003. "Divine Secrets of the Cultural Studies Sisterhood: Women Reading Rebecca Wells." *American Literary History* 15 (1): 134–161. https://www.jstor.org/stable/3567972.

Walker, Callum. 2021. *An Eye-Tracking Study of Equivalent Effect in Translation: The Reader Experience of Literary Style.* London: Palgrave Macmillan.

Wright, David. 2006. "Cultural Capital and the Literary Field." *Cultural Trends* 15 (2/3): 123–139.

CHAPTER 13

What translation
and interpreting practices do
Field research on human differentiation
in a German reception centre for refugees

Dilek Dizdar & Tomasz Rozmysłowicz
University of Mainz

The aim of this chapter is to introduce a new theoretical framework for field
research in translation studies. The framework is centred around the
concept of 'human differentiation' (Hirschauer 2017; Dizdar et al. 2021).
Drawing on original data gathered during field research carried out at a
German reception centre for refugees, the chapter demonstrates and
discusses the analytical benefits of adopting the proposed framework. By
doing so, it hopes to increase the discipline's capacity to observe what
translation practices *do* in specific social situations — other than enable
communication. The central idea is that translation also creates differences
between people and that field research is particularly well suited to
investigating how this occurs.

Keywords: translation practices, human differentiation, asylum seekers,
interpreter recruitment, participant observation, interviews, document
analysis

1. Introduction

Ethnographic field research has been of increasing methodological interest in
translation studies ever since the cultural and social turns. It has been used as
a way to study translation[1] as a situated practice under 'real-life' instead of laboratory conditions. As a result, our knowledge of the production and functioning of translation in specific areas of the socio-cultural world — such as courts

---

1. If not indicated otherwise, the term 'translation' is used generically to encompass both translation and interpreting.

https://doi.org/10.1075/btl.165.13diz
Available under the CC BY-NC 4.0 license. © 2025 John Benjamins Publishing Company

(Kinnunen 2010), hospitals (Angelelli 2004), the EU parliament (Koskinen 2008), translator's workplaces (Risku, Rogl, and Milosevic 2019), and many others more (e.g., Flynn 2004; Flynn and van Doorslaer 2016; Gustafsson 2023) — has grown, making us more and more aware of the complex interrelationships between translation and the socio-cultural world.

The purpose of this chapter is to contribute to this growing body of ethnographic field research in translation studies by offering a new conceptual framework based on the notion of 'human differentiation' introduced by German sociologist Stefan Hirschauer and elaborated in transdisciplinary cooperations (Hirschauer 2017; Dizdar et al. 2021). This notion unfolds a perspective in which the complex interrelation between translation and the socio-cultural world can be studied empirically and systematically under a specific aspect in order to better understand what translation *does* — other than enable communication. The central idea is that translation also *creates* differences between people and that field research is particularly well suited to investigating how this occurs.

In this chapter, we first introduce the conceptual framework of human differentiation and relate it to translation. This sets the stage for demonstrating its application in ethnographic field research that we carried out at German reception centres for asylum seekers — facilities where newly arrived asylum seekers are accommodated and provided for until their official asylum hearing. The choice of going to such reception centres was motivated by the research interest of finding out empirically how translation catalyses the production of differences between human beings. Because reception centres for asylum seekers are — by their very nature — highly multilingual and very intense "translation spaces" (Koskinen 2014), they make particularly fruitful sites for field research interested in the difference-making effects of translation. In this sense, the contribution that this chapter aims to make does not consist in describing a translation space which has not been studied before in translation and interpreting studies. On the contrary, much valuable research into the asylum-related translation spaces and practices has been carried out for some while now (Lagnado 2002; Pöllabauer 2004, 2005, 2006, 2007, 2008, 2013; Inghilleri 2005; Merlini 2009; Macfarlane et al. 2009, 2020; Maltby 2010; Daniyan 2010; Bourke and Lucadou-Wells 2016; Iacono, Heinisch, and Pöllabauer 2024, see also Todorova, Chapter 14, this volume, on practices of self-translation by asylum seekers and refugees in Hong Kong). Rather, we want to offer a specific perspective on these translation spaces which, in combination with ethnographic field research, can yield interesting results.

Based on our data gathered through participant observation, interviews, and document collection, we will discuss how translation acts as a *catalyst* for acts of *language-related* human differentiation — that is, the institutional sorting of people into 'language boxes' for the purposes of translation. The chapter closes with a few remarks concerning the analytical benefits of the proposed perspective.

2. Conceptual framework

2.1 Language-related human differentiation

Human beings continuously differentiate between themselves and others according to a variety of criteria, such as nationality, ethnicity, religion, age, sexual orientation, or language. The categories which emerge as a result of such processes of differentiation are contingent and dynamic; some turn out to be stable and durable to the extent that they are treated as natural (such as nation or ethnicity) while others are transient. The concept of 'human differentiation' covers all kinds of such difference-making processes in which human beings are involved either actively or passively and takes a critical distance towards approaches working with presupposed categories or categorial hierarchies. Within this framework, categories are not taken as given, instead they are conceptualised as constructions which create social affiliations and belongings and gain socio-cultural relevance under certain circumstances (Hirschauer 2017, 2021, 2023; Dizdar et al. 2021).

Seen from this perspective, the self-assignment and external assignment of people to languages is to be understood as a form of human differentiation which interacts with other differentiation forms and potentially assumes different positions in hierarchies of relevance. We call this *language-related human differentiation*. Most typically, people are sorted according to language using explicit categories such as 'German', 'Arabic', or 'Chinese'. Such categories generalise an act of distinction by grasping it linguistically and thus making it available for further situations. In this way, for example, a waiter in a pub can hand the appropriate menus to guests: he recognises 'English' and reaches into the right compartment — 'English'. Similarly, employees of immigration authorities can categorise the newcomers in forms according to language in order to arrange for an appropriate interpreter. The categorisation of people according to language makes use of linguistic indices, when, for example, many front round vowels (ü, ö) lead to the conclusion that the language spoken is 'Turkish'. Language-related categorisation can also occur as part of or as the result of a chain of attributions without anyone having spoken. For example, a physical marker can produce language-related inferences. This happens when someone concludes from a headscarf that the person must be a speaker of Arabic. Similarly, eye shape, skin colour, and nonverbal behaviour (such as when someone bows politely in greeting) also lead to the attribution of language affiliations.

People also use self-assignment practices to signal belonging to a certain community. They use specialised lexemes to mark their profession and employ eloquent syntax and stylistics to indicate intellectuality. The varieties of speech can, in principle, serve as markers for the most diverse classifications of people, and their hierarchy is variable: the mastery of a slang is more important for the acceptance of young newcomers among their peers than speaking the standard variety flawlessly, which they in turn need for good grades in their classes.[2]

The scales of human differentiation and the size of the communities they form vary as much as the 'language unit' and its relevance to the speakers. The continuum ranges from family languages, e.g., the sign languages that develop in families with deaf children (Hill, Lillo-Martin, and Wood 2019), to transnational lingua francas. This diversity and situational mutability of language-related human differentiation experienced in everyday practices is intersected by institutional forms of categorisation. Generally, the way language is institutionally processed in Germany and other European countries reifies the nation-state bias and monolingual norms, a perspective from which multiple affiliations are seen as exceptions and linguistic hybridity is considered a deficiency ("one person, one language"; Busch 2010:10).

2.2 The role of translation in language-based differentiation processes

The notion that translation takes place 'between' homogeneous and sharply demarcated languages or linguistic communities proves to be constitutive of the monolingual norm: Translation is also an indirect affirmation of imagined national and ethnic communities, each of which is held together by a common language. In this respect, translation even supports the emergence of national, ethnic and linguistic units (Sakai 2018) to which people 'belong'. Human beings are then members of a nation, a people, and a language community that can encounter each other in translation processes as 'foreign' to each other.

For human differentiation research, the question of how speakers fit into 'existing' individual languages must be preceded by the question of what 'a language' means to the participants in each case, where it begins and ends (Derrida 2003:21–22), and how 'language drawers' with labels like 'English' or 'Dari' come into being in the first place. Instead of assuming language structures and distinct language units to which speakers are assigned, the focus is thus shifted to the people who categorise themselves and others. Language concepts in which the membership of people in monolingual language communities in the form of a nation state appears as an always already regulated and 'natural' order (Silverstein 1996;

---

2. This section draws on earlier work (Dizdar 2019, 2021).

Bonfiglio 2010) have to be replaced by an approach in which the question is not answered authoritatively, but opened up empirically. The criticism of concepts of language as if they were things in the world (Davidson 1992: 256), however, is opposed by the everyday and institutional handling of language, which does just that.

2.2.1 Listing languages: Glottonyms

Languages are not only 'used' by people, e.g., 'inhabited', 'mastered' and 'controlled'. They 'survive', have to be 'saved' and 'maintained', they are 'collected' and 'listed', 'taught', 'deleted' and 'added'. Their diversity is compared to biodiversity, they are praised and condemned as cultural assets and as storage media for the collective memory; many are doomed to death. For their recording and processing, it is necessary for languages — and all objects of categorisation (Hirschauer 2021: 159) — to have a name. Not all make it onto official lists, and the circumstances of naming are highly complex. In everyday life, people do not or rarely think about what language they are speaking — they simply speak as they breathe or swim. Only on the basis of factual or anticipated reactions from others does this come into consciousness as a particular language. In this context, glottonyms, much like labels on drawers or bells, serve to sort out speakers in heterolingual constellations, to secure the way for them to access communication, and to make them approachable — for example, when the right language button on the audio guide has to be pressed during a visit to a museum so that the information can be understood. Speech names reduce complexity and ensure the manageability of communication.

2.2.2 Linguistic and language-related differentiation

As language-related categories are expressed linguistically ('Japanese', 'Uzbek'), they stand in a double relationship to language: they sort people by using language and according to 'language(s)'. However, most forms of human differentiation, including those based on gender, age, nationality, etc., are carried out linguistically. Therefore, speech as a marker is to be separated from language as the modus operandi of differentiation. While all categorisations of humans by 'language' are performed linguistically, conversely, not all human differentiations are language-related. Through their linguistic nature, human differentiations can draw on all layers of language (Hirschauer and Nübling 2021). While there is no need for a multiplicity of languages for linguistic human differentiation, the statement of language difference (i.e., a recognition of at least two codes/idioms/dialects/languages/etc.) is a prerequisite for language-related human differentiation.

2.2.3 Translation motivating institutional categorisations

Translation plays a fundamental role not only in the theoretical sense described above, namely that the determination of a difference between languages presupposes contact, comparability, and translatability. The observation of translation practice also provides reason to conceive of translation as a catalyst for language-related human differentiation. Indeed, the need for translation and interpretation services requires a workable sorting of addressees and interpreters in advance and motivates the categorisation process. Interpretation can only be commissioned if it is clear for which language it is to be used (Dizdar 2019, 2021).

In the context of dealing with language difference — understood as the result of language-related human differentiation — in everyday and institutional contexts, translation usually takes on a crucial function. The need for translation leads to a categorisation of speakers that precedes the actual translation or interpreting process. In many institutional contexts, if translation is needed, the speakers to be addressed are first assigned to a language recorded in the directory so that translators or interpreters can be appointed. In the run-up to the actual translation, an initial translation takes place in the form of a transfer of the individual or collective cases into the official structure — and the "seemingly universalistic language of the state" (Mokre 2015: 22). Different ways of speaking are thus first rendered 'translatable'; the bureaucratisation leads to the levelling of differentiated speech practices in favour of an institutionally and pragmatically grounded effort to achieve 'sufficient' understanding. The monoglottistic framing of languages (Silverstein 1996), in which national languages are prioritised not only for symbolic reasons (Bourdieu 2012) but primarily because they stand for clarity and transparency (Blommaert 2009: 421), thus proves to be a prerequisite for the institutional processing of translation. Non-determinable language boundaries and an excessive number of individual languages would make the organisation of translation impossible. The infrastructures of the bureaucracies provide the framework for the options and the selection processes. As in other areas, the following applies here: the more differentiated the division, the more difficult it is to deal with categories. Categorisations follow the principle of economy. The Arabic variety spoken by the applicants in an institutional proceeding is irrelevant for the instrumental processing of information. Information material, forms, etc. are produced in 'Arabic', under which all varieties are subsumed. If a national language cannot be determined and a recognised 'standard language' is lacking, a variant must be chosen which is thereby indirectly elevated to the status of standard (e.g., 'Kurmanci' to 'Kurdish'). The bureaucratically motivated tendency toward standardisation does not mean, however, that differentiations which have disappeared cannot become relevant again: if, in the context of asylum procedures, the credibility of applicants is to be verified in relation to their region of origin, the distinction between the varieties itself acquires informational value — it rises in the hierarchy of relevance.

3. Field research in German reception centres for asylum seekers

3.1 Approaching the field

Our field research to date has been carried out at two German reception centres for asylum seekers.[3] In Germany, reception centres for asylum seekers are state-run institutions where those seeking asylum are required to go after entering the country.[4] Reception centres differ in size, location, resources, and nomenclature. But they all have in common that they are the official place in Germany at which asylum seekers find shelter, are registered, and apply for asylum. Moreover, reception centres provide not only accommodation and provisioning, but also medical care, psychological counselling, and legal advice concerning the asylum procedure. The asylum procedure itself, in which a decision on the application for asylum is made, does not fall under the purview of the reception centres. It is the sole responsibility of the *Bundesamt für Migration und Flüchtlinge* (BAMF) (Federal Office for Migration and Refugees). Even so, the BAMF often maintains sub-offices on the grounds of reception centres where the asylum procedures take place. Taken together, they form a bureaucratic complex of *people-processing organisations* (Hasenfeld 1972).[5]

3.2 Methodology

In total, three field trips were undertaken in 2021 and 2022. Two of these field trips took place at the first reception centre (RC A) we gained access to. They lasted two and five days respectively. Three research team members plus one Arabic-speaking assistant went on the first field trip, two members plus the same assistant on the second. The third field trip to the second reception centre (RC B) lasted

---

3. Depending on the state, these reception centres have different names (such as *Ankerzentrum, Aufnahmeeinrichtung für Asylbegehrende, Ankunftszentrum*). For the purposes of this paper, we will refer to them in English generically as "reception centres for asylum seekers" or just "reception centres".

4. A legal exception has been made for refugees from Ukraine.

5. Hasenfeld distinguishes between *people-processing* and *people-changing* organisations. The former differ from the latter in that their "explicit function is not to change the behavior of people directly but to process them and confer public statuses on them" (1972: 256).

one day and was undertaken by two research team members. This reception centre's management only gave us permission to do field research for one day. The official explanation was that, due to the high influx of refugees during that time (October 2022), the reception centre was running at maximum capacity, drastically diminishing the time and attention that could be afforded to researchers.

The reception centres were located in the same state. There are several reception centres in each state, and they differ in size and role within each state system of reception centres. In our case, the first reception centre was intended to house approximately 500 asylum seekers, the second to accommodate approximately 3000. The difference in size or housing capacity also reflects a difference in roles. The bigger reception centre was also the central reception centre of the state, which means that, typically, all asylum seekers arriving in that state are required to go there first.[6] After being registered there, they can be sent to smaller reception centres, like the first one we visited.

During our field trips, a variety of ethnographic methods were used. Participant observation was employed to observe practices of language-related human differentiation in different situations (related to translation), such as the official registration process and the waiting room of the reception centre's "info point". Qualitative, semi-structured interviews were conducted with asylum seekers, the reception centre's management, and staff of the private contractor responsible for accommodation and provisioning, as well as with medical personnel and social workers. Also, spontaneous informal interviews were conducted with staff members of the reception centre's registration office. In total, fifteen semi-structured interviews were conducted. Seven of them were recorded and transcribed using MAXQDA. Notes were taken for the other eight.[7] The research team was only able to record seven interviews for different reasons: In some cases, the wish to record was explicitly rejected. In other cases, the team members felt that asking for permission to record the conversation would compromise the interviewees' willingness to participate in the interview as the setting of the reception centre was (and still is) under political observation. After a close reading of the transcripts and notes, the interview data was coded according to analytic themes related to questions of language-related human differentiation. The interviews lasted between 20 and 60 minutes and were conducted by individual research team members alone or as a pair. Two of the interviews with asylum seekers were interpreted by our Arabic-speaking team member.[8]

---

6. Exceptions were made during the pandemic. During that time asylum seekers could also go directly to other reception centres in the same state.

7. All quotations from interviews appearing in this chapter were translated from German into English by the authors.

Our material also comprises two walking interviews or "go-alongs" (Kühl 2016; King and Woodroffe 2017) with the receptions centre's management and one staff member of the private contractor. These interviews consisted in accompanying the participants on their everyday paths through the reception centre whilst talking about their work. They covered the compound and housing facilities of the first reception centre and were carried out in order to reconstruct the way the reception centre is experienced as a particular place. Finally, linguistic landscaping, the photographic recording of "publicly visible bits of written language" (Blommaert 2013: 1), was applied to capture the multitude of multilingual signs found all over the reception centre and its sub-organisations. Approximately 170 multilingual (and monolingual) documents (such as brochures of the different sub-organisations in the reception centre, registration forms, information about rights and obligations, and orientation materials) were also collected for document analysis. Documents are an important form of material for the research project as they constitute an essential part of the communicative and bureaucratic reality encountered in reception centres. This is why they are methodologically treated not (only) as sources of information about this reality, but as interesting objects of analysis in their own right that are produced and used within the organisational context of the reception centre (Prior 2003).

The types of data resulting from the fieldtrips thus comprise interview recordings and transcriptions, field notes, photos, and written documents. In this chapter, we will mainly draw on field notes from participant observation, verbal interview data, and document analysis. What do these data tell us about what translation does and how translation is done with regards to language-related human differentiation?

3.3 Language-related human differentiation before and for the purposes of translation: Recruiting interpreters

Because of their explicit function to register and accommodate asylum seekers, reception centres for refugees find the question of which language(s) the latter speak to be doubly relevant. It is, on the one hand, important for the process of *identification*. 'Language' is used by the BAMF to verify an asylum seeker's claim of country of origin for the determination of refugee status. It is part of the procedure to determine whether a person is a refugee. However, the question of which

---

8. This means that we too engaged in acts of language-related human differentiation for the purpose of translation. In order to 'capture' these moments methodically, we arranged special team meetings with our Arabic-speaking team member in which we discussed her interpreting experiences on the basis of the recordings.

language(s) someone speaks is also asked to enable communication between asylum seekers and BAMF employees through an interpreter. For interpreting to occur, an act of language-related human differentiation is necessary to determine the languages for which an interpreter is to be employed. Because the asylum hearing at the BAMF is based on personal data of asylum seekers first collected by reception centres, it is important to look at these institutions and figure out how language-related human differentiation is intertwined with translation practices there.

Sorting asylum seekers according to the language(s) they speak for the purpose of translation is particularly relevant for reception centres as they are dealing with asylum seekers on a daily basis and in all their sub-organisations. In fact, as our data shows, translation is an on-going concern for reception centres. They are characterised by a permanent need for translation. This is why translation is not only omnipresent as the *modus operandi* through which reception centres communicate with asylum seekers: in order for translation to occur, it has to be constantly planned, organised and managed by the reception centre. In contrast to translating institutions such as the EU parliament, where the languages for which translation is needed are known in advance because of its policy to include the national or official languages of its member states, reception centres are confronted with a highly dynamic environment and fluctuating linguistic repertoires for which it is difficult to plan. For instance, as we were told by the local authorities of RC A, in 2020 about 90 percent of the asylum seekers came from Nigeria, Cameroon, and Guinea. In this situation, interpreters were not or rarely considered necessary because most of the communication could be carried out in English or French (which members of the registration office spoke). However, one year later most asylum seekers came from Syria and Afghanistan and predominantly spoke either Arabic, Dari or Pashtu, for which interpreters were needed. With the arrival of refugees from Ukraine in 2022, suddenly interpreters were needed for Ukrainian or Russian.

One of the main problems that reception centres are therefore routinely confronted with is the *recruitment of interpreters*. How do they do this? And what role does language-related human differentiation play in this? A particularly conspicuous solution could be observed in RC A. There, interpreters are recruited from the population of asylum seekers themselves. This is, of course, a potentially conflict-laden solution because being categorised as speakers of the same language does not prevent asylum seekers from categorising each other as members of different hostile ethnic or religious groups. During our stay, asylum seekers categorised as Arabic *and* English speakers were highly sought after to establish communication between other asylum seekers and the administrative staff.[9] Asylum seekers are

Chapter 13. What translation and interpreting practices do 307

renumerated for their interpreting activity; however, they receive less than one Euro per hour and no training whatsoever. The recruitment of interpreters typically occurs during the registration process.

3.3.1 Recruiting interpreters in reception centre A

The registration process consists of several steps. First, an 'unofficial' registration is undertaken at the "info point" by the private contractor's staff right after newly arrived asylum seekers have passed the reception centre's gates guarded by the security team. Members of the security team are the first ones to undertake an act of language-related human differentiation in order to pass on information to the info point about the language(s) spoken by the asylum seekers. This is relevant for carrying out the unofficial registration which is undertaken for assigning rooms to asylum seekers. From informal interviews with the security team and semi-structured interviews with the staff of the info point, we were able to gather that this initial act of language-related human differentiation is based on indexical cues such as documents (passports, ID cards) or overall outward appearance. At the info point, personal data of asylum seekers is recorded in a form. This form includes the name (or number) of the building, room number, family name, first name, date of birth, religion, country of origin, 'mother tongue', time of arrival, date of arrival, and the name of the staff member responsible for the registration (in this exact order). As the first two points "building" and "room number" indicate, this form serves the purposes of the private contractor tasked with accommodation and meals. It is later transferred to the contractor's internal database.

Of particular interest to us is the fact *that* language is explicitly recorded and *the way* in which it is done: as *mother tongue* (German: *Muttersprache*). This very culture-specific (Western) concept of language is based on the assumption of an inherent link between nation, state, and language. It posits languages as clearly distinguishable units congruent with the territories governed by particular states of particular nations (cf. also Blommaert 2009; Busch 2010). This idea becomes overtly problematic once the self-categorisation of asylum seekers does not correspond to it. For example, asylum seekers from Syria told us in an interview that actually they were Kurdish and that Arabic is not their first language as was initially and automatically assumed by the staff of the info point. A possible con-

---

9. One of the staff members contrasted the situation in 2021 with the situation in 2015/16, during the so-called 'refugee crisis' in Germany. At that time, RC A was housing between 2000 and 3000 asylum seekers. Interestingly enough, this was also one of the few times where the reception centre did not suffer from a shortage of translators because it had such a large pool to recruit from. As the staff member reported enthusiastically, all languages were covered: they even had 7–8 *Ganztagsdolmetscher* (full-day interpreters).

sequence of such practices of human differentiation can be that Syrian nationals are put together in the same room because they are believed to 'understand' each other on the basis of a common language. However, these persons can categorise themselves and each other as belonging to different ethnic groups who are in conflict with one another.

Recording the "mother tongue" in the contractor's database is, however, not only consequential because it lumps people together in a potentially conflictual way. The entry under "mother tongue", in fact the whole registration form, later serves as a basis for the official registration with the local authorities. There, another form is used to record personal data more extensively which is then, in a further step, entered into two digital databases. We were able to observe how this is done.

Present were an asylum seeker from Turkey, two members of the administrative staff, and two members of the research team. One of the staff members filled in the form by asking questions concerning each category in order to verify the data of the unofficial registration form. The form, the questions, and the answers were all in German. The other staff member interpreted their colleague's questions in German and the asylum seeker's answers in Turkish. German and Turkish (also Macedonian and English) were part of the interpreting staff member's linguistic repertoire. The question of language(s) was again part of the registration process and to be recorded in the official form. However, this form not only contained an entry for "mother tongue", but also for "further languages". This point is also verified by the administrative staff by looking at the initial and unofficial registration form. However, as the person filling in the form told us afterwards in an informal interview, staff members carrying out the official registration usually assume that whatever answer is given to the question of "mother tongue", it is indeed the "mother tongue". They do not call into question nor are they able to determine the level of proficiency with which someone is able to speak a given language.

According to the staff member who was handling the interpretation, the asylum seeker said during the registration process, when asked what further language(s) he spoke, that he only spoke a few scraps of English. The question of which further language(s) someone speaks is a central moment in the recruitment of interpreters from the population of asylum seekers. This is where the administration of RC A determines whether the asylum seeker's linguistic repertoire is relevant for the reception centre's translation needs. Typically, they are looking for English and ask asylum seekers who speak it whether they would be willing to act as an interpreter in the reception centre. If so, their name is entered into a list of interpreters available to the reception centre. They join the centre's 'interpreter pool' which is managed by the same person who carried out the registration described above. In this specific case, however, the asylum seeker did not wish to serve as an interpreter. In fact, when it came to entering his personal data into the official digital databases, he wished no entry in the section "further languages" – so that it would not become "his undoing",[10] as the staff member filling in the form later told us. Apparently, the asylum seeker was anxious about having to speak English during the asylum procedure, thus lowering his chances of a positive outcome because of the inability to properly express himself. This goes to show how the self-categorisation according to language(s) can be undertaken consciously by asylum seekers in anticipation of potential negative outcomes – in this case: the legal categorisation as not entitled to asylum.

Recruiting interpreters by means of language-related human differentiation from the population of (newly arrived) asylum seekers is, as we have hinted at, not the only way RC A meets its translation needs. Interpreters are also recruited from the staff of the security team and the private contractor responsible for accommodation and provisioning. In addition to this, volunteer interpreters are recruited from among local residents by a special volunteer coordinator. Moreover, medical care, counselling psychology, and social workers offering social and legal advice, also work with external, paid interpreters. When hiring staff for the security team or the private contractor, it is ensured that they are multilingual (by already placing this requirement in the job ad). In fact, the manager of the interpreter pool said that he "could not use" people working for the reception centre who only spoke German. And, last but not least, translation machines (Google Translate) are conscripted into translation service in the case of "exotic languages" (as the same staff member called them) for which no human translator is available on the ground. In rare cases, remote interpreting is also used in RC A. This solution seems to be based upon friendly relationships between the reception centre's manager and former asylum seekers who have been granted asylum and now are living in Germany. However, remote interpreting also occurs when travelling to the reception centre is not possible or reasonable.

We can gather several important aspects from these observations. In order to fulfil its explicit function of registering, accommodating and providing for asylum seekers until their asylum hearing, RC A recruits interpreters from various sources: asylum seekers, staff, and local residents. This means that the functioning of RC A, and of reception centres in general, does not only depend on trained interpreters. It also depends on an on-going practice of language-related human differentiation for interpreters to be there in the first place. This means that RC A is constantly engaged in sorting people into 'language boxes' and categorising them as speakers of particular languages in order to know for which language an

---

10. German original: "damit es ihm nicht zum Verhängnis wird".

interpreter is needed and in order to recruit interpreters to meet this need. In this sense, people (asylum seekers, staff, local residents) appear to the reception centre as speakers, as language-using beings who need or provide translation and interpreting.

RC A's practice of primarily internal recruitment of interpreters can be understood as a pragmatic solution to an on-going communication problem. But because recruitment is primarily internal, those who are recruited as interpreters are inevitably burdened with taking on *additional roles* beside the primary roles assigned to them by the reception centre: either as asylum seekers or staff members. As we will see when looking at RC B and their reasons not to use the same approach as RC A (see Section 3.3.2), this can create all sorts of secondary problems, including role ambiguities and conflicts.

Another important aspect of recruiting asylum seekers as interpreters during the official registration process is the relationship between the external categorisation of asylum seekers according to language by the reception centre and their self-categorisation. The description of the unofficial and official registration process has shown that language is an explicit category of human differentiation. If we also take into account the initial act of language-related human differentiation by the security team members at the reception centre's gate, we can observe a logic of an increasing solidification of 'language': it starts from the situated and perceptual differentiation of speakers based on cues such as outward appearance or documents. From there, information about the language a given asylum seeker is perceived to speak is communicated to the info point where it is recorded in writing for the first time. During the official registration, the written fixation is iterated under "mother tongue" and "further languages" in the registration form and, finally, the digital databases. In each step, the category of language becomes more and more solidified: Whereas entries under "language" in the forms can still be changed locally, entries in the digital databases can only be changed by the BAMF.

Furthermore, it is not at all clear what asylum seekers understand when being asked about 'their' language, especially when asked about their 'mother tongue': is it the language spoken by their mother (Blommaert 2009: 417)? By their family? Based on an interview with a social worker (responsible for social and procedural advice) we suspect that this bureaucratic chain of language-related human differentiation can remain uncontested (and thus unproblematic in the eyes of the reception centre) right up to the asylum hearing itself where an official (legally recognised) interpreter is booked based on this categorisation history. According to the social worker, asylum seekers sometimes request a different interpreter because they cannot understand them (see Pöllabauer 2005 for similar findings). Since interpreters are booked by the BAMF with prior knowledge of an asylum seeker's linguistic repertoire, the categorisation practices of reception centres offer one explanation for these occurrences. What this refers to is the question of agency and materiality in practices of language-related human differentiation for the purpose of translation: to what extent can asylum seekers be not only objects but also subjects of their categorisation? And what influence do media and technology such as writing, bureaucratic forms, and digital databases have in this regard?[11] The materiality of the media and technologies in use appears to have a significant effect upon the rigidity of categories of human differentiation.

3.3.2   *Recruiting interpreters in reception centre B*

As these observations only pertain to RC A, it is useful take into consideration a second reception centre: RC B. There, we can see that the translation management observed in RC A is not practiced in all reception centres for asylum seekers. The most conspicuous difference between them is that RC B does *not* recruit interpreters from asylum seekers or the security team (or other staff members). The communication problem of the reception centre is instead resolved in different ways. One solution is the employment of multilingual staff who speak the languages needed for their task. This is the case in the registration office, where the linguistic repertoire of each staff member is important information for internal planning and is displayed on schedule sheets in national language categories. The other observed solution to the communication problem is the use of interpreter pools consisting of *external* interpreters (freelancers). This is the case in RC B's medical facility as well as for its social and procedural advice provider responsible for making sure asylum seekers understand their rights and duties in the asylum procedure sufficiently to make informed decisions. These sub-organisations each manage their own pool of interpreters. In fact, the medical facility even has its own translation manager who plans and schedules interpreters (one week in advance), so that the medical staff is able to carry out its duties. To a lesser degree, this is also true for the social and procedural advice provider. Although they do not have a separate position for translation management, they also plan and organise translation in order to offer their services. They work with a schedule that shows the availability of external, paid freelance interpreters or, more precisely, of *languages* during the day and week. Languages are differentiated by different colours for quick recognition. Meetings with asylum seekers are arranged according to the interpreter/language schedule. This means that meetings are scheduled according to the availability of interpreters instead of commissioning interpreters according to the meeting plans.

---

11. See Bowker and Star (2000), and also Schabacher (2021), for the role of infrastructures in classification and categorisation processes.

When we told RC B's manager about RC A's translation policy of recruiting asylum seekers as interpreters, this solution was dismissed outright. The reason given for this rejection was that letting asylum seekers interpret would run the risk of arousing suspicion of unequal treatment among those asylum seekers who were not working as interpreters. They might think that those interpreting receive some kind of special treatment by the reception centre. Moreover, giving an interpreting job to an asylum seeker might raise their expectations concerning a positive outcome of the asylum procedure. The head of the medical facility in turn told us, when we mentioned RC A's practice of also using security-team staff as interpreters, that they "had no business" interpreting there.

These reactions can be interpreted as an awareness in RC B of the secondary problems the recruitment practice of RC A creates. Appointing asylum seekers as interpreters is perceived as creating a *distinction*, a special and privileged category within the population of asylum seekers, violating the norm of equal treatment. Entering the category of 'interpreter'[12] means that asylum seekers take on an additional role, which is viewed as inviting conflict among asylum seekers and raising false expectations among those who interpret. Appointing security staff as interpreters, on the other hand, is perceived as creating role ambiguities in sensitive situations such as medical examinations or psychological counselling. Here, too, someone in a different role entering the category of 'interpreter' is judged as dysfunctional.

The concerns voiced in RC B seem to be explainable through the differences in size, role, and resources between both reception centres. RC B is much bigger that RC A. And, within the federal state, RC B is the central reception centre through which all asylum seekers in that state must go. We assume that for this reason it has more financial resources at its disposal. It can therefore afford to dispense with recruitment practices such as those observed in RC A. They seem to be primarily a function of economic resources.[13]

---

12. German: 'Dolmetscher', 'Sprachmittler'.

13. Our findings match the observations that Kujamäki and Pasanen (2019) made in their historical analysis of Finnish prisoner of war (POW) camps during WW II. Not only were Russian-speaking refugees recruited as interpreters for establishing communication between the Finnish military and Russian prisoners. The POW camps were also marked by a "clear shortage of interpreters" (2019:180), which led to recruiting POWs "with the most elementary Finnish skills" (2019:188): "The POWs were, from the very establishment of the camp network, a crucial part of its multilingual resources which the POW unit commanders held tightly onto when necessary" (2019:189). Apparently it is a rule that, under conditions of scarcity, the linguistic requirements for someone to act as an interpreter can be lowered to a minimum. Interestingly enough, this recruitment system caused similar secondary problems as the ones

3.4 Categorisation as interpreter/translator

This brings us to our final analytical point: the category of 'interpreter'/'translator' itself. This category is vital to the functioning of reception centres for refugees. However, as we have seen, recruiting people for that category is not only a matter of their availability. It is also relevant for reception centres *who* takes on that role – and who does not. This means that the category of 'interpreter' can take on additional social meanings beside 'communication aid', such as 'special status' (not only an asylum seeker anymore). Or it may make it difficult for asylum seekers to distinguish between the categories of interpreter and security staff in certain situations. In some cases, as a member of the social and procedural advice team told us, asylum seekers even prefer translation machines to humans because they attribute a sense of neutrality and disinterestedness to machines. The extent to which reception centres are able to determine who may enter the category of interpreter seems to be dependent on their economic resources (and thus on state policy and internal funding allocation). The smaller the reception centre and its budget, the more often it has to recruit interpreters *internally*. And the more it has to recruit internally, the more language-related human differentiation is triggered by the centre's interpreting and translation needs. In this sense, we can say that interpreting and translation perpetuates the production of differences between human beings.

Moreover, not all occurrences of translation and interpreting seem to entail the category of translator/interpreter. This poses a similar methodological problem as the one described by Kujamäki and Pasanen (2019: 177). In their historical analysis of Finnish POW camps, they notice that "'translators' or 'interpreters' usually do not manifest themselves as organisational categories in the folders and particular databases". In our case, however, the possibility of observing communicative practices allowed for spotting translation even where it is not explicitly highlighted as such. The multilingual staff in RC A's and B's registration offices also translate documents to be handed out to asylum seekers. And, although RC B claims not to use interpreters during the registration process because its staff is able to communicate with asylum seekers without an intermediary, they actually do translate the asylum seeker's answers when entering them into the German database. Apparently, these translation activities are considered *tasks* within their job profile without necessarily implying an explicit categorisation as translators (see also Koskinen, Chapter 1, and Steinkogler, Chapter 6, this volume, on paraprofessional translation and interpreting).[14]

---

anticipated by RC B's management: From the perspective of their fellow inmates, POW interpreters could quickly be categorised as traitors (2019: 190).

What these observations point to is a spectrum of translational practices, only some of which are reflected as such and considered to be carried out by 'translators' or 'interpreters'. They range from occasional and ephemeral or 'habitual' translation (Wolf 2012) that is produced routinely to planned and organised interpreting practices involving a third party as a linguistic intermediary (see also Koskela et al. 2017 on "translatoriality" in institutional contexts).[15] Thus, not only the decision of who is allowed to enter the category of translator/interpreter reflects the structure, size and role of the "translating institution" (Koskinen 2008) that uses translation to solve its problems, but also its meaning: what counts as an act of translation/interpreting by a translator/interpreter is determined by the reception centre in question.

4. Conclusion

The aim of this chapter was to demonstrate the analytical benefits of adopting the perspective of human differentiation when carrying out field research in translation studies. Of course, this perspective can also be adopted in research branches of translation studies where ethnographic methods are hardly applicable, such as translation history. The perspective of human differentiation is not bound to a specific methodology. And it is not reserved for the investigation of particular contexts of translation, such as reception centres for asylum seekers. But it can illuminate the translational complexity of reception centres particularly well.

An ethnographic approach makes it possible to observe the diversity of translation-related practices in these highly intense "translating institutions" (Koskinen 2008), "translation sites" (Simon 2019) or "translation spaces" (Koskinen 2014), as well as their functions and effects. In the case of reception centres, this is of particular importance because the sole analysis of official language and translation policies or of media discourses about translation in the context of migration does not suffice to account for the 'messy' social reality of translation practices. The perspective of human differentiation allows for an

---

14. This observation belongs to and confirms findings in research on 'non-professional translation and interpreting' (Antonini et al. 2017; Grbić and Kujamäki 2018). If we consider Paloposki's historical analysis of the translator-category, we can come to the conclusion that such phenomena seem to be the norm, rather than the exception. She convincingly writes: "We may have been applying our present understanding of translators (as members of a profession we know, train and study) to a heterogenous group of people from the past, trying to tie them up with our project of professionalisation" (Paloposki 2016: 28).

15. Also cf. Grbić (2020) for the distinction between habitual and organised translation with reference to sign-language interpreting in Austria.

analysis of this reality by breaking down supposedly stable and durable categories into practices of human differentiation through which these categories arise in the first place. By studying translation ethnographically as a catalyst of (manifold forms of) human differentiation, we can grasp how translation is involved in the construction of the socio-cultural world in which it occurs (Dizdar and Rozmysłowicz 2023).

The combination of participant observation, interviews, and document collection proved particularly useful. Since translation and human differentiation are always situated practices, being present while they occur is an adequate methodological response. However, using only participant observation would not have been enough as we would not have been able to take into account factors that transcend specific situations, such as their path dependency on other situations. For instance, the official registration during which interpreters are recruited in RC A is based on the unofficial registration at the info point on the form that is used there. Practices of language-related human differentiation for the purposes of translation or recruiting interpreters thus turn out to be distributed across several situations. The sequence of these situations is in turn a result of the functional structure of the reception centre (as divided into sub-organisations that play different roles in the registration and accommodation of asylum seekers). This structure was something that we only got to know through interviews with different staff members whose accounts helped to understand how a reception centre 'works' and thus to contextualise situated practices of translation and human differentiation. Moreover, interviews in RC B helped us to identify a dependency of interpreter recruitment systems on variables such as size, role, and economic resources of reception centres. In this way, translators and interpreters became visible as *human categories* dependent on the structure and function of specific reception centres. Finally, the collection and analysis of documents such as bureaucratic forms turned out to be an important part of our research design as it added a further layer of meaning that the participants were not necessarily aware of: the aspect of materiality. As we have demonstrated, the written fixation of 'languages' in combination with other categories such as nationality plays a consequential role in sorting speakers into 'language boxes'.

Our findings contain manifold empirical and theoretical connections to ongoing, sociologically oriented research in translation studies — especially to research on non-professional translation and interpreting (Antonini et al. 2017; Grbić and Kujamäki 2018), interpreting in the context of asylum procedures (Lagnado 2002; Pöllabauer 2004, 2005, 2006, 2007, 2008, 2022; Inghilleri 2005; Macfarlane et al. 2009, 2020; Merlini 2009; Maltby 2010; Daniyan 2010; Bourke and Lucadou-Wells 2016), translation spaces (or sites/zones) (e.g., Koskinen 2014; Cronin and Simon 2014; Simon 2019), and translator/interpreter recruitment systems (Kujamäki and Pasanen 2019; Grbić 2020, 2023). A discussion of the benefits of using the concept of 'human differentiation' (in combination with an ethnographic approach) for these research fields would be a further step towards an intra-disciplinary debate about appropriate tools for the analysis of the roles of translation in the construction of the socio-cultural world.

Funding

This research was funded by the Deutsche Forschungsgemeinschaft (DFG, German Research Foundation) — SFB 1482/1-2021-442261292.

References

Angelelli, Claudia V. 2004. *Medical Interpreting and Cross-Cultural Communication.* Cambridge: Cambridge University Press.

Antonini, Rachele, Cirillo Letizia, Linda Rossato, and Ira Torresi (eds). 2017. *Non-Professional Interpreting and Translations: State of the Art and Future of an Emerging Field of Research.* Amsterdam & Philadelphia: John Benjamins.

Blommaert, Jan. 2009. "Language, Asylum, and the National Order." *Current Anthropology* 50 (4): 415–441.

Blommaert, Jan. 2013. *Ethnography, Superdiversity and Linguistic Landscapes. Chronicles of Complexity.* Bristol: Multilingual Matters.

Bonfiglio, Thomas P. 2010. *Mother Tongues and Nations: The Invention of the Native Speaker.* Berlin: De Gruyter Mouton.

Bourdieu, Pierre. 2012. *Was heißt sprechen? Zur Ökonomie des sprachlichen Tausches.* Translated by Hella Beister. Wien: new academic press.

Bourke, John F., and Rosemary Lucadou-Wells. 2016. "Interpreters, Translators and Legal Practitioners: A Perspective of Working Together for Refugee and Asylum-Seeking Clients in Australia." *Redit — Revista Electrónica de Didáctica de La Traducción y La Interpretación* 2: 1–10.

Bowker, Geoffrey, and Susan Leigh Star. 2000. *Sorting Thing Out. Classification and its Consequences.* Cambridge, MA & London: The MIT Press.

Busch, Brigitta. 2010. "...und Ihre Sprache? Über die Schwierigkeiten, eine scheinbar einfache Frage zu beantworten." *Stichproben. Wiener Zeitschrift für kritische Afrikastudien* 19 (10): 9–33.

Cronin, Michael, and Sherry Simon. 2014. "Introduction: The City as Translation Zone." *Translation Studies* 7 (2): 119–132.

Daniyan, Femi. 2010. "Interpretation in Irish Asylum Law: Practical Problems — Real Solutions." *Community Interpreting in Ireland and Abroad,* 18 (2): 127–142.

Davidson, Donald. 1992. "The Second Person." *Midwest Studies in Philosophy* 17 (1): 255–267.

Derrida, Jacques. 2003. *Die Einsprachigkeit des Anderen oder die ursprüngliche Prothese.* Translated by Michael Wetzel. München: Fink.

Dizdar, Dilek. 2019. "Translation und Grenze. Versuch einer translationswissenschaftlichen Neufiguration." In *Übersetzung. Über die Möglichkeit, Pädagogik anders zu denken*, ed. by Nicolas Engel, and Stefan Köngeter, 57–74. Wiesbaden: Springer.

Dizdar, Dilek. 2021. "Translation als Katalysator von Humandifferenzierung. Eine translationswissenschaftliche Bestandsaufnahme." In *Humandifferenzierung: Disziplinäre Perspektiven und empirische Sondierungen*, ed. by Dilek Dizdar, Stefan Hirschauer, Johannes Paulmann, and Gabriele Schabacher, 135–159. Weilerswist: Velbrück.

Dizdar, Dilek, Stefan Hirschauer, Johannes Paulmann, and Gabriele Schabacher (eds). 2021. *Humandifferenzierung: Disziplinäre Perspektiven und empirische Sondierungen.* Weilerswist: Velbrück.

Dizdar, Dilek, and Tomasz Rozmysłowicz. 2023. "Collectivities in Translation (Studies)." *Translation in Society* 2 (1): 1–14.

Flynn, Peter. 2004. "Skopos Theory: An Ethnographic Enquiry." *Perspectives, Studies in Translatology* 12 (4): 270–285.

Flynn, Peter, and Luc van Doorslaer. 2016. "City and Migration: A Crossroads for Non-Institutionalized Translation." *European Journal of Applied Linguistics* 4 (1): 73–92.

Grbić, Nadja. 2020. "Autorisierte Translator*innen und un_übersetzte Subjekte: Rekrutierungsformen des Gebärdensprachdolmetschens in der Geschichte." In *Übersetztes und Unübersetztes: Das Versprechen der Translation und ihre Schattenseiten*, ed. by Nadja Grbić, Susanne Korbel, Judith Laister, Rafael Y. Schögler, Olaf Terpitz, and Michaela Wolf, 55–82. Bielefeld: transcript.

Grbić, Nadja. 2023. *Gebärdensprachdolmetschen als Beruf: Professionalisierung als Grenzziehungsarbeit: Eine historische Fallstudie in Österreich.* Bielefeld: transcript.

Grbić, Nadja, and Pekka Kujamäki. 2018. "Professional vs Non-Professional? How Boundary Work Shapes Research Agendas in Translation and Interpreting Studies." In *Moving Boundaries in Translation Studies*, ed. by Helle V. Dam, Matilde Nisbeth Brøgger, and Karen Korning Zethsen, 113–131. London: Routledge.

Gustafsson, Kristina. 2023. "The Ambiguity of Interpreting: Ethnographic Interviews with Public Service Interpreters." In *The Routledge Handbook of Public Service Interpreting*, ed. by Laura Gavioli, and Cecilia Wadensjö, 32–45. London: Routledge.

Hasenfeld, Yeheskel. 1972. "People Processing Organizations: An Exchange Approach." *American Sociological Review* 37 (3): 256–263.

Hill, Jospeh C., Diane C. Lillo-Martin, and Sandra. K. Wood. 2019. *Sign Languages: Structures and Contexts.* London: Routledge.

Hirschauer, Stefan. 2017. *Un/Doing Differences: Praktiken der Humandifferenzierung.* Weilerswist: Velbrück.

Hirschauer, Stefan. 2021. "Menschen unterscheiden. Grundlinien einer Theorie der Humandifferenzierung." *Zeitschrift für Soziologie* 51 (3–4): 155–174.

Hirschauer, Stefan. 2023. "Telling People Apart: Outline of a Theory of Human Differentiation." *Sociological Theory* 41 (4): 352–376.

Hirschauer, Stefan, and Damaris Nübling. 2021. "Sinnschichten des Kulturellen und die Aggregatzustände der Sprache." In *Humandifferenzierung: Disziplinäre Perspektiven und empirische Sondierungen*, ed. by Dilek Dizdar, Stefan Hirschauer, Johannes Paulmann, and Gabriele Schabacher, 58–83. Weilerswist: Velbrück.

Iacono, Katia, Barbara Heinisch, and Sonja Pöllabauer (eds). 2024. *Zwischenstationen / Inbetween. Kommunikation mit geflüchteten Menschen / Communicating with Refugees.* Berlin: Frank & Timme.

Inghilleri, Moira. 2005. "Mediating Zones of Uncertainty: Interpreter Agency, the Interpreting Habitus and Political Asylum Adjudication." *The Translator* 11 (1): 69–85.

King, Alexandra C., and Jessica Woodroffe. 2017. "Walking Interviews." In *Handbook of Research Methods in Health Social Sciences*, ed. by Pranee Liamputtong, 1–22. Singapore: Springer.

Kühl, Jana. 2016. "Walking Interviews als Methode zur Erhebung alltäglicher Raumproduktionen." *Europa Regional* 23 (2): 35–48.

Kinnunen, Tuija. 2010. "Agency, Activity and Court Interpreting." In *Translators' Agency*, ed. by Tuija Kinnunen, and Kaisa Koskinen, 126–164. Tampere: Tampere University Press.

Koskela, Merja, Kaisa Koskinen, and Nina Pilke. 2017. "Bilingual Formal Meeting as a Context of Translatoriality." *Target. International Journal of Translation Studies* 29 (3): 464–485.

Koskinen, Kaisa. 2008. *Translating Institutions. An Ethnographic Study of EU Translation.* Manchester: St. Jerome.

Koskinen, Kaisa. 2014. "Tampere as a Translation Space." *Translation Studies* 7 (2): 186–202.

Kujamäki, Pekka, and Päivi Pasanen. 2019. "Interpreting Prisoners-Of-War. Sketches of a Military Translation Culture in Finnish POW Camps During World War II (1941–1944)." *Chronotopos* 1: 173–197.

Lagnado, Jacob. 2002. "Beyond Neutrality: The Translator-Interpreter and the Right to Asylum in Britain." *Íkala* 7 (13): 63–71.

MacFarlane, Anne, Zhanna Dzebisova, Dmitri Karapish, Bosiljka Kovačević, Florence Ogbebor, and Ekaterina Okonkwo. 2009. "Arranging and Negotiating the Use of Informal Interpreters in General Practice Consultations: Experiences of Refugees and Asylum Seekers in the West of Ireland." *Social Science & Medicine* 69 (2): 210–214.

MacFarlane, Anne, Susann Huschke, Kevin Pottie, Fern R. Hauck, Kim Griswold, and Mark F. Harris. 2020. "Barriers to the Use of Trained Interpreters in Consultations with Refugees in Four Resettlement Countries: A Qualitative Analysis Using Normalisation Process Theory." *BMC Family Practice* 21: 1–8.

Maltby, Matthew. 2010. "Institutional Identities of Interpreters in the Asylum Application Context: A Critical Discourse Analysis of Interpreting Policies in the Voluntary Sector." In *Text and Context. Essays on Translation and Interpreting in Honour of Ian Mason*, ed. by Mona Baker, María Calzada Pérez, and Maeve Olohan, 209–233. Manchester: St. Jerome.

Merlini, Raffaela. 2009. "Seeking Asylum and Seeking Identity in a Mediated Encounter: The Projection of Selves through Discursive Practices." *Interpreting* 11 (1): 57–93.

Mokre, Monika. 2015. *Solidarität als Übersetzung: Überlegungen zum Refugee Protest Camp Vienna.* Wien: transversal texts.

Paloposki, Outi. 2016. "Translating and Translators Before the Professional Project." *The Journal of Specialised Translation* 25: 15–32.

Pöllabauer, Sonja. 2004. "Interpreting in Asylum Hearings: Issues of Role, Responsibility and Power." *Interpreting* 6 (2): 143–180.

Pöllabauer, Sonja. 2005. *"I Don't Understand Your English, Miss": Dolmetschen bei Asylanhörungen.* Tübingen: Narr.

Pöllabauer, Sonja. 2006. "'Translation Culture' in Interpreted Asylum Hearings." In *Sociocultural Aspects of Translating and Interpreting*, ed. by Anthony Pym, Miriam Shlesinger, and Zuzana Jettmarová, 151–162. Amsterdam: Benjamins.

Pöllabauer, Sonja. 2007. "Interpreting in Asylum Hearings: Issues of Saving Face." In *The Critical Link 4: Professionalisation of Interpreting in the Community. Selected Papers from the 4th International Conference on Interpreting in Legal, Health and Social Service Settings, Stockholm, Sweden, 20–23 May 2004*, ed. by Cecilia Wadensjö, Birgitta Englund Dimitrova, and Anna-Lena Nilsson, 39–52. Amsterdam & Philadelphia: John Benjamins.

Pöllabauer, Sonja. 2008. "Forschung zum Dolmetschen im Asylverfahren: Interdisziplinarität und Netzwerke." *Lebende Sprachen* 53 (3): 121–129.

Pöllabauer, Sonja. 2013. "Interpreting in an Asylum Context: Interpreter Ttraining as the Linchpin for Improving Procedural Quality." In *Interpreter Training in Conflict and Post-Conflict Scenarios*, ed. by Lucía Ruiz Rosendo, and Marija Todorova, 129–145. London & New York: Routledge.

Pöllabauer, Sonja. 2022. "The Interpreter's Role." Translated by Ursula Stachl-Peier. In *Handbook for Interpreters in Asylum Procedures*, ed. by UNHCR Austria, and Sonja Pöllabauer, 50–71. Vienna: UNHCR Austria.

Prior, Lindsay. 2003. *Using Documents in Social Research*. London, Thousand Oaks & New Delhi: Sage.

Risku, Hanna, Regina Rogl, and Jelena Milosevic (eds). 2019. *Translation Practice in the Field. Current Research on Socio-Cognitive Processes*. Amsterdam & Philadelphia: John Benjamins.

Sakai, Naoki. 2018. "The Modern Regime of Translation and Its Politics." In *A History of Modern Translation Knowledge: Sources, Concepts, Effects*, ed. by Lieven D'hulst, and Yves Gambier, 61–74. Amsterdam & Philadelphia: John Benjamins.

Schabacher, Gabriele. 2021. "Infrastrukturen und Verfahren der Humandifferenzierung. Medienkulturwissenschaftliche Perspektiven." In *Humandifferenzierung. Disziplinäre Perspektiven und empirische Sondierungen*, ed. by Dilek Dizdar, Stefan Hirschauer, Johannes Paulmann, and Gabriele Schabacher, 287–313. Weilerswist: Velbrück.

Silverstein, Michael. 1996. "Monoglot 'Standard' in America: Standardization and Metaphors of Linguistic Hegemony." In *The Matrix of Language: Contemporary Linguistic Anthropology*, ed. by Donald Brenneis, and Ronald K. S. Macaulay, 284–306. Boulder: Westview Press.

Simon, Sherry. 2019. *Translation Sites: A Field Guide*. London: Routledge.

Wolf, Michaela. 2012. *Die vielsprachige Seele Kakaniens. Übersetzen und Dolmetschen in der Habsburgermonarchie 1848 bis 1918*. Wien: Böhlau.

CHAPTER 14

Lives in translation

Listening to the voices of asylum seekers

Marija Todorova
Hong Kong Baptist University

This chapter discusses the methodological implications of conducting ethnographic research on interpreting and (self-)translation practices performed by asylum seekers and refugees, based on the author's study conducted in Hong Kong involving events showcasing refugee talents. The ethical implications of conducting ethnographic research with vulnerable populations, especially women, are discussed, along with this researcher's recommendations. The chapter investigates the difficulties refugees and asylum seekers in Hong Kong face, highlighting the emergence of grassroots non-profit organisations founded by and for refugees and asylum seekers as essential support structures facilitating integration, promoting cultural exchange, and addressing challenges faced by marginalised individuals, thereby fostering a more inclusive, compassionate, and diverse society.

Keywords: refugees, asylum seekers, women, ethnography, cultural mediation, ethics

1. Introduction

In my previous research on interpreters in conflict-related scenarios, I have extensively explored the experiences of professional and non-professional interpreters working in refugee camps (Todorova 2020), informed by personal observations during my work experience as a UNHCR interpreter and through conversations with other fellow interpreters. In this context, I have highlighted the fact that interpreters engaged in humanitarian interpreting are often refugees themselves, employed not only for their linguistic skills but also for their capacity to comprehend cultural codes and empathise with refugees due to shared experiences (Todorova 2021a; Tedjouong and Todorova 2023). However, asylum seekers and refugees not only interpret for others, they also translate themselves and their identities in order to mediate between their native culture and the host country's

https://doi.org/10.1075/btl.165.14tod
Available under the CC BY-NC 4.0 license. © 2025 John Benjamins Publishing Company

culture in an effort to belong and forge meaningful connections with the local population (Todorova 2022). Building upon these previous studies and the current state of research on the topic of interpreting and translation in refugee contexts, the research presented in this chapter aims to delve further into these practices, but this time from the perspective of a researcher applying field research in capturing the translation practices undertaken by refugees as an integral part of their integration process. By adopting an ethnographic approach, the asylum seekers' activities and experiences are placed at the centre of the analysis, enabling the researcher to gain a comprehensive understanding of social practices embedded within structural constraints. Translation, for the purposes of this chapter, will be understood as a broad practice incorporating both oral interpreting and written translation activities, as well as "the human ability to understand and transform meaning" (Ciribuco 2020:179) including the lived experiences of asylum seekers representing their identity in a foreign language.

The analysis presented in this chapter is grounded in field observations of activities undertaken by asylum seekers and refugees in Hong Kong, in association with several non-profit organisations, including *Grassroot Futures, RUN Hong Kong, Centre for Refugees, Africa Center in Hong Kong* and others. This research encompasses personal observations of events wherein asylum seekers and refugees interacted with the local Hong Kong population, including food-sharing events, hiking trips, fashion shows, music and storytelling events, and other informal gatherings of a similar nature. These personal observations have provided me with insight into how such events serve as translation occurrences that empower refugees and asylum seekers to negotiate their position within the local community and establish meaningful relationships with the local public (Todorova 2022), in the process often serving as cultural mediators (Todorova 2023). However, as a participant in these field activities, I have also become aware of the constraints of conducting observations and interacting with members of a highly vulnerable group within Hong Kong's population. Based on that personal experience, in this chapter, I aim to elaborate on the utilisation of ethnographic methods designed to capture translation practices by asylum seekers and refugees as they occur in real time. In particular, the chapter will discuss the ethical implications and considerations of conducting ethnographic research with vulnerable refugee women.

2. Ethnographic study of translation practices for the vulnerable

Critical ethnography is a research approach that applies ethnographic methods to the study of shared experiences within cultures or subcultures in specific settings, rather than across entire communities (Hammersley and Atkinson 2007). In this context, field research, and particularly ethnographic research and participant observation, are qualitative research methods that involve researchers immersing themselves in the natural environments of the researched subjects to gather data and insights. Within the process of ethnographic research, the goal is to make visible what is typically invisible, critique underlying assumptions, and highlight what is taken for granted in social fields. Additionally, this research seeks to highlight that ethnographic accounts of human action should challenge socially constructed labels and categories to foster a more inclusive understanding of the experiences of marginalised populations.

Employing ethnography in translation studies has yielded valuable insights into the translation processes of professional or non-professional translators operating in vulnerable populations' working environments, primarily within humanitarian non-governmental organisations (Tesseur 2014, 2019, 2023) and the realm of immigration law (Jacobs and Maryns 2022). In particular, Tesseur (2023) has investigated translation policies and practices within non-governmental organisations, focusing on the role of translation in promoting social justice. In the context of immigration and asylum encounters, Jacobs and Maryns (2022) have employed a linguistic-ethnographic approach (Tusting 2020; on linguistic ethnography, see also Koskinen, Chapter 1, and Napier, Chapter 2, this volume) to examine the dynamics of lawyer-client interactions in the field of immigration law, focusing on how agency and vulnerability are constructed and negotiated through communicative practices.

Based on observations and interpreter interviews in refugee camp settings, I have previously reflected on the importance of empathy, cultural awareness, and specialised training for interpreters in these crucial yet challenging contexts (Todorova 2020). In these contexts, it often happens that linguistic assistants, who have knowledge of the languages involved but are not trained in interpreting, are former or current refugees themselves, who share not just a language but also similar experiences with the refugees requiring immediate assistance. A distinctive aspect of interpreting for refugees in emergency situations is the interpreters' propensity to feel a strong connection and identify with the refugees for whom they interpret. As explained by my research, although interpreters agreed that they should remain invisible, most of them take a proactive role, working independently and suggesting remedial activities (Todorova 2016). This position of humanitarian interpreters is important to consider because of its implications for the interpreting process, as it "would indicate that while they may be intuitively aware of their agency in the process, the dominant education narrative still works to cancel that out" (Todorova 2016: 238). To be thoroughly effective in their work, humanitarian interpreters should "perceive their role as powerful and visible" and acknowledge the agency they possess (Angelelli 2004: 3).

More recently, within translation studies research, the method of ethnographic participant observation has been seen as particularly suited to observing and documenting linguistic and non-linguistic practices of asylum seekers and refugees as they understand and navigate their new surroundings. Ciribuco investigated the role of everyday translation practices in the lives of asylum seekers living in Italy, examining how "transfer between different meaning-making systems" (2020: 197) shapes their experiences and contributes to the construction of social relations in the local context. Elsewhere, I have also drawn on personal observations, supplemented by interviews, to explore the translation practices of refugee culinary cultures in Hong Kong, analysing how food-sharing events serve as translation encounters that contribute to the integration processes of asylum seekers in Hong Kong (Todorova 2022). The study revealed the significance of this type of (self-)translation in fostering cultural exchange and understanding within diverse communities.

This fairly extensive use of ethnography as a tool for rendering visible the ordinarily invisible, scrutinizing underlying assumptions, and emphasizing aspects taken for granted in social fields, has been reflected in research on how to use ethnographic methodologies in translation studies (Koskinen 2006) and examining the position of the researcher in these types of studies (Milošević and Risku 2020). Examining the interaction between the researcher and the subjects of observations conducted in translation-related workplace environments, Milošević and Risku (2020: 125) point to the various factors that influence the events and subsequently the interpretation of results. In another example, Tesseur (2023: 158) reflects on the role of the researcher as an activist who aims at raising awareness and achieving change in language and translation practices and policies in international non-governmental organisations. Tesseur also points to the need for "critical re-examination of the role of the researcher in social sciences and ethnographic research designs and methodologies in order to ... produce high-quality and ethical research with valid results" (2019: 201).

3.   The ethics of conducting ethnographic research with vulnerable refugee women

The methodological implications of conducting ethnographic research with asylum seekers have come into the focus of reflexive analysis only in the past couple of decades. To begin with, researchers in these contexts stress the need to be mindful of the ethical considerations involved in studying marginalised populations, as they may "inadvertently deny their basic human need for recognition — that is, to be heard and seen as human — by relying solely on testimonies from individuals working with asylum seekers rather than engaging with asylum seekers directly as research subjects" (Bloom 2010: 60). Engaging with asylum seekers directly, rather than with their community interpreters or community facilitators and mediators, and empowering such individuals may facilitate empathy in the reader and contribute to reinforcing the recognition of the human status of an otherwise disenfranchised and mistreated population.

Bloom (2010) has further critically examined the ethical implications of conducting research involving asylum seekers, questioning whether they are treated as subjects or objects in the research process and calling for a more equitable and participatory approach. Goodkind and Deacon (2004) have discussed methodological challenges faced when conducting research with refugee women in particular, and have come up with principles aimed at recognizing the needs and experiences of this multiply marginalised population. They propose six principles to consider when conducting research with refugee women, based on the challenges they encountered and their successes and failures in addressing them. These principles include: (1) developing strategies for involving marginalised refugee women in research; (2) weighing the advantages and limitations of quantitative and qualitative methodologies and innovatively combining them; (3) preparing for the extensive time and effort required in quantitative measure construction; (4) considering gendered decision-making structures in refugee women's lives and their potential impact on the research process; (5) planning for refugee women's common triple burden of working outside the home, managing their households, and adjusting to life in a new country; and (6) attending to refugee women's cultural norms and unfamiliarity with the concept of interviewing (Goodkind and Deacon 2004: 728–729). Similarly, Leaning (2001), looking at international instruments for ethics and protection of refugees, has addressed the ethical considerations involved in conducting research with refugee populations, emphasising the importance of ensuring their welfare, dignity, and informed consent throughout the research process. Moreover, Smith (2009) has examined ethical considerations and effective methods in ethnographic research, utilising a case study involving Afghan refugees in California. The study underscored the importance of cultural sensitivity, informed consent, and rapport building to ensure ethical and accurate data collection.

The ethical dilemma faced by researchers in this context involves striking a balance between protecting vulnerable participants and fostering dialogue and recognition of asylum seekers as fellow human subjects (Zion, Briskman, and Loff 2010). Furthermore, Mackenzie, McDowell, and Pittaway (2007) have argued that adhering to the principle of "do no harm" is insufficient in refugee research, and have explored the complexities of constructing ethical relationships with research participants in this context. According to them, researchers must attend to and respond to the effects of forced displacement, encampment, and dependence on humanitarian assistance on refugee participants' capacities for autonomy while also recognizing and respecting their resilience and agency.

In conclusion, critical ethnography offers a valuable framework for studying the experiences of marginalised populations, such as asylum seekers and refugees, in specific settings. By adhering to the principles outlined by Goodkind and Deacon (2004) and addressing the ethical challenges involved in this type of research, researchers can construct meaningful, inclusive, and responsive research relationships that contribute to a greater understanding of the complexities surrounding the experiences of these vulnerable populations. Ethnographic research can thus play a crucial role in fostering empathy, challenging socially constructed categories, and advocating for the recognition and inclusion of marginalised individuals in the broader human circle as rights-bearing participants.

4. Ethnographic work with asylum seekers and refugees in Hong Kong

Drawing on applied linguistics and its recent intersection with translation in multilingual contexts (Creese, Blackledge, and Hu 2018; Baynham and Lee 2019), this study places individual translation activities at the forefront of integration research, thereby fostering a perspective on integration rooted in individuals actively negotiating and compromising between divergent worldviews. In particular, it seeks to understand how asylum seekers and refugees in Hong Kong translate their cultures and identities for the local host population.

4.1 The study

Despite its longstanding history of refugee flows, Hong Kong has been characterised as one of the regions with the slowest pace of asylum claims processing and one of the lowest acceptance rates globally (Todorova 2021b). Since 2004, a mere 65 out of nearly 30,000 cases have been deemed substantiated, representing less than 0.4 per cent of applications (Lau and Gheorghiu 2018). According to the Hong Kong Immigration Department, there are currently 10,477 outstanding protection claims within the Hong Kong Special Administrative Region. These asylum seekers originate from diverse ethnic backgrounds, fleeing violent conflicts and political persecution from various regions in Asia, Africa, and the Middle East.

One of the primary challenges faced by asylum seekers in Hong Kong is the prohibition of working, leaving them without income and reliant on welfare and charity. This dependence, coupled with limited interaction with the local population, has contributed to a negative perception of asylum seekers in general in the eyes of the local population. In response, refugees and asylum seekers have begun establishing grassroots non-profit organisations, such as *Refugee Union, Harmony, Art Women,* and most recently *Humanity Seekers.* These organisations facilitate opportunities for refugees and asylum seekers to engage in activities that promote integration into the local community and represent their culture in a manner that is palatable to the local population. Activities range from designing clothes and organising dinner parties to participating in hiking events aimed at introducing Hongkongers to refugee cultures.

The field research referenced in this study was conducted over a period of two years in Hong Kong between 2021 and 2023. During this time, as a researcher, I attended more than ten events organised by charity organisations involving mainly women asylum seekers and refugees. The events were documented by photographs, avoiding photographing the faces of the asylum seekers to protect their identity. Rather than their faces, the photographs include images taken from the back, one quarter portrait, or a face under a mask (particularly during fashion shows). In addition, my personal observations were supplemented with insights gained from four in-depth interviews conducted with asylum-seeking women from four different countries, who had lived in Hong Kong for around 10 years each while waiting for the result of their non-refoulement applications, to better understand their experiences and challenges in Hong Kong. The researcher met and got to know these women during the observed events, but they were also referred by the relevant charity organisation. Subsequently, they agreed on a more in-depth personal interview. The interviews were conducted at public venues and lasted for about an hour. Based on consent from the interviewees, some of the interviews were recorded in audio format, yet other interviewees were reluctant to use recording equipment, so I took notes during interviews and later confirmed the written notes with each respective interviewee. The notes were taken in English, which was the language in which each interview was conducted. It is important to note here that English is a second language for both the researcher and the interviewees. The interviews were structured around questions related to the background and culture of the interviewees, their feeling of belonging in Hong Kong, activities they have been involved in while in Hong Kong, and how Hong Kong society can provide more assistance in making them feel more welcome. The interviews were analysed based on themes including the use of language in everyday activities, misunderstandings and feeling of belonging.

The observed events were organised by different charities. As the charity behind the *Table of Two Cities* project, *Grassroot Futures* invites refugee women to cook their national and traditional dishes to be shared at dining events intended for the local population. They also run a multiyear project, *Crochet for Well-being*, where they exclusively work with asylum seeking women on developing their crocheting skills, but also share the crocheted products with the local community. *RUN Hong Kong* helps asylum seekers in Hong Kong overcome trauma and fight depression by running, hiking, and generally spending time outdoors. They collaborate with other organisations to arrange English and Cantonese classes for refugees, thereby facilitating their integration into Hong Kong society. *Christian Action Centre for Refugees* is another organisation that provides a range of support services to refugees in Hong Kong, including language classes. They offer English classes designed to help refugees and asylum seekers develop practical language skills necessary for daily life and communication in Hong Kong. Additionally, the organisation provides other services such as counselling, vocational training, and general educational support. While not directed exclusively towards the asylum seeking and refugee community in Hong Kong, the *Africa Center* was established by a refugee from Zimbabwe and organises cultural sharing activities between African migrants in Hong Kong and the local population. They organise regular food sharing events, among other occasional activities, sometimes involving asylum-seeking women.

These grassroots non-profit organisations try to help refugees and asylum seekers overcome negative perceptions about them through various strategies and activities aimed at fostering understanding, promoting cultural exchange, and challenging stereotypes. By organizing events and activities that showcase the rich cultural heritage of refugees and asylum seekers, these organisations provide an opportunity for the local population to engage with and learn about different cultures. By involving refugees and asylum seekers in community-based activities, these organisations help them build social connections and foster a sense of belonging within the local community (Todorova 2022). This engagement helps challenge the notion that refugees and asylum seekers are a burden on Hong Kong society, instead portraying them as active and contributing members of the community.

By raising awareness about the challenges faced by refugees and asylum seekers and advocating for their rights, these organisations help to counter negative perceptions and promote empathy and understanding among the local population. They provide platforms for refugees and asylum seekers to share their personal stories and experiences, bringing back to the fore their humanity and helping the local population better understand their struggles and aspirations. Personal narratives help challenge preconceived notions and stereotypes, fostering empathy and encouraging more positive attitudes towards refugees and asylum seekers. However, the challenges remain in the use of translation, especially translation into Chinese as the dominantly used language by most of the Hong Kong local population (Todorova 2025).

This research explores the activities of asylum seekers and refugees through the lenses of (self-)translation and community cultural mediation, as previously analysed in Todorova (2023). The following sections will delve into the ethnographic research processes and their ethical implications, derived from observing these encounters and engaging in conversations with participants. Additionally, the discussion will address the rationale behind choosing to conduct research with asylum seekers and refugees, providing insights into the motivations and considerations that underpin this research focus.

4.2 Ethical implications of ethnographic research

Researchers can balance protecting vulnerable participants and fostering dialogue with them by adhering to several key principles and practices that prioritise ethical considerations, participant well-being, and open communication.

4.2.1 *Engaging asylum seekers in translation studies*

In conducting translation and interpreting ethnographic research, studies are usually directed towards the interpreter or translator, regardless of whether they are professional or non-professional, who serves as a linguistic and cultural mediator between the asylum seekers and refugees and the representatives of their host communities. Research in translation and interpreting rarely includes the service users (Tekgül-Akın, Chapter 12, this volume, makes a similar observation referring to the readers of translations), especially the asylum seekers, often in an attempt to protect their safety. However, asylum seekers and refugees frequently find themselves in a position to serve as cultural mediators for other refugees, sometimes family members. Additionally, they are involved in practices of self-translation as a strategy of adaptation to their new life in the host country. Thus, in this research project, the focus shifted to these practices of self-translation and to the asylum seeker as a self-translator. In telling their own stories, the narratives of asylum seekers are intrinsically linked to the concept of self-translation (Todorova and Poposki 2022), as they are involved in talking about their experiences in their second language, which they often learned only after moving to a new country. The narrative, closely based on the interviewee's personal experiences of migration, trauma and experiences, uses the techniques of self-translation where the source culture is distinctly preserved and some of the original words are present in the dialogues (Todorova 2023).

The self-translator also acts as a cultural mediator, explaining the asylum seeker's culture to the researcher and the audience. During this research project, these practices of culture mediation often took shape as explanations of national dishes and food items. *Table of Two Cities* and *African Centre Hong Kong* organised a range of African *Soirées*, private dining experiences, or African cooking workshops. Each event frequently centred on a single country and was intended to showcase traditional dishes chosen by the (self-)designated asylum-seeker-cook from that country, who also served as the menu's curator. The translations involved in these refugee dishes have tended to change the original dishes for the benefit of a non-familiar audience by adapting the traditional recipes to more locally accepted and modern variants. This is because the cooks were aware that they were preparing food not just for themselves but for a multi-ethnic and multicultural community (Todorova 2022). The asylum-seeker-cooks were able to share their culture and culinary heritage with the community while also adapting their dishes to suit a local audience.

In my research, although all four interviewed asylum seekers chose to use pseudonyms, two of them pointed out that they would "like to be treated as human beings who can contribute to society" (Sofia) and "have the same needs any human being has to be recognised for their skills" (Nana). Engaging directly with the asylum seekers as self-translators and primary subjects of study was my deliberate choice as a researcher.

4.2.2 *Establishing ethical relationships*

A significant ethical issue encountered when conducting ethnographic research with asylum seekers is establishing ethical relationships with the women included in the study. The position of asylum seekers in Hong Kong is extremely precarious and frequently changing. Asylum seekers are often going through prolonged and difficult legal and appeal procedures that have significant consequences for their lives. In these circumstances, as a researcher I had to adapt my research methods or practices in response to participants' needs, concerns, or feedback. This required building trust and rapport with the participants, being sensitive to their cultural and linguistic backgrounds, and ensuring their safety and confidentiality. For this purpose, I shared my own stories of life in crises and conflict during the breakup of ex-Yugoslavia, creating a sense of closeness and shared experiences. However, I had to navigate power dynamics between myself and the participants, acknowledging my current position of privilege as a university employee.

In addition, Oakley (1981) has critically examined the gendered dimensions of interviewing in research, particularly with women as participants. On one hand, for Oakley, the shared trust built between women can lead to developing a real friendship (1981:46), while for other feminist critics (Thwaites 2017:np) "feminist interviewing can become contradictory and opaque", essentialising gender. However, both agree that the feminist interview can be framed by rules of showing genuine interest and compassion. In order to follow these rules, I not only engaged in interviewing the participants for the purposes of the project but also interacted with them outside of project activities in other shared activities and experiences, involving more members of the family and joint interests.

In the first instance of my research, when seeking to establish relationships with the asylum-seeking community in Hong Kong, initial connections were established through various gatekeepers. The first points of contact were the staff of the charities and organisations that provide assistance to asylum seekers. Establishing ethical and trustworthy relationships with the gatekeepers was of utmost importance for explaining my research motivations and gaining the trust of the community of asylum seekers themselves. The gatekeepers' knowledge of the community and individual situations was very important in selecting participants who were comfortable sharing their personal narratives. The relationship with the gatekeepers also allowed me to finetune my research questions and aims. Additionally, having several different entry points from different organisations was also helpful, as asylum seekers with different cultural and linguistic backgrounds tend to establish closer relationships with kindred organisations. In this way, the research secured diverse representation of the asylum-seeking community in Hong Kong, which includes members of various communities, such as Indonesian, Vietnamese, Filipino, Bangladeshi, Pakistani, Yemeni, Rwandan, Somali, Sri Lankan, Egyptian, Congolese, and Cameroonian nationals (in order of size of the community from the biggest to the smallest). Overall, the gatekeepers played a crucial role in facilitating access to the community. By providing additional information about the background of the interviewee and their particular situation (for example, being a single mother when divorce is a culturally taboo topic for the interviewee), they helped conduct the research in a culturally sensitive manner. Their support also helped extend the trust they have with the participant to include the researcher, which was essential for obtaining more details about the lives of the asylum seekers in Hong Kong, the obstacles they faced, and how they overcame these obstacles.

When conducting observations with asylum seekers, the field researcher is often a community outsider (Smith 2009). In this particular study, as a researcher, I found myself to be distanced twice, (1) as an outsider of the community of refugees and (2) as an outsider in the host country, being a migrant scholar from North Macedonia living in Hong Kong since 2011. However, this positionality has allowed me as the researcher to reflect on my own position as a newcomer, navigating and learning the local customs and going through a process of self-translation myself. Despite these points of convergence, an extensive secondary literature review was conducted about the asylum seekers' circumstances. Furthermore, I spent extended time developing cultural competency and building relationships with the community.

Finally, the notion of researcher objectivity and neutrality have long been contested in the social sciences, particularly in ethnographic research (Clifford and Marcus 1986). As a researcher, I aimed to validate the voices and the agency of the participants in the study, by explaining to them the objectives of the research to highlight their knowledge, skills, language and cultural diversity. Thus, the participants felt encouraged to share their experiences, perspectives, and opinions, "because they want the local community to know they can be productive community members" (Sofia). Whenever possible, I involved the participants in the research process, through participatory research methods such as sharing draft versions of analyses and accepting feedback, in order to help foster a sense of ownership and engagement. Involving the participants in the research process not only helped to ensure that their voices were heard but also helped to reduce power imbalances between the researcher and participants. This approach allowed for a more collaborative and respectful research experience, which ultimately led to richer and more nuanced findings.

4.2.3 Informed consent as a process

Researchers have a responsibility to maximise potential benefits and minimise potential harm to participants. This entails carefully considering the research design, ethical considerations, and potential consequences, as well as providing appropriate support or resources to participants if needed. Moreover, researchers should also prioritise obtaining informed consent from participants and ensuring confidentiality and anonymity throughout the research process. These ethical considerations are crucial for maintaining trust and respect between researchers and participants, and for upholding the integrity of the research findings.

Several volumes on research methodology in the field of interpreting and translation (e.g., Hale and Napier 2013; Saldanha and O'Brien 2013) have provided ample suggestions on how to write an informed consent form. They have also discussed the issues that might arise when collecting informed consent. Informed consent implicates notifying participants of all aspects of the research and acquiring their written or oral permission to use their outputs for research purposes in anonymised or non-anonymised form (Tiselius 2021:133). Using pseudonyms, aggregating data, and securely storing research materials protects participants' identities and personal information. Researchers should avoid sharing identifiable information in research findings or publications, to minimise the risk of stigmatisation, discrimination, or other negative consequences.

Ethics approval for the study presented in this chapter was granted by the relevant university research ethics committee, and all participants read and signed an informed consent form. According to university standards, the consent form was provided in the English language in a standard format, explaining the objectives of the study, anonymity, the possibility to withdraw their participation from the study and who to contact in a situation of misunderstanding. However, in order to be fully understood by the participants whose knowledge of English is at a basic level, the consent form still required some site translation in the form of an explanation in a plain language statement provided by the researcher. The use of plain language might offer some techniques to achieve a certain extent of improved readability and comprehension (Burger and Stadler 2019).

Finally, the question remains whether the research participants should be made aware of and able to read and contest the researcher's account of their sharing (Angrosino 2005). When data analysis is done and raw data has been used for findings, the participant cannot claim the right to findings (Iphofen 2020). For the purposes of my research, some of the interviews were digitally recorded to be additionally used as material for editing podcasts and creating comics, which constitute part of the project outputs. The participants felt a strong inclination to be involved in the whole process of using the recorded material, photos, and observations. Checking for consent before any of the project outputs were published contributed to building ongoing relationships with the participants. Similar to understanding informed consent as a process where the consent needs to be re-established during every step of the research process (Saldanha and O'Brien 2013: 44; see also Riondel, Chapter 8, this volume), before every public presentation the consent given by asylum seekers needs to be reconfirmed, as the status of the participant in the study might change and their circumstances might become more or less risky.

It is important to note that obtaining consent from asylum seekers is not a one-time event, but an ongoing process that needs to be revisited throughout the research project. Additionally, ensuring that participants have agency and are involved in the decision-making process regarding the use of their data can help build trust and foster positive relationships between researchers and participants.

4.2.4 Working with an interpreter

As a final ethical consideration, in my research, I had to make a decision on whether to use interpreters, especially in recorded interviews that may be used for further podcasts or other project activities. While some refugees may possess rudimentary language skills in Chinese or English, they might not have the advanced proficiency necessary to accurately convey intricate cultural concepts or nuances. This linguistic deficiency could give rise to misunderstandings or miscommunication between asylum seekers and local Hong Kong residents, further exacerbating the already complex process of cultural integration.

Tesseur (2023) has reported on the positive impact of visiting interviewees with a local interpreter who spoke English as well as both Russian, the more widespread, traditionally dominant language, and Kyrgyz, the local native language of most participants. In my context, this meant engaging an interpreter who speaks English and the native language variety of the participant (rather than the dominant language of the host community). In the case of Arabic, for example, an interpreter with knowledge of the Arabic dialect spoken by the participant would be viewed more positively.

Additionally, in my ethnographic research with asylum seekers in Hong Kong, I found it recommendable to ask the participants who requested or agreed to use interpreters for consent to use a certain interpreter. As the presence of an interpreter has a significant impact on the outputs of participants and can influence the relationship that the researcher builds with the participants over a period of time, participants feel more at ease when allowed to participate in the decision as to who will interpret for them. In my research, an additional limitation was the lack of interpreters in the language combinations that were required. Thus, very often, participants chose a member of their own community, either a community leader whom they could trust or a fellow asylum seeker who knew the culture and the languages.

Asylum seekers with knowledge of both their native culture and the host country's culture can act as cultural mediators, serving as a critical bridge between the two disparate cultures. By elucidating cultural norms, customs, and expectations for both refugees and locals, they facilitate mutual understanding and contribute significantly to the integration process. However, Lai and Mulayim have highlighted the obstacles encountered in training refugees to perform interpreting for their communities due to insufficient interpreting staff with expertise in these particular "rare and emerging languages" (2010: 48).

Many refugees who assume the role of cultural mediators may not have received formal training in translation, interpreting, or cultural mediation (see also Dizdar and Rozmysłowicz, Chapter 13, this volume). This lack of professional expertise can result in difficulties when attempting to convey complex cultural concepts or addressing sensitive issues, potentially undermining the efficacy of the mediation process. Furthermore, acting as a cultural mediator can be emotionally taxing for refugees, as they may find themselves caught between their own cultural identity and the need to adapt to their new environment. Managing the expectations of both their own community and the host community can prove to be an arduous endeavour especially for the non-professional refugee interpreter.

Refugees who undertake the responsibility of assuming the role of cultural mediators may also be grappling with personal challenges related to the integration process, such as securing employment, housing, and accessing essential services. This additional burden can strain their well-being and limit their ability to effectively mediate between cultures. Therefore, it is important for organisations and governments to provide adequate support and training for refugee interpreters to help them navigate these challenges. This can include mental health resources, language classes, and professional development opportunities to enhance their skills as cultural mediators.

5. Conclusion

This chapter examines the methodological implications of a study on asylum seekers and refugees in Hong Kong and the challenges faced by this community in their host country. The ethnographic research encompasses personal observations of events in which asylum seekers and refugees interacted with the local population as well as personal conversations with four women asylum seekers. The findings of the study suggest that such interactions can help bridge the gap between asylum seekers and the host community, fostering a sense of community and reducing social isolation. However, more research is needed to understand the long-term impact of these interactions on both refugees and host communities.

The chapter highlights the importance of considering the ethical implications of conducting research with vulnerable populations such as refugees and asylum seekers. It emphasises the need for researchers to prioritise the safety and well-being of participants, as well as to engage in ongoing dialogue with them to ensure that their voices are heard and their perspectives are accurately represented.

In summary, researchers engaging with vulnerable populations through the deployment of ethnographic methods must remain cognizant of their ethical responsibilities to maximise potential benefits and minimise potential harm to participants. This entails careful research design, considering potential consequences, and providing appropriate support or resources to participants. Obtaining informed consent, ensuring participant anonymity, and involving participants in decisions regarding interpreters are crucial aspects of ethical research conduct. By adhering to these principles and practices, researchers can protect vulnerable participants while fostering open, respectful dialogue and promoting a more accurate, nuanced understanding of marginalised populations' experiences and perspectives.

Moreover, it is important for researchers to acknowledge and address power imbalances that may exist between themselves and the participants, and to prioritise the needs and perspectives of the participants in their research. Additionally, researchers should engage in ongoing reflexivity and critical self-reflection to ensure that their own biases and assumptions do not negatively impact the research process or outcomes.

References

Angelelli, Claudia V. 2004. *Revisiting the Interpreter's Role*. Amsterdam & Philadelphia: John Benjamins.

Angrosino, Michael V. 2005. "Recontextualizing Observation: Ethnography, Pedagogy, and the Prospects for a Progressive Political Agenda." In *The SAGE Handbook of Qualitative Research*, ed. by Norman K. Denzin, and Yvonna S. Lincoln, 729–745. Thousand Oaks: Sage.

Baynham, Mike, and Tong King Lee. 2019. *Translation and Translanguaging*. Oxon: Routledge.

Bloom, Tendayi. 2010. "Asylum Seekers: Subjects or Objects of Research?" *The American Journal of Bioethics* 10 (2): 59–60.

Burger, Johanna Maria, and Leon de Stadler. 2019. "Plain Language: Can It Ever Be Plain Enough?" *Southern African Linguistics and Applied Language Studies* 37 (4): 325–338.

Ciribuco, Andrea. 2020. "Translating the Village: Translation as Part of the Everyday Lives of Asylum Seekers in Italy." *Translation Spaces* 9 (2): 179–201.

Clifford, James, and George E. Marcus. 1986. *Writing Culture: The Poetics and Politics of Ethnography*. Oakland, CA: University of California Press.

Creese, Angela, Adrian Blackledge, and Rachel Hu. 2018. "Translanguaging and Translation: The Construction of Social Difference Across City Spaces." *International Journal of Bilingual Education and Bilingualism* 21 (7): 841–852.

Goodkind, Jessica R., and Zermarie Deacon. 2004. "Methodological Issues in Conducting Research with Refugee Women: Principles for Recognizing and Re-Centering the Multiply Marginalized." *Journal of Community Psychology* 32 (6): 721–739.

Hale, Sandra, and Jemina Napier. 2013. *Research Methods in Interpreting: A Practical Resource*. London: Bloomsbury.

Hammersley, Martyn, and Paul Atkinson. 2007. *Ethnography: Principles in Practice*. 3rd edition. London: Routledge.

Iphofen, Ron. 2020. *Research Ethics in Ethnography/Anthropology*. European Commission. https://ec.europa.eu/research/participants/data/ref/h2020/other/hi/ethics-guide-ethnoganthrop_en.pdf

Jacobs, Marie, and Katrijn Maryns. 2022. "Agency and Vulnerability in the Field of Immigration Law: A Linguistic-Ethnographic Perspective on Lawyer-Client Interaction." *Journal of Law and Society* 49 (3): 542–566.

Koskinen, Kaisa. 2006. "Going into the Field: Ethnographic Methods in Translation Studies." In *Übersetzen – Translating – Traduire: Towards a 'Social Turn'?* ed. by Michaela Wolf, 109–118. Berlin: LIT.

Lai, Miranda, and Sedat Mulayim. 2010. "Training Refugees to Become Interpreters for Refugees." *The International Journal of Translating and Interpreting Research* 2 (1): 48–60.

Lau, Pui Yan, and Iulia Gheorghiu. 2018. "Vanishing Selves Under Hong Kong's Unified Screening Mechanism." *Cultural Diversity in China* 3 (1): 21–35.

Leaning, Jennifer. 2001. "Ethics of Research in Refugee Populations." *Lancet* 357 (9266): 1432–1433.

Mackenzie, Catriona, Christopher McDowell, and Eileen Pittaway. 2007. "Beyond 'Do No Harm': The Challenge of Constructing Ethical Relationships in Refugee Research." *Journal of Refugee Studies* 20 (2): 299–319.

Milošević, Jelena, and Hanna Risku. 2020. "Situated Cognition and the Ethnographic Study of Translation Processes: Translation Scholars as Outsiders, Consultants and Passionate Participants." *Linguistica Antverpiensia* 19: 111–131.

Oakley, Anne. 1981. "Interviewing Women: A Contradiction in Terms." In *Doing Feminist Research*, ed. by Helen Roberts, 30–58. Boston: Routledge & Kegan Paul.

Saldanha, Gabriela, and Sharon O'Brien. 2013. *Research Methodologies in Translation Studies*. Oxon: Routledge.

Smith, J. Valerie. 2009. "Ethical and Effective Ethnographic Research Methods: A Case Study with Afghan Refugees in California." *Journal of Empirical Research on Human Research Ethics* 4 (3): 59–72.

Tedjouong, Ebenezer, and Marija Todorova. 2023. "Training Needs of Interpreters in the Refugee Crisis in Africa." In *Interpreter Training in Conflict and Post-Conflict Scenarios*, ed. by Lucia Ruiz Rosendo, and Marija Todorova, 101–113. Oxon: Routledge.

Tesseur, Wine. 2014. "Institutional Multilingualism in NGOs: Amnesty International's Strategic Understanding of Multilingualism." *Meta* 59 (3): 557–577.

Tesseur, Wine. 2019. "Listening, Languages and the Nature of Knowledge and Evidence: What We Can Learn from Investigating 'Listening' in NGOs." In *Learning and Using Languages in Ethnographic Research*, ed. by Robert Gibb, Annabel Tremlett, and Julien Danero-Iglesias, 193–206. Bristol & Blue Ridge Summit, PA: Multilingual Matters.

Tesseur, Wine. 2023. *Translation as Social Justice: Translation Policies and Practices in Non-Governmental Organisations*. Oxon: Routledge.

Thwaites, Rachel. 2017. "(Re)Examining the Feminist Interview: Rapport, Gender 'Matching,' and Emotional Labour." *Frontiers in Sociology* 2: Art. 18.

Tiselius, Elisabet. 2021. "Informed Consent: An Overlooked Part of Ethical Research in Interpreting Studies." *INContext* 1 (1): 83–100.

Todorova, Marija. 2016. "Interpreting conflict mediation in Kosovo and Macedonia." *Linguistica Antverpiensia* 15: 227–240.

Todorova, Marija. 2020. "Interpreting for Refugees: Lessons Learned from the Field." In *Interpreting in Legal and Healthcare Settings*, ed. by Eva Ng, and Ineke Crezee, 63–81. Amsterdam & Philadelphia: John Benjamins.

Todorova, Marija. 2021a. "Pressing Issues and Future Directions for Interpreting in Conflict Zones." In *Interpreting Conflict: A Comparative Framework*, ed. by Marija Todorova, and Lucia Ruiz Rosendo, 305–316. London: Palgrave Macmillan.

Todorova, Marija. 2021b. "Interpreting Refugees in Hong Kong." In *Interpreting Conflict: A Comparative Framework*, ed. by Marija Todorova, and Lucia Ruiz Rosendo, 273–289. London: Palgrave Macmillan.

Todorova, Marija. 2022. "Translating Refugee Culinary Culture: Hong Kong Narratives of Integration." *Translation and Interpreting Studies* 17 (1): 88–110.

Todorova, Marija. 2023. "Refugee Life Stories in Translation: Translators as Cultural Mediators." In *Community Translation: Research and Practice*, ed. by Erika Gonzalez, Katarzyna Stachowiak-Szymczak, and Despina Amanatidou, 181–193. London: Routledge.

Todorova, Marija. 2025. "Living in a Limbo: Translation in Hong Kong Narratives of Asylum in the Digital Space." In *Routledge Handbook of Translation and Migration*, ed. by Rita Wilson, Loredana Polezzi, and Brigit Maher, 293–305. Oxon: Routledge.

Todorova, Marija, and Zoran Poposki. 2022. "Rehumanizing the Refugee Crisis." In *Translating Crises*, ed. by Federico Federici, and Sharon O'Brien, 65–78. London: Bloomsbury Academics.

Tusting, Karin (ed). 2020. *The Routledge Handbook of Linguistic Ethnography*. Oxon: Routledge.

Zion, Deborah, Linda Briskman, and Bebe Loff. 2010. "Returning to History: The Ethics of Researching Asylum Seeker Health in Australia." *The American Journal of Bioethics* 10 (2): 48–56.

CHAPTER 15

Exploring interspecies translation and interpreting through multispecies ethnography

Xany Jansen van Vuuren
University of the Free State

Against the background of the recent enlarging of translation studies to include the more-than-professional (Tymoczko 2007), more-than-verbal (Petrilli 2016) and more-than-human (Cronin 2017; Marais 2019), this chapter explores the opportunities that accompany multispecies translational research by focusing on multispecies ethnography as a research design. It will provide examples from a recent multispecies translation and interpreting project that involved the application of such a design in an animal welfare context.

By taking an ecosemiotic approach to conceptualising the process of translation and interpreting, this chapter assumes that all forms of semiosis are, in essence, translational processes (Petrilli 2016) that are "shaped by available conditions, encumbered by their history, yet at the same time ... partly autonomous and independent" (Maran 2020:1).

Keywords: multispecies ethnography, translation, interpreting, intersemiotic translation, interspecies translation, ecosemiotics

1. Introduction

Animal welfare outreach events in South Africa consist of multiple processes of multicultural, multilingual, and multispecies interaction where numerous verbal and non-verbal translational (and, by implication, interpreting) processes take place. These events are arranged to provide (otherwise inaccessible) healthcare and food provision to animals in lower income communities, whereby animal owners bring their animals for check-ups and medical care to centralised, temporary mobile clinic/outreach setups. However, due to the country's linguistic make-up of 11 official languages, verbal communication between participants often becomes challenging. As a result, non-professional interpreters (who are

https://doi.org/10.1075/btl.165.15jan
Available under the CC BY-NC 4.0 license. © 2025 John Benjamins Publishing Company

either fellow animal owners, veterinarians, welfare workers or passers-by) often interpret anything from a few words to lengthy conversations. In addition to the inter-human communication, many instances of interspecies communication and translation take place where humans act on behalf of the animals by translating non-verbal communication. The multispecies make-up of the research context requires not only post-anthropocentric *theories* that transcend anthropocentrism, but subsequent post-anthropocentric *methodologies* as well, in order to conduct a comprehensive study of multispecies interactions within the broader field of translation studies. One such way is within an ecological, and in particular, ecosemiotic, theoretical framework where the contribution of both human as well as non-human (and environmental) participants to the translation processes is regarded as equally important and meaningful.

Divided into two sections, this chapter attempts to build on existing and emerging research on the relationship between semiosis and translation. The first section approaches translation and interpreting theoretically from within an ecosemiotic framework as a foundation for the inclusion of linguistic as well as non-linguistic data collection. It will also address the benefits of opening up translation studies to the so-called Animal Turn in humanities and related fields, after which the methodological grounding for the study is provided.

Section two builds on the first, allowing for the theory and methodology to interact to form an emergent, multispecies research design. In particular, it will present the challenges and opportunities in a project that uses multispecies ethnographic research design (Jansen van Vuuren 2022). The first-person narrated discussion will reflect not only on the positionality of the participants in an animal welfare setting, but also the positionality of the researcher within a multicultural, multispecies research project. It furthermore provides brief findings on the processes of verbal and non-verbal translation and interpreting (I will from hereon use "translation" to refer to any translational process — which can include interpreting).

2. Exploring human/non-human relationships in the Animal Turn

Humans and non-human animals co-exist in various settings, and as a result, their respective forms of communication with and about one another have become progressively intertwined, a phenomenon that has been explored by scholars from various fields such as ecocriticism (Garrard 2012), ecolinguistics (Stibbe 2001, 2015), and ecofeminism (Buckingham 2004; Adams 2010), amongst many others. Such studies often start out from the premise that while nature is no longer independent of humans and is, in fact, deeply influenced by humans (Drenthen

2016: 109), it is still valuable to consider that "humans are not the only agents in the world of the Anthropocene"[1] and that non-human agency is equally significant (Drenthen 2016: 110). Agency in these fields is regarded as not only the ability of an animal to exert change on itself or the environment, or ability to act, but also to be sentient. Approached in this way, it emphasises the continuity between humans and non-humans, rather than the discontinuity and differences between humans and non-humans (McFarland and Hediger 2009).

A semiotic approach to agency would imply a recognition of all organisms' (both human and non-human) ability to make choices in relation to their interpretation of signs. This chapter, then (in line with an ecosemiotic approach to translation and interpreting, which will be addressed in the next section), regards both human as well as non-human agency on equal footing, while concurrently considering the unavoidable ubiquity of human culture in nature (or, more simply put: the effect that humans can have on non-humans and their environments).

The escalation of similarly-themed studies has culminated in the recently termed *Animal Turn* in academia, which involves the "recognition of the fact that human and animal lives have always been entangled and that animals are omnipresent in human society on both metaphorical and practical, material levels" (Andersson Cederholm et al. 2014: 5). Used for the first time in 2003 (as noted by Simmons and Armstrong 2007), the term *Animal Turn* refers not only to the increased focus on non-human animals in research as subjects, but also to the cognizance of non-human animal agency (amongst others). It has brought with it wide-ranging, active attempts at reconceptualising and addressing human-animal relations in various scholarly fields that include feminism (Buckingham 2004; Adams 2010), psychology (Kasperbauer 2018), semiotics (Maran 2020), literature (Parham and Westling 2016), and, the topic of this chapter, translation studies (Marais 2019; Jansen van Vuuren 2023).

Lestel (2014: 62), describes the non-human animal as "a hybrid creature with whom humans have an extraordinary multiplicity of relations, from the most superficial to the most complex, that engage with the very foundations of what an animal is and what it is believed to be". These relations vary not only in terms of complexity, as Lestel argues, but also in terms of the willingness of both parties to form and maintain relations. One such example, one could argue, is the willingness of wild birds to become accustomed to humans in their immediate environment, such as urban birds that often happily move around humans in search of human food morsels. Or feral cats that become less feral, and relatively tame,

---

1. The *Anthropocene* is a term used to describe the geological impact that humans have on the environment; rather than biological entities, humans and their collective impact on the planet are regarded as the source of the next geological epoch (Crutzen and Stoermer 2013).

around humans. In humans, this willingness can be seen in the vast array of roles that have been assigned to dogs, for instance (guard dog, working dog, companion, dog show prize-winner, etc.). As such, exploring features of animal ownership and animal welfare within the Animal Turn can reveal the complexity of human understanding of the non-human other, and particularly take into account that non-human animals are very often not participants in their own social construction, which regularly results in exclusions from discussions about them (Stibbe 2001: 146). This exclusion often extends to their rights to welfare and care. One prevalent example of this is that many decisions regarding environmental conservation and other animal protection decisions stem from the perceptions that people have of other species (Maran et al. 2016). Human language and culture (in the broadest and narrowest sense of the words) are therefore (often unintentionally) used to impose control over non-human animals and their place in human frames of reference. This can be observed in the many linguistic and lexical mechanisms that create a divide between humans and non-human animals. For example, with regards to animals as food in the English language, Peter Singer (1990: 95) argues that "[t]he very words we use conceal [meat's] origin, we eat beef, not bull ... and pork, not pig". We also wear leather, not skin, and eat meat (not flesh) from a carcass, not a corpse. As such, it can be argued that "[c]ultural constructs determine the fate of animals" (Lawrence 1994: 182). And as a result, the concept of the non-human animal is often represented differently by respective human cultures and societies. Similarly, humans' opinions of respective non-human animal species often vary, resulting in complex patterns of interactions between different species of non-human animals and humans (Mäekivi and Maran 2016: 211). The purpose of animal welfare work, then, is often to perform mediating roles between the non-human animals and their human custodians. This mediative role requires cognizance of the varying approaches to, and understanding of, the non-human animal by these aforementioned custodians, which at times is highly complex and in conflict with the views of animal welfare mediators.

Sociologists Arluke and Sanders used a *sociozoological scale* to explain the culturally biased ranking of animals based on their usefulness to humans and "how well they seem to 'fit in' and play the roles they are expected to play in a society" (1996: 169). In essence, the scale ranks humans at the top, after which pets are ranked as a close second, for whose welfare humans generally have an overwhelming concern. Instrumental animals such as horses are third in the ranking. They are not regarded as characteristically close to humans as their pet counterparts, but "because they are necessary cogs in the wheels of society, there is interest in their welfare" (Arluke and Sanders 1996: 171). While often unintended, such rankings stress two important conditions that enforce human domination of non-humans: the emphasis on differences, as opposed to similarities, that distinguish non-human animals from humans, as well as the (pre-supposed) inferiority of the non-human animal (Stibbe 2015:150).

It is this hierarchical ranking of species and the emphasis on differences between humans and non-humans that most often predetermine the provision of healthcare and welfare of non-humans. As such, the idea of animal welfare is not a universally agreed-upon concept, and no country has the same approach to animal welfare, or even the same level of interaction with specific non-human animals. For instance, in much of the Global North, especially in urban contexts, physical encounters between humans and non-human animals that are not pets have mostly diminished (Cook 2015), which is contrary to many Global South contexts such as South Africa, where humans and non-humans live and work in the vicinity of, and consistently depend on, each other to survive. Often, the welfare of non-human animals is determined by human welfare, survival, and needs, and in many contexts animal welfare is only a priority if it supports the output and survival of a particular community (Eadie 2012). This means that the welfare of non-human animals is inextricably linked with the welfare of the human carers, "because happy, healthy animals will be able to assist humans best in their struggle for survival" (Eadie 2012:vii).

In this light, doing research within the *Animal Turn* implies not only a shift in the focus on the place of non-human animals within a human world, but also a shift in the place and purpose of the human/non-human relationship within the Anthropocene and, by extension, the human in the non-human world. It also implies a shift in the abovementioned mediating role (which includes acts of intersemiotic, interlingual and intralingual translation) between humans and non-humans. The question, then, that should be asked when doing research on the human/non-human relationship is not so much "what kind of knowledge we can produce in the 'animal turn' but what we *do* with this knowledge — that is; how we put it to work, and for whose benefit" (Pedersen 2014:16). The answer to this question would most probably be along the lines of recognising not only the sentience of non-human animals, but also their individuality and agency and, conversely, as argued by Wheeler and Williams (2012), the 'animal part' in human consciousness.

Nevertheless, doing research in a context where animals are primarily used as tools (as in the case of this chapter) seems to be in contradiction with the original purpose of the *Animal Turn*, in that this is not a critical approach to animal welfare and animal ownership as such, particularly with regard to (in the case of this study) the horses that are non-consensual participants in the research for this chapter, nor in the welfare outreach context. However, the purpose of the chapter, I would like to argue, merges with the purpose of the *Animal Turn*, in that it argues that animal welfare work is regarded as an act of translation on a macro level, which has ultimately allowed for an exploration into the translation of non-human agency. It is also important to add that the complexity of social landscapes, such as that of the Global South, often makes it difficult, and at times impossible, to advocate for complete emancipation of non-human animals, given the prevalence of non-human animals and their roles in the human environments. In this instance, where animals are going to be used as tools, for example, enabling a solid foundation for their health and welfare is essential. Not ideal, but essential.

## 3.	Semiotics, ecosemiotics and the non-human animal in translation studies

The scholarly interest in the non-human animal comes at an important time, given our shift into the Anthropocene, which has certainly prompted a change in the way in which the non-human animal's positioning and agency are being investigated in several fields of research (see Crutzen and Stoermer 2013; Robin, Sörlin, and Warde 2013; Tønnessen and Armstrong Oma 2016; Cronin 2017). Fields such as translation studies, which have previously leaned towards a linguistic bias, are no exception, and scholars like Petrilli (2016), Marais (2019, 2021), and Torop (2003) have used Peircean semiotics (Peirce 1935a, 1935b; De Waal 2013) as a foundation to encourage the breaking of linguistic bonds of translation studies by equating the process of translation to both verbal and non-verbal semiosis.

As a field of study, semiotics examines sign processes. A sign, in terms of Peircean semiotics, is "any mark, bodily movement, symbol, token, etc., used to indicate and to convey thoughts, information, commands, etc." (Danesi 1994:vi). Semiosis, by extension, is the meaning making process of a particular sign, and has been argued to take place in a similar manner as translation (Petrilli 2016; Marais 2019). Simply put, the argument for this is that, in the same way that a sign stands in the place of something else, translation also stands in the place of something else. Adding to this, Marais's biosemiotic theory of translation (2019) claims that not only is translation ultimately semiosis but also, since semiosis is not purely a human phenomenon, non-humans also partake in translational processes (2019, 2021). This argument is largely based on the reasoning that meaning creation or semiosis transpires on as much a linguistic level as a non-linguistic level, given that the meaning making process is made up of multiple sign systems, of which only one is linguistic (others include human and non-human non-verbal sign systems). Furthermore, the translational process is not only linked to, but also dependent on, the context in which it takes place, where semiosis becomes an oscillation of multiple sign processes within other sign processes, within which translation takes place continuously. By approaching translation processes as semiotic processes and including animals in translation studies, our understanding of non-human animals and the non-human world can be broadened. In support of this move, Marais argues that "[i]n a post-humanist paradigm of thinking, where humans are no longer regarded as the center of either the universe or earth, it is crucial that a theory of translation is able to explain not only human semiosis, but also non-human semiosis" (2019: 41). As a result, when doing interspecies research, non-human animals and their non-linguistic sign systems can and should be regarded as part of the translational processes that form part of the research.

Further building on the Peircean school of thought, the field of ecosemiotics explores human and non-human interaction and semiosis in a given environment. More specifically, however, within ecosemiotics "signs are treated not as fully conventional and arbitrary means of human culture, but as partly rooted in the natural world and in our corporality" (Maran 2020:1). In other words, ecosemiotics explores the vastness of human/non-human relations from the viewpoint that culture is part of nature and not separate from it, and approaches interspecies relationships from this viewpoint as well. Within this foundation, ecosemiotically framed studies have looked at wildlife management (Tønnessen 2011; Drenthen 2016), landscape studies (Lindström, Kull, and Palang 2011), geography (Maran and Kull 2014), and urban life (Magnus and Remm 2018). While diverse in their approaches, these studies have in common their exploration of human/non-human relationships in various contexts and on various levels. The significance of an ecosemiotic approach to studying interspecies translation is that both humans and non-humans are seen as makers and experiences of their own experiential worlds. The purpose of translation between species would be to bridge the gap between the two subjective lifeworlds.

4. First steps towards multispecies ethnography: From paradigm and approach to design for interspecies translational research

From the onset of this study, an ethnographic methodology seemed like the most appropriate way to observe translational processes where both humans and non-human animals are involved. Contrary to more positivistic approaches to data collection, ethnographic studies are often iterative in nature due to cyclical, and at times simultaneous, occurrences of data collection and integration with the theory — the progression of which will follow below.

The theoretical ecosemiotic approach ultimately opened up an exploration of the interaction of subjective realities of both humans and non-humans through various translational processes. This further highlighted the interpretivist nature of this study, since "semiotics is not about the 'real' world at all, but about complementary or alternative actual models of it and ... about an infinite number of anthropologically conceivable possible worlds" (Sebeok 1991: 12) which reveals a unique understanding of that which is explored through the particular method of questioning.

Adding to this, an interdisciplinary research project studying the relations between nature and culture is often "schematized as having four intertwining aspects: theoretical framework, research object, cultural and natural context" (Maran 2014: 79). The first one of these (the theory) "can be considered to carry academic identity and historical legacy, whereas the latter three are rather dependent on a particular research object and its local conditions" (Maran 2014: 79). Building from the interpretivist research paradigm, this study naturally progressed towards a qualitative research approach, since one of the identifying characteristics of a qualitative approach is often the natural setting(s) where the research is conducted in order to understand the social actions of the participants (Babbie and Mouton 2001). However, while the human social aspect and aforementioned social actions were regarded as a given in this study, an additional non-human social awareness was required to expand the methodology into a multispecies study, and more particularly a multispecies research design. This expansion implies an expansion of the meaning of 'social actions' to include both human and non-human semiosis, and by extension, actions. The result of this was a further progression towards an emergent multispecies ethnographic design.

The term 'emergent', in the context of this research design, "involves a process that is ongoing, changeable and iterative in nature" but at the same time implies "that choices [with regard to research] will be purposeful and carefully considered prior to, during, and after, implementation" (Wright 2009). The emergent characteristics of this study, which were mainly guided by the dynamic nature of the outreach events and the concurrent development of the theoretical framework, furthermore allowed for a progression of ideas and methods to arise during the research process, rather than unilaterally following a predetermined set of methods and approaches in order to answer the research question. This is often the case with ethnographic studies, since the control of the research context does not lie with the researcher, but rather with the participants themselves. For instance, after observation of and participation in the first few outreach events, I realised that my initial idea of doing semi-structured interviews would not be conducive to the setting, since the event occurred under time constraints; the horse owners were eager to continue with their day and would not have been able to spend an extra 30 minutes answering questions. As such, I worked spontaneous interviews into the existing conversations between the participants.

Broadly speaking, ethnography entails the study of social interactions, behaviours, and perceptions that transpire within particular communities through the means of the researcher emerging herself in 'the field'. Building on these characteristics, multispecies ethnography involves their study beyond anthropocentric boundaries. This means that, in addition to viewing non-humans as co-participants and agents, a conscious decentralising of the human and recognition of non-humans as fellow "sense-makers" (Wels 2020:344) is necessary in multispecies ethnography. Ethnographic concepts such as 'social' and 'sensemaking' should therefore be expanded "to include and integrate non-human animals" (Wels 2020:344).

The move towards methodologies (and of course theories) that accommodate the more-than-human world is necessary if the non-human animal is to be recognised as an active participant in various multispecies communities. As such, by including non-human animals in the ethnographic design (and subsequent execution) of this study as meaning making agents forming part of the communication process, it was possible to shift the perceptions of the non-human participants from the periphery to a more central positioning in human/non-human relations. As emphasised by Kirksey and Helmreich (2010:545):

> Creatures previously appearing on the margins of anthropology — as part of the landscape, as food for humans, as symbols — have been pressed into the foreground in recent ethnographies. Animals, plants, fungi, and microbes once confined in anthropological accounts to the realm of zoe or "bare life" — that which is killable — have started to appear alongside humans in the realm of bios, with legibly biographical and political lives.

Multispecies ethnography furthermore accepts that human and non-human research participants do not exist in isolation, and as such concerns itself with "seeing interaction [between humans and non-humans] as a two-way (or multiple way) process that impacts the bodies, minds, behaviors, social lives, and natures of all involved organisms" (Singer 2014:1283). Such a study, then, disrupts the anthropocentric borders that separate humans from non-humans and enables a comprehensive approach to human/non-human relations.

Nevertheless, as a design, multispecies ethnography shares characteristics with the more general ethnographic approach. Some of these key features as identified by Hammersley and Atkinson (2019) include:

- Actions and accounts are studied in everyday contexts, and not under conditions created by the researcher.
- While data can be gathered from a range of sources, participant observation and informal conversations [or interactions with the non-human] are usually the main sources of data.

- Data collection is relatively 'unstructured' in terms of not having an initial fixed research design or fixed data analysis categories at the start of data collection process. These emerge during the course of data collection and analysis, respectively.
- The focus is generally on a single, or a few, case(s) in order to facilitate an in-depth study.
- The data analysis is based on the interpretation of meanings of the participants' actions, and how these are implicated in particular contexts. The result is the production of descriptions, explanations, and theories.

The recognition of non-human agency is a key characteristic of multispecies ethnography (as opposed to other non-human animal related research). Often, non-human animals are studied in contexts such as laboratories, for instance, where their ability to function as decision making, thinking agents is suppressed (Blattner, Donaldson, and Wilcox 2020). To some extent, this can be said about animal welfare contexts as well, since animals are not always regarded by their human counterparts as agentive beings. However, a fundamental difference between laboratory-based research and animal welfare contexts is the need for (and ability of) one party (such as animal welfare workers) to acknowledge and translate animal agency. However, even if this were not the case, acknowledging non-human animal agency in contexts where the non-human participants are not able to exercise their agency (because of restraints, confinement, etc.) is essential for expanding formerly anthropocentric approaches to such contexts.

5. Description of the research context and its participants

This section provides a reflexive description of the data collection, analysis and findings regarding translational processes in the multispecies animal welfare context, where the ability of non-human animals to exercise their own agency was limited. The data that I ultimately analysed consisted of the photographs that I took over three years (2018–2021) of attending the outreach events as well as cell phone video recordings that I recorded during the last six months of attending the events. The reasoning for the use of these two types of data will be discussed in section 6 of this chapter.

Most research in translation and interpreting studies as well as semiotics that make use of interpretivist methodologies emphasise the significance of context, since "an understanding of the context in which any form of research is conducted is critical to the interpretation of the data gathered" (Willis 2007: 99). By observing humans (and in this case non-human animals) in a particular context, "being themselves" (Danesi 2004: 41), researchers at the intersection of semiotically driven fields attempt to determine what a sign means, how it means what it means, and why it means what it means (Danesi 2004: 41).

The animal welfare context in South Africa consists of a variety of organisations with different approaches working in various settings. The particular context of this research was a succession of outreach events that took place in the semi-rural town Thaba Nchu, Free State, South Africa. Spanning a surface of 36.39 km², the town consists of a central district and roughly 42 villages that surround it. The undeveloped land is communal and divided into land for grazing, residential and agricultural purposes (Goitsemodimo 2015). According to official census data (Statistics South Africa 2011), Thaba Nchu had a population of roughly 70,000 residents in 2011. However, due to a declining population growth, it is estimated that the current population is roughly 56,000 (World Population Review 2020).

The three most widely spoken languages are Sesotho, which is the first language of 47% of the residents, Setswana, which 40% of the residents speak as a first language, and English, which only 4% of the residents speak as a first language. However, many of the residents can speak, or at least understand, all three languages as well as Afrikaans, one of the other official languages. Thaba Nchu is regarded as a semi-arid area, and as a result there is, at times, limited grazing for the (mostly) free roaming livestock. This often has far-reaching consequences for both humans and non-humans, since, due to the low employment rate and poor economy of the town (see Goitsemodimo 2015), many horse owners do not have the financial means to buy additional feed for the horses when grazing becomes scarce. As a result, subsidised feeding programmes such as the cart horse outreach events often constitute a large source of sustenance for the horses and are therefore not only essential for the welfare of the horses but also provide some socio-economic relief to the horse owners.

Figure 1 represents a typical outreach scene. The cart horses stand and wait their turn, while horse owners interact with other owners and the animal welfare workers. The welfare workers will move from horse to horse, interacting with the animals as well as their owners while they do health checks and document the overall health of the horse in order to keep track of the treatment that each animal receives as well as any improvement/deterioration in their health. After all the horses have been checked by a veterinarian, horse feed is distributed and the event concludes. The duration of each event is about 3–4 hours.

Figure 2 shows a typical example of human/human and human/non-human interaction. One welfare worker is having a discussion with the horse owner while another welfare worker assesses the health of the horse by means of a physical examination.

Figure 1. A typical outreach scene

Figure 2. A typical interaction at an outreach event

6. Researcher positionality as photographer participant observer

My access to, and knowledge of, the outreach events happened serendipitously. I got to know the welfare worker who organised these events on an animal activist social media platform. Upon seeing that I am a hobby photographer, she asked me to do a photoshoot of her rescue horses for a calendar to raise funds for the outreach events (which I did), after which I offered to take photos of her outreach events. I decided to do my PhD research at these events when I noticed the different forms of translation and interpreting that occurred during interactions at these events. My request to do the research was informal at first, when I mentioned the possibility to do research during a collegial conversation, after which I followed up with a formal request via my institution. While she, as the organiser, granted the initial access to these events, I also requested permission from all the human participants at the events (which included the other animal welfare workers, the horse owners, and the community members) to collect data in the form of photographs and video recordings. As a show of gratitude for allowing me access, I shared my photographs after each event with the welfare worker, who would share it with the horse owners as well as with the broader public on different social media platforms.

Photographs and recordings can simultaneously serve as a data collection method and as documentation of a particular event during research (Holm 2014). During the data collection process, taking photographs documented the event for myself as well as for the animal welfare organisation and animal welfare workers (obviously with different end results in mind). However, the video recordings were used solely for research purposes (to serve as sources of data for semiotic analysis).

The photographs aided in the documentation of both intentional and non-intentional sign (translational) processes that were observable visually (symptoms of illness and injuries, interactions, non-verbal communication and even verbal communication). The video recordings, while also documenting visual data, added access to auditory data (conversations between humans and verbal communication with and on behalf of the horses, and non-verbal communication by the horses). However, while providing visual evidence of the participants and their actions, it should be noted that, as Barthes (1964) argued, photographs (and by extension videos, in this case) are polysemic; they contain more than one meaning. Building on this, Schwartz (1989: 120) warns against the tendency to regard photographs as objective evidence, since that would lead to a disregard for "the convention-bound processes of both image making and interpretation". As such, the photographs would always firstly be from the perspective of my own observation and my own subjective positionality as a researcher, and in particular as a participant observer.

Participant observation is widely regarded as a core data collection method for ethnographic research designs (DeMunck and Sobo 1998; Bernard 2006) and as such played a major role in the data collection process for this project. Sandiford (2015) highlights two characteristics of participant observation. Firstly, in most contexts, researchers tend to be physically and socially close to the participants of the phenomenon that they are researching, which leads to scattered interviews and questioning rather than separate interviews. Secondly, researchers experience first-hand many of the same experiences as the participants. For this study, being a participant observer provided a direct personal observation of all the relevant (human and non-human) interactions and non-verbal forms of communication, together with their duration and the specific manner in which activities were executed (Schmuck 1997). Furthermore, this particular multispecies context enabled an observation of not only how humans behave towards non-humans and other humans, but also how non-humans behave in (and react to) a human-created environment. Adding to this, being an observing participant in multispecies contexts is a complex process that requires awareness of one's own ability and inability to interact with the respective participants. For instance, in an animal welfare context, which is always created by humans and involuntarily attended by non-humans, human participants have more autonomy than the non-humans that share the context. The researcher's participation is therefore more in line with the other human participants.

My level of participation was at times moderate (participating in some of the outreach activities, like holding a horse's reins) and at other times active (actively experiencing what the participants were experiencing by assisting in fundraisers, for instance). These two types of participation are based on five scaled types of observation identified by Spradley (1980), namely non-participation, passive participation, moderate participation, active participation, and complete participation. Alternating between the two aforementioned types of participation allowed access to wide-ranging data, and also allowed easy navigation of the setting since it provided opportunities to build relationships with the human participants. The reason for this was that I was able to, at times, stand back and allow the process to happen without hindering the flow of the process. It implied that I often became less visible, and consequently less imposing. At other times, my visibility resulted in conversations with participants (often initiated by the participants), allowing me to gain more in-depth information about a particular situation.

In addition to becoming aware of limitations with regard to interaction with non-human participants, attempting to investigate interspecies relations often forces a researcher to confront her own often subconscious biases regarding animal agency, animal ownership and interspecies relationships. In my case, recognising my own bias about animal ownership within the broader social context proved challenging at first. My own ideas of horses' roles and positioning in nature-culture relationships were different from that of the welfare workers, veterinarians, and horse owners, in that I am an animal activist. This prompted a conflict between my animal activist background and the animal welfare context (where the use of animals is regarded as acceptable if their welfare is taken into consideration). Animal sentience is central to my moral compass, and I believe that horses should not be ridden or used for human gain. However, I feel the study might not have happened if it had not been for this stance, since animal sentience and agency is what triggered my interest in human/non-human interaction.

The extent of any researcher's participation is steered by several constraints which can generally include age, ethnicity, gender, and socio-economic background, amongst others, and will have a direct impact on the way in which a researcher participates in a particular event. This became clear in many instances where I could not participate as much as I would have liked: I was not a cart horse owner, I do not work with horses outside of my research, I was not from the same socio-economic background as the cart horse owners, we did not share the same mother tongue, or level of education (which meant that I was inadvertently grouped with the welfare team). However, these constraints guided the study and my positionality as observer and researcher into what it eventually became.

7. Analysing data and 'finding' findings with multispecies ethnography

Emergent qualitative data analysis is generally associated with a bottom-up approach in which the collected data provide a foundation from which themes can emerge. This approach was followed during the thematic analysis of 27 video recorded interactions between humans and non-humans. As stated, my agreement with the animal welfare worker who organised these events was that I would document the event by taking photographs for her to use on her welfare organisation's social media pages and for her own record-keeping purposes. Consequently, I photographed all of the participants and their interactions for the full three years that I attended these events. I video recorded various forms of interactions between all (multispecies) participants, which I could do quite easily since as with almost all ethnographic studies, the dynamic context (as a result of the unpredictability of human — and in this case non-human — participants "being themselves" [Danesi 2004: 41]) naturally allowed for video recordings of various forms of interaction to happen.

That said, this section is not merely a discussion of the data and findings as such (see Jansen van Vuuren 2022), but also a post-research reflection of the analysis process and a very brief description of the findings in order to show how the process of multispecies ethnography flowed from immersion in the field, to data collection, and eventually, analysis and writing up of findings.

8. Identification of the theme: Agency of meaning makers

In this section, I will briefly discuss one theme that arose from the analysis: agency. The success of an animal welfare outreach event is based on the interaction and interpretation of human and non-human behaviours by both humans and non-humans through their positioning in the outreach event and their resultant agency. While the data revealed many examples of agency in human/human interaction and human/non-human interaction, I will present instances where non-human agency (both directly and indirectly) is translated by human participants and where human agency directly affects the human/non-human relationship, respectively. In the first example, the welfare worker translates a horse's behaviour for the horse's owner, while in the second one a community member translates the cultural practices of horse owners (that form bonds between horses and their owners) for the animal welfare community.

Figure 3. Three humans surround a distressed horse

During an incident where a horse was incorrectly assumed (by the horse owner (middle), one welfare worker (right) and a community member (left)) to be obstinate, another welfare worker and a non-professional interpreter step in to intersemiotically translate the behaviour (by observing the non-verbal bodily communication — body language in layman's terms) as fear of humans due to pain that he (the horse) was experiencing.

From Figure 3 (a screenshot from a 2-minute recording), the reader can see three humans attempting to approach and touch a visibly scared horse. The ears of the horse are pulled back (which, together with widely opened eyes, indicates fear) and his head is raised high (in an attempt to avoid humans touching him).

The horse appears agitated from the humans being so close. Regardless of this, the humans are still attempting to move right up to the horse. The horse constantly pulls against restraints while walking backward, which the humans see as an indication to also move forward.

Figure 4. The welfare worker (right) performs intersemiotic translation

At this point, the non-professional interpreter (obscured in Figure 3 and partially obscured by the middle right participant in Figure 4) and one of the welfare workers walk up to this interaction (see Figure 4). The welfare worker (front right) intersemiotically translates the behaviour of the horse to the owner by explaining (in English) that the actions of the horse imply that he is in pain and fearsome of human touch. She also adds that, in addition to treatment, the horse needs to rest in order to heal. This is conveyed by the interpreter (obscured by the other welfare worker, middle right) in Sesotho to the horse owner.

As a result of this intersemiotic translation, the humans changed their confrontational approach towards the horse, and rather allowed the horse to get used to their presence and calm down before advancing and attempting to touch him. After a while, the horse allowed the humans to approach and touch him (as can be seen from Figure 5).

The horse in this instance was an active participant in the communication process, without which no translation of behaviour, and resultant interpreting from English to Sesotho would have been necessary. The translation and interpreting became a collaborative process between humans and non-humans.

In other instances of collaborative translational actions, the translation of knowledge that directly impacts the interspecies relationship between horse and

Figure 5. A visibly calm horse undergoing physical assessment by a welfare worker

human was facilitated by several participants simultaneously. The following instance is an example:

> *What seems like rope made out of horsehair is tied to the horses' bits,[2] and also placed in the horses' mouths (see Figure 6). A conversation about this between the researcher (R), welfare worker (W1), interpreter (INT1) and community members (CM4, CM5, CM6) follows:*[3]
>
> R: [in English to welfare worker and interpreter] It looks like horsehair?
>
> INT1: [in English to welfare worker and researcher] Like a tape.
>
> W1: [in English to no one in particular] What is the purpose?
>
> INT1: [in English to W1] I don't know what it means.
>
> INT1: [in English to no one in particular] Where is the owner?
>
> INT1: [in Sesotho to CM4] What is this?
>
> CM4: [in Sesotho] I don't know?
>
> INT1: [in Sesotho] Really?
>
> CM5: [in English] These guys, huh-uh. [indicating that some people do strange things]

---

2. A bit is the part of the bridle that is inserted into the horse's mouth in order to aid communication between a human and horse when the horse is being ridden or pulling a cart.

3. The passages originally in Sesotho and Afrikaans were translated into English by the author.

More community members join in the discussion — no one knows what the purpose of the hair is.

INT1: [in English to W1] No one knows.

CM6: [who had arrived during the discussion] [in Afrikaans] We Bantu people... when we want the horses to be strong... we do this...

W1: [in English] Oh I was wondering if it was something like this.

W1: [to CM6, switching to Afrikaans] Is it just to make the horses stronger?

CM6: [in Afrikaans to W1] It is our religion.

W1: [in Afrikaans to CM6] But why do you do it?

CM6: [in Afrikaans] So that the horses listen to the new owner.

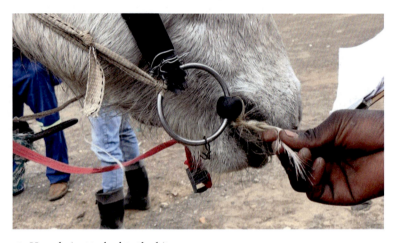

Figure 6. Horsehair attached to the bit

This example shows how not only the regular non-professional interpreter's agency beyond that of merely interpreting comes to the foreground in the above conversation, but also the agency of the other participants who act as translators and interpreters, as well as the (albeit more passive) agency of the horse in fostering an interspecies relationship by wearing altered tack that would foster a human/non-human bond. While the interpreter interprets verbally, the community member [CM6] provided an intersemiotic translation of cultural practices that connect humans to their horses by means of the metaphysical to the welfare workers.

9. Findings: Moving away from linguistic and anthropocentric biases

The data collected at these outreach events showed multiple instances of interlingual, intersemiotic and intralingual translational processes, amongst which were diagnoses of illnesses and injuries, verbal interpreting between and within languages, and non-verbal interpreting and translation. The analysis of the data and the interpretation of it into workable findings yet again demanded a shift away from an ingrained linguistic and anthropocentric bias.

By enlarging the concept of translation to include non-verbal data, and the concept of the translator to include and/or translate on behalf of a non-human animal, the data revealed numerous translational processes that ultimately benefitted the welfare of the non-human animal. From the reconceptualisation of translation and interpreting as semiotic processes, the process of explaining a horse's behaviour by means of assessing body language, as well as explaining cultural practices, can be seen as an act of translation. Based on the context, the successful translation of these actions took place, based on the time and space (when they were presented, and by whom), in order to assist interspecies relationships.

The instances of interlingual, intralingual and intersemiotic interpreting and translation showed that all participants, not only human participants, participate in the translational event. With regard to the purpose of interpreting and translation in animal welfare as a whole, humans' attitudes toward respective non-human animal species often vary, resulting in "complex pattern[s] of interactions between different interest groups" (Mäekivi and Maran 2016: 211). As such, the purpose of animal welfare work is often to perform translation as mediation between the non-human animals and their human custodians. This mediative role requires cognizance of the varying approaches to, and understanding of, the non-human animal by humans, which at times is highly complex and conflicting with their own views of human-animal relationships.

Here also it is worth noting that the expansion of translation to include non-human animals has allowed for the opening up of translation studies to consider animals as not merely being *translated*, but also as *translators*, which is a topic well worth exploring in subsequent research.

10. Conclusion

Doing multispecies research in an animal welfare context broadens exploration into, and conceptualisation of, interlingual, intralingual and intersemiotic translation by including both human and non-human participants. In line with recent novel theories and conceptual shifts in translation studies (Petrilli 2016; Marais

2019), this chapter was an attempt at discussing the empirical observation of these aforementioned translation processes. Enlarging the concept of the translator and interpreter and the resultant translational processes in which they engage has enabled an identification of several translational processes, and the agents who engage in them, that work together to make a particular context work. When explored within the Animal Turn, and in particular with ecosemiotic lenses, multispecies ethnography allows for the reconceptualisation of the non-human participant as an active participant in the research process. The act of performing welfare then links with the act of translation, in that the needs of the non-human animal are translated into something more understandable for the human owner, and in other cases for the welfare workers.

References

Adams, Carol J. 2010. *The Sexual Politics of Meat*. New York & Hove: Continuum.

Andersson Cederholm, Erika, Amelie Björck, Kristina Jennbert, and Ann-Sofie Lönngren. 2014. "Introduction." In *Exploring the Animal Turn: Human-Animal Relations in Science, Society and Culture*, ed. by Erika Andersson Cederholm, Amelie Björck, Kristina Jennbert, and Ann-Sofie Lönngren, 5–11. Lund: The Pufendorf Institute for Advanced Studies.

Arluke, Arnold, and Clinton R. Sanders. 1996. *Regarding Animals*. Philadelphia: Temple University Press.

Babbie, Earl R., and Johan Mouton. 2001. *The Practice of Social Research*. Cape Town: Oxford University Press South Africa.

Barthes, Roland. 1964. "Rhetorique de l'image." *Communications* 4 (4): 40–51.

Bernard, H. Russel. 2006. *Research Methods in Anthropology: Qualitative and Quantitative Approaches*. Walnut Creek: AltaMira Press.

Blattner, Charlotte, Sue Donaldson, and Ryan Wilcox. 2020. "Animal Agency in Community: A Political Multispecies Ethnography of VINE Sanctuary." *Politics and Animals* 6: 1–22.

Buckingham, Susan. 2004. "Ecofeminism in the Twenty-First Century." *The Geographical Journal* 170 (2): 146–154.

Cook, Guy. 2015. "'A Pig Is a Person' or 'You Can Love a Fox and Hunt It': Innovation and Tradition in the Discursive Representation of Animals." *Discourse & Society* 26 (5): 587–607.

Cronin, Michael. 2017. *Eco-Translation: Translation and Ecology in the Age of the Anthropocene*. Oxon: Routledge.

Crutzen, Paul J., and Eugene F. Stoermer. 2013. "The 'Anthropocene'." In *The Future of Nature*, ed. by Libby Robin, Sverker Sörlin, and Paul Warde, 479–490. New Haven: Yale University Press.

Danesi, Marcel. 1994. "Introduction." In *An Introduction to Semiotics*, auth. Thomas A. Sebeok, xi–xvii. London: University of Toronto Press.

Danesi, Marcel. 2004. *Messages, Signs, and Meanings: A Basic Textbook in Semiotics and Communication Theory*. Toronto: Canadian Scholars' Press.

De Waal, Cornelis. 2013. *Peirce: A Guide for the Perplexed*. London: Bloomsbury.

DeMunck, Victor C., and Elisa J. Sobo. 1998. *Using Methods in the Field: A Practical Introduction and Casebook*. Walnut Creek: AltaMira Press.

Drenthen, Martin. 2016. "Understanding the Meaning of Wolf Resurgence, Ecosemiotics and Landscape Hermeneutics." In *Thinking about Animals in the Age of the Anthropocene*, ed. by in Morten Tønnessen, Kristin Armstrong Oma, and Silver Rattasepp, 109–126. Lanham: Lexington Books.

Eadie, Edward N. 2012. *Understanding Animal Welfare: An Integrated Approach*. Heidelberg: Springer.

Garrard, Greg. 2012. *Ecocriticism*. New York: Routledge.

Goitsemodimo, Relopile G. 2015. Socio-cultural Dynamics of a Rainwater Harvesting Project in Rural Thaba Nchu. Unpublished MA dissertation. Bloemfontein: University of the Free State.

Hammersley, Martin, and Paul Atkinson. 2019. *Ethnography: Principles in Practice*. New York: Routledge.

Holm, Gunilla. 2014. "Photography as a Research Method." In *The Oxford Handbook of Qualitative Research*, ed. by Patricia Leavy, 380–402. Oxford: Oxford University Press.

Jansen van Vuuren, Xany. 2022. "Non-professional Interpreting in Animal Welfare: Towards an Ecosemiotic Understanding of Interaction." Unpublished PhD Thesis, University of the Free State.

Jansen van Vuuren, Xany. 2023. "Translation Between Non-Humans and Humans." In *Translation Beyond Translation Studies*, ed. by Kobus Marais, 219–230. London: Bloomsbury.

Kasperbauer, Tyler J. 2018. *Subhuman: The Moral Psychology of Human Attitudes to Animals*. New York: Oxford University Press.

Kirksey, S. Eben, and Stefan Helmreich. 2010. "The Emergence of Multispecies Ethnography." *Cultural Anthropology* 25 (4): 545–576.

Lawrence, Elizabeth. 1994. "Conflicting Ideologies: Views of Animal Rights Advocates and their Opponents." *Society and Animals* 2 (2): 175–190.

Lestel, Dominique. 2014. "Hybrid Communities." *Angelaki* 19 (3): 61–73.

Lindström, Kati, Kalevi Kull, and Hannes Palang. 2011. "Semiotic Study of Landscapes: An Overview from Semiology to Ecosemiotics." *Sign Systems Studies* 39 (2/4): 12–36.

Mäekivi, Nelly, and Timo Maran. 2016. "Semiotic Dimensions of Human Attitudes Towards Other Animals: A Case of Zoological Gardens." *Sign Systems Studies* 44 (1/2): 209–230.

Magnus, Rinn, and Tiit Remm. 2018. "Urban Ecosemiotics of Trees: Why the Ecological Alien Species Paradigm Has Not Gained Ground in Cities?" *Sign Systems Studies* 46 (2): 319–342.

Marais, Kobus. 2019. *A (Bio)Semiotic Theory of Translation: The Emergence of Social Cultural Reality*. New York: Routledge.

360   Xany Jansen van Vuuren

Marais, Kobus. 2021. "Tom, Dick and Harry as well as Fido and Puss in Boots Are Translators: The Implications of Biosemiotics for Translation Studies." In *Translating Asymmetry — Rewriting Power*, ed. by Ovidi Carbonell i Cortés, and Esther Monzó-Nebot, 101–121. Amsterdam & Philadelphia: John Benjamins.

Maran, Timo. 2014. "Place and Sign. Locality as Foundational Concept for Ecosemiotics." In *Re-Imagining Nature: Environmental Humanities and Ecosemiotics*, ed. by Alfred K. Siewers, 79–89. Lewisburg: Bucknell University Press.

Maran, Timo. 2020. *Ecosemiotics: The Study of Signs in Changing Ecologies*. Cambridge: Cambridge University Press.

Maran, Timo, and Kalevi Kull. 2014. "Ecosemiotics: Main Principles and Current Developments." *Geografiska Annaler: Series B, Human Geography* 96 (1): 41–50.

Maran, Timo, Morten Tønnessen, Riin Magnus, Nelly Mäekivi, Silver Rattasepp, and Kadri Tüür. 2016. "Introducing Zoosemiotics: Philosophy and Historical Background." In *Animal Umwelten in a Changing World: Zoosemiotic Perspectives*, ed. by Timo Maran, Morten Tønnessen, and Silver Rattasepp, 10–28. Tartu: University of Tartu Press.

McFarland, Sarah E., and Ryan Hediger (eds). 2009. *Animals and Agency: An Interdisciplinary Exploration*. Leiden: Brill.

Parham, John, and Louise Westling (eds). 2016. *A Global History of Literature and the Environment*. Cambridge: Cambridge University Press.

Pedersen, Helena. 2014. "Knowledge Production in the 'Animal Turn': Multiplying the Image of Thought, Empathy, and Justice." In *Exploring the Animal Turn: Human-Animal Relations in Science, Society and Culture*, ed. by Erika Andersson Cederholm, Amelie Björck, Kristina Jennbert, and Ann-Sofie Lönngren, 13–18. Lund: The Pufendorf Institute for Advanced Studies.

Peirce, Charles S. 1935a. *The Collected Papers of Charles S. Peirce (Vol 2)*. Cambridge: Harvard University Press.

Peirce, Charles S. 1935b. *The Collected Papers of Charles S. Peirce (Vol 3)*. Cambridge: Harvard University Press.

Petrilli, Susan. 2016. "Translation Everywhere." *Signata* 7: 23–56.

Robin, Libby, Sverker Sörlin, and Paul Warde (eds). 2013. *The Future of Nature: Documents of Global Change*. New Haven: Yale University Press.

Sandiford, Peter J. 2015. "Participant Observation as Ethnography or Ethnography as Participant Observation in Organizational Research." In *The Palgrave Handbook of Research Design in Business and Management*, ed. by Kenneth D. Strang, 411–443. New York: Palgrave Macmillan.

Schmuck, Richard. 1997. *Practical Action Research for Change*. Thousand Oaks: Sage.

Schwartz, Dona. 1989. "Visual Ethnography: Using Photography in Qualitative Research." *Qualitative Sociology* 12: 119–154.

Sebeok, Thomas A. 1991. *A Sign is Just a Sign*. Bloomington: Indiana University Press.

Simmons, Laurence, and Philip Armstrong. 2007. *Knowing Animals*. Leiden: Brill.

Singer, Merrill. 2014. "Zoonotic Ecosyndemics and Multispecies Ethnography." *Anthropological Quarterly* 87 (4): 1279–1309.

Singer, Peter. 1990. *Animal Liberation*. New York: New York Review.

Spradley, James P. 1980. *Participant Observation*. New York: Holt, Rinehard & Winston.

Statistics South Africa. 2011. "Census 2011: Key Statistics Thabanchu." https://www.statssa.gov.za/?page_id=4286&id=7354

Stibbe, Arran. 2001. "Language, Power and the Social Construction of Animals." *Society & Animals* 9 (2): 145–161.

Stibbe, Arran. 2015. *Ecolinguistics: Language, Ecology and the Stories We Live By*. London: Routledge.

Tønnessen, Morten. 2011. "Umwelt Transition and Uexküllian Phenomenology: An Ecosemiotic Analysis of Norwegian Wolf Management." Doctoral dissertation, University of Tartu.

Tønnessen, Morten and Kristin Armstrong Oma. 2016. "Introduction: Once upon a Time in the Anthropocene." In *Thinking about Animals in the Age of the Anthropocene*, ed. by Morten Tønnessen, Kirstin Armstrong Oma, and Silver Rattasepp, vii–xix. Lanham: Lexington Books.

Torop, Peeter. 2003. "Intersemiosis and Intersemiotic Translation." In *Translation, Translation*, ed. by Susan Petrilli. Leiden: Brill.

Tymoczko, Maria. 2007. *Enlarging Translation, Empowering Translators*. London: Routledge.

Wels, Harry. 2020. "Multi-species Ethnography: Methodological Training in the Field in South Africa." *Journal of Organizational Ethnography* 9 (3): 343–363.

Wheeler, Wendy, and Linda Williams. 2012. "The Animals Turn." *New Formations* 76: 5–7.

Willis, Jerry. 2007. *Foundations of Qualitative Research*. Thousand Oaks: Sage.

World Population Review. 2020. "Thaba Nchu Population 2024." https://worldpopulationreview.com/world-cities/thaba-nchu-population

Wright, Hazel R. 2009. "Trusting the Process: Using an Emergent Design to Study Adult Education." *Educate~*: 62–73.

Index

A

activist translation 161
actor 18, 255–256
actor-network theory 254–259
    enrolment 258, 263–269,
      271
    interessement 257–258, 265,
      269–271
    intermediary 256
    mediator 256, 264
    mobilisation 258, 264, 267,
      269, 271
    obligatory passage point
      (OPP) 257–258, 264,
      268–269, 271
    problematisation 257–258,
      263, 266, 268, 270
    spokesperson 256–257, 271
    translation 256–258,
      270–271
affect *see* emotion
affective labour *see* emotional
    labour
affordances 231
agency 18–19, 340, 353–356
    non-human 340, 347,
      353–356
Animal Turn 340, 342
animal welfare 341–342
animal, non-human 340–341
Anthropocene 340
artefact 230–231 *see also*
    cognitive artefact
artefact analysis 48–49, 227, 231
artistic research 49
asylum seekers 320–321 *see also*
    refugees
    in Germany 303–304
    in Hong Kong 325–330
    reception centres for
      refugees 303
Auslan 61
Australia 61, 65
Austria 138–140

autoethnographic narrative 108,
    160
autoethnography 11–12, 81–82,
    105, 108, 159–161
    autoethnography in
      translation and
      interpreting studies
      160–161
    autoethnography vs.
      ethnography 160–161

B

bias 11, 129, 132, 351–352
boundary spanners 39
boundary work 141, 147, 153
    cultural boundaries 141,
      146–147, 149
    moral boundaries 141, 150
    socioeconomic boundaries
      141, 147, 149–150

C

Callon, Michel 257–258, 264,
    270
Caritas 138–140
case study 118
    single case study 208
church interpreting *see under*
    interpreting settings
citizen science 49
client-specific guidelines (CSG)
    209–220
cognitive artefact 204–205,
    219–220 *see also* artefact
cognitive labour, distribution of
    227–228, 232–233, 239–246 *see*
    also distributed cognition
cognitive practices 205
collaboration 18, 41, 202
committed research approaches
    161
communicative validation *see*
    member checking

community radio, South
    African 261
conference interpreters 75
conversation analysis 201,
    206–207
cooperation in translation work
    see collaboration
co-researching 49
COVID-19 pandemic 14–16, 162,
    278
cultural authority 285–286
cultural cognitive ecology 205
cultural mediators 328–329,
    333–334
culture concept 205

D

deontic authority 208, 219
discourse analysis 227, 234–235
distributed cognition 203–204,
    219, 227–228 *see also* cognitive
    labour, distribution of

E

ecosemiotics 344
emancipatory research agenda
    44
emotional labour 100–103
    altruistic "false self" 103
    commercialised affect 99,
      103, 112
    deep acting 100–101, 109,
      111
    emotion regulation 99–102,
      109–112
    feeling rules 100–101, 110
    surface acting 100–101, 111
emotional recall 108
emotions 13, 86–87, 99
    documenting emotions 165
    emotions and field notes
      165–167
epistemic stance 208
epistemic status 207–208

364 Field Research on Translation and Interpreting

ethics *see* research ethics
ethnographic methods and data
    digital methods and tools 16
    informal conversations 87,
      149–150
    linguistic analysis 57–59,
      232–236
    photographs 349–350
    remembered data 84, 106
    types of ethnographic data
      46
    video recording 350
    written texts 228
ethnography 3, 10, 45, 56, 66–67,
  78–80
    critical ethnography
      143–144, 321–322
    diachronic ethnography 83
    didactic relevance of
      ethnography 21
    ethnographic fieldwork 3
    ethnography in translation
      and interpreting studies
      4–5, 79–80, 142
    ethnography on reading
      translated fiction
      281–283
    ethnography vs.
      autoethnography
      160–161
    multi-sited ethnography
      8–9
    multispecies ethnography
      344–347
    netnography 163, 288–290
    online ethnography 9
    patchwork ethnography
      7–8
    reflexive ethnography
      81–82, 84
    retrospective ethnography
      83–84
    (socio-)cognitive
      ethnography 44–45
    transformational power of
      ethnography 21
    virtual ethnography 163
etic and emic perspective 17
European Parliament 63–64

F
field access 15, 123, 146–147
field concept 6–9

field diary 13, 130–132
    and emotions 165–167
    as a tool for academic
      productivity 170–171
    for ethical reflection
      130–132, 168
    in autoethnography
      158–159
    therapeutic role 166–167
field exit 151–152
field interviews 5, 46, 140,
  149–150
    responsive interviewing
      191–192
    semi-structured interviews
      88–89
field notes 159 *see also* field
  diary
field observation 3
    feasibility 140
    participant observation
      57–58
    types 351
field relationships 124, 148–151,
  191–192
field research 2–5
    and contingency planning
      15
    and flexibility 11, 15
    as a journey 9
    in translation and
      interpreting research 4
    messiness of field research
      10, 16
fieldwork 2–3, 7
    disembodied 163 *see also*
      remote fieldwork
    ethnographic fieldwork 3
    with readers of translated
      fiction 279
Finland 103–104
Finnish 233–234, 244–245
food 329

G
gatekeeper 146–147, 330
Geertzian dilemma 80 *see also*
  researcher role
Germany 303
Gieryn, Thomas F. 141
glottonym 301
grounded theory 89–90

H
healthcare interpreting *see under*
  interpreting settings
Hirschauer, Stefan 298–299
Hochschild, Arlie 100–101
Holz-Mänttäri, Justa 40–41, 44
Hong Kong 325–328
human differentiation 298–301
    categorisation of translators
      and interpreters 313–314
    language-related human
      differentiation 299–301,
      305–306
human rights 75–76
Hutchins, Edwin 203–205, 219

I
informant feedback *see* member
  checking
informed consent 183, 194–195,
  331–332
insider/outsider role of the
    researcher *see under*
    researcher roles
interaction 209–211
    institutional 207–208
interpreter confidentiality 87
interpreters
    (lack of) training 80, 85,
      89–90
    recruitment 306–313,
      333–334
    working with interpreters
      332–333
interpreters' roles and selves
    blended roles 111–112
    private selves 99, 103,
      111–112
    service roles 99, 102–103,
      111–112
interpreting concept 17–18
interpreting settings
    church 99, 101–102, 108–110
    conflict zones 74–75
    international organisations
      75, 88
    healthcare 59, 61
    humanitarian contexts
      320–323
    legal institutions 65–66
    political institutions 63–64
    welfare 139–140
    workplace 61–62

interspecies translation 344–345
intersubjectivity 84
interviews *see* field interviews

J
journalation 41
journalistic translation *see* news
translation

K
Knorr-Cetina, Karin 11

L
laboratory studies approach in
science and technology
studies 11
Lamont, Michèle 141
language service provider (LSP)
209, 229–230
Latour, Bruno 254–261
legal interpreting *see under*
interpreting settings
life story 86
linguistic analysis *see under*
ethnographic methods and
data
linguistic ethnography 17, 55–67
parallels with interpreting
studies 58
translatorial linguistic
ethnography 38–39,
44–50
linguistic landscapes 48

M
marketisation of research 14
member checking 192–193
mixed methods research 62–63
mother tongue 307–310
multilingualism 47
multi-methods research 62–63
multiprofessionals 140 *see also*
paraprofessional translators

N
narrative inquiry 81, 85–87
netnography *see under*
ethnography
news translation 251–252,
262–271

non-governmental organisation
(NGO) 139–140, 152, 162,
321–322, 326–327
non-professional translators and
interpreters 18, 138, 140,
147–148
as a hidden population 147

O
observation *see* field observation
Office of the United Nations
High Commissioner for
Human Rights (OHCHR)
75–76

P
paraprofessional translators and
interpreters 18, 39–41, 47, 138,
140
paratranslator 39, 252
participant observation *see*
under field observation
past presencing 77, 84
Peirce, Charles 343–344
Pentecostal church 103–105,
109–110
photographs *see under*
ethnographic methods and
data
positionality of the researcher
11–12, 80–81, 119, 131–132, 134,
144–145, 349–352 *see also*
researcher roles
changed positionality
98–99, 105–107
multiple positionalities 107
post-humanist paradigm 344
practices *see* cognitive practices
practisearcher 9, 11–12, 78,
140–141, 145 *see also* researcher
roles
professional translators and
interpreters 18, 40, 149–150
public translation studies 49

Q
qualitative data analysis 352
questionnaire 47–48

R
reading

ethnographic research on
reading 281–282
reading as a social practice
281–282
reading group 280
reception centres for asylum
seekers 303 *see also* asylum
seekers
reception research 283
reflexivity 6, 11, 13, 57, 82, 84,
107, 126, 131–132, 138–139, 143
collective nature of
reflexivity 144
reflexivity and emotions 13
reflexivity in translation and
interpreting studies
144–146
refugee women 324, 329–330
refugees 320–321 *see also* asylum
seekers
remembered data *see under*
ethnographic methods and
data
remote fieldwork 15–16, 162–163,
165
remote interpreting *see* video
interpreting
representational crisis 5, 142
research confidentiality 168,
186–191
external 187, 190
internal 187, 190
open approach 188
restrictive approach
187–188
research design, emergent 345
research diary 158 *see also* field
diary
research ethics 13–15, 133
clearance 179–184, 332
in ethnographic research
328–331
in reading research
283–286
in studying marginalised
populations 323–325
reciprocity 185, 192
regulation 181–182
relational approach 13–14
utilitarian approach 182
situated and reflexive
approach 13–14, 184

research ethics committees
  (RECs) 179–184
research ethics journal 130–132
research funding 14
researcher identities 169
researcher roles 121–122 *see also*
  positionality
    convert researcher 122
    dual role, multiple roles
      11–12, 122, 126–127, 134,
      145 *see also* practisearcher
    going native 128
    insider role 123–128, 133
    insider–outsider
      continuum 12, 118, 122,
      133–134, 148–149
    outsider role 330–331
    over-familiarisation 128,
      132
    role conflicts 106–108,
      127–128, 133
    role transparency 132–133
researcher subjectivity 11, 80
researcher-participant
  interactions *see* field
  relationships

S
semiosis 343
semiotics 343, 345
  sign 343
sign language (interpreting)
  60–66
situatedness 1
socio-cognitive view 1
socio-cultural ethnography
  44–45

socio-zoological scale 341
South Africa 261, 338, 348
Sweden 201, 209
Swiss Federal Chancellery 119
Swiss Federal Office of Justice
  119
Switzerland 118–119, 158, 162,
  185–186
systemic functional linguistics
  227, 232–236, 247
    ideational metafunction
      233, 244–245
    in translation research 234
    interpersonal
      metafunction 233–234,
      244–245
    textual metafunction 233,
      244–245

T
translanguaging 43
translation concept 17–18, 41–43
translation memory (TM) 202,
  204
    TM matches 211–218
translation revision 185–186,
  189, 227
    quality assurance 117
    reviser 227
    revision files as data
      227–230, 236–237
    revision policy 186
    translator-reviser
      relationship 189,
      227–228
translation space 298
translation workplace 202, 209

translatorial action, theory of
  40–41, 44
translatorial linguistic
  ethnography *see under*
  linguistic ethnography
translatoriality 38–39, 41–44
translators and interpreters as
  (non-)authors 111–112
translatorship 41

U
United Kingdom 280
United Nations (UN) field
  missions 75–77, 80, 85–89
United Nations Office at Geneva
  (UNOG) 76–77, 85, 88–89

V
veganism 162
video interpreting 64
video recording *see under*
  ethnographic methods and
  data
visibility of translation and
  interpreting 251–252
volunteer church interpreting
  99, 101–102, 108–110
volunteer translation 162–164

W
welfare organisation *see under*
  interpreting settings